W9-AYH-619

BLACKED OUT

Signithia Fordham

BLACKED OUT

Dilemmas of Race, Identity, and Success at Capital High

THE UNIVERSITY OF CHICAGO PRESS
CHICAGO & LONDON

Signithia Fordham, formerly assistant professor of anthropology at Rutgers University, is assistant professor of anthropology in the Department of Education at the University of Maryland, Baltimore County.

The University of Chicago Press, Chicago 60637
The University of Chicago Press, Ltd., London
© 1996 by Signithia Fordham
All rights reserved. Published 1996
Printed in the United States of America
04 03 02 01 00 99 98 97 96   1 2 3 4 5

ISBN: 0-226-25713-4 (cloth)
0-226-25714-2 (paper)

Library of Congress Cataloging-in-Publication Data

Fordham, Signithia.
Blacked out : dilemmas of race, identity, and success at Capital High / Signithia Fordham.
p.   cm.
Includes bibliographical references and index.
1. Afro-Americans—Education (Secondary)—Case studies.
2. Academic achievement—United States—Case studies. 3. Afro-Americans—Race identity—Case studies. 4. Afro-American students—Psychology—Case studies. 5. Educational anthropology—United States—Case studies. I. Title.
LC2779.F67 1996
373'.08996'073—dc20   95-33036
                                                CIP

This book is dedicated to the memory of my wombmate, confidante, friend, and chief mudpie assistant, whose untimely death compels me to sing both alto and soprano and to fly this uncharted journey with only one wing.

You may write me down in history
With your bitter, twisted lies,
You may trod me in the very dirt
But still, like dust, I'll rise. . . .

Just like moons and like suns,
With the certainty of tides,
Just like hopes springing high,
Still I'll rise. . . .

You may shoot me with your words,
You may cut me your eyes,
You may kill me with your hatefulness,
But still, like air, I'll rise.

Maya Angelou

CONTENTS

ACKNOWLEDGMENTS

Exile and sequestration are the two words that best describe the configuration of my institutional life during the remaking of what was my dissertation. Exile is rarely self-selected; sequestration can be either self-selected or imposed. As I write these lines, I am sitting in the tiny windowless office where I was both exiled and sequestered. This stigmatized space became my *primary* residence—my prison and sanctuary, the site where I spent the greater part of virtually every working day. Fortunately, the spatial restrictions of this evolved "primary residence" were repeatedly erased by the love and support of so many wonderful people, people who repeatedly peeled my bruised and battered psyche from the floor, pushing and kicking me toward the achievement of my goal. While I have enjoyed many forms and sources of support during the long and often difficult process of writing this book, the most crucial has been the love and counsel of kith and kin, friends and family. These individuals became my hidden collaborators and fellow conspirators, compelling my visions and insights to transcend the spatial limitations I was forced to endure. Thus, in the tradition idealized in the African-American community, "I" became "we," with the completion of my manuscript the presumed commodity of exchange. Through the medium of giving, I adopted the eyes, ears, insights, and fortitude of the people who supported me. They contacted me on my lifelines—the telephone and e-mail—to advise me that the sun was shining, night had become day, and day had become night. They urged me to go home in inclement weather; escorted me to my car; got food to me through the chunnels; unlocked my office door when I repeatedly locked myself out; gave me keys to their homes so I could eat my way down the East Coast, thus nourishing not only my physical being but my battered self-esteem as well. They continually consoled me, providing big shoulders for me to cry on when my wombmate died and waterless tears bruised my face;

repeatedly moved me with my rapidly shrinking worldly possessions; located obscure research sources and materials; read virtually incomprehensible drafts of various chapters; beat off the sharks who sought to consume my professional body; assured me that the mountains I saw before me were really only molehills; taught me computer skills beyond the rudimentary level; connected me to their powerful and influential professional networks; helped me to keep abreast of the inquiries regarding my research findings; typed drafts from my virtually incomprehensible handwriting; transcribed interview data, fieldnotes, and so forth; and generally served as mediators and involuntary research assistants. These were the voices, hands, eyes, and ears that quelled my fears and bolstered my sense of what I could do, compelling me to revisit the powerful dictum from the significant others in my childhood: "You can do it, Black girl, you can do it." I have been so fortunate. So blessed. The support of my kith and kin has been so powerful that I have begun to think of it as "hands across Signithia." Indeed, the power of my kith and kin has erased and nullified the negative forces in my life. It is therefore with the *greatest* pleasure associated with this book that I acknowledge them here; that I publicly thank them for being there for me when I stumbled (which was often), helping and even demanding that I "straighten up and fly right." I want these people to know that I am getting credit beyond what I deserve and I want to assure them that I know they are the "wind beneath my sail."

My heartfelt thanks are extended to the District of Columbia Public School System and, more specifically, the students and adults of the small community I fictiously label Capital High. This book would not have been possible without the cooperation and support of school officials and the parents and children of that community. I survived and thrived because of their goodwill, their willingness to allow me not only to peep into the crevices of their lives but also to gawk and stare. Their belief in the potentially transformative power of the findings that were likely to emerge from this study propelled them to share with me intimate aspects of their lives and, in so doing, reveal the way they construct cultural meaning. Meanwhile, the cultural information they voluntarily and involuntarily shared transformed me as a person, altering and even transforming my anthropological perceptions. My agreement with the District of Columbia Board of Education does not allow me to identify the individual participants either here or elsewhere in this book. I lament and respect this limitation. In order to protect the study participants' privacy, throughout the book the images presented are composites, combined portraits of the actual participants, and all names are fictitious. Despite these limitations, I want to thank each of them publicly and let them know that in this ethnography they were my hidden collaborators, the anonymous voices in the pages that follow, the people who taught me what I needed to know about how African-Americans achieve success—academic and otherwise—in contemporary Washington, D.C., and perhaps in the United States in general.

There was also financial support, which freed me from the usual intense workload of the academy. The American University awarded me a dissertation research grant during the spring semester of 1982. I also received a research grant from the Office of Educational Research and Improvement's Unsolicited Grants Program (formerly the National Institute of Education, Grant No. NIE-G-82-0037). This grant enabled me to collect the data during the first year of my fieldwork. The Spencer Foundation supported my research by awarding me a regular Spencer Foundation grant in 1984–85. Without this grant I would not have been able to complete the research on which this book is based. The year after I defended my dissertation, the Spencer Foundation also awarded me the Spencer Postdoctoral Fellowship. With the help of Professor Edmund Gordon, I spent the year of that fellowship at Yale University in the African-American Studies Department. I thank him for his support. At Yale, I was able to write and think and interact on a daily basis with such intellectual giants as Professors John W. Blassingame and the late Sylvia Boone. In 1992–93 I was also the beneficiary of a Minority Research Initiation and Career Advancement Awards Planning Grant (SRB-9154501) from the National Science Foundation. This NSF grant enabled me to look more critically at the gender issues that emerged in both the ethnographic and quantitative data. Richard McCormick, the erstwhile dean of the Faculty of Arts and Sciences at Rutgers University, awarded me a Henry Rutgers Research Fellowship, for which I thank him. I was also the recipient of a one-semester "minority research grant" that allowed me to devote more time to the crucial task of deciphering meaning. I am especially grateful to the faculty of the prestigious African-American Studies Program at Princeton University: Professors Kevin Gaines, Wahneema Lubiano, Toni Morrison, Nell Irvin Painter, Arnold Rampersad, Carol Swain, Howard Taylor, Walter Wallace, and Cornel West. As the recipient of the program's first Presidential Fellowship in 1991–92, I spent an entire academic year working with these supportive and intellectually unmatched academicians, all of whom were willing to read and critique my inchoate thoughts and ideas. They read my drafts and suggested I rewrite. They reread the revisions and suggested I rewrite. They shared their powerful professional networks and intellectual knowledge—unconditionally. They invited me into their homes; took me to lunch; and insisted that I attend their classes, lectures, and seminars. For similar kinds of support I am also grateful to Professors Hildred Geertz and Kay Warren in the Department of Anthropology at Princeton, and to Professor Deborah Tannen, who was visiting in the department that year. To all of these people, I extend my sincere appreciation.

At each of the institutions identified above, I relied upon the goodwill, professional skills, and personal warmth of the support and secretarial staff. These individuals corrected my mistakes, ignored my frustrations, and forgave me when my unreasonable expectations made it difficult for them to perform their job successfully. It is a real pleasure to thank them: Janet Bascom, Hattie Black, Carolyn Boston, Shirley Frederick, Janet Giarratano, Shirley Mero, Gayle Pemberton, Dorothy Randolph, Edwina Segledi, Evelyn Snipes, Rosa Urena, and Gwendolyn Williams.

At these same institutions, I also relied upon a group of people who are often ignored: those who prepare the meals, scrub the floors, and guard the doors. Some of them I know by name; most I do not. Nevertheless, they know me and they know what they did for me. They were the people who removed the discarded papers from my cluttered office; tried—often unsuccessfully—to find floor space in order to clean; replaced light bulbs; checked the areas where I was working late at night to be assured that I was unharmed; turned on the heat to keep me from freezing, the air conditioning to keep me from liquefying; escorted me to my car and gave me rides home when my old car died and I had stayed too late to walk home alone; warmed cold bagels; heated tepid soup; and gently and sometimes not so gently reminded me that sleep is essential to good health. They talked and talked and talked. They told me stories about the difficulties associated with their jobs. They shared their hopes and dreams, not only for themselves but for their children as well. I remember and appreciate their many acts of kindness and support. I hope, therefore, despite the lack of specificity here, that each of them will be able to see him- or herself depicted in this brief description and conclude: "She is describing me!"

Institutions of another category—libraries—were essential to the completion of this book. I benefited immensely both from the collections and from the vast skills and knowledge of reference librarians and media specialists. I am indebted to the late Senator Charles Mathias of Maryland for making a reference desk at the Library of Congress available to me. I also made use of the libraries at the American University, the University of the District of Columbia, and Yale University; Princeton University's Firestone Library; and all branches of the library and information system at Rutgers. While I thank all of the people who helped me obtain the desired resources and information, there are a few individuals who unwittingly became unpaid research assistants and therefore deserve special recognition. Here I must single out Melba Broom, Bruce Martin, Catherine Geddis, Marie Maman, Nancy Putnam, Elizabeth

Scherff, and Thelma Tate. Among this elite group, Marie Maman, Nancy Putnam and Thelma Tate deserve gold stars for convincing me that the library system could be truly "user friendly."

It is far more difficult adequately to thank the numerous colleagues whose mentoring, interest in my work, concrete suggestions, and stimulating conversations have shaped the construction of this book. While I have tried to acknowledge how they have influenced my thinking in the pages that follow, some people deserve special mention here, most notably the members of my dissertation committee: William L. Leap, Brett Williams, and John U. Ogbu. I would not have been able to complete the dissertation or write this book without their sharing their expertise in support of my professional advancement. Their willingness always to be there for me professionally has been their most consistent and significant contribution to my professional life. I thank each of them— unconditionally.

I am also indebted to a wide range of people whose support blurs the distinction between the intellectual and the personal. They include Brenda Allen, Herman Blake, John Blassingame, Liz DeBold, Lisa Delpit, Marta Bermudez-Gallegos, Wesley Brown, Margaret Eisenhart, Catherine Emihovich, Vivian Gadsden, Bernice Howard, Herman Howard, Michelle Fine, Michele Foster, Lynn Isbell, Brenda Jones, Donald Gibson, Kay Hunter, Gloria Ladson-Billings, Joyce King, Peter McLaren, Ceasar McDowell, Prathiba Joshi, Adel Patton, Yolanda Moses, Lauckland Nicholas, Mildred Lockhart, Howard McGary, Elmer Redfern Moore, George Pieczenik, Sara Rhoden, Robin Roberts, Mohamed Sessay, Christine Sleeter, Laura Smith, Ian Straker, Rick Turner, Vanessa Siddle Walker, Antoinette Washington, Wendy Weis, Deborah Gray White, and Jane White. I am especially grateful to Iris Carter Ford, whose anthropological knowledge and expertise combined with her willingness to listen to my "subaltern" ideas are apparently unending. I am grateful to John Johnson, who continually buttressed my willingness to take risks by challenging my thinking and encouraging me never to "blow" an opportunity to make a difference. I thank Renee Larrier for enduring my endless ramblings and tactfully helping to clarify my thinking. I am also grateful to Carmel Schrire, a senior colleague, who was braver than the people with whom she worked. I thank Ken Carlson, Francine Essien, Tom Figueira, Karla Jackson-Brewer, Walton Johnson, Cheryl Wall, and Cornel West for taking on my fight and in the process earning my deepest respect and admiration. I thank the American Association of University Professors (AAUP) chapter at Rutgers for trying to stigmatize injustice. Special thanks are extended to Linda Chalfant, who worked with me during the data-gathering stage of this ethnography, transcribing reams of interview data and typing numerous drafts. Her varied research skills and professionalism strengthened the manuscript immeasurably. Lynissa Stokes deserves my thanks because she kept me from drowning in my "snail" mail, performing many clerical tasks that I found difficult or impossible to do. I am grateful to Michael Barney for unconditional support, including a willingness to teach me cyberspace skills—gratis. I thank him for being prepared to do whatever tasks needed to be done to get my manuscript to the publisher. I am also grateful to Joan Phalen and Chuck Cowderey for modeling the best of what it means to be "liberal": practicing what they preach.

And then there is my dear friend Sylvia Weathers, whose friendship, love, and support were constants in an otherwise largely chaotic life. I hope Sylvia knows how much I value her friendship and how critical her support was to the completion of this book. I also appreciate the understanding of her husband Frank and their children, Nathan and Alexis.

I also want to express my gratitude to David Brent of the University of Chicago Press. His unwavering belief that my manuscript should and could become a book was extremely gratifying. And I am grateful for the excellent copyediting of Wilma Ebbitt.

Finally, I wish to thank my parents—my mother and my late father—and my sisters and brothers as well as my numerous nieces and nephews, aunts, uncles, and cousins on both sides of my parentage. I thank my father for sharing the stories of how individual members from different generations of our family resisted enslavement. I thank my mother for modeling Black womanhood and the life she knew awaited me. I thank my big sisters for teaching me to read before I went to school and forever encouraging me to "Go, little sister, go!" I thank my niece and her daughter for being the Fordham family heirlooms. I thank my entire family of orientation because over the years they have repeatedly forgiven me for not being present at certain critical family gatherings and ceremonies. In addition, I seek their forgiveness because often when I was at these gatherings I was really absent, engrossed in thinking about "the book." It is to my family of orientation that I owe the biggest debt of gratitude, for it was in their bosom that I learned the centrality of respect in African-American womanhood.

This book is about the dreaded R-word and its impact on the academic performance of African-American adolescents. No, the word is not *race* or *racism;* it is *representation*. *Representation* is the word because it compels us to see those who differ from us as "Other," as very different in some important ways. Even more significant, this representation—this imaging—is based primarily on written or visual portraits, on watching as a kind of violence imposed on the watched. I am, therefore, self-consciously using the word *watch* rather than *observe* in talking about ethnographic observations, because *watch* is a stronger verb, suggesting scrutiny or surveillance rather than merely noticing.

Undoubtedly, how and by whom people are *watched* are major issues in contemporary anthropological analyses. Watching is so central to anthropology that the discipline requires anthropologists-in-training to engage in participant watching as the major prerequisite to full professional status. One might argue then that participant observation, or participant watching, is really about rape, rage, and rapaciousness, the issues often underlying and fueling ethnographers' representations or misrepresentations of those they watch. Unfortunately, real anthropologists frequently misrepresent by both focusing on and indulging in rape, rage, and rapaciousness. As I use it here, *rape* obviously carries a much broader meaning than the physical violation of a woman's body, although that is certainly a central component of it. Rape might also be seen, however, as an important element in the way anthropologists have (mis)represented the Other, as the act of (re)presenting people in such a way that their humanness is both violated and brought into question. For example, Malinowski's watching or observing of the Trobrianders in the book *The Sexual Life of Savages: An Ethnographic Account of Courtship, Marriage, and Family Life among the Natives of the Trobriand Islands* (1929) compels us to "see" them as not quite equal to the people who share the knowledge, culture, and sexual behavior of the 1 ethnographer. Indeed, in this approach the ethnographer's civilized status is confirmed by his or her ability to situate the population being studied as his or her opposite. One of the cardinal factors fueling Malinowski's (re)presentation of the Trobrianders is their "difference," their "Otherness."

Similarly, in conveying inter- or intragroup rage, ethnographers have often neglected to juxtapose this human sentiment—rage—with the other emotions visible among the populations they study. This omission breaches the humanness of the people being studied. For example, ethnographies about headhunting among the Ilongot of the northern Philippines highlight expiatory rituals and the attendant grief and rage. Ethnographers' depictions of the centrality of rage among these people in the wake of the death of a member of the community is so compelling that a western reader will likely see the Ilongot solely as headhunters. Clearly, the Ilongot are more than the rage fueling their response to grief. Indeed, I would speculate that they—like most human groups—experience a full range of human emotions—love, anger, hate, depression, anxiety, and so forth.[1] Nevertheless, the way they are (re)presented textually and ethnographically precludes the possibility of their having other emotions and sentiments.

Rapaciousness is a third element underlying real anthropologists' application of the R-word. Both in the subjects and issues ethnographers choose to write about and in the constructions and representations of the groups they study, rapaciousness is a concern. While the world globalization process has had and continues to have a profound effect on anthropology as a discipline, the primary way anthropologists have historically represented their subjects remains virtually unchanged: watching as a kind of violence imposed on the watched. The subjects become objects.

Like most other academic disciplines, anthropology does not exist without writing. Written texts and anthropology are inseparable. Erase writing as a form of representation, and anthropology is immediately extinct, erased. Historically, anthropologists' heavy reliance upon detailed, written cultural descriptions based on the ethnographer's observation of primarily nonliterate peoples in Africa, Asia, and other non-Western contexts, positioned the discipline in such a privileged manner that anthropologists were, in many instances, the sole authorities on certain nonliterate peoples. Thus, anthropologists were free to represent the Other as they chose.[2] The "partial truths" of such analyses were never seriously debated, primarily because the anthropologists' claims were based on long-term watching, and the consumers of this knowledge were totally dependent upon the ethnographer's interpretations and subsequent representations.

The anthropological pen, as well as the anthropological gaze, has been influential in transforming the world in many socially important ways. It has maintained and transformed our images of the world's populations and the existing world order. It has made us aware of existing global poverty, including the huge chasm between the haves and the have-nots. It has made us sensitive to the concept of culture and its powerful impact in shaping the lives we live. More specifically, it has made us extremely conscious of divergent worldviews. Nevertheless, as Torgovnick notes in her book *Gone Primitive: Savage Intellects, Modern Lives* (1990), contemporary ethnographers have managed to maintain the notion of the primitive and primitivism in their analyses. Thus, among ethnographers the globalization process has come to mean substituting one form of colonialism for another. Although writing up one's observations of nonliterate, formerly nonliterate, and/or non-Western peoples is no longer the province of a single anthropologist, the written word remains the civilized weapon that maintains the status quo in a postmodern form of colonialism.

Not surprisingly, then, writing ethnography is suddenly[3] and irrefutably a source of heated debate *within* the discipline, with an entire legion of practitioners joining the debate. Some anthropologists have fueled and exaggerated this debate by asserting that ethnographic representations are invariably partial truths. Thus, how anthropologists construct and/or "make" texts is a much discussed issue, with "symbolic violence" one of the major subtexts of the debate. Still further, the "stickiness" of the concept of culture as well as the growing "literariness" of ethnography generates a real need for understanding how ethnographies are created. This is necessary, in part at least, because, as one scholar argues so convincingly, "An ethnography is written representation of a culture (or selected aspects of a culture) . . . [that] carries quite serious intellectual and moral responsibilities, for the *images of others inscribed in writing are most assuredly not neutral*" (Van Maanan 1988:1).

I take this claim seriously. How I write about the people I studied in the Capital community is a form of representation, and the resulting images are not impartial. In this ethnography, I focus on both "selected aspects of a culture" and the multilayered problems attendant on those aspects, when constructed by "halfies"—anthropologists who are "blocked [in their] ability to comfortably assume the self of anthropology" (Abu-Lughod 1991). The "self of anthropology" is rigidly scripted, and a member of the profession who does not fit neatly into this constructed identity—that is, is neither a pristine self nor an Other—is inevitably suspect, questioned, or questionable. The resulting "split selfhood" marks one as perpetually marginalized.

I am an anthropologist. I am also racially identified as African-

American. I am involuntarily diasporic—a wanderer. Therefore, I embody and reflect this "halfie" status, both in terms of the anthropological self and the Black Self. In constructing this ethnography, I became keenly aware of the duality of my "split selfhood," of the imperative to use data based on watching and the violence attendant on trying to "make a way out of no way" in my chosen profession.

The scholarly literature, including anthropology, has not been kind in its representations of African-Americans—an involuntarily diasporic people. Some of the most violent representations of them are riddled with images of *lack*: difference, intellectual inadequacy, hostility, aggressiveness, and so on. Frequently, these images have been "scientifically" documented; that is, scientists and the principles of the scientific method are highlighted in these representations, compelling us to silence, to remaining uncritical of the authors' claims. The cumulative effects of this kind of negative imaging are displayed in the academic performance and responses of African-American adolescents, as is plainly evident in the narratives recorded in this book.

While this ethnography grows out of a widespread concern regarding the "images of others inscribed in writing," it is also evoked by a growing preoccupation with the nature of ethnographic texts and with how what is written censures Blackness. Thus, a central feature of this ethnography is African-Americans' multiple responses to the primary ways they are represented in anthropological (and other) texts. I document my concern by focusing on the current resistance of African-American adolescents to much of what is taught in school.

As a people[4] whose culture and background are repeatedly represented in ways that validate the claim that images are not neutral, African-American adolescents' self-consciously contrived response to school is a prime example of how memories shape the present, how the students seek to both retain and reclaim a Black Self while concurrently embracing a world ordered by (an)Other. Indeed, as many African-Americans envision it, the pen is a double-edged sword. Their school performance is impaled on this sword in at least two significant ways: first, because the students align themselves with a social group whose history and representation were conceived and constructed by an Other; and second, because they seek to take control of the imaging of Black people by creating from this fraudulent representation an acceptable Black Self. They seem to know that these factors are likely to sandbag them at any given moment. I am struck, for example, by how often African-American adolescents cite the claims of such notorious researchers as Herrnstein and Murray, Shockley, Jencks, and Jensen as typical of the way African-Americans are constructed as Other in texts. I am equally surprised at how often the personal fears of these students are unconscious, unacknowledged, unarticulated, or—even when conscious—denied. Thus, the historical practice of using written words based on watching to both construct and dehumanize (an)Other enhances the power of certain segments of a multiethnic, multiracial society. Academicians and other researchers are able to engage continuously in this symbolic warfare because of their access to the pen. This compels other segments of the society—African-American adolescents, for example—to avoid constructing themselves in a similar manner. The following account, drawn from my classroom experience, illustrates how the academic effort of one group of African-American students—and by extension my role and performance as a professor—was negatively affected by their perceptions and fear of anthropological representations.

In an interdisciplinary undergraduate class comprising third- and fourth-year African-American students, I assigned a fifteen-page ethnographic paper as the major course requirement. I provided copious guidelines and additional text sources (including examples of both professional and student-generated ethnographic work) because I was asking each student to engage in a kind of research—based on watching—with which he or she might not have been familiar. I also wanted to give students no excuse for objecting to the assignment. But resistance surfaced immediately, even before I was able to complete the instructions. Ironically, the more written assistance I gave the students and the more I urged them to visit my office, the more anxious they appeared to become.

Our struggles centered around the legitimacy of the writing assignment. Was it appropriate to ask them to reproduce their lives and experiences by watching and then writing about the Black Self as it is represented in major academic texts? The students' reactions could be characterized in the following ways: (1) they did not know what I wanted them to watch (this they asserted even though I gave them oral and written directions); (2) they had never before heard of, or at least completed, such a task (suggesting that if an experience was not a part of their existing repertoire, it was not legitimate); (3) they had very little to no experience in writing academic papers—especially ethnographic ones; (4) they did not want to become anthropologists; and, most important, (5) they thought I was being grossly unfair in asking them to (re)present themselves in text form.

As the instructor of the class, I tried unsuccessfully to convince them that they were capable of completing the assignment. When, at the beginning of one class session, I asked, in utter frustration, "How many of you came to class today without a weapon?" silence ensued. Finally, one female student reluctantly admitted that she was uncertain about the meaning of the term *weapon*. She asked, "What do you mean by weapon?" Again, a pregnant silence. Eventually, a male student took a knife from his pocket and, with the appropriate amount of bravado, assured us that he "always had a weapon."

This response was what I had anticipated: students thought of weapons as embracing only the cultural category identified with guns, knives, machetes, and so forth. I pointed out that there is such a thing as "psychic," or "symbolic," violence, a kind of violence in which this category of weapons—guns, knives, machetes—is not applicable. I went on to point out that in the academy the weapon of choice is the pen. Further, I insisted, the pen has both negative and positive capabilities. On the one hand, it will inevitably freeze the images of their subjects, including even images that distort or misrepresent; on the other hand, it is capable of compelling the reader to edit and revise his or her prior knowledge and belief system in such a way as to realign existing social relations and worldviews. I implored them to think of the pen as this potentially transformative or liberating weapon. I then asked if there was anyone in the class who did not have on his or her person such a weapon—a pen. There was no one who did not possess a pen. Nevertheless, the students' responses to the required written assignment suggested a kind of uneasiness, a discomfort with this "weapon," and, beyond that, fear of the consequences of watching and "talking back" (perhaps even a learned inability to "talk back"); their responses suggested, too, a latent fear that their academic writing was likely to misrepresent their subjects, reinscribing them as Other, thereby denying the existence of a humanness outside the western gaze.

The day I outlined the details of this writing assignment, I was impaled on the fulcrum of my students' anxieties and hostilities. My relationship with them was permanently altered, frozen in a struggle for the right to determine the course agenda as well as the trajectory of their evolving collegiate, academic identities. More to the point, when I would not renegotiate my expectations vis-à-vis that assignment, several students dropped the course. Those who remained continued to challenge the legitimacy of my requiring a fifteen-page ethnographic study for the final assignment. They continued to suggest, by their questions and responses, that writing such a research paper was potentially implosive, likely to misrepresent their subjects, reinscribing themselves and the people they represented as Other. The students argued incessantly that I was biased in a basal sense, in that I was insisting upon a written text based on the violence of watching. Curiously, their initial, pre-class rage and indignation, which was directed at the residual colonial structures in America, was redirected, now aimed at my public persona rather than at a critique of the assigned readings.

I tried not to take their attacks personally. Nevertheless, in accusing me of being prejudiced and unfair, they used code words that I (and they) fully understood. To be both racially identifiable as a person of African ancestry and accused of imposing on others the kind of psychic violence that has consistently dogged Black existence in this country ripped the core of my being.

The students understood the power of the words they chose—how they both represented and misrepresented me. They also knew they were accusing me of a kind of rape (violence) in that (as they perceived it) I was bringing into question their humanness as well as the humanness of their potential subjects. The words the students chose—*prejudiced, unfair*—were carefully selected for their likely emotional effect. They also knew (and so did I) that they were accusing me of having become an Other—a transformation which their college attendance suggested they aspired to but which they also feared. Indeed, their accusations were so painful that I felt as if my soul were murdered, bludgeoned by the demonizing effects of their words. Fortunately, my dark skin camouflaged most of my embarrassment and semester-long humiliation. The blood continually draining from my face went unnoticed.

The language the students used indicated their rage: they felt betrayed, "dissed" by a woman who they assumed—based on phenotypic features—shared their racialized identity. For this group of Black undergraduates, the quintessential issue appeared to be embodied in the notion that, like a "real" (as opposed to a symbolic) dominant Other, I was compelling them to assume the gaze of an Other, to appropriate (an)Other identity, in order to succeed. Thus, as the students constructed and would subsequently represent me, my refusal to alter the written course requirement symbolically transformed my gaze from victimized to perpetrator of violence, from "Us" to "Them," from Black to "book-black Black."[5] Hence, as *the* professor, I became *(an)Other*.

I write about this painful experience because, as the narratives presented in this book demonstrate, similar issues resonated in the student-teacher relationships I had discovered years earlier among the students and teachers at Capital High. Also, as these narratives reveal, one of the biggest issues confronting the student-teacher relationship is student resistance to what is perceived as the violence attendant on identity appropriation and the other representations so central to Black adolescents' academic success.

Indeed, cultural representations of the Other verify the dramatic ways in which writing—based on watching—is used to construct and appropriate normal and abnormal models for "imaging" social reality. Writing thus becomes the central instrument through which America's social order and its gaze can be apprehended. The resulting representations are potentially more powerful and destructive than the egregious violence associated with the gun and other culturally sanctioned weapons. As a "civilized" weapon, the pen's benign designation also means that it can engage in horrific social warfare under a cloak of innocence. African-American students' sense of appropriation and/or (mis)representation of the Black Self in the academy has its origin in a deep distrust of what appears in print, of what is written as well as of those who write. Still further, there is some evidence that contemporary Black students' distrust of the written word was initially evoked by the larger society's practice of making laws and even constitutional protections (all written documents) inapplicable to African-Americans. Indeed, the mere act of assuming that African-Americans were entitled to such protections led to the fully documented lynching and raping of the Black Self, males and females. The legacy of such gross injustice is evident in what has been labeled "the rage of the privileged class." It produced the desired distrust about which I speak. Further, I argue that these societal rapes generated the rage and the subsequent documented loss of desire to learn from what was printed and deemed official and true.

While what is written is almost always used as a weapon against the Black Other, it is not regarded as abhorrent or repulsive. For centuries, writing has been central to the commodification of the Black Self; it was—and still is—the fuel that drove social science research. What is written thus penetrates and impregnates the ideology of the larger society. Indeed, it is on negative images of Black people that representations of societal power are commonly focused. *Time* magazine, 6 April 1970, acknowledges this reality: "Whites often assume that civil rights acts and court decisions made law the black man's redeemer. In practice, many blacks see the law [that is, what is written] as something different: a white weapon that white policemen, white judges and white juries use against black people."

African-American students beyond the elementary level appear to understand the power of writing in the larger society. They seem to know—despite the draconian efforts of school officials to keep this knowledge from them—that African-Americans have been repeatedly misrepresented in the nation's major "public transcripts," their identities bludgeoned and blurred in ways that rape them of their humanity and fuel their rage as well as the rapaciousness of those who (mis)represent them in written documents. They also appear to know how these documents have been repeatedly used in connection with the practice of symbolic violence, at the center of which are allegations of genetic inequality. Hence, central to these students' construction of a Black identity is the practice of distancing the Black Self as a sacred cultural space, that is, a place where one's sense of identity is unassailable. The students' response to the writing assignment in my college class as well as the documentation of a similar response pattern among the students at Capital High suggests that this space is a cultural imperative. These responses also indicate the existence of an unconscious or, at most, a partially conscious fear of becoming (an)Other, capable of committing atrocities on the Black Self similar to those that are taken for granted in the dominant community.

In many ways, then, writing in the school context compels African-American adolescents to confront the notion of being identified as contemporary griots, actively engaging the pen's double-edged perception.[6] Thus, the pen's constructions and representations of the Black Self as Other are powerful deterrents to the academic success of African-American students.

The narratives presented in this ethnography are uncensored evidence of this dilemma. Engendered by my experience as an anthropologist, a "halfie," a teacher, and someone who is represented in two contested ways—a body that is racialized and (mis)represented as Other juxtaposed with that of the dispassionate, carefully trained anthropologist—these narratives scrape against my skin, bleeding the anxieties, the pain, and the suffering attendant on my own experience. More important, they celebrate and make permanent the varied identities and emotions of the school and the entire community. This is significant because, as I indicated above, images inscribed in ethnographic texts are not neutral. Rather, ethnographic texts are stained with the violence, the biases, and the partialities that are inevitably (although perhaps unconsciously) frozen in the vision of the writer.

For years I have struggled with this dilemma. I sought to develop a discourse that would not only capture and illuminate my findings at Capital High, but would also minimize the violence connected with the watching and writing process. Documenting how the students' efforts to represent and reflect the sacredness of the Black Self are repeatedly suffocated in the context of school learning, I wanted to show how their efforts to alter existing representations of the Black Self unwittingly ⌐ P. Willis impale them on existing images. Further, I sought—some will conclude unsuccessfully—to find a way to write about how the members of the Capital community contested my (re)presentations of them. As I see it, then, the following ethnographic narratives are embedded in the improvisational nature of the life I and the non-elite people I studied are compelled to live. They are also evidence of the omnipresent issue of watching as violence, with the constant threat of the students' identities imploding.

As a marginalized member of the academy, I am aware of my complicity in the development of a discourse of anthropology that emphasizes the instability and heterogeneity of racialized categories and meanings. I am also at least partially aware of how what I write is policed and challenged, especially "out there in the real world." Understandably, I grapple endlessly with the development of a discourse that accurately captures the ways in which the students I studied and those I teach police their own racialized identities while concurrently seeking the prestige traditionally defined as the rightful prerogative of persons whose geographical place is regarded as European in origin. Consequently, this ethnography presents a discourse that captures the impact of the students' self-(re)presentations scraping up against an image that constructs them as intruders; it also documents how their academic effort is affected by the constant surveillance of their peers and cohorts for signs of misrepresentation and appropriation of images of the Other. More important, it chronicles how the Capital community residents—students, parents, teachers, and everybody else—are compelled to "make a way out of no way" by forging a way of life in the school context that is both contrived and tentative, changing yet remaining unchanged. Among the students I have taught and observed, resistance as both conformity *and* avoidance is evident.

If the Capital High research findings and my personal experience as a teacher are typical, African-American students perceive the pen as the quintessential instrument of representation, appropriation, and oppression—the "stealth bomber" implicated in the construction of Black people as Other. This perception leads inevitably to a fear of imminent immolation or rape of Self. What provokes and sustains this widespread student perception and response, as well as how and why it persists, is still not widely understood. This ethnography is a first tentative step in the unraveling of that enigma.

In the ethnography, I document—in the words of parents, students, teachers, other school officials, and other adults not connected with the school—the effects, both intended and unintended, of "attitude adjustment," that is, acquiescence to privileged-class social norms and a growing dependence on oral rather than written interpretations of what was in print about the academic performance of contemporary African-American adolescents. I reveal how African-American adolescents' partial or unconscious understanding of how what is written and declared legally binding on all American citizens is, and was historically, repeatedly abrogated in the case of African-Americans, propelling them to a distrust of what is written as an accurate representation of what they can expect as citizens of this country.

These narratives show how the formal school curriculum and its omissions and deletions are implicated in the development of appropriate(d) identities and how the students resist this fraudulent construction. Admittedly, this genre of narratives—rape, rage, and rapaciousness—is never included in the formal curriculum, though surely embedded in the informal one. I disclose how African-American students "read" American history in hapless consternation as their ancestors, parents, and other Black adults fight for what is known as civil rights—rights that some Americans take for granted. In addition, I describe the childrearing practices of the parents, highlighting how they connect with and abrogate the dominant imaging and imagining of African-Americans. I argue that Black people's linguistic practices are central instruments in this process. I also unravel the students' gender-differentiated response patterns and perceptions.

The analysis presented in this book foregrounds narratives of how African-Americans at Capital High and in the Capital High community conceptualize and internalize the school experience. This analysis also shows how the students' understandings of the ways they are represented and tortured by these so-called scientific analyses of the racialized Other affect their academic performance. Further, I reveal why it is appropriate to view the responses and reactions of the adults and students at Capital High and within the Capital community as in many ways deliberately and self-consciously contrived in order to protect and accurately represent the Black Self. Compromises and negotiations are endlessly evident. Masking is rampant, and individuals tend to know when it is expected, expedient, and necessary. They also seem to have a kind of intuitive sense of when it is not acceptable to breach conventions of school and society. Language usage and voice are, for example, hotly contested, with school officials and employment agencies uncompromising in their insistence on employing only those members of non-elite populations who are able and willing to speak the standard English dialect. This policy scrapes up against what many Black people think of as the sacred Black Self.

Understanding the narratives in this ethnography against a backdrop of corrective representation will go a long way toward disabusing the reader of two free-floating yet unfounded notions: (1) African-Americans, especially African-American adolescents who seek to maintain the Black Self as a safe cultural space, are "weird," "radical," and do not want to do well in school or achieve the good American life; and (2) success is an unproblematic social process fueled only by desire and ability. The Capital High data suggest that success is a more complicated process for African-Americans. Indeed, the data document that success—as defined by the larger society—is so complicated that it might be useful to read the following narratives as having at their core the mandate that the individuals involved accept the abnormal as normal, the unreal as real, and the strange as familiar. My desire to assist readers in understanding the representations included in this ethnography compels me to forewarn them that the psychological costs of academic success for African-American adolescents constitute the jugular vein of my entire analysis.

But let me postpone further discussion of the response of African-American adolescents to the R-word and its effect on their academic performance until I have discussed the following: my ambivalent role as an ethnographer; the city of Washington as a research site; African-American parents' gender-differentiated childrearing practices, including their most dominant linguistic codes; and the problems of Black teachers as people who are compelled to "pass" while remaining connected to divergent communities—Capital High, the larger Black community, and American society writ large. It is my hope that the multiple representations presented here mute the violence attendant on watching and writing. I also hope they accurately reflect the community I studied, the many voices—some positive and some negative—existing in the community, and the many valuable lessons I learned from a population that had so very much to teach me. I hope also that some of what I learned is accurately conveyed in this text and made accessible to the reader.

BIBLIOGRAPHICAL NOTE

In developing the Prologue, I have been influenced by the ideas and publications of the following ethnographers and other researchers (for details, see the Bibliography, pp. 373–96): Lila Abu-Lughod (1991); Michael H. Agar (1980); Arjun Appadurai (1990, 1991); Mary F. Berry and John N. Blassingame (1992); Pierre Bourdieu and J. C. Passeron (1977); Caroline B. Bretell (1993); Louis A. Castenell and William F. Pinar (1993); Napoleon A. Chagnon (1968); Chinweizu (1987); Rey Chow (1993); James Clifford (1983, 1988, 1994); James Clifford and George E. Marcus (1986); Celeste Condit (1993); Ellis Cose (1993); Michel de Certeau (1980); Russell Ferguson and others (1990); Richard G. Fox (1991); Morris Freilich (1978); Clifford Geertz (1973, 1988); Hildred Geertz (1959); Paul Gilroy (1991); Donna J. Haraway (1989); Richard J. Herrnstein and Charles Murray (1994); bell hooks (1989, 1994); Charlayne Hunter-Gault (1992); Fredric Jameson (1990); Christopher Jencks (1972); Arthur R. Jensen (1969); William L. Leap (1993); Catherine Lutz (1988); Catherine Lutz and Geoffrey A. White (1986); Bronislaw Malinowski (1987); George E. Marcus (1984); Margaret Mead (1961); Patricia Morton (1991); Sherry B. Ortner (1991); Nell Irvin Painter (1995); Paul Rabinow (1991); Michelle Rosaldo (1980); Renato Rosaldo (1980); Edward W. Said (1978, 1989); James C. Scott (1990); William Shockley (1970); Audrey M. Shuey (1966); Edward H. Spicer (1980); Paul Stoller (1994); Gregg Tate (1992); Michael Taussig (1987); Marianna Torgovnick (1990); Haunani-Kay Trask (1991); Michel-Rolph Trouillot (1991); John Van Maanen (1988); Joan Vincent (1991); Cornel West (1990, 1993); and Brett Williams (1988).

Stalking Culture and Meaning and Looking in a Refracted Mirror

William, my then 4-year-old son, announced while riding a department store escalator: "I want to be white. Whites are good. If my family is white, then I would be white."

"Being black . . . being an African-American isn't good. That's the reason why," he said as I explored what prompted this revelation.

In response to a question about what is wrong with being a black person, he pointed his finger and pretended to shoot.

Somewhere along the line, my son had received messages that being a black person in America was not something to be proud of, that his cultural heritage was not something to cherish, that his smooth caramel-colored skin made him one of the undesirable. Somewhere in his 4-year-old psyche he had come to the conclusion that to be happy, to achieve success, to reap life's bounty he needed to be white.

My conscious efforts to imbue my son with a positive sense of himself and his race had failed. The books, the plays, the paintings, the historic sites that bespeak a proud past and a promising future seemed to have made no impact.—Yvonne Shinhoster Lamb, *Washington Post*, 9 September 1991.

EYEWITNESSING: BRAIDING PAST AND PRESENT

The small southern community in which I was reared and the large urban community where I did my anthropological fieldwork are hundreds of miles apart, both geographically and temporally. Culturally, however, they are virtually indistinguishable: externally constructed as *lacking*, they evoke appropriate(d) identities forged in the crucible of a race-specific humanity. In both communities, individuals are compelled to

13

slip in and out of a culturally specific perception of Blackness. This continuous, forced identity migration, especially in institutions like my high school, is equated with survival, not only for the individual but for the larger "imagined [Black] community" as well (B. Anderson 1991:6). Consequently, when I walked into Capital High School[1] that first day, there was something both culturally familiar and strange about this unfamiliar place, something which indicated that much of what I saw and heard was self-consciously constructed and policed.

My familiarity with this pattern and its implication propelled me to a familiar cultural space. I was suddenly transfixed in time, awash in a sea of ambivalent cultural memories, convinced that I had been granted a second life as an adult to relive my childhood and schooling experiences. I felt as if I had been reincarnated but allowed to maintain my previous karma. It was as if I had been traveling for many years to get to this place, to bring an ethnographer's eye—braided to my adult status—to what I had not been able to understand as a young Black girl.

These divergent feelings flooded my psyche as I drove my old car slowly down the street that would become as familiar to me as the darkness of my skin. Hunter Avenue, the street nearest the school, was crowded with adolescents even though they were not officially scheduled for school on this day. As I watched the students from my car window and listened to the sounds of their laughing voices, powerful memories of my own schooling experiences came alive in my mind. Remembering how constrained my early school days had been, suddenly I was a little girl again, giving the correct responses in classes; obeying every rule in elementary school; honoring my parents' demand that regardless of what the other students did, it was imperative that my sister and I remain silent while in school;[2] enduring beatings by my classmates on the way home from school virtually every day of the week for answering my teachers' school-related questions; most important, not learning soon enough that my willingness to obey school norms was seen by my classmates as representing the Other.[3] I remembered how every activity was carefully choreographed to avoid angering the White community or endangering someone in the Black community. My parents' First Commandment, "Do not try to act like those White girls," evoked memories of emotional pain. I remembered the pervasive, rarely verbalized message of difference and exclusion—the "erasure" of my cultural, racial, and gendered "Self" from what I read, studied, and subsequently came to consider important. I seemed to recall every social ache I had experienced as a young Black girl. What I remembered most, however, was the sense of containment and suppression; and the attendant sense of responsibility that my ability to see through "the veil" placed on me and on everyone I knew (DuBois 1970 [1903]).

Embarking on this unknown journey at Capital High was both exciting and frightening. I was excited by the sense of discovery inherent in the pursuit of the unknown. I was fearful because for African-Americans success is a problematic concept, for in the larger American context it has been unilaterally appropriated and unevenly sutured to human and resource domination. My fear was also driven, in part at least, by my desire not to be involved in any acts that could be constructed to mean human domination of others. Ironically, my fear was generated by and anchored in my prior experience of the institution of schooling and my sense of a Black cultural space. In fact, it was the feeling of déjà vu—the familiarity of schooling—that was so unsettling.

As I got out of my car and walked toward Capital High School, where I was about to begin my anthropological research project, I realized that I could now try to braid my childhood experiences with my present knowledge as an anthropologist. Intellectually, I relished the opportunity; from a practical point of view, however, I entered this environment as "the naked anthropologist," ambivalent about what it would mean to imbue my life with the wisdom and knowledge I would surely acquire from my research (DeVita 1992: xvi). I was also unsure of what might happen and fearful that what I dreaded most—rejection—might become a reality.

Viewing schools and schooling as *the* American symbol of upward mobility had structured my school behavior and academic effort when I was a child. It was this meritocratic perception of schools and schooling that compelled me to deny the humiliation of the many racially denigrating experiences I had endured as a young Black girl in the southern United States. It was also this perception that led me to believe that despite the Black/White difference all around me, America was the land of opportunity for all and that education was the social and intellectual equalizer. As an adult, I became far less certain that schools could deliver all they have traditionally promised. I especially doubted the widely accepted axiom that schooling mitigates caste, race, gender, and class issues. In fact, it was this skepticism that initially persuaded me to propose my research project at Capital High School. I wanted to determine whether, as a cultural symbol, blackness was still imaged as a barrier to academic achievement. A number of anthropologists had reported on the implications, for nondominant groups, of the role of schooling in cultural transmission, and I had studied their reports.

SCHOOLING AS CULTURAL TRANSMISSION

From its inception, anthropological studies of schools and schooling—in both colonial and "native"[4] contexts—have had as a central theme the idea that education (schooling) and cultural transmission are in many ways synonymous (see Diamond 1971; Henry 1957; Ogbu 1982a; Spindler 1955). They have also consistently noted that this conflation has proved to be problematic for African-Americans and other nondominant cultural groups (Leacock 1969; Rosenfeld 1971). It is also widely implicated in the massive underachievement of Black students and some other nondominant groups in high school.

Anthropologists have frequently noted that such an orientation in the school context leads to what they have termed "cultural discontinuities" (Ogbu 1982a; Wolcott 1973). This is true, Ogbu argues, because in the system of schooling made available to nondominant groups they are generally expected to learn and embrace the culture and mores of the group with the power in the society and at the same time to discard the native mores and values they bring with them to the school context.

Studying Black children and the children of some other nondominant groups outside of school, anthropologists have found a significant consensus among school officials. M. Wax and R. Wax (1971), for example, found what they describe as a "vacuum ideology" in the teaching strategies and interactional styles of school officials among the Sioux Indians in South Dakota. That is, in planning school programs and curricula, school officials did not feel compelled to consider the influence and power of the Sioux children's existing culture. Instead they started with the assumption that the culture of the Sioux was not a factor to be incorporated into the core curriculum, teaching practices, or teacher expectations. School officials behaved as if Sioux children had lived in a cultural vacuum. Given such an orientation, these officials were free to reconstitute the Sioux, to change them into White Indians or at least into Indians who could "act white" in order to achieve a modicum of success in the larger American society. Those students who resisted or showed other evidence of a reluctance to redefine themselves were slated for academic failure.

Wolcott (1967) describes a similar response to the Indian students at Blackfish Village in his study of the Kwakiutl Village and School. There he found the Indian students responding to what they apparently saw as efforts to transform them as "headstarts to nowhere." They became unwilling participants in a schooling process that "transmit[ted] elements of White culture only" (Wolcott 1967:127). Their resistance took many forms, including truancy, tardiness, bullying the teacher and other students, and working cooperatively in completing classroom assignments that were intended to test their individual skills and knowledge. In response to these strategies, school officials frequently gave failing marks to students who were resisting. Wolcott notes that virtually none of the students who attended the Blackfish Village school graduated. The students' general response was to "appear to but not to" become a part of the school's transformation ethos (Holt 1972:154); they remained at the school until they were sixteen—the age at which they were no longer legally compelled to go to school—but they would not allow their psyches to be violated by what was sanctioned in the school context. As soon as they could, they left school, regardless of their grade level at the time.

In an ethnographic study of Black students' schooling in Harlem, Rosenfeld (1971:107) concludes by declaring that "the failure of education in Harlem is the failure of cultural transmission." He buttresses this assertion by noting that most of the teachers—White and Black—see the students' responses to the demands of their school as "foreign" and "improper." This generally shared view leads most teachers to fail those students who do not behave in ways that are familiar to them.

When I sought permission to study the academic achievement of Black adolescents in the nation's capital, I intended to follow the scholarly leads that had been initiated by the anthropologists mentioned above. I was certainly not prepared to relive my own early school experience. Yet it became imperative for me to both face and understand the powerful feelings that had surfaced on my first day because, like many of the students who would become the focus of this study, I had been labeled a high-achieving student. In addition, there is no other way to describe accurately how my membership in the Black community, as well as my intuitive understanding of what it means to be Black and American, affected my reaction to the onset of my research.

Prior to arriving at Capital High that fateful September morning, I could imagine the students I would study as Other, not as extensions of me. My actual arrival at the research site, however, dissolved all these pretensions. I knew immediately that it was not the fear of my connectedness to the students, but the actual recording and reporting to the external Other that was suddenly stripping me of my confidence that I could complete the project. Essentially, my fear was grounded in the notion that engaging in this research effort would inevitably lead to one more construction of the traditional Other.

When I entered the main office at Capital High, I was frightened by a feeling of the enormous responsibility my project entailed. I realized that I was also afraid because I was uncertain about the power of my writer's "voice." Would my pen be mightier than the sword or would my voice be ignored? Clearly, I would not be able to inhabit the minds of the Capital community residents. This was true despite our racial and cultural similarities. So I wondered and worried: Would my voice be an extension of the voices of Black teenagers? If I were moderately successful in capturing their voices, would my resulting analyses be heard by policymakers and school officials who believed wholeheartedly in the validity of test performance and who might harbor notions of racial inferiority? I was about to undergo a series of personal trials.

A FIERY ANTHROPOLOGICAL BAPTISM

Suddenly I realized that the number of people in the office of Capital High School had grown tremendously. My fear had not abated, yet I tried to present an image of confidence and poise. I sat up straighter in the chair I occupied. I tried not to stare.

Looking at my watch, I knew it was almost time for the meeting to begin. The principal had asked me to prepare a brief talk about what I planned to accomplish at Capital during the academic year. He had argued that it was absolutely essential for the teachers and staff to hear me verbalize my research plans. I had agreed. In conjunction with his request, I had written a brief speech which I had almost memorized. Prior to leaving my apartment that morning, I had made a promise to the image in my bathroom mirror not to read the speech. Suddenly I knew I might have to admit to myself that I had lied to the image in the mirror.

My anxieties were growing rather than dissipating. The muted voices of the teachers were becoming louder. Everybody but me appeared to know everybody. It was clear that I was visible to them only as background. Most of the people in the office appeared to equate me with a lack of importance; hence, no one approached me.

Then, suddenly, the voices of the people in the office were lowered. I could barely see Mr. McGriff as he hurriedly entered the office and greeted everybody with a repeated, thunderous "Good morning!" Very few returned the greeting. I tried to rise from my chair to make my way through the crowd to where I had seen Mr. McGriff enter the room, but the chair clung to my dress, scraping the floor and then falling back against the wall with a thud. I was horrified! These noises punctuated the muted sounds in the office. Absolutely certain that everyone was looking at me, I glanced up. Only one person was, and she smiled benignly. The wooden chair kept clinging to the blended cotton and polyester dress I wore. I eased back into the chair, trying to be as inconspicuous as possible while attempting to dislodge my dress from the splinters that were holding it. The air conditioning was on in the room, but the growing number of people in the office, as well as my heightened sense of visibility, raised the room temperature geometrically. I tried to be calm and not panic as I sought to break the chair's hold on my garment. Finally, the splinters in the chair lost their grip on my dress. I tried to smooth out the pulled threads, patting the garment next to my body in order to determine if any of the splinters were still clinging to it. After satisfying myself that I was chair-free and splinter-free, I walked as rapidly as possible around the various groups of teachers toward Mr. McGriff's office. When I looked in, he was standing behind the desk, with some papers in his hands. I knocked on the opened door; he looked up, recognized me (we had met earlier, when I visited the school this summer), greeted me by name, and invited me to enter his office. His warm greeting reassured me, and some of my anxieties melted away. As had been the case the first time we met, Mr. McGriff appeared genuinely happy to see me. He apologized for being late and invited me to have a seat. His energy was refreshing. He sensed my anxieties and assured me that everything would go well. He insisted that I *would* be able to get the data I needed to complete my proposed study.

His office was buzzing with people demanding answers to all kinds of questions and concerns, from the custodian to the assistant principals. He appeared unfazed by the constant interruptions and the seemingly insatiable demands for answers to a multiplicity of questions. Soon he requested that I follow him to the library where the faculty had gathered for the annual opening meeting. He reminded me, once again, that he had included my planned presentation on the agenda and that I would have a few minutes to address the faculty near the end of the meeting. To think of verbalizing what we already knew regarding my presence in the building increased my anxieties.

The ambience of the meeting room—the school's library—was inviting and relaxing. Mr. McGriff and the other school officials who spoke used a podium and I was pleased to see that it would be available to me just in case my legs became too weak to support my trembling body. As a veritable parade of speakers addressed an equally varied number of issues, I sat on the edge of my seat, both wishing that they would observe the five-minute limit imposed by Mr. McGriff so that I could get my presentation behind me, and dreading the rapidly evaporating agenda because it meant that I would be forced to convince a very tough audience that what I proposed to do during my year at Capital would lead to insights that would inevitably improve the school performance of African-American adolescents.

In what appeared to be both forever and a nanosecond, Mr. McGriff was introducing me as "the doctoral student from George Washington [The American University] who is here to study our students." I managed to make the five steps to the podium where I read verbatim the short presentation I had prepared, outlining my research goals and objectives. The faculty applauded politely as I made my way back to my seat. Mr. McGriff followed me to the podium and reinforced the idea that I was an invited guest and that everyone should welcome me with open arms. He informed them that I would be working directly with the counselors in order to obtain the desired research sample.

At the conclusion of the meeting, several members of the faculty—all females—introduced themselves and welcomed me to Capital High. They wished me well and invited me to stop by their classrooms and offices if I determined that there was something that they could help me with. On the other hand, several other faculty members assured me that they were absolutely capable of telling me—today—what I would learn during the year and could spare me the time and energy I was going to spend trying to learn what they already knew about why some African-American adolescents are successful in school. I muzzled my desire to explain that what I planned was a systematic inquiry into the worldview of the students, their parents and teachers and other members of the community. This was my objective, I silently voiced, because I was practicing the scientific method.

Later, as I made my way toward my car in the hot Washington sun, I vowed to remember to muzzle my nonprovincial thoughts; to avoid, whenever possible, plagiarizing their thoughts and ideas; and to regard as sacred their creative ideas and energy. As I slowly drove from the campus, I wondered if, at the end of these experiences, I would look in the mirror as I did that morning and smile at the face that looked back at me, or if I would look at her and wonder who she was. (Fieldnotes, September 3, 1982)

THE RESEARCH PROBLEM

Following the lead of the anthropologists mentioned earlier, I shall argue in this text that schooling is largely a system that reinforces the norms sponsored by the dominant group in American society. In the process of reinforcing the values and norms of the larger society, schooling—perhaps unwittingly—alters and negates the values and beliefs that the children of subordinate cultural groups bring with them to school, and thereby grafting onto their presumed naked bodies a lacking imagery. One of the primary goals of schools and schooling is to implant the values and cultural norms of the dominant Other. At the same time, I shall make explicit what one can infer from earlier anthropological analyses: Schools transmit existing cultural norms; therefore, in attempting to teach the children of nondominant peoples, schools inevitably deconstruct racial and cultural identities.

It is important to emphasize that this is not a comparative study of the academic performance of different cultural groups. It does not seek to compare, juxtapose, or evaluate the academic behavior and achievements of different social/cultural/ethnic groups. Consequently, it does not address the issue of why some "model minority" groups outperform African-American students. The focus of this study is on the "logic" of the responses of African-American students at one high school in Washington, DC.

I was baffled both personally and professionally by the numerous stories I heard from friends and colleagues about the seeming unwillingness of Black students to put forth a great deal of effort in certain critical subjects. The varied descriptions of the general response of Black adolescents to schooling since the Civil Rights Movement were often confirmed but sometimes clashed with my vivid recollections of how my peers responded to my efforts to do well in school. But it was the growing magnitude of the problem as I was experiencing it that truly distressed me. Everybody was talking about it—parents, teachers, colleagues, researchers, academicians, newspaper columnists, politicians, and preachers—everybody.[5]

To my way of thinking, the reported resistance to academic learning among Black adolescents was a total rejection of our forebears' courageous struggle to establish schooling and the right to attend school as a basic human right in this country. This current response, if it were as widespread as reported, needed to be examined systematically and scientifically, I reasoned, in order to bring about changes in policy that could reverse it.

This book explores the complex nature of the problem of Black adolescents' academic performance in the wake of a two-dimensional cultural revolution—the Civil Rights and Black Power movements—in a school where achieving academic success is constructed as "acting white."[6]

Within the African-American community, "acting white" is generally used as an epithet to convey the response of African-Americans to the institutionalization of norms that are generated and maintained by the larger, dominant community. As Capital students defined it, "acting white" entailed representing the "Other" in the presence of Black people. They labeled this response an acceptance of dominance, a political statement about whose views and ideas are to be promulgated. Most Capital students are consciously or unconsciously engaging in an effort to avoid dominating the Black Other and evading domination by the Black Other. The idea of dominating the Black Other is both a powerful issue for these students and a deterrent to academic excellence because the school's core curriculum is perceived as "racial text" (Castenell and Pinar 1993), inevitably compelling undesired alterations and transformations in their perceptions of an appropriate Black Self. Further, as Michelle Wallace (1990:41) asserts, "schooling has always been, first and foremost, a means of transmitting social values, not knowledge or power," and the individualistic, capitalistic values sanctioned by the school are often in conflict with the idealized collective, egalitarian values attributed both to the African-American community in general and the Capital community in particular. At Capital, students had an inordinately long list of ways in which it was possible to act white, many of them directly related to behaviors in and outside the school and some directly related to the pursuit of academic achievement.

Acting white embodies the idea of becoming the Other, but at the same time, because Black Washingtonians are both African and American, the *Other* is not totally *other*. The notion of a pristine or authentic racialized identity, uncontaminated by contact with another culture, is not at issue here. Acting white presupposes contact. It is therefore more than a set of behaviors; it is even more than the reluctance to act in ways that mimic white people. Central to the idea of "acting white" is Gramsci's notion (1971) of hegemony, that is, the maintenance of the existing system of power and domination through the celebration of practices and an ethic put in place by people who migrated primarily from Europe. While these powerful people may have appropriated and incorporated a Black or an African ethic in their writings (see, for example, Fishkin 1993) and normalizations, their failure to publicly acknowledge a "multiplicity of voices" in either the "public transcripts" (J. Scott 1990:2) or the footnotes of these transcripts negates the idea of a multiple ethic that includes the Black Self.

Acting white is both unavoidable and inevitable, the inescapable outcome of American citizenship, American schooling, employment in America, and, as J. Scott asserts, the embodiment of "the dialectic of disguise and surveillance that pervades relations between the weak and the strong . . . domination and subordination" (1990:4). While becoming White or the Other is not literally possible, that is not *the* issue. Rather, the issue is how the Black Self is symbolically dissolved and reconstituted (Kondo 1986, 1990) as an Other in the ideological celebration of what is known as an American ethic, the daily practices of living in America (see Gramsci 1971; Castenell and Pinar 1993). For many African-Americans, acting white implies (1) acceptance of an ethic that is normed by the dominant society and inevitably practiced by African-Americans in the process of living in America; (2) tacit endorsement of that which is written (text) as embodying African-Americans' social realities; and (3) unwitting practice of the dominant ideology (Foucault 1977) by controlling and dominating an Other, possibly including the domination of other Black people. Many African-Americans find this last possibility particularly abhorrent.

Accordingly, my inquiry migrates between an analysis that seeks to "give voice" to Black Americans' culturally and politically inventive and contested visions of Blackness and group identity and the more traditional ethnographic practice of seeing Blackness—and to a lesser degree Whiteness—as a seamless whole. It examines how those students who are doing well academically are able to do so and how the students who are underachieving manage to avoid academic success. More specifically, this book looks at how Black adolescents achieve school success in a setting where the latent, though dominant, socially sanctioned ethos—at least as constructed by the Black students at Capital High—seeks to reconstruct them to minimize their perceived connectedness to Blackness and the African component of their hyphenated, hybridized identity.

GOALS OF THE STUDY

An overarching goal of this analysis, then, is to offer a culturally sensitive representation of the factors—other than higher scores on school measures of success—implicated in the success of Black adolescents. An equally important goal is to have the reader reassess the impact of the school's core curriculum (ideological hegemony) on Black adolescents' academic motivation. While the study took place in a high school, *it is not a study strictly about academic success*. It is instead a study of *success* in the Black community that uses a high school as a research site. A high school appears to be an appropriate site for this kind of study because it is society's incubator: the critical context where this social process is first imagined, constructed, and marketed in the lives of impressionable, future Black workers.

I went to Capital High School and the Capital community after a protracted period of negotiating entry into the Washington, DC Public School System. I went in search of answers to, or at least some insight into, several naggingly persistent questions: (1) Why do Black students resist school-sanctioned learning?[7] (2) What, apart from high performance on school measures of success, differentiates Black adolescents who do well in school from their less successful peers? (3) What are some of the costs associated with school success for African-American adolescents? (4) Why do African-American students appear to include betrayal in their evaluation of African-American teachers who assess them in ways that, in their minds, parallel the assessment process of non-African-American teachers? (5) Why is this so clearly gender-differentiated? I thought that if I could get information to help me to answer these questions, not only would I become a better teacher in the college classroom but, more important, I would be able to help other people persuade larger numbers of Black students to seek academic excellence.

METHODOLOGY

In the tradition of social and cultural anthropology, the research I proposed included an extended period of study in the field. Fieldwork and a focus on the language, practices, categories, rules, beliefs, and social organization of a bounded culture group—African-Americans and Black adolescents in particular—are the sources upon which my subsequent interpretations are based. I believe that ethnography and ethnographic methods are the best reporting devices. Because in ethnographic studies, the researcher is inseparable from the research problem, he or she is always a part of the resulting analyses. And, as an American of African descent, I am keenly aware of a latent but powerful aversion in the Black community to the obligatory school-sanctioned transformation ethos.

I was involved in a formal study of the Capital Community for more than two years; informally, I was there two additional years. In some ways I am still very much connected to the school. My formal study included thirty-three students who served as key informants during the first year. This group of students was unevenly divided into high-achieving and underachieving students, with most of the sample—twenty-one—fitting my definition of underachieving students. The remaining twelve students constituted the high-achieving segment.

All the parents signed consent forms granting their children permission to participate in the study. Most signed eagerly. Those who hesitated were troubled by my hyphenated identity,[8] and, more important, by the violence attendant on watching. A few of the parents were extremely suspicious of me because, while they were not familiar with the anthropological method, they intuitively understood that it entailed watching (we anthropologists use the more polite term *observation*), a practice they rightly feared. For example, Maggie's mother was reluctant to allow her daughter to participate in the study. I called her several times trying to convince her that I was not dangerous. My fieldnotes of that first phone call are revealing:

> I finally reached Maggie's mother at her office. I told her that I had spoken with Maggie earlier and that she mentioned that you had reservations about allowing me to visit your home. However, if that was not a component of the study, you would allow her to participate. Maggie's mother responded by noting that home visitation was troublesome for her because she worked all day and did not get home until about 6:30. I responded by saying that if that was the only concern she had—home visitation—I thought we would be able to modify that component of the study to meet the unique needs of her family. That seemed to allay her fears (I detected an undercurrent which was not related to the lack of time at home but simply the lack of desire to have a stranger watch their family interactions) and she agreed that she would sign the form granting me permission to employ Maggie as an informant in the study, if the home visitation component of the study were modified or eliminated. I should note that this did not make me happy, but this component of my proposed study does seem to bother a number of parents. Hence the need to compromise. I must remember that I am not in the Trobriand Islands like Malinowski, who had complete and unobstructed access to the community. (Fieldnotes, November 2, 1982)

The selected student informants enabled me to study the Capital High Community and its "moral and meaning" systems in ways I had not envisioned. Initially, I was fearful that none of the students would talk to me. At the same time, I worried about the authenticity of their responses. Would they give me standard responses to questions that focused on race and race-sensitive issues? Would they see me primarily as a researcher and not as an African-American? Would the students "act white" in social settings where the preexisting norms compelled this "abnormal" response? And, most important, would they ever talk to me and to each other in my presence in "Black voice"?[9] Arriving at that state of interaction with the students was one of my most sought-after goals. Hearing them in this familiar "voice" was like a guarantee: an assurance of product reliability.

All of these concerns haunted me constantly during the first weeks of my research. As time passed, they bothered me less, yet they were omnipresent throughout the period of my research. I knew the likely consequences of all my options. None was good. I tried to give as much time to the underachievers as I did to the high-achieving students. Fortunately, most of the students viewed their involvement in a school-sanctioned research project about their academic behavior as a very positive factor. Hence, while they were initially less open and even taciturn, my primary problem became how to keep from drowning in the data with which they drenched my professional persona.

In time the students talked freely and openly about all aspects of their lives and those of their cohorts. They told me about their hopes and aspirations, their frustrations with school and school officials; how they coped with what many of them described as the unrealistic expectations of their parents; their struggles with their peers; their perceptions of who they were racially and culturally; how they differentiated between the true role and the idealized function of schooling for Americans of African descent; and how they saw Capital High operating in defiance of that idealized function. They also shared with me their feelings about what it meant to be Black and American in a society where being Black is disvalued and often equated with a lack of humanness. Most important of all, as time passed, they talked to me in Black voice.

The data upon which the following analysis is based were collected in two stages. The first data set was collected from a small sample of the students at Capital High—thirty-three key informants—and their parents and the school officials. *Data* is here broadly defined to include formal and informal interviews; documentary sources (J. Scott's [1990] "public transcripts"); participant watching both within and outside the school (in the homes of students, at their work and play sites), in classrooms, in churches, at community rituals including holiday celebrations and baptisms, and at recreational activities such as football and basketball games. I also collected data from the students' peers and nonfamilial adult members of the Capital Community. During this time, I "lived" at Capital High School and in the community in which it is embedded. I went to the school every day of the week, arriving shortly after eight most mornings and staying until late afternoon, early evening, or late night. The actual number of hours spent at the school on a daily basis was determined by the progress or stage of the research. For example, during the initial stage of the study, I left the building shortly after the teachers and the students. During the final phases, I left it or the homes of the student informants as late as eleven or twelve o'clock at night. I often returned to their individual homes as early as 6:30 in the morning in order to walk or ride the bus to school with them or to chauffeur them in my car. In a few instances, I walked with the students from their homes to Capital. In general, what I did was dictated by the pattern the students assured me was typical of how they went to school.

Since I had naively assured the students that during the time I spent observing (watching) them individually, I wanted to follow their undeviated after-school schedules, I was tested on that score in several ways. The most persistent and uncomfortable test was offered by the male high achievers, who invariably wanted to test my assertion that I did not want them to revise their after-school schedules for me. If I were unable to do what I said I wanted to do—that is, follow their after-school schedules regardless of what those schedules entailed—I would be judged in ways that assured them that I was just another "book-black Black."[10] The testing of my self-proclaimed racial and cultural identity by virtually everyone at the school was inevitable. Consequently, the high-achieving males repeatedly took me to a well-known sex store in Georgetown, in part to test the truthfulness of my stated intention—"I want to follow your typical schedule, regardless of what it entails"—but also to assure me that they were real men and to see my reactions to this alleged aspect of their lives. Every time one of them said that going to the sex shop was what he typically did after school, I took deep breaths, bit my tongue, smiled weakly, and went with him.[11]

Most weekends found me spending some of my time in the community, participating in the activities there and talking with the students' parents, other Black adults, and community leaders.

These data constitute the ethnographic component of the study. The second set of data was collected through the use of survey questionnaires developed in situ and administered to a large sample of the students (650). Questionnaires were also developed and administered to the teachers and counselors of the key informants. Only a small portion of the quantitative data informs the analysis that follows.

In the tradition of anthropology, I dutifully recorded daily fieldnotes as soon as possible after I left the research site. Most often, they were written at the desk I was assigned at the Library of Congress. My notes covered everything I saw and heard during my daily immersion in the school and community activities. In some instances, they included my interpretations and responses to formal meetings of the school board, faculty, parents, and parent-teacher meetings. My notes were more than just a log of the day's observations. They also included my understanding of my informants' "silences, resistances, dissimulations, avoidances, and hedging." (Coughlin 1988:1).

In summary, the bulk of the data used in this analysis comes from the ethnographic component of the study. It includes a synthesis of my fieldnotes and the formal and informal interviews with the key student informants, their teachers, counselors, and other school officials. I have also included the perceptions of the students' parents and community leaders. Most important, this analysis is based primarily on watching—a nonbenign activity.

I made a special effort to get at the community's indigenous definitions and understandings of success. These definitions and understandings are important because they inform Black adolescents' assessment of the relationship between what is expected of them as adult members of the workforce and academic success. I also tried to garner as much folk theory as possible in order to be sure that I was not just getting official information regarding what was and was not important in the Capital community. In order to minimize the possibility of being accused of distorting the residents' perceptions and worldview, I spent between ten and twelve hours every school day at Capital High and in the Capital community. Some census data and official school data are also a part of this analysis.[12]

THE RESEARCH SETTING

The Social Context

Capital High School—the locus of the study—is near the center of the community both geographically and culturally. The tensions, controversies, and conflicts there are representative of those that are apparent everywhere in the community but are not publicly acknowledged by most residents. The school as an institution is both embraced and rejected by the members of the community. School officials and the larger society tend to see it as the institution that will transform the community residents from their marginal human status to almost full membership in Euramerican civilization. This ambivalence is everywhere apparent. It is discernible in the almost universal parental command: "Go to school" and in their simultaneous reluctance to become involved in school and school-related activities. Lack of participation by parents in the Parent-Teachers Association meetings is widespread, and there is almost unanimous adoption of the warning to children: "Don't make me have to come up to that school."[13] This command also embodies a plea that most students, especially the high achievers, hear and understand. Failure of the child to obey leads almost invariably to punishment both for his or her violation of school-sanctioned norms and for making it necessary for his or her parent(s) to have to come to the school and in some symbolic way unmask the Black body in the presence of (an)Other. This latent, nonverbalized fear of schools and schooling structures the response of most Capital High parents.

A similar response pattern is evident in the behaviors of the students at the school. Like their parents, most of the students at Capital High proclaim a strong relationship between schooling and achievement of the aspirations of African-Americans. Verbally, they insist that schooling mitigates issues of race, class, and gender. However, as I shall point out with the data from the Capital High community, in many ways their behaviors negate their verbal declarations.[14] In noting the lack of congruence between declarations and behaviors, I am not suggesting that the members of the Capital community are significantly different from most human populations. They are not. In fact, many of these existing inconsistencies document how indistinguishable they are from other human populations, sharing this very human tendency to fall short of professed ideals.

Despite these shortcomings, the Capital community is not a bad place to live. Unfortunately, it is embedded in a section of the city where what is categorized as violent crime is regularly publicized by the news media. In consequence, Capital residents are perceived negatively by most Washingtonians. Often they are constructed in such a racist way that their humanness is questioned.

Efforts directed at distinguishing the Capital community residents from the general perception of the political ward in which they live are invariably futile. This is the case primarily because it is not possible for them to separate themselves from this larger social context. Some segments of the community simply try to cope with the stigma attached to living in this segment of the city; others contest the racialized imaging. It was this latter segment of the Capital community that was influential in getting an advanced placement program instituted at Capital High.[15] In their view, this is their finest achievement. The establishment of this program has led to the busing of students from all segments of the city, including Strawberry Hill;[16] this in turn has reinforced their perceptions of the efficacy of their efforts, thereby strengthening their commitment to broadening and expanding their agenda.

Meanwhile, the conditions that influenced the emergence of the larger community's perception of the Capital community residents persist. The community's reputation has always been a source of conversation. Because of its pockets of poverty, the community has been forced to take on an image that may be true for a segment of the ward in which it is embedded but that ignores the cultural knowledge, aspirations, and lifestyles of the community's residents. They are most often constructed *big emphasis on how outsiders react — is this just to illustrate reputation or is there a lot of interaction across wards?*

in this image when interacting with outsiders, and are compelled to endure looks of pity, disgust, anxiety, and fear when others learn where they live. This response, however, is muted when directed at the students who declare that they attend Capital High. This is true in part because the school has its widely recognized advanced placement program.

Even so, when a child or an adult identifies himself or herself as a resident of the community, the response is generally negative. This salient reaction on the part of those persons who are not members of the Capital community, and even those persons who make distinctions within the community, has consequences for students' motivation and ultimately for their achievement. Achievement here indicates school-related effort, not intelligence or the willingness to seek self-realization in other aspects of life.

Capital High: The School and Community

Capital High School is located in a predominantly African-American section of the city of Washington, DC. It is a school within a school, and as such it attracts students from all socioeconomic segments of the city of Washington. Its recruitment efforts are quite successful. More than a fourth of the students travel from various parts of the city to participate in the school's advanced placement and humanities programs. Hence, Capital High is not a school that can be accurately labeled low-income or inner-city. The school's complex student body and diverse, rudimentary class structure do not lend themselves readily to such uncomplicated labeling.[17] It is far more accurate to call Capital a "magnet school" in that through its multiple-level, rigorous curriculum it accurately reflects the diverse population of the city.

The main thoroughfare near the school—Hunter Avenue—is lined with fast-food restaurants, such as McDonald's, Bojangle's, Kentucky Fried Chicken, and Popeye's. There are two major Catholic and Protestant churches, both having either a predominantly White or a predominantly Black congregation. There are banks and grocery stores. There are gasoline stations, liquor stores, and small convenience shops.

The admixture of homes, including apartment buildings, and businesses gives the community a kind of patchwork appearance. Detached single-family homes with small yet well-cared-for front yards are often adjacent to fast-food restaurants, laundromats, and other small businesses. During the spring, many of these yards are abloom with begonias, petunias, and tulips, as well as other flowering plants, complementing the luscious green of the grass and shrubbery in front of Capital High.

Directly across the street from the school is an undeveloped, wooded area about which the principal was constantly admonishing the students. He was fearful of their tendency to use the area at lunchtime and before and after school as a place where they could escape the watchful eyes of the school personnel. In this area they were able to drink and smoke cigarettes and do anything else they wanted to without asking each other, "Is Mr. McGriff coming?"

During the two-year study reported here, the streets surrounding the school were the arena where the fastidiousness of the school principal, Mr. McGriff, could be seen, evaluated, and appreciated. They were also the arena where he and the older males competed for psychological and physical control of the female students. Every day, during the lunch period and the periods immediately before and after lunch, Mr. McGriff walked the streets ordering the males to "beat it." He discouraged them from parking their cars and enticing the young girls at the school to join them. While he was not always successful in his efforts to control this daily run on the female students, his high visibility soothed the fears of the people who lived near the school and minimized the selling of dope and other illegal or toxic substances on or near school property. His visibility also reduced the practice of cutting class during those critical class periods immediately before and after lunch.

This, then, is the general configuration of the environment where the study took place. It is also the context where I learned to appreciate the sociopolitical significance of resistance in a contemporary African-American community.

The Students

Capital is a predominantly Black high school—more than 99 percent—in a historically Black section of Washington, DC. Most of the students come from one-parent homes; many live in public or low-income housing. Their parents' lack of income makes them eligible for either the free or the reduced lunch program. In fact, according to the official school data submitted to the Superintendent's Office, of the nearly 2,000 students at the school in November of 1982, almost 500, about one-fourth of the student body, were eligible for the program. According to the DC Public Schools' official statistics, Capital had a total school population of 1,886 students as of 14 October 1982, a month after this research study began. The racial composition of the student body was listed as indicated in table 1. Graduates in 1982 numbered 476—75 percent of the twelfth-graders. Twenty-two percent failed to graduate. Four hundred ninety students entered Capital during the regular fall registration of 1982. There were 130 voluntary discharges as of 22 November 1982.

While the above data describe the geographical and some of the socioeconomic realities of the Capital community and the school, they do not present a complete picture of the student population. This is the

TABLE 1. MEMBERSHIP IN CAPITAL SENIOR HIGH SCHOOL AS OF OCTOBER 14, 1982

Race	Grade 10	Grade 11	Grade 12	Total
Black	723	616	529	1,868
White	7	3	6	16
Hispanic	—	—	2	2
American Indian	—	—	—	—
Asian or Pacific Islander	—	—	—	—
Total	730	619	537	1,886

Source: District of Columbia Public Schools, Division of Research and Quality Assurance.

case, in part at least, because Capital High is a school within a school, and because, as with every other senior high school in Washington, students at the high school level are not required to attend their neighborhood school. Indeed, more than a fourth of the students are not community residents but travel from various parts of the city to participate in the advanced placement program. Throughout my analysis, I will be making the point that Capital High cannot be accurately labeled low-income or poverty-stricken. In fact, the school includes all segments of the Black community in Washington.

The Staff

The administrative staff during the base year of the study consisted of a principal; 4 assistant principals; 5 counselors; 2 librarians (although the school was without a certified librarian until after the spring break of 1983); 123 regular classroom teachers; 4 Special Education teachers; 1 Transition teacher; and 2 teachers in the Skills Lab—one for Mathematics and one for Reading.

All of the administrators were permanent (tenured) members of the DC Public Schools. One hundred twenty of the 130 classroom teachers were tenured; 5 were probationary and 5 were temporary. Most teachers at Capital had from six to ten years of classroom teaching experience. The support staff consisted of 10 cafeteria workers, 5 clerical aides, 2 community aides, 12 custodians (including the engineering staff), and 1 school nurse.

The school is predominantly Black in terms of teachers as well as students. The English Department had the largest number of White teachers (4 females). Most departments, including special education, had at least one White member, and generally they were the teachers of the more advanced or "difficult" courses—e.g., physics, chemistry, and advanced placement[18] courses in English and mathematics. They were also the teachers who served as sponsors for the clubs such as JETS (for engineering students), It's Academic (for high achievers), Mathematics, and Chess.

The Curriculum

The school has a four-tier curriculum—two enrichment programs, the regular curriculum, where most of the nearly 2,000 students are centered, and a program for those students in need of special education. Additionally, where the regular curriculum and the two special academic programs overlap, students are grouped according to performance on standardized examinations and, based on the test results, are permitted or required to take the appropriate courses for their skills levels. Those students in English 050 are performing well below grade level; those in English 051 are at or just below grade level; and those in English 052 are performing above grade level. This is necessary, it is argued, because all students are required to take English in each grade level and they benefit from the homogeneous groupings.

In selecting courses, students in the regular curriculum are urged by their counselors not to drop the courses that the students generally feel are difficult—algebra, geometry, computer programming, chemistry, physics, biology, and foreign languages. Unfortunately, students usually ignore this advice and drop the so-called difficult courses once they have been given a "letter of understanding" apprising them of the Carnegie Units needed for graduation. In the rare instances when a senior does not have the courage to go against the suggestion of his or her counselor, and remains in the "difficult" course or courses not needed to complete the requirements for graduation, the student resorts to behaviors that make him or her "appear to but not to" (Holt 1972:154), remaining enrolled in the course but rarely going to class and thus virtually assuring lack of success in that course; or taking the body to class but depositing the mind somewhere other than in the classroom. Since class attendance is so important in teachers' assessment of students at Capital High, going to class every day enhances the possibility that students will earn a final grade of at least a D if they put forth even minimal effort.

In the regular curriculum of the school, the operative student norm appears to be to take only what is required for graduation. Students who sign up for more courses than they need are generally thought of by their peers as "strange" or "crazy." Usually, though, these few students are able to convince their peers that they could not get out of the class or classes, attributing their deviation from the norm to the intractability of their counselors: "Man, Mr. Collins would not let me drop this class."

Students in the special programs are few in number (the larger of the two special programs has just over 400 of the nearly 2,000 students enrolled in the school) and are subjected to a curriculum that far exceeds the minimal requirements of the regular one. For example, in the regular curriculum, students scheduled to graduate in June of 1983 were required to have taken only one course in the natural sciences and one in mathematics between the tenth and twelfth grades; they were not required to have taken a single course in a foreign language. In the larger of the two special programs—advanced placement—students who were anticipating graduation in June of 1983 had to complete a mathematics course and a science course at each grade level—ninth, tenth, eleventh, and twelfth—and to take two years of a foreign language. While it should be noted that this list of requirements changed during the second year of the study, this was the situation during the base year of the research, and it had been the case for several years.

Divergent response patterns among the high-achieving and under-achieving students at Capital are readily apparent. This response-variability is clearly illuminated in the riposte of Martin, a high-achieving male student who camouflages his academic effort. He was responding to my queries about school officials' efforts to transform his racial identity.

> They tried to get me in advanced placement when I was in the ninth grade, when I made straight As and one B. I was mad! They asked me to fill out a form. I said, "No, I don't want to get in 'cause they ask too much out of you." That's why I'm not goin' join . . . , 'cause I don't want to change, change myself. (Interviews, February 28 and March 23, 1983).

Embedded in the response of this student is much ambivalence about the value of schooling as well as a reluctance to participate in the trans-forming of the racial, cultural, and gendered "Self" that, as he sees it, is sanctioned by school officials. This response pattern is evident in both high- and underachieving students.[19] While many students define education as a commodity that will enable them to own big cars, fabulous homes, lots of jewelry, and money (that is, the American Dream), many also display an overwhelming yearning to maintain their ongoing relationship to the Capital community.

SUCCESS AS LEGITIMIZER OF DOMINATION

Capital's students were variously aware of how difficult it was to achieve the success that was heralded in the school and in the popular media, including television. They were also acutely aware of how the Capital community's established institutions defined success. In most instances, these competing versions of success tormented their psyches. Each student juggled the norms of community and school and the norms of the larger society, trying to achieve or retain citizenship in both worlds while alienating neither.

The students at Capital High did not share a monolithic view of success, nor did they agree how, or even if, they should be transformed by their schooling. Nevertheless, their perceptions of what sort of transformation was permissible could be categorized in terms of achievement and identity. All the students at Capital High—both high- and under-achieving—acknowledged the existence of a transformation ethos at the school and their struggle to resist it. Consequently, this social field—the school—was riddled with difficulties and tensions; it was a caldron of divergent social forces, some designed to maintain existing social conditions and others designed to produce racial and cultural change.

The members of the Capital community were compelled to live and construct their identity in a social field that most Washingtonians perceive in terms of the Black Other. But, as C. Geertz (1973) asserts, the residents share a "system of meaning"; they are culturally bonded, fused to an image of the Self that differs from the Other. Hence, the notion of *communitas*—"the [temporary] escape from structure" (Kaprow 1992: 222)—is useful here because it enables us to understand the porous nature of both community membership and the ongoing efforts of group members to avoid the larger society's externally defined structure (Kaprow 1992; M. Williams 1974). M. Williams, for example, argues that *communitas* enables us to appreciate the idea that although the members of a community are externally defined, their social field is much broader in scope than that "landlocked" definition implies.

It is the Capital community residents' cultural repertoire, or meaning system, that is landlocked rather than the geographical location or the people's perception of the social structure. In this analysis, people of African ancestry living within and outside Capital's geographical contexts, are constructed in ways that suggest similar constraints—both structural and cultural—in their behaviors. Consequently, avoiding externally defined social structures is expected of all members, regardless of their geographical location. Avoiding this structure is a quintessential characteristic of group membership. In many ways, then, the meaning system that exists in the Capital community is best characterized as a fictive kinship system. This porous system enables members of the community to gain prestige, obtain status, survive, and, in some instances, thrive in a social context filled with obstacles and impediments to success. As an organizational structure and idealized cultural feature, fictive kinship is not problematic. Like all features of culture, its continued existence suggests that it is supportive of Black people's efforts to survive. Fictive kinship thus becomes problematic only because it interacts with the larger intrusive forces of the dominant society, competing for the loyalty and allegiance of the students at Capital High as well as the members of the larger Black community.

During my first walk through the community, I was struck by the startling contrast between the way in which the Capital Community is imaged and the predominantly White middle-class community that I am here identifying as Strawberry Hill, with which it is frequently contrasted.

THE CHALLENGES

Although this book is not exclusively about my response to doing fieldwork at Capital High, I must acknowledge that throughout the project, my identity as an African-American affected my research in that I experienced—often concurrently—both estrangement and identification. This cultural baggage was forever present, structuring and obstructing my research agenda. I hope that in this account of what happened at Capital High, I am able, despite my conflicting roles and identities, to adequately freeze on paper what I learned about the people I studied there. At the same time, however, I hope it is clear that in writing about the culture of a particular population group, the ethnographer rarely captures the changing nature of the culture. What I describe in the pages that follow is the social field as it was constructed *at that time*.

Throughout my research and subsequent analysis, I have been plagued by a number of questions. Did the massive social and cultural changes ushered in by the Civil Rights Movement have some unintended consequences in the academic behavior and performance of Black students, none of which was anticipated by the members of either the Black or the White communities? Would my subsequent accounts and interpretations of the cultural knowledge, behaviors, and actions of the residents of the Capital Community, as well as their "moral meanings," be defined in some ways and at some levels as plagiaristic? Was I to become at least an adequate spokesperson for today's Black adolescents? Would our similarities limit my success? Or, conversely, would our shared histories and contested understandings make me more effective? Would my marginalized status as an anthropologist transform me—in the perceptions of the Capital residents—into a "book-black Black," unable to accurately translate or understand their "oral meaning" system and the values and beliefs fueling their behaviors? More important, would the unintentional "voice" inflections generated by my schooling make it likely that I could be legitimately accused of plagiarizing the views and perceptions of the Capital Community residents, inevitably offering a distortion of their lived reality?

So many questions haunted me: Did I want to have to relive my segregated-integrated school experience? Would I be able to detach my personal school experience from the experiences of the students at Capital High? As an anthropologist and an African-American, would I be able to manipulate these varied statuses and roles in ways which would illuminate the schooling dilemmas of contemporary Black teenagers? Would I be able to freeze in printed materials—reports, journal articles, and perhaps a book—authentic yet fluid descriptions of the perceptions of the Capital High residents? Would I be able to capture the dynamic and magnetic nature of the consensuses and conflicts welding and splitting the Capital Community into the energized cultural field it apparently is? Finally, would I be able to carry out this study in ways that might lead policymakers and school officials to make drastic changes in the way schools are currently structured?

Before presenting the ethnographic data that document how and why school success is sought and achieved by only a small segment of the student population at Capital High, this book offers a limited discussion of the history and perceptions of African-Americans in Washington, DC, and my theoretical claims regarding fictive kinship. This discussion is necessary, I believe, if we are to understand—from a broad perspective—why African-American students born and reared since the passage of civil-rights legislation resist the academy's silent but powerful message to achieve academic success and in the process become a dominant Other.

ONE

Schooling and Imagining the American Dream: Success Alloyed with Failure

One of the guys I met in the West End was called JuJu. A jeweler, he was known all along the East Coast as one of the finest in his profession. I don't know what had happened in life to make JuJu so bitter, but he refused to even talk to white people. He let his wife do any negotiations that required interaction with whites. There were many whites trying to do business with JuJu. A prominent white-owned store chain offered him a lucrative contract to make jewelry exclusively for its stores nationwide, but he turned it down because it would require too much involvement with baldheads. He could have made a lot of money if he'd been willing to venture into the white world, but he said money was less important to him than his sanity. (McCall 1994:322)

Among contemporary African-Americans, resistance is constructed as power and appears to take two primary forms: conformity and avoidance. As conformity, it is interpreted as unqualified acceptance of the ideological claims of the larger society; within the African-American community, it is often perceived as disguised warfare in which the Black Self "passes" as (an)Other in order to reclaim an appropriated humanity. In the dominant community, resistance as avoidance is defined by the larger society as failure or incompetence, the inability to acquire and display culturally appropriate skills (Ogbu 1981c; Inkeles 1968). Within the African-American community, avoidance is constructed as willful rejection of whatever will validate the negative claims of the larger society regarding Black people's academic abilities. Thus constructed, avoidance enables its adherents to retain a sense of power and agency. As Kohl (1994:2) convincingly argues, it is imperative that we not confuse a *"willful refusal to learn [with] failure to learn"* (emphasis added).

Most people are familiar with resistance as avoidance in that it is generally constructed as oppositional and even antagonistic, and researchers have repeatedly noted that this form of resistance negatively affects the academic performance of adolescents, including African-American adolescents (Fordham 1993; Giroux 1983; MacLeod 1987; Payne 1988; Solomon 1992; Wolcott 1967). But there appears to be less familiarity with resistance as conformity. Indeed, nominal conformity to school rules is often equated with acceptance and, in some instances, even acquiescence to a dominant ideology. However, as I shall argue throughout this book, at Capital High conformity to school norms and values could be and often is interpreted as resistance. Indeed, I shall argue that African-American "success" writ large can be so constructed. It is against this background that the following general historical overview of Washington, DC, is presented as a site where the long-term construction of success among African-Americans can properly be seen as resistance through conformity.

To understand the reasons for the primacy of resistance as a response and the particular imaging of the Black Self among the students at Capital High, one needs a brief overview of the social history of Black people in Washington, DC. That history can best be discussed in the context of the two major emancipations that have occurred in the social and cultural life of Black people in America, particularly among Black Washingtonians.

I offer a four-layer typology. Central to it is the postulate that African-American history can be divided into four historical eras. African-Americans' enslavement has been followed by two distinct revolutions: the First Emancipation following the Civil War and a Second Emancipation following the Civil Rights Movement. The final phase—neosegregation—is just emerging and is not yet clearly defined.[1]

BLACK AMERICANS' FIRST EMANCIPATION

Trying Not to Appear Black
Washington has always been a site of Black resistance, of resistance manifested as conformity, because the Black population that migrated to the city sought to transform Washington's imaging of the Black Other. Black people's primary weapon of resistance was—and still is—conformity to the existing but constantly changing ideology.

Further, Washington has always had a significant Black population (see Associates for Renewal in Education 1983; L. Brown 1972; C. Green 1967; Hutchinson 1977). However, Americans of African ancestry did not become the majority population in the city until after the Civil Rights Movement of the 1960s.

Historically, Washington attracted Black people who actively resisted the changing yet constant ideological hegemony of the larger society. They came in large numbers from other American cities because, despite the fact that Washington was the nation's capital, the city's White elected officials and government bureaucrats did not find it an attractive place to live (B. Williams 1988). Second, the relatively wide range of jobs available to people of African ancestry and the lack of a competing White population for the lower-status jobs in the city made it preferable to other American cities (L. Brown 1972; C. Green 1967).

Even though Black people were not the majority population in the city until after the Civil Rights Movement, Washington had a large free Black population much earlier, whose resistance was initially manifested in its opposition to slavery. According to L. Brown (1972:17), Washington's free Black population in 1790 represented more than one-third of the entire free Black population in the United States.[2] This population exercised its influence in the city both before and immediately after the Civil War in ways that were unheard of in other cities in the United States (C. Green 1967; Hutchinson 1977). C. Green notes that the existence of this large free Black population was in many ways the catalyst for the heightened aspirations and hopes of the Black community in the nation at large. Certain patterns of social behavior were also manifested in conjunction with those newly formed aspirations.

Imaging a White Middle-Class Life

In my proposed typology, the First Emancipation encompasses the Civil War and the following 130 years when people of African ancestry struggled to "act white" although forbidden to do so. Initially, their newly achieved legal freedom from slavery evoked a response that denied the "permanence of racism" (Bell 1992). Nevertheless, during this entire historical era, being Black was a burden and was frequently conceptualized as an identity to be opposed through conformity to existing dominant norms and values. The following example from an anonymous document is typical of Black conformity in the city and the undermining impact of race on the efforts of an African-American male to find and retain jobs and careers in Washington, DC:

> I am personally acquainted with one of the most skilful laborers in the hardware business in Washington. For thirty years he has been working for the same firm. He told me he could not join the union, and that his employer had been almost forced to discharge him, because the union men threatened to boycott his [employer's] store if he did not. If another man could have been found at the time to take his place he would have lost his job, he said. When no other human being can

bring a refractory chimney or stove to its senses, this colored man is called upon as the court of last appeal. If he fails to subdue it, it is pronounced a hopeless case at once. And yet this expert workman receives much less for his services than do white men who cannot compare with him in skill. (What It Means to Be Colored in the Capital of the United States 1907:185)

In another example from the same source, the consequences of resisting dominant imaging of the Black Other (also known as passing) are highlighted.

Some time ago a young woman who had already attracted some attention in the literary world by her volume of short stories answered an advertisement which appeared in a Washington newspaper, which called for the services of a skilled stenographer and expert [typist]. It is unnecessary to state the reasons why a young woman whose literary ability was so great as that possessed by the one referred to should decide to earn money in this way. The applicants were requested to send specimens of their work and answer questions concerning their experience and their speed before they called in person. In reply to her application the young colored woman, who . . . [was] very fair and attractive . . . , received a letter from the firm stating that her references and experiences were the most satisfactory that had been sent and requesting her to call. When she presented herself there was some doubt in the mind of the man to whom she was directed concerning her racial pedigree, so he asked her point blank whether she was colored or white. When she confessed the truth the merchant expressed great sorrow and deep regret that he could not avail himself of the services of so competent a person [and] admitted that employing a colored woman in his establishment in any except a menial position was simply out of the question. (ibid., 182)

Is this what modern African-American parents mean when they admonish their children to be "twice as good in order to go half as far"? In both these examples, existing notions of race took precedence over all other factors, including education, training, skills, even experience. At the same time, however, acting white was socially forbidden because it entailed encroaching on what White America defined as its prerogatives: going to school, learning to read and write, and seeking and obtaining jobs above the then extant "job ceiling." The era was also characterized by the emergence of a system of schooling which essentially enslaved once again the newly freed Black population (see J. Anderson 1973, 1975; Ogbu 1978; Spivey 1978:16).

During the First Emancipation, Black people constructed acting white as characteristic of those group members who resisted affiliation with Blackness, with the slave experience, and with other Black people in exchange for success. Such a strategy compelled an uncritical resistance—manifested as conformity—to the then dominant ideology. Whites generally deemed this response inappropriate because it negated a "scientific" postulate of the time—that the fundamental social and cultural practices of Black people are conveyed unaltered from generation to generation. Therefore, the stigma of Blackness was unavoidable, and those members who breached existing social etiquette (that is, behaved in ways that paralleled the behaviors and lifestyles of the dominating White community) were subjected to a gender-specific system of institutionalized violence, including lynching, rape, and maiming. Thus, as Michael Wallace (1970–71) notes, racial violence was a perennial weapon used by the dominant community to maintain the ongoing subordination of Black people, especially that segment judged guilty of acting white.

In Washington, DC, which did not become a predominantly Black city until 1959, "colorphobia had been an admitted fact" since the arrival of the first Black residents (C. Green 1967:316). Colorphobia existed in the fire and police departments as well as in the federal and local governments. It was also evident in the 1956 median income figures of Black and White Washingtonians when compared with those of 1950:

In midcentury [1950, four years before the *Brown* v. *Board of Education* decision] median white income was $3,425, [Black] $2,190, six years later $6,643 and $3,918 respectively, a drop of 6 percent in [Black people's] relative position. In federal employment itself, 85 percent of the city's 25,840 [Black people] in white-collar jobs were in grades 1 through 4, with base pay ranging from $2,690 to $3,415 a year. The proportion of [Black people] in Washington in the interval had risen from 35.5 to 44 percent of the population, an increase of which an estimated 45 percent was due to in-migration. (C. Green 1967:320)

Green paints a similar picture of the relative economic positions of Black and White Washingtonians in 1960:

The 1960 census showed a slight further decline in [Black people's] income compared to white—a median of $4,800 a year over against $7,692. By the end of 1960, on the other hand, Washington contained 22,000 nonwhite families with an income above $8,000 and 10,800 with more than $10,000 a year (C. Green 1967:321).

BLACK AMERICANS' SECOND EMANCIPATION

Imaging: "Looking White on Paper"
Looking white on paper—that is, behaving in ways and displaying the skills, abilities, and credentials that were traditionally associated with White Americans—became the way to "pass" during the Second Emancipation (circa 1960–1986). Those African-Americans who were able to become White, at least on paper, were embraced by the integration ideology. "Looking white on paper" became the impetus for school integration and for such social programs as the war on poverty, allegedly designed to eliminate the socioeconomic distinctions between Black and White Americans. What "looking white on paper" did not anticipate was the parallel emergence of the Black Nationalist Movement with its commitment to the maintenance of an "uncontaminated" Black identity.

I argue that this brief historical period is critically important because it enables us to look, for the first time, at a generation of Black people born and reared in a maelstrom of cultural forces that provided official support to the humanness of Black people, if only they would conform to the newly extant integration ideology. Prior to the Second Emancipation, there existed both legal (de jure segregation) and extralegal (de facto segregation) means of denying the humanness of people of African descent. I argue that the Second Emancipation forged a revolution within a revolution—a double-layered reformation. I make this claim because, though overlooked, dismissed, and discounted, this double-layered revolution evoked unprecedented social changes and an internal revolution: an identity implosion. The co-occurrence of the Black Nationalist Movement and the integration ideology, manifested in the Civil Rights Movement, created an unprecedented revolution, signaled most boldly by Black people's subsequent imagining of a Black nation (B. Anderson 1991) just as the larger society (the nation-state) was deciding not only to discontinue its "separate but equal tradition" but to include Black people as full citizens of the nation-state. Moreover, as Anderson convincingly argues, a critical element in the formation of modern state systems was the privileging of writing over oral presentations.[3] Thus, the successful imagining of the Black Nationalist Movement—with its parallels to the imagining of state systems—was (and is) contingent upon the successful development of a population committed to writing, or textuality, and the bureaucratized aims of schooling.

Hence the centrality of the Second Emancipation to this analysis. The period was the first in American history in which African peoples born and reared in America were declared legally indistinguishable from their Euramerican counterparts. Ironically, as the legal barriers fell and the integration ideology was promoted, internal cultural barriers embodied in a racialized identity soared. Acceptance of the re-imaging of Blackness, as in "Black is beautiful," emerged. Thus the convergence of the Black Power movement and the fear of the disappearance of a Black identity in the midst of the emergence of the integration ideology evoked concern with how to retain a Black identity in a context where an infantile Black identity was overwhelmed by a flood of White normalizations. The central issue for Black Americans became integration and assimilation, vis-à-vis the struggle for the preservation of Blackness.

Black students born during this period would find themselves facing both unparalleled opportunities and subtle limitations. Unfortunately, most social scientists tend to emphasize the former rather than the latter. Officially, Black adolescents are growing up in a social context which values integration[4] of all segments of American society. At the same time, however, there are definite indicators of continuing racism and other forms of human degradation. There is also the development within the African-American community of an imagined Black nation. The goal of the Black Power movement was never fully realized; many of its proponents were killed or left the country. Nevertheless, the emergence of a wealth of symbols—for example, adopting African names, wearing African dress and practicing African religions, choosing natural hair styles rather than the customary Euramerican styles, returning to the more collective or egalitarian lifestyle that characterized their foreparents' way of life in most of the African countries from which they involuntarily came—these symbols that African-Americans understood and were able to relate to during the 1950s and 1960s forged the development of an imagined Black nation. Hence, for many of these teenagers, coming of age during the Second Emancipation has entailed imaging oneself as a citizen in two competing state systems and having to choose one as primary or central. Moreover, it means that in the Second Emancipation these Black students are compelled to live an improvised life in that the adult population, including their parents, do not fully appreciate the psychological implications of imagining and re-imaging a Black racialized identity in postmodern America and its effect on school-sanctioned learning (Herbert H. Denton and B. Sussman, *Washington Post*, 25 March 1981, A2.

Imagining Washington, DC: The Black Nation's Capital

Today nearly 70 percent of Washington's population is Black (see Mary Jordan, *Washington Post*, 23 May 1933, A1; see also Paul Farhi, *Washington Post*, 25 May 1990, F1).[5] This suggests that among African-Americans Washington is still seen as a relatively hospitable city by the significant segment of the Black population that conflates conformity and success. The Washington, DC Standard Metropolitan Statistical Area (SMSA) has the highest median income for Blacks in America (V. Martin 1983; Maxwell 1985). Yet the median income of the residents in the city proper is lower than that of both Black and White Americans in the surrounding suburban communities (Washington Urban League 1985).

There is an enormous gap between the median family income of Blacks and Whites within the city, with the White families, at the time this study was undertaken, earning more than twice as much as the Black families in the city: $36,000 and $16,000 annually, respectively (V. Martin 1983). Further, one in every six residents of the city and one family out of every six was living below the government's official poverty line. The high unemployment rate prevalent in the city during the base year of the study reported here was headed by Black males, whose training and skills are notoriously underutilized in the unfolding service-based marketplace by both the private and the public sector employers (Grier and Grier 1985; McCall 1994).

For Black adults who were born and schooled just before and during the heyday of the Civil Rights Movement, ambivalence and bitterness are the most frequent responses to the life most have led since then. Many of these adults have given up on integration (Matusow 1989). Indeed, Denton and Sussman (1981) argue that in this "crossover generation" are the most unhappy and conflicted Black adults alive today. Since most of the parents of the students participating in the Capital High study are members of the crossover generation, it was not surprising to discover that they displayed the ambivalence and anger noted by Cose (1993), Denton and Sussman (1981), and Matusow (1989). Moreover, as I am postulating here, these adults' consistent conformity must be seen as a kind of resistance to the continuing imaging of the Black Self as Other by the larger society.

In general, these parents' perceptions of the opportunity structure in America are riddled with uncertainties and confusion. As the generation of Black people most influential in promoting the Civil Rights Movement, they are the most vested in its consequences. These adults resisted the continuing imaging of Black people as an Other, an imaging that was most prevalent before and during the First Emancipation. They have some personal evidence to support their perceptions of the dramatic changes in opportunity created by the Civil Rights Movement: jobs and income that far surpass those of most other Black people both in Washington and elsewhere in the United States. By resisting dominant imaging of the Black Self, many of these adults have been able to achieve personal goals that were unthinkable for their parents' generation. At the same time, however, there is an intensely powerful feeling among this segment of Black Washingtonians that while their conformity has benefited them financially, they have not achieved the segregationist goals of the Black Nationalist Movement or the integration ideology of the Civil Rights Movement. The degree to which they attribute this perception to the imaging of race and a Black racialized identity varies.

> All of the black women seated around the table move comfortably in the white world. They live in integrated neighborhoods and their children attend integrated schools. Lynn French went to Wellesley and is a DC housing administrator. Amy Goldson, a Smith alumna, is an attorney, as is former TV personality Carol Randolph. Gladys Vaughn heads the public affairs office of the American Home Economics Association. Roscoe Dellums, in whose Chevy Chase home they have gathered, is the wife of Congressman Ron Dellums and works on Capitol Hill.
>
> As a group, they epitomize the dream Martin Luther King had for his people, but when these women begin to talk about race relations, it is with anger, not optimism. (Matusow 1989:153)

According to Matusow, this perception is widespread among Black middle-income professionals in Washington.

> They seem convinced that integration hasn't worked. Increasingly, black unity is more important to them than blending into the white world. "We as a people thought that integration was going to solve a lot of our problems, but the opposite is true," says Randolph.
>
> Dellums tells of warning her college-educated sons, ages 25 and 27, to stay in the house when she hears that the police are looking for a young black male. French describes how her brother, a student at the University of Virginia, was attacked last year by a group of whites and thrown through a 7-Eleven plate-glass window in Charlottesville. Vaughn says she is routinely ignored by clerks in stores and that her husband, a Prince George's County physician, can't get a check cashed un-

less he points out the MD next to his name [on the check].
(Matusow 1989:153)

This perception of enduring failure while achieving is not limited to
"high visibility" Black people in Washington. It is strikingly evident in
the lives of African-Americans who have chosen careers or who have
been denied opportunities to achieve dreams that do not necessarily lead
to visibility. In fact, resistance to the continuing imaging of Black people
as an Other in spite of their acknowledged conformity is a common
theme in the auto-ethnographic snapshots of contemporary, middle-
income Black people (see Cose 1993). This imaging is no stranger to
Black Washingtonians. There is a constant struggle to present the Black
body as an Other in order to maximize the leverage which is inevitable
in being so scripted. This episodic "enactment of hybridity" is unending
(Narayan 1993; McKnight 1993). In concurrently conforming to existing imaging and resisting the dominant imagining of the Black Other,
the Black body becomes America's postmodern ATM machine: it is continually consumed.

The central dilemma confronting African-Americans in Washington
is the coexistence of the valorizing of race and its deconstruction as a
significant social and cultural category (Shanklin 1993). While African-
Americans seek to become an Other by meeting or exceeding all existing
expectations for success, they frequently discover that their efforts are
thwarted and their ability to both imagine and dominate is hyphenated
and fragmented. One's ethnicity and ethnic identity becomes even more
"situationally" constructed (A. Epstein 1978). That is, one's inability to
transform the stigma attached to race becomes a consuming passion,
making the individual more inclined to be what he or she needs to be in
order to "pass" in a particular context. Dissonance is inevitable, primarily because the individual meanders between two imagined state systems
(see B. Anderson 1991; Bhabha 1990a, 1990b; Renan 1990), displaying
cultural competence in each but, as a result of the competing cultural
competencies acquired in each, treated as a noncitizen in both (Neira
1988:337). For example, in his book *Best Intentions: The Education
and Killing of Edmund Perry,* Anson (1987) briefly discusses his interactions with one of Perry's African-American female cohorts—a former
student Anson calls Carolyn Jones—in the program A Better Chance
(ABC). She outlines the mandatory meandering she and other Black students like Perry were compelled to endure, highlighting both the familiar
hostility from the Black community and the overt, unfamiliar, institutionalized racism of the elite preparatory schools where they matriculate.
She emphasizes how her academic acumen was constantly assailed and

brought into question, making her doubt her intellectual abilities, compelling her to think of herself as smart but not smart enough.

> There was a faculty member once who gave me a present. Now anyone who knows anything about me knows that the present I like best is a book. But that's not what this faculty member gave me. Oh, no. What he gave me was a very sexy dress, off the shoulder, slit up the front . . . He was trying to be nice. I wonder, though, how he would have felt if someone had given his daughter a dress like that. I guess he just thought that anyone from a quote-unquote deprived background has gotta know about sex. *You know those niggers— they just love to fuck.* (Anson 1987:91–92)

Jones then shares with Anson another instance when she was constructed as a nomad, not just different but very different:

> I remember the . . . dinner at school. To my right was an heiress to a cosmetic fortune. To my left was an heiress to a department-store fortune. Across the table from me was an heiress to an oil fortune. And they were talking about the places they had been, the things they had bought, the vacations they were going to take, as if I wasn't there. Finally, one of the girls—it was the department-store heiress—tapped me on the elbow and said, "You better be nice to me, because I'm paying for half your scholarship." I almost got sick to my stomach. I didn't say anything. I just got up from the table and walked out. It was two weeks before I could bring myself to go back into the dining hall. What had happened was that I had met "the man" face to face. (Anson 1987:90–91)

Because it is so difficult to mask "blackness" both as a racial category and as a cultural system of meaning, imaging the Other is enormously difficult. Appropriating Otherness embodies mirroring behaviors and competencies that are simultaneously revered and detested, implying "assimilation and contamination" (Bullivant 1987:190; Tatum 1987). Bullivant argues that among the factors accounting for this situation is something he calls "ethnic closure" or resistance to the domination of those who are in power. Consequently, in the high school context one of the primary concerns of contemporary African-American adolescents is resisting the possibility of "contamination," that is, somehow escaping the threat of reflecting the imagined Other.

Further examples of this shared perception among Black Washingtonians abound. Ironically, whether the individual seeks to collapse his or her identity in ways that parallel the example cited above, or whether he or she is more openly resistant to imaging the Other, the outcome appears to be the same. The following life histories of two Second Emancipation African-American males graphically illustrate both the reification and the futility of efforts to deconstruct issues germane to race and ethnicity in Washington, DC. These cases show how success and failure are alloyed in a disfiguring alliance in the lives of Black Washingtonians.

McBride—the last son of his White mother's first two marriages to Black males—was born and reared in New York City and attempted to enact the hybridity—to live his life concurrently in Black and White—he imagined himself entitled to, coming to Washington as a young professional journalist in order to escape the limitations of race as manifested in New York City. He also came because, like many other African-Americans, he perceived Washington to be a place where deconstruction of his racial and cultural identity was least likely to occur and reclamation of his appropriated African identity would flourish. His perceptions were wrong.

> Washington is a town split straight down the middle—
> between black and white, haves and have-nots, light-skinned
> and dark-skinned, and full of jive-talkers of both colors . . .
> There's no middle ground. No place for a guy like me to
> stand. Your politics is the color of your face, and nothing else
> counts in Washington, which is why I have to get out of here.
> (McBride 1988:27)

McBride imagined that it was skin color that had stymied his growth and development in New York. Hence the move to the Black mecca—Washington—the site where he would be able to display and celebrate his perceived racial hybridity. The presence of so many Black politicians led him to assume that race was not the consummate obstacle it was and still is in other parts of the United States. He was wrong. Stigmatized racial imagining is the same inescapable barrier in Washington that it is elsewhere in the United States.

> I'm a black white man and I've been running all my life. Some-
> times I feel like my soul just wants to jump out of my skin
> and run off, things get that mixed up. But it doesn't matter, be-
> cause what's inside is there to stay, no matter how fast you
> sprint. Being mixed feels like that tingly feeling you have in
> your nose when you have to sneeze—you're hanging there
> waiting for it to happen, but it never does. You feel com-
> pletely misunderstood by the rest of the world, which is proba-
> bly how any 16-year-old feels, except that when you're

brown-skinned like me, the feeling lasts for the rest of your life . . . I hate it when people see my brown skin and assume that all I care about is gospel music and fried chicken and beating up the white man. I could care less. I'm too busy trying to like myself. (McBride 1988:26)

It should be clear that Washington is merely a *mirror reflection* of the larger American society, African-Americans' imaging or imagining to the contrary notwithstanding. Anthony Walton (1989), a Black writer and filmmaker who is not a Washingtonian, makes the point:

I am a black man. I am a young black man, born let's say, between Brown v. Board of Education . . . [and] before the murder of Dr. Martin Luther King Jr. I am one of the young black Americans Dr. King sang of in his "I Have a Dream" speech . . . I don't remember the speech. I do remember my parents, relatives, teachers and professors endlessly recounting it, exhorting me to live up to the dream, to pick up the ball of freedom, as it were, and run with it, because one day, I was assured, we would look up and the dream would be reality. I like to think I lived up to my part of the bargain. (Walton 1989:52)

As in the case of the young lawyer in Washington, Walton reluctantly admits that his conformity as resistance to dominant ideological claims was futile. He acknowledges that the primary strategy he used to minimize the stigma of race was to try to disconnect himself from the negative imagining of the African-American Self by obtaining school credentials, which, as he understood it, would connect him to the world of the Other. It did and it did not.

I stayed in school and remained home many nights when I didn't have the interest of "staying out of trouble." I [suffered] a lonely Catholic school education because public school wasn't good enough. At Notre Dame and Brown, I endured further isolation, and burned the midnight oil, as Dr. King had urged. I am sure that I represent one of the best efforts that . . . black Americans have made to live up to Dr. King's dream. *I have a white education, a white accent, I conform to white middle-class standards in virtually every choice* [emphasis added] . . . But as I get older, I feel the world is closing in. I feel that I failed to notice something, or that I've been deceived. I couldn't put my finger on it until I met Willie Horton . . . I think we, the children of the dream, feel as if we are holding 30-year bonds that have matured and are suddenly worthless. There is a feeling, spoken and unspoken, of having been suckered. This distaste is festering into bitterness. I know that I disregarded jeering and opposition from young blacks in adolescence as I led a "square," even dreary life predicated on a coming harvest of keeping-one's-nose-clean. And now I see that I am often treated the same as a thug, that no amount of *conformity* [emphasis added], willing or unwilling, will make me the fabled American individual. I think it has something to do with Willie Horton.[6] (Walton 1989:52)

Being unable to escape the symbolic violence visited on their ethnic group and powerless to escape the inconsistencies in status from being Black and male shattered the common dream of Walton and McBride. As they look at the broken pieces of their individual dreams, each reluctantly concludes that he has been terribly misled and even lied to by well-meaning members of both the Black and the White communities. The lie is encapsulated in the ideological claim that race is no longer a socially significant signifier.

As with Walton and McBride, countless female as well as male citizens of African ancestry, regardless of the degree of their conformity, have been unable to overcome the limitations associated with being constructed as the Black Other. "Success alloyed with failure" is not gender-specific, nor is it a recent phenomenon. This is as true today as it was a hundred years ago, even though the meaning of race has constantly changed during this century (see Gossett 1980; Shanklin 1993; see also Cose 1993). Race as blackness, even today, is still a powerful deterrent to complete self-actualization. Thus, for African-Americans, conformity as resistance is alloyed with underachievement or what some respondents describe as failure (Cose 1993).

This "contradictory unity" (Bahktin 1981)—success and failure; past and present—is fused in the lives of Black Washingtonians in ways that are not paralleled in the social life of other contemporary social groups (for example, Jewish Americans and Mormons), making what is not supposed to be even remotely associated with success an endemic component of it: the coexistence of underachievement and a sense of failure even when African-Americans uncritically conform and appear to be successful.

Despite the evidence above, Washington—the geographical space—is still widely imaged[7] as *the* American city for Americans of African ancestry. It is Black America's Strawberry Hill. Contemporary Washington, with a Black population of close to 70 percent, has more Black Americans living in it than any other racial group. It also has more elected Black politicians than most other American cities: a Black mayor;

a predominantly Black city council; a Black police chief; a predominantly Black public school board. The school superintendent and most of the teachers in the city's public school system are Black.[8]

The local government is a visible employer of Americans of African ancestry. African-Americans live in every ward and section of the city, from the least affluent to the wealthiest, in the Capital community and in Strawberry Hill.

WASHINGTON, DC: IMAGING AND IMAGINING RACIALIZED IDENTITIES AND SUCCESS

In Washington today there is a merging in the Black community of two diametrically opposed worlds: affluence and poverty, success and failure. This is not a new social reality; historically, it has always been true. These contested realities emerge as fused, hybrid elements in the lives of Black Washingtonians primarily because of the continued saliency of race in American life and particularly among Americans of African ancestry. Among Black Washingtonians, one's racialized identity is imaged as indistinguishable from achievement.

In the imaginings of most White Washingtonians, low-income African-Americans are invisible; they do not exist. This manufactured invisibility means that it is not difficult for public officials to continue to promulgate an integration ideology in which the existence of low-income African-Americans is denied. On the other hand, when their presence cannot be denied, their wretched existence is defined as a consequence of their individual and/or group inadequacy. African-Americans, it is argued, are individually responsible for their deplorable lives.

Despite African-Americans' imaging and imagining of Washington as the land of opportunity for Americans of their ancestry, the vast majority of its Black residents live in the least desirable sections of the city, work at the most menial jobs, and commute to work, not in the sleek new cars of the recently completed subway system, but on the poorly maintained buses that take them to upper Northwest and the domestic, custodial, and semiskilled jobs in private homes, clubs, and restaurants, and the nonmanagerial jobs available in the federal and District governments. Like their Black middle-income counterparts who live in the actual Strawberry Hill area or in a metaphorical Strawberry Hill in other parts of the city, lower-income Black Washingtonians share systematic exclusion from realization of the American Dream. It is this common theme in their lives—exclusion or only marginal acceptance regardless of achievement—that fuels their resistance to and avoidance of an imagined Other.

Imaging a Racialized Identity in the Black Community
The consequences of conflict between the intrinsically valued racial identity and the externally stigmatized racial identity are everywhere apparent. While race is an important cultural category among both Black and White Washingtonians, its level of importance as a cultural category is neither unanimous nor uniformly predictable. Indeed, the influence of race among individual African-Americans varies across important intragroup categories and among individual Black Washingtonians, making its application and influence both alterable and unalterable, consistent and inconsistent, even coherent and incoherent. For some Black Washingtonians, the effect of a racialized identity is manifested in the commingling of hope and rage; for others, it is evident in the coexistence of accommodation and vengeance. For still others, it is evident in the soldering of defiance and acquiescence and the merging of adaptation and retaliation. This is Black Washingtonians' convoluted and tangled reality, despite widespread acknowledgment of the acceptance of a racialized identity among most persons of African ancestry in the United States and of the "official" denial of race as an important cultural category by the powerful members of the society (Shanklin 1993; West 1993).

Capital High Teachers and Imagining the American Dream
Contradictory feelings, especially those relating to success alloyed with underachievement, are expressed by many of the teachers and administrators at Capital High. Most of them have unpleasant stories to tell of their own failure to realize the American Dream, even though they conformed to the larger society's rules and norms and, as they perceive it, worked hard at achieving the credentials and training necessary to obtain mobility in their chosen careers. The sense of a lack of accomplishment is pervasive.

> Two English teachers declared that all one needs in order to teach high-school students is a good high-school education with one or two additional classes. Further, they argued, most of what one learns in college is not utilized in this context. (Fieldnotes, October 13, 1982)

In a second passage from my fieldnotes:

> Mr. Telly teaches a variety of math courses. He is quite annoyed with the increasingly low expectations of students' capabilities which are reflected in the courses students are expected to take. What bothers him even more is the constant inclusion of weaker and weaker math and science courses. For example, he maintains that the newly created "Lab Skills" course in the

DCPS is a clear example of the weakening of the science curriculum. He believes that this weakened curriculum is implicated in the fact that very few Black people pursue majors in the physical sciences. Instead, they pursue degrees in the biological sciences. Hence the teachers in the public school system in the natural science area are biologists rather than physical scientists, which, he claims, has its own unique set of problems, leading to some crazy and in his view illogical curriculum inclusions like Lab Skills. In his view, the course represents a corruption of what is biological and physical science. Moreover, it represents a diminution of the expectations of students. (Fieldnotes, October 14, 1982)

Capital High Parents and Imagining the American Dream
Most middle-income African-American parents face a dilemma similar to that of the teachers at Capital. As adults who have reared children utilizing middle-income and sometimes middle-class norms and standards, they have generally taught their children to conform to established social rules and norms as a way of resisting society's low expectations for African-Americans. Indeed, the most cherished dream shared by these parents is to pass on to their children their own level of income and of status, making it possible for them to live lives that are less contained and constrained. For many parents this is not what is transpiring. Their children are not achieving in the ways they had envisioned they would.

The parents at Capital High have conflicting perceptions regarding the importance of school and schooling. Wendell's mother is a case in point. Wendell is her oldest child and only son. She is a native Washingtonian; her former husband—Wendell's father—was born and reared in North Carolina. She dissolved her marriage when Wendell was about a year and a half old, returning to Washington and the Capital Community. Her low-level job skills have forced her to accept public assistance and housing in "the projects." Because of these experiences, she wants a great deal more for Wendell, one of the high-achieving male students in the study. She has always insisted that he conform to school rules and norms. At the same time, she indicates that in some ways education can be and often is detrimental to African-Americans:

Time's too short to be playing. And even—I found that even now, different [African-Americans] you meet that . . . got a education got [underpaid] jobs. Even in a sense, the education don't make no sense. You know. It hurts to see people got all that education, and some people can't cope, for being down.

A lot of people have taken their lives because of it. But at least you know you got it. (Interview, June 13, 1983)

In similar contradictory ways, the parents of one of the underachieving females—Dawn—insist that schooling is essential for African-Americans:

> *Mother:* I think Black people should get as much education as they can. I want all of my children to get as much as they can.
> *Father:* Well, there's definite disadvantages if you don't have an education. You know. 'Cause the White people been using that so long—you know, that . . . Black people are not qualified, so—you know, if you don't have it, the way I look at it, if you got to compete with a White, you got to be twice as good as he is. Or else you got two strikes against you to start. One is being Black, I mean—and they always think all—they think all Black people are dumb. (Interview, June 17, 1983)

Dawn's father's assertion that if African-Americans are forced to compete with White Americans they have to be "twice as good" suggests that being only "as good" will result in failure. Further, he insists that African-Americans, including his children, have to resist these low expectations by achieving more than what is expected of them. This philosophy documents the central claim I am making here: Among Black Washingtonians, there is a widely held perception of the commingling of success and failure for individual African-Americans. Thus, adults of African ancestry who are the parents of the students who participated in this ethnographic study share the experiences of the people whose life stories were condensed above, even though the vast majority of them do not earn middle-income salaries.

Black Students Imagining White Dreams

The imaging and imagining embodied in the Second Emancipation resonates in the formal school curriculum. Contemporary Black adolescents are regularly and officially taught to imagine the American Dream in the same way that White teenagers are taught this dream. At the same time, however, unintended lessons are subtly taught and learned (Foley 1990; Peshkin 1991). These lessons are also conveyed by the socioeconomic limitations that characterize these students' lives. Since two critical components of success in the larger society are wealth and "vulgar" material comforts (West 1990, 1993), Black teenagers are victimized in that they are also imaging race as the consummate obstacle to social mobility.

Not long after I began the study, I realized that at Capital High most of the students' dreams had died, were dying, or would soon die.

Art's dreams died in junior high school. Wendell's are in the process of dying. So are Nekia's. But while Wendell's modest dreams are dying silently, Nekia's are dying openly and ferociously, with a rage so violent that it threatens to limit not only her already "small future" (deLone 1979) but those of the persons who teach her or interact intimately with her. Korey's dreams are similarly affected. His dreams died yesterday. Or was it today? He is uncertain. He only knows that his future is not bright. And, in response to that mental image, he seeks to resist this imaging through avoidance. He minimizes his efforts in school, doing only those things that are familiar and comfortable and avoiding those aspects of the school curriculum that are unfamiliar and strange.

Fortunately, at Capital High not every student's dreams are imagined in this manner. A few students believe the claim that America offers equality of opportunity regardless of one's social or economic background, and in most instances those who cling to that dream are the high achievers. They use their perceptions, their belief in the fairness of the system, to resist the negative imaging of Black people as (an)Other by performing beyond the level of expectation. Even among this small group of dreamers, however, conformity is alloyed with uncertainty. Lisa works very hard to obtain good grades in school, yet she refuses to become an "official" member of the advanced placement program. Paul acknowledges that racism and racial discrimination negatively affect the lives of African-Americans. But his knowledge is abstract and decontextualized, discounted because these social problems have not been significant factors in his own life.

In general, these high-achieving students believe that performing well in school will mitigate the stigma of race. In response to their perceptions and beliefs, this small subgroup of students conforms wholeheartedly to school-sanctioned norms and values, even though its members are frequently accused of acting white. Indeed, they are so certain of the efficacy of schooling that they are caught in a dialectic that seeks to change their reference group from Black to White.

This response was *not* characteristic of all of the high-achieving students at the school. Indeed, a central premise in this book is that at Capital High, both high- and underachieving students maintained and abandoned, created and annihilated, and reconstructed and demolished a race-based identity. In the process of constructing and reconstructing this racialized identity, resistance was the fulcrum. This response occurred after both the First and Second Emancipations. That is, resistance has always been a central force in the cultural history as well as the imagings and imaginings of African-American students. Capital's students were actively, although often unconsciously, engaged in this process. Moreover, I argue, they attempted to decorate the outrage associated with dehumanization by either selectively masquerading as the dominant Other or, alternatively, evading all official efforts to engage them in an academic process that attempted to transform and reconstruct them as an imagined Other.

WASHINGTON, DC: SOCIAL TRANSFORMATION STRATEGIES

Stigmatized Race as a Barrier to Social Mobility

The complex nature of African-Americans' understanding of race as a deterrent to social mobility is established in each person's imaged past and personal sense of identity. The resulting dynamic nature of the struggles embodied in issues of identity formation, as well as the tensions endemic to socioeconomic conditions, are made manifest in virtually every aspect of the lives of Black Washingtonians.

> "I thought I would be rich," he says. "I thought I would be leading an upper-middle-class lifestyle, working for a big corporate law firm, married to another professional, four kids, vacations. You know, the American Dream."
>
> Today [the lawyer] and his wife, an office manager for a defense contractor, and his five-year-old daughter live in a modest bungalow-style home in Glenarden, a working-class neighborhood in Prince George's County [Maryland], and he is struggling to get his law practice off the ground. [He] and his partner, who is white, rent downtown space at a law firm on I Street, which gives them a good address and attractive surroundings, but they can't yet afford their own secretary or computer system. A tall man with erect carriage, [he] is starting to get some good cases, but he still depends heavily on representing indigents as a court-appointed lawyer.
>
> Twice a month he takes his portable Compaq computer to the Superior Court, where he is assigned three clients he first meets at the central cellblock. He gets paid $35 an hour to defend them—"probably less than other attorneys bill for word-processing services," he notes with more than a trace of bitterness. (Matusow 1989:153–154)

All his life, this young Black lawyer has used conformity to social rules as a way of resisting the dominant imaging of the Black Other. He has repeatedly sought to transform and invert the impact of a racialized identity by imagining an abundance of that which is supposed to alter the limitations of a stigmatized, racialized[9] identity: education. Born and reared during the Second Emancipation, he laments the ironies in his life: success fused to failure. It is, in his mind, increasingly ironic that while he has devoted virtually his entire life to obtaining schooling as a mantra assuring solvency, inherent in the small success he has experienced is a powerful sense of economic failure and social underachievement (Cose 1993).

The son of Alabama schoolteachers and the grandson of sharecroppers, this young lawyer, who graduated from Princeton University and Howard University Law School, is the recipient of greater opportunities than were ever before experienced by Americans of African ancestry, and yet he has also endured unimagined socioeconomic limitations. His inability to achieve the same or comparable goals as White lawyers with similar school credentials, academic skills, and training has led to a growing sense of disillusionment as well as a disavowal of his earlier, more raceless understanding. He is bitter and angry that his consistent conformity to society norms, including his investment in education, has not produced the same social benefits enjoyed by his White schoolmates. Further, since they—he and his erstwhile classmates—have the same kind of "academic breeding," the only reasonable explanation for their widely differing levels of achievement is, in his mind, race.

> He can't help but think that his life wasn't supposed to turn out this way.
>
> Always a top student, he was one of three black children chosen to integrate an elementary school for gifted children in Birmingham, Alabama. His first day there he was sent home for punching a kid who called him "nigger." The next day at band practice, a white boy let him try out his trumpet, and another boy said, "Are you going to let him touch your trumpet with those nigger lips of his?" [He] got sent home for fighting again. He cried and begged to go back to his old school, but his parents wouldn't let him. They said he should be proud to be a "soldier in the struggle." (Matusow 1989:154)

Becoming a soldier in the struggle implies both a "burning drive to prove the racists wrong" (Carter 1993:76) and the acceptance of what appears to be an academic imperative for African-American adolescents: resistance to the hegemonic claims of the larger society by suffering or enduring race-associated indignities as a prerequisite for academic distinction (E. Brown 1992; hooks 1989).[10] Moreover, it suggests the existence of Black Nationalism as an "imagined community" among African-Americans (see B. Anderson 1991; see also Davis, cited in hooks 1989:10). It further insinuates that writing rather than wisdom or experience is the privileged way of "knowing." This response by his parents continues a practice that has been a part of the historical experience of African-Americans but that became widely "routinized" (Weber 1978) with the passage of the Brown decision. In the wake of that decision, African-American parents actively encouraged their children to endure the pain and suffering attendant on integrating formerly all-white schools in order to make the goals of the Civil Rights ideology reality (see E. Brown 1992; Goldfield 1990). E. Brown, for example, describes how this mandate propelled her to imagine herself as a dominant Other at a predominantly White elementary school in Philadelphia:

> I became a biddable little wretch. I did anything to belong among them, those white children and white teachers. I was the first to offer to beat overchalked erasers or run messages around the school, or answer a question, or clean up after a party. I jumped at the chance to trade or give away my lunch treats, my Tastykakes or my Welch's grape juice, to my school friends. Soon I was convinced I was actually beginning to join them, leaving York Street behind. "You know, Elaine, you're not like the other coloreds. You're different. You don't even talk like one." My white friends and teachers at Thaddeus Stevens were telling me that all the time . . .
>
> Finally, I became white. At least until 2:17 P.M., when school was let out . . . The rule was simple: The closer to white, the better. We derided girls who had short "nappy" hair, or thick "liver" lips, or protruding, high behinds, or skin "so black it's blue." . . . [L]ike most girls on York Street, [I was] a few shades "too dark," [but] I had good hair and white facial features. I was really not like the other colored girls. My mother had told me that. White people were telling me that [at school]. I did not belong on York Street. I belonged in their world. I had not only learned to talk white and act white, I could do white things. I could play classical music . . . There were other white things in my repertoire. I was learning ballet . . . Moreover, there were my theater excursions . . . Everything considered, I believed I was really becoming white. So much of my life was white, except when I was returned to York Street . . . York Street threw me back, back to the realization that I might not ever really be white. (E. Brown 1992:30–33)

In the South, school integration mandated enormous sacrifice on the part of the African-American adolescents chosen to be soldiers in the struggle. Goldfield (1990) vividly details the first-day experience of one of the nine African-American children selected to become soldiers in the struggle to integrate Central High School in Little Rock, Arkansas.

Elizabeth Eckford was one of the nine black students to be admitted to Central High that day. She had scarcely slept the night before, excited about her first day of school. She rose early the next morning and pressed the dress she had made for this occasion. The reports she heard of a crowd gathering around the school caused concern in the Eckford household, and before Elizabeth left her mother called the family together for a brief prayer. Her bus dropped her off one block from Central, and she walked toward the school and saw the soldiers guarding the entrance. Some in the crowd followed, taunting her as she walked up to the entrance. A guard raised his bayonet, barring her way, and other guards with bayonets fixed surrounded her. Somebody in the crowd yelled, "Lynch her! Lynch her!" As they closed in on her, she looked desperately for a friendly face and suddenly saw a kind-looking elderly [White] woman. The [White] woman leaned forward and spat on Elizabeth: "No nigger bitch is going to get in our school. Get out of here!" [Elizabeth] retreated down the steps and down the block toward a bench by a bus stop, all the while trailed by the mob hurling threats and obscenities. She made it to the bench and sat down to wait for the bus. A white man sat down beside her, patted her shoulder, and said, "Don't let them see you cry." A white woman came over and escorted Elizabeth to her bus while the mob continued their taunts. Her first school day was over. (Goldfield 1990:109).

In her book *Warriors Don't Cry*, another of the female students, Melba Beals (1994), juxtaposes her long-held visions of her impending sixteenth birthday with her entrance into what she describes as the "furnace that consumed [my] youth and forged [me] into [a] reluctant warrior" (p. xx):

"Sweet Sixteen?" How could I be turning sweet sixteen in just a few days and be a student at Central High . . . Looking around, I wanted to take care that no one would bang me on my head or trip me up. I had relished so many dreams of how sweet my sixteenth year would be, and now it had arrived, but I was here in this place. As I walked deeper into the dim passageway, I thought about how I had always hoped that my sixteenth birthday would be second only to my wedding day as the most perfect moment of my life. I had planned every detail . . . beginning at school with my friends, a party at home with a new dress, red and white balloons all over the house, and "Sixteen Candles" playing on the hi-fi . . . Sixteen was also going to be my debut year—I had planned to launch my campaign to become a popular girl about school . . . None of that was going to happen now—nobody would let me even say "good morning" at Central, let alone sing on stage. "Hey, nigger, . . . you here again?" A boy's voice pulled me from my thoughts. A strong hand grabbed my wrist and doubled my arm up behind my back, like a policeman arresting a criminal. Frantically I looked for a teacher or guard. There was none. "Hey, we got a nigger to play with." He was shouting to his friends. Soon I'd have several of them on me. I struggled against him, but it was no use. Then I remembered I'd always been told, "If a fellow's got so little manhood he'd hit a woman, it's up to that woman to relieve him of what few morsels of his masculinity remain." I bent my knee and jammed my foot backward, up his crotch. "Damn you, bitch," he shouted. "You'll be a dead nigger before this day is over." Grabbing my purse, I raced down the hall, leaving my textbooks behind. I felt the power of having defended myself. I walked up the stairs to homeroom, only to be greeted by the same two boys who had been taunting me every day. I squared my shoulders and glared at them as I whispered, "I will be here tomorrow and the next day and the next." (Beals 1994:211–212)

Years after the first wave of soldiers in the struggle, the response is less obvious but unchanged. Black students' conformity as resistance is still excoriated in the school context. Indeed, the social pressure to conform is so great that some of these students—the high-achievers, for instance—are able to imagine themselves as Other, not totally Other but very nearly (Kondo 1986:75; 1990).

How do people whose academic achievement is stigmatized become successful? How do they transform their group identity in a context where success has been marked, marred, and appropriated as the prerogative of a dominant Other, that is, a group or groups having the language and power to institutionalize, define, label, and assign meaning? In order to maintain group sanctity, how do these stigmatized populations decorate the horrors that accompany oppression? In an era when essentialized identities are discredited and negated, how do they reclaim that part of themselves that they declare has been appropriated?[11] In the specific case of African-Americans, how do they transform the meaning of race as a cultural category so that it is no longer the essence of who they are? How do they demonstrate that Black "success" is often "alloyed with hypocrisy and blank-faced lies?" And how do they avoid the perception of dominating and being dominated by other, more educated[12] Black Americans?

Black Peoples' Belief in the Value of Schooling

For Americans of African descent, belief in the power of public schooling to make dreams come true is not new. Our ancestors shared this perspective: schools mitigate racial barriers. What is different today is both the context in which this belief now functions and the attendant social forces. "Successful" Black people, also known as role models, are sometimes accused of being the Other and/or acting white.

As the first generation whose entire schooling has taken place *since* the culmination of the Civil Rights Movement, today's Black adolescents dream dreams that are broader and more deeply embedded in the values of the larger society than those of earlier generations. Their social and cultural experiences differ from those of other Black Americans primarily because they are the "beneficiaries" of profound cultural change advocated by Americans of African ancestry and because they are reaching adulthood in a social context which leads them to believe that race is no longer the consummate barrier it once was (Wilson 1978). Today's Black adolescents are growing up in the wake of the most deeply rooted cultural changes affecting people of African ancestry in this country—that is, unlimited free public schooling, access to tax-supported public higher education, the opportunity to compete for most low-status jobs, and the emergence of the imagining of a Black nation-state. They are also coming of age in an era in which racism persists in a more subtle but no less degrading form (Cose 1993; McCall 1994).

Racism as a negative factor affecting the lives of Americans of African ancestry in the United States is obviously not new (Myrdal 1944; Drake and Cayton 1970). The premature announcement of its death (Wilson 1978) has been particularly troublesome for the Black adolescents of the Second Emancipation. It has resulted in the emergence of a new and totally unfamiliar form of segregation that tends to strangle the life chances of Black adolescents, depriving them of the impetus to resist the precocious death of their dreams. The Second Emancipation in Black Americans' cultural history gave rise to the practice of attributing differences in the academic performance of Black and White students to class rather than to racial differences.[13] As I shall document, however, class as a structural phenomenon in the Capital community was traditionally mediated by behaviors that, during our earlier cultural history, effectively guided and influenced African-Americans' perception of what it means to be human (see Benjamin 1991; Cox 1948; Landry 1987; Ogbu 1988b; Zweigenhaft and Domhoff 1991:138–177).

Schooling as a Process of Status Transformation

Historically, African-Americans have been taught that equality of status is best achieved through the process of schooling. They are repeatedly assured that if they will just perform well in school, the blackness of their skin will not matter. They have also been taught that schooling is the quintessential feature of humanness, the commodity, the ornament, and the currency that inoculates every individual and every population group against an undesired and degrading nonhuman status. What is not fully understood, however, is that, ironically, complete human status is conferred only on those groups or individuals who not only perform well in school but who are also both able and willing to dominate others. Consequently, in complex nation-state contexts where identity formation is invariably contested and fragmented, the central issue is how schooling purports to deracialize a people whose primary identity is both stigmatized and racialized. How do these groups avoid institutionalizing the very norms that mark their identity and culture as in some ways nonhuman? How do they both conform to existing expectations for academic achievement and resist dominant ideological claims regarding the Black Other?

In America, schooling gives status to one cultural face: "Whiteness," in all its varieties.[14] These include rituals like baptisms, family gatherings of all kinds that mimic the practices of the dominant population, holidays (St. Patrick's Day, Columbus Day, Christmas, Easter), and so forth. Thus, whatever is affiliated with Whiteness becomes what is normalized—the essence of what is labeled knowledge, goodness, and so on, and is therefore human and virtuous. Whiteness as a cultural symbol and category is at the center of racial discrimination. It is both the commodification and institutionalization of schooling that is so powerfully wedded to racism. It is the social glue that maintains existing racial practices. And it is central to the process that equates Whiteness with rightness.

By contrast, among African-Americans race is neither valorized nor empowering. Nevertheless, it is an important cultural category and a meaningful, if stigmatized, component of a shared identity. Indeed, it is the element that makes it possible for African-Americans to imagine themselves members of an imagined community—A Black nation-state. For Black people, race sets in motion a process that braids success and failure in an unequal and seemingly unalterable alliance. This lack of racial valorization emerged in the Black community because most Black people construct race as a stigma rather than a privilege.[15]

The amalgamation of two generally dissimilar and incompatible cultural categories—success and failure, Blackness and Whiteness—in the body of the Black community clearly distinguishes these cultural categories and processes from their operation and isolation in the economically dominant White community, where these categories exist solely for the pursuit of an atomized existence. The process of alloying success with failure persistently affects the lives of Black Washingtonians and subverts the normalized and expected impact of socioeconomic factors.

Becoming the Other: A Problematic Transformation

What it means to be Black in America has undergone enormous social and cultural change. That change, however, has not resulted in the total elimination of the stigma of race. Nor have changes in the nature and configuration of what Ogbu (1978) has called the "opportunity structure" radically altered the impact of race. This is the current reality for African-Americans in spite of their herculean efforts to expunge the racialized "Self" and in the process image it with aspects of the dominant Other. Thus, as the above autobiographical data suggest, learning to act white or be like the dominant Other has not obliterated race as a cultural category for African-Americans. Paradoxically, in many ways acting white has both altered and rearticulated the issue of race in their lives.

> [The young lawyer] learned to feel at ease among whites . . .
> "I was a National Merit finalist, a national achievement
> scholar, and I ranked among the top 2 percent of high school
> students in Alabama when I graduated." (Quoted in Matusow
> 1989:154)

His conformity suggests resistance to society's low expectations for Black achievement. At the same time, there is an emerging, unfolding sense of failure as the lawyer attempts to dissolve his racialized identity and become the individual, though imaged, Other. This proved to be both impossible and counterproductive:

> "I realized . . . that no matter how smart I was or how hard I
> was willing to work, that it wasn't going to happen for me."
>   "Don't get me wrong," he says. "Integration has been
> great for my life. Without it I would be playing on a much
> more restricted field . . . At the same time, there's no doubt in
> my mind that I would be much more successful today if I were
> white." (Matusow 1989:154)

Finally, as I shall document, virtually every student informant at Capital indicated that a central problem confronting African-Americans both in the school context and the larger society is the widely held perception and African-Americans' subsequent internalization of the claim that they are less intelligent than the dominant white population. Capital students shared the view that this perception is influential in the consignment of African-Americans to low-status jobs, inferior schooling, and so forth. The following examples from two of the high-achieving males is typical of how the perceptions of African-Americans have shaped the group's collective response:

> 'Cause [white folks] look down on Blacks . . . They think we ignorant or something. Something like that. They think we ignorant . . . Animals or . . . I don't think nobody really ignorant—unless their mind gone or something. (Wendell, interview, March 2, 1983)

> Well, [Black people] supposed to be kind of stupid . . . We perform poorly in school, 'cause we all have it thought up in our heads we're supposed to be dumb, so we might as well go ahead and *be* dumb. And we think that most of the things we learn won't help us in life anyway, like some people say, "What good is the quadratic equation gonna do me if I'm picking up garbage cans?" We don't even think about performing in school 'cause it won't help us . . . 'Cause people feel that since they Black they're not 'sposed to get good jobs. They're 'posed to get the blue-collar jobs all the time, and the menial jobs and everything—sweeping streets and being garbage collector, I mean trash man—whatever you call them people. (Norris, interview, February 18, 1983)

Humanness is thus the term used here to capture the Capital Community's angst, its struggle to recapture and reclaim an appropriated identity. It is also the term of choice because it embodies the affective nature of their struggle and hence the depth of their attachment and resistance to compulsory school norms.

TWO

Becoming a Person: Fictive Kinship as a Theoretical Frame

My parents' ambivalence about my love for reading led to intense conflict. They (especially my mother) would work to ensure that I had access to books, but would threaten to burn the books or throw them away if I did not conform to her expectations. Or they would insist that reading too much would drive me insane. Their ambivalence nurtured in me a like uncertainty about the value and significance of intellectual endeavor which took years for me to unlearn. While this aspect of our class reality [race] was one that wounded and diminished, their vigilant insistence that being smart did not make me a "better" or "superior" person (which often got on my nerves because I think I wanted to have that sense that it did indeed set me apart, make me better) made a profound impression. From them I learned to value and respect various skills and talents folk might have, not just to value people who read books and talk about ideas. They and my grandparents might say about somebody, "Now he don't read nor write a lick, but he can tell a story," or as my grandmother would say, "call out the hell in words." (hooks 1989:79)

DENYING HUMANNESS: GENETIC AND INTELLECTUAL INFERIORITY

In the academy, being able to "call out the hell in words" is of very little value. Rather, one must be able to read, write, and compute in the prescribed discourses. African-American students who are either unwilling or unable to engage in such practices are likely to be described as *lacking* in important social skills and therefore intellectually inferior. Researchers have offered many explanations for Black students' comparatively lower academic achievement, explanations that range from genetic inferiority (Herrnstein and Murray 1994; Jensen 1969; Shockley 1970) to Ogbu's (1978) cultural ecological model. Not surprisingly, then, the souls of African-Americans have been bludgeoned by many of these theories, particularly those based on biological distinctions.

Unfortunately, while varied explanations have been offered for why Black students are *not* performing well in school, few of these theorists have addressed the question of how and why some Black students achieve academic *success* and, more important, what the psychological costs of that success may be.[1] This relative paucity of recognition in the existing research literature of the success in school of Black adolescents is extremely troubling.

In accounting for the differences in academic performance between Black students and White students, the "scientific fact" of genetic or intellectual inferiority is revisited periodically in grandiose, ill-refuted scientific studies and reports (see, for example, Dreger 1973; Herrnstein and Murray 1994; Jensen 1969, 1973; Shockley 1970), by scholars whose credentials and skills are presumed impeccable. These explanations generally reinforce a perception widely held among some segments of American society: to be human is to be White or, alternatively, to be able to do and accomplish what White Americans have done and accomplished, both in and out of school.[2] African-Americans have either not been able to or have been deliberately unwilling to replicate these "achievements." Therefore, it is argued, African-Americans are not human or, at the very least, not as human as White Americans.

While there are other explanations for this difference in academic performance, including the cultural conflict model (Baratz and Baratz 1970; Hale 1977), the lack of educational equity model (Kozol 1966, 1991; Stein 1971), and everything in between (S. Baratz and J. Baratz 1970; Coleman et al. 1966; Hale 1982), none of these explanations is as persuasive or as pervasive as the genetic inferiority model.

AFFIRMING HUMANNESS: THE CULTURAL ECOLOGICAL MODEL

An anthropological paradigm postulated by John Ogbu (1978) challenges the validity of the genetic inferiority model. Ogbu advances the notion of an equivalent humanness among Black and White Americans in the current academic response to schooling by African-American adolescents. His paradigm offers an explanation not only for lower school performance but for lower Black achievement in American society in general.

A cardinal feature of Ogbu's cultural ecological model is his postulate that while work is the most salient symbol in a human population, the group that controls the definition of work—what work is and what work is valuable—and the representation of work is able to reinforce or negate the image of any segment of that population.

Ogbu's explanation (1978) includes historical and contextual factors in Black adolescents' response to schooling. Initially, he suggested that the disproportionately high rate of school failure among Black Americans was an "adaptation" to their limited social and economic opportunities. He argued that this failure was, in effect, a fait accompli, given the imperatives of the Black ecological structure. More recently, he has modified his cultural ecological explanation by reducing the emphasis on the instrumental limitations in the opportunity structure (1988b; Fordham and Ogbu 1986). What he proposes instead is a systematic analysis of the expressive responses within the internal structure of the culture of Black Americans. In this way, he is able to look more intently at the "lifeblood," the evolutions and relentless metamorphoses of the culture of African peoples as they have been dispersed geographically.

Ogbu's claims (1978) regarding the impact of a "job ceiling" on Black students' school performance make an extremely appealing explanation. The schooling offered Black students, he says, tends to undermine their sense of an acceptable Black historical past. Hence, they learn both to avoid seeking certain categories of jobs and, at the same time, to resist the legitimizing of such categories. Indeed, a primary response of Black Americans to their ascribed low status during the Second Emancipation is a commitment to the creation of an acceptable historical past. Resistance becomes the fulcrum on which that past is impaled.

Using data obtained from an ethnographic study of one high school in Washington, DC, Fordham (1988) and Fordham and Ogbu (1986) insist that factors within groups are also implicated in the continued underachievement of Black adolescents in the high school context. Further, I have asserted (Fordham 1988) that because Whites decide upon and impose the norms in the larger society, in order to be judged "successful" in that society, African-American students are compelled to develop a "raceless persona" (see also Carter 1993).

RESISTANCE: IMAGINING PEOPLEHOOD, FICTIVE KINSHIP, AND AFRICAN-AMERICANS

Working with Ogbu (Fordham and Ogbu 1986), I sought to modify his cultural ecological model, moving beyond his focus on instrumental exploitation (limitations in opportunity structure, such as job ceilings) and instrumental responses to examine the expressive dimension of the relationship between the dominant culture and Black Americans. I also sought to explain African-American adolescents' academic success rather than their failure. Indeed, examining and explaining success became the linchpin in my work. Looking at the expressive dimension of African-American life which, as I envisioned it, was embodied in resistance, was important, I reasoned, because, as I understood it, the cultural ecological model did not address that component. It was also important because, as Trask (1991) and other anthropologists assert, peoples who are engaged in constituting or reconstituting themselves do not seek to liquidate their pasts. Indeed, constructing an acceptable past *in the present* is central to their definition of who they are (Trask 1991:164; see also Friedman 1992:851). Contemporary African-American adolescents appear to replicate this pattern in that they are committed to imagining a past that meshes with their perceptions of an appropriate contemporary Black identity. Thus, a critical feature of the Second Emancipation is preoccupation with reclaiming an appropriated Black identity through the use of resistance, both as conformity to dominant norms and values and as avoidance of Self-immolation through acceptance and internalization of negative images of the Black Self.[3]

The cross-cultural literature on dominant/nondominant (colonizer/colonized) relationships highlights the dyadic, oppositional processes generally characteristic of such associations. These conflicts often provoke the subordinate members of the dyad to develop oppositional social identities and oppositional cultural frames, which lead ultimately to the emergence of a "people," or what Spicer (1971) describes as "peoplehood." A people is not to be equated with a racial or ethnic group (see Spicer 1961, 1971, 1980; Castile 1981; Castile and Kushner 1981; V. Green 1981; Leone 1981). While it may share with such groups the idea of distinctiveness, a human population's designation as *a people* is broader and more inclusive. What determines that designation is the unique nature of the historical experiences to which a human population attaches significant meaning. This is likely, Spicer (1980:347) argues, because each human population has a "historical experience which no other group has [endured]." Even though a social group may share a human experience with another social group—other social groups have been enslaved at various times—no two social groups have experienced a particular historical event in the same way. Consequently, it is both the uniqueness of the historical heritage of a particular social group and the meaning the group attaches to common identity symbols that are influential in its emergence as a people.

A people or peoplehood appears to be the appropriate imaging for African-Americans during the Second Emancipation (V. Green 1981). It is especially appropriate because the cultural upheavals evoked by the co-occurrence of the Black Nationalist Movement and the Civil Rights Movement encouraged unprecedented feelings of nationalism among African-Americans, forging what B. Anderson (1991:6) has identified as an "imagined community." Further, as he notes, a nation-state is of necessity an "imagined community" in part because, despite the claims of comradeship and deep feelings of patriotism among the people who comprise it, members of the community will never meet and, therefore, their commitment to the nation is largely a consequence of the privileging of language and printed materials coupled with their impact on mass communication (Bhabha 1990a, 1990b; Renan 1990).

Black people's "history"—that is, the images Black people created and absorbed during the revolutions of the 1960s—evoked an imagined community within a preexisting imagined community, the United States of America. This imagined Black community did not disappear with the culmination of the Civil Rights Movement and the emergence of the integration ideology. Indeed, as Castile notes (1981: xv–xxii), the emergence and continued existence of a people is not contingent upon most of the indicators previously imaged as prerequisites for designating a population as an ethnic or racial group: a homeland, a separate language, an unchanging culture, and so forth. Hence, my analysis is rooted in the "imaginings" of people of African ancestry and their constructions of Self. As is true of the residents in the imagined nation-state, African-Americans' imagining is hinged to a perception of territoriality that is not geographically real. As a diasporic people, African-Americans are compelled to live their lives on the margins of America's imagined community. Moreover, their own efforts to construct a sacred cultural space within this marginalized existence provokes them to even greater "dissemiNation" (Bhabha 1990a: 291).

The important questions become these: How is the imagined community concept connected to the existence of fictive kinship in the Black American community?[4] What is the role of fictive kinship in African-Americans' emerging perceptions of peoplehood or imagined community and their notions of success? How is kinship implicated in the academic performance of Black adolescents? And how is resistance central to this process?

PRESTIGE IN THE AFRICAN-AMERICAN COMMUNITY

Fictive Kinship: A Definition

Traditionally, anthropologists used the umbrella term *fictive kinship* to refer to people within a given society to whom one is not related by birth but with whom one shares essential reciprocal social and economic relationships (Brain 1972; Fortes 1969; Freed 1973; Norbeck and Befu 1958; R. Staples 1981). In this analysis, I am postulating that among Americans of African descent, this connection extends beyond the social and economic to include a political and prestige function as well. Thus, the hypothesized fictive kinship system is African-Americans' premier prestige system in their imagined nation-state, conveying the idea of brotherhood and sisterhood of *all* African-Americans, regardless of class, gender, or sexual orientation. A sense of peoplehood or collective social identity exists within the group. This collective, appropriate(d) identity is evident in the various kinship terms that Black Americans use to refer to one another, such as "brother," "sister," and "blood" (Folb 1980; Liebow 1967; Stack 1974; Edward Sargent, *Washington Post,* 10 February 1985, D1). It is also evident in the way Americans of African descent interact (see, for example, Gates 1994: xii–xiv).

Here I am postulating that fictive kinship is, first, a prestige system through which most African-Americans apprehend reality; and second, the ideology and organizational structure that undergirds and permeates Black social life—the subtext, so to speak. It denotes a cultural symbol of collective identity among African-Americans based on more than just skin color. The fictive kinship system also implies a particular mind-set, a specific way of being human. It reflects and embodies the moral judgment the group makes on its members (Brain 1972; Gates 1994; McCall 1994). The concept suggests that merely possessing African features or being of African descent does not automatically make one a Black person. One can be black in color but choose not to seek membership in the fictive kinship system. One can also be denied group membership because critical group-specific behaviors, attitudes, and activities are perceived to be at variance with those thought to be appropriate to the group. These significant characteristics are culturally patterned and serve to distinguish "us" from "them." A particularly relevant example is the tendency for African-Americans to emphasize *group loyalty* in situations involving conflict or competition with White Americans. The Congressional Black Caucus is an example par excellence of Black people stressing group loyalty over competition with Whites.

Fictive Kinship and the Egalitarian Ethos

In the Black community the hypothesized fictive kinship fulfills reciprocal social, economic, and political relationships. It also evokes a form of resistance that has sociopolitical significance and meaning (Giroux 1983; Solomon 1992; MacLeod 1987). As manifested in the African-American community, the Black fictive kinship system resonates in and deviates from the form anthropologists have traditionally associated with egalitarian societies (Flanagan 1989; R. Lee 1969, 1974). Because it is fused both to an externally imposed hierarchic structure and the imagined community of a racially subordinated population, egalitarianism *within* the diasporic African-American community not only functions differently but over the years has evolved as an oppositional, hybridized force that permanently adheres to and conflicts with the hierarchical structure celebrated in the larger American society. For example, anthropologists have repeatedly described how egalitarian societies function *without* conflict or contestation of existing norms (R. Lee 1969; Flanagan 1989). Among the !Kung Bushmen, R. Lee notes, one must never become a braggart even when he has killed the most awesome animal in the forest. I argue that within the African-American community a similar worldview is idealized but that in contemporary America it is fused to what West (1993) refers to as vulgar materialism—an unending quest for what makes one wealthy and successful in America. Hence the hybridity and opposition noted above as well as the deviation from the reported ethnographic data.

Thus, egalitarianism within the African-American community, pregnant with hybridity, is more complex in its relation to the existing dominant hierarchy than earlier polarized schemata suggest.[5] Central to this complexity is the merging or coupling of components of social life affiliated with both hierarchical and egalitarian structures. In contemporary African-American communities, the claims of a hierarchical structure coexist with notions of egalitarianism, which is then rearticulated through the Black community's fictive kinship system. Individuals are categorized and ranked. Age, sex, and individual characteristics are the general distinguishing elements. At the same time, individuals are compelled to embrace an idealized organizational structure in which individuation, as conceptualized in the larger society, is blurred. Among Black Americans, the usual polarized distinctions between egalitarianism and hierarchy are not only blurred but are sutured to the fictive kinship system, accidentally forging the "enactment of hybridity" (Narayan 1993). Interestingly, as in unhybridized egalitarian groups, members of the Black community negotiate areas of dominance and status and the contexts in which they will mark these characteristics.

The idealization of an egalitarian ethos within the African-American community does not imply the absence of "historical tensions . . . and the interpersonal power struggles that form a part of daily existence" (Flanagan 1989:247). Black people's interactional patterns are riddled with surface tensions and power struggles. Indeed, there is some evidence to suggest that in order to imagine the Black community one has to also imagine impermanence, controversy, and power struggles. These features are much more visible in the Black community than they are in the dominant society. Their existence does not, however, negate the centrality of the claim I am making in this analysis: Within the African-American community, a primary way to gain prestige, honor, and status is through encapsulation in the group's premier prestige system—fictive kinship. This means that for most African-Americans, self-actualization is realized only insofar as the individual is able to create an image of himself or herself as embracing the group's idealization of a sacred cultural space, an imagined Black community. Whether this is or is not what he or she is actually doing is immaterial. The goal is to create an image of oneself that emphasizes a positive role within the fictive kinship community. At the core of this imaging is validation through other kin or Black people, a process that entails reflecting an appropriate(d) identity. Consequently, the most highly valued group strategies are those that enable the individual to be seen as embodying those qualities and characteristics most critical to fictive kinship: the egalitarian ethos.

Fictive Kinship and Imagining the Black Community

Historically, among African peoples transplanted to America, tensions and the struggle for power were provoked by the coercive nature of their lives as chattel. As property, they were certified nonhuman. The erasure of humanness compelled these people to discover alternative ways of survival. They established a reward or prestige system that not only preserved their embryonic imagined community (peoplehood) but was also inaccessible to their enslavers.

Indeed, according to J. Scott (1985), these are the quintessential "weapons of the weak" of an enslaved population:

> *Everyday* forms of . . . resistance—[are] the prosaic but constant struggle between the [weak] and those who seek to extract labor, food, taxes, rents, and interest from them. Most of the forms this struggle takes stop well short of collective outright defiance. Here I have in mind the ordinary weapons of relatively powerless groups: foot dragging, dissimulation, false compliance, pilfering, feigning ignorance, slander, arson, sabotage, and so forth. They require little or no coordination or planning; they often represent a form of individual self-help; and they typically avoid any direct symbolic confrontation with authority or with elite norms. To understand these commonplace forms of resistance is to understand what much of the [weak] does "between revolts" to defend its interest as best it can. (J. Scott: 1985:29)

As slaves, African-Americans were stigmatized as nonhuman. To mute the effects of this stigma, they were encouraged and expected to distinguish themselves by the amount of work they completed every day. Work production was *the* externally imposed criterion for humanness, suggesting, ironically, that the most obedient, hardworking, and productive slave—the individual who was most willing to forswear his appropriated humanness—had in fact transformed his lowly status. In his or her new status, while not human in the same way as the White enslaver, he or she was, nonetheless, different from those slaves who were defined as less industrious and less obedient.

Meanwhile, an internal definition of what it means to be human was sprouting and rapidly unfolding *within* the enslaved community. It appears to have begun as an inversion of the dominant society's meaning of humanness for slaves. It also appears to have been invoked by the drive for prestige, also known as the hunger for approval, within the community. Researchers have identified and documented this phenomenon (see Blassingame 1979; Holt 1972; Johnson 1934; Rawick 1972). Holt argues that during the period of Black enslavement, language usage among African-Americans reflected the group's desire for prestige and survival and their understanding that survival was contingent upon their ability to create a subversive humanness.

> Blacks gradually developed their own ways of conveying resistance using The Man's language against him as a defense against sub-human categorization . . . The function of white verbal behavior toward Blacks was to define, force acceptance of, and control the existing level of restraints. Blacks clearly recognized that to master the language of whites was in effect to consent to be mastered by it through the white definitions of caste built into the semantic/social system. (Holt 1972: 153–54)

The resulting "linguistic guerrilla warfare" (Holt 1972:154; Felicia R. Lee, *New York Times,* 5 January 1994, A1) became a primary weapon of the weak, enabling African-Americans to survive with some degree of integrity despite their imaged invisibility. This linguistic practice meant assigning an intrinsic value to the importance of group survival and doing whatever was necessary to minimize the risk of cruelty to community members. In contexts controlled by (an)Other, it was necessary to behave as a collective Black Self while suppressing the desire to promote the individual Self. This internal definition of humanness has evolved with ecological transformations in the African-American community. While the definition changes constantly, even if almost indiscernibly, it remains an inviolable component of the group life of people of African ancestry. Holt goes further, arguing, quite convincingly, that during the period of enslavement, and for years following "official" manumission, African-Americans' oral language was a way of concurrently reproducing or expanding their image of what it means to be Black. Language also provided a way of resisting the larger society's efforts to shrivel their perceptions of an appropriate(d) Black identity. Holt's argument suggests that African-Americans have consistently and diligently guarded and protected their linguistic practices even though they were—and still are—severely stigmatizing. Her analysis indicates that those Black people who self-consciously policed their linguistic practices so that they spoke only the standard version of English deviated from the norm in the Black community and were in effect behaving "abnormally." Ironically, it was (and is) these individuals' acceptance of abnormality and their willingness to be seen as abnormal ("You are not like other Blacks") that led to their designation as "models of success."

Presenting an identity that minimized individual distinctions strengthened the possibility of community stability; it also promoted survival in a system not designed for Black survival.[6] Hence, African-Americans learned to suppress their desire to compete with each other in arenas defined as work or to compete with White Americans in arenas Whites had appropriated and declared their prerogative—that is, teaching in the most prestigious institutions, working as researchers in major research laboratories, seeking high political office, and so on. In these "White" contexts, Black Americans suppressed their desire to make their individual personas different from similar racialized bodies.

Rawick (1972) asserts that the emergence of an imagined *community* among African peoples during enslavement resulted in a weakened sense of attention to family, class, and class-related concerns. Black enslavement was such a powerfully intrusive force, he argues, that it compelled group members to become dependent upon each other in profoundly intimate and unprecedented ways. African-Americans learned to share unequivocally the values, beliefs, and norms of their entire imagined community, locally and nationally. Consequently, according to Rawick, this imagined Black community rather than the immediate family became the center of life on the plantation.

It is against this background that Black people learned to disvalue individual competition, to mask their distinctive abilities and skills by limiting the opportunity to cultivate specific skills and expertise to one member or a few members of the community. The state's enslavement of Black people evoked the notion of mutual dependence and "statehood." Members who learned to live in this mutually dependent manner were respected, embraced, and awarded prestige by the community at large, regardless of their inability or refusal to reflect the values sanctioned by the larger society. To become human, to obtain prestige in the Black community, one had to accept unambiguously the notion of sharing and mutual dependence.

African-Americans' imagined community of fictive kin (rather than the nuclear family), with its focus on the survival of the group rather than the individual, was evoked by the group's will to survive. Fictive kinship stimulated and incited an emphasis on the value of cooperation, collaboration, and solidarity. These values thus became institutionalized in this diasporic context.

Why Fictive Kinship Persists

For most African-Americans, egalitarianism means that everybody is equal—literally. As thus idealized, status distinctions are nonexistent. This meaning of egalitarianism within the Black community was engendered by the oppressed group's historical relationship to the dominant American hierarchical structure. For some Black folks, then, to be human is to be equal to and therefore indistinguishable from any other person or population group, absorbed in the prestige system endemic to the Black fictive kinship system, and successful in resisting the constraints and strictures of the dominant social structure.

African-Americans' development and elaboration of fictive kinship is neither neat, tidy, nor static. Indeed, it is frequently inexplicable, unpredictable, and sometimes even incoherent, assuming new forms and creating new antagonisms in different historical eras. This evolution is not to be equated with its disappearance. The "imagined" fictive kinship system survives. As a symbol of resistance, fictive kinship embodies the guerilla-like nature of Black life in America. It is sutured to existing social conditions and structured by the oppressive forces confronting African-Americans during any historical era. Consequently, while its form and configuration are constantly changing, the "permanence of racism" (Bell 1992) in America assures and promotes its persistence.

FICTIVE KINSHIP DURING OFFICIAL ENSLAVEMENT: RESISTANCE DISGUISED AS CONFORMITY

While the resistance of African-Americans to the established norms of the larger society has varied in depth and intensity over time, some measure of defiance has consistently been employed as a way to reclaim an appropriate(d) Black humanness. Such resistance was directed at both the society's legal and extralegal means of Black dehumanization. Ironically, at no time was resistance (disguised as conformity) more apparent than during the period of official enslavement. J. Scott (1985) insists that the history of American slavery is in effect a history of resistance,[7] manifested in

> foot dragging, false compliance, flight, feigned ignorance, sabotage, theft, and, not least, cultural resistance. These practices, which rarely if ever called into question the system of slavery *as such*, nevertheless achieved far more in their unannounced, limited, and truculent way than the few heroic and brief

armed uprisings about which so much has been written. The slaves themselves appear to have realized that in most circumstances their resistance could succeed only to the extent that it hid behind the mask of public compliance. (J. Scott 1985:34)

Blassingame (1979) earlier made a similar claim by asserting that while the response of the enslaved population was both "complex and contradictory," resistance was a pandemic element.

[In the antebellum literature] the major slave characters were Sambo, Jack, and Nat. The one rarely seen in literature, Jack, worked faithfully as long as he was well treated. Sometimes sullen and uncooperative, he generally refused to be driven beyond the pace he had set for himself. Conscious of his identity with other slaves, he cooperated with them to resist the white man's oppression. Rationally analyzing the white man's overwhelming physical power, Jack either avoided contact with him or was deferential in his presence. Since he did not identify with his master and could not always keep up the facade of deference, he was occasionally flogged for insubordination. Although often proud, stubborn, and conscious of the wrongs he suffered, Jack tried to suppress his anger. His patience was, however, not unlimited. He raided his master's larder when he was hungry, ran away when he was tired of working or had been punished and was sometimes ungovernable. Shrewd and calculating, he used his wits to escape from work or to manipulate his overseer and master. (Blassingame 1979:224–25)

The complex nature of the slave community's reaction pattern is widely documented. Nevertheless, very little has been written about the gender-specific nature of the enslaved population's resistance (for exceptions, see Fox-Genovese 1986a; Hine and Wittenstein 1981; Terborg-Penn 1986; White 1990). Indeed, much of what has been written about Black resistance addresses either explicitly or implicitly how males resisted enslavement. I want to alter this male-dominated imaging by emphasizing that Black women were doubly oppressed, economically and sexually (see Hine 1993; Hine and Wittenstein 1981; Mullings 1994; White 1985). African-American females have historically worked outside the home both for pay and not for pay (see Davis 1971; Jewell 1993; Moses 1985; Palmer 1989; Rollins 1993; White 1985; Zinn and Dill 1994). This was not the ideal pattern for White American women (see, for example, Clark-Lewis 1992; Davis 1971; Fox-Genovese 1986b; Palmer 1989; Rollins 1993; J. F. Scott 1965; Zinn and Dill 1994). The ideal pattern for White women was *lack* of employment outside the home (Ostrander 1984; Palmer 1989; Rollins 1993). Hence, gender diversity *within* American society is a reality that has long existed but is "officially" underreported and largely unacknowledged in the research literature.

Hine and Wittenstein (1981:291–98) describe the three primary ways enslaved African-American women resisted economic and sexual oppression: sexual abstinence, abortion, and infanticide. These three forms of female resistance seriously endangered the continued existence of the desired slave pool.

Much has been written about the enslaved community's response to the unwillingness of White Americans to allow them to attend school during both the antebellum and postwar periods (J. Anderson 1973; Berry and Blassingame 1982; Spivey 1978). The community's resistance was manifested in subtle and not so subtle ways. During the period of actual enslavement, for example, resistance was evident in group members' willingness to risk obtaining what had been forbidden: the ability to read, write, and compute. It was also visible in their tendency to engage in systematic, wholesale dissimulation.

> When I come along niggers didn't know nothing 'bout writing.
> Arch [a fellow slave] was the only nigger 'round who could
> write. He done learned carrying the white folks' chillun to
> school. When Master found Arch could read he fainted. And
> he didn't find out till after the war. He said, "Arch, you done
> been to war wid me, slept wid me, and eat wid me. If I'd a
> knowed you could read I woulda had your arm tuk off."
> When come time to sign warrants to keep on working for Mas-
> ter after emancipation, the white folks would write our names
> down and we would make signs, 'cause we couldn't write. But
> Arch could write and that was when Master 'scovered it and
> fainted. He said, "All de niggers done sign to stay this year,
> but you git off [leave]. You done stayed in war wid me four
> years and I ain't know that was in you. *Now I ain't got no
> confidence in you.*" (Johnson 1934:131; emphasis added)

In this particular example, an African-American obtained that which was forbidden and which unambiguously symbolized the dominant perception of humanness: literacy. Literacy skills were considered the prerogative solely of those persons who were both White and free. Arch, the former slave, knew that he possessed skills and expertise that were forbidden to someone of his race and status. His fear of the slaveowner's response led him to conceal this information. As he suspected, once it was known that he had obtained skills thought to be the prerogative of White Americans, he lost his job and his connectedness not only to his

genealogical family but, more important, to his known fictive family—
the imagined African-American community.

Learning to do the things that White Americans had traditionally
done but which had always been off-limits to African-Americans—for
example, reading and writing—disqualified Arch and all other African-
Americans for the stigmatized status they occupied and were expected
to continue to occupy. Consequently, during the actual period of enslavement, schooling for African-Americans was not considered appropriate
because it tended to undermine the existing status system: White Americans as human and African-Americans as nonhumans. But African-
Americans resisted the denial of schooling by laboriously seeking to obtain it. Their quest for schooling was galvanized and fermented by its
legal prohibition. Fortunately, the cumulative effects of a long-term subordinated relationship between Black and White Americans had not yet
imploded, producing the kind of negative impact it appears to be having
today.

FICTIVE KINSHIP DURING THE FIRST EMANCIPATION: RESISTING ENFORCED GRATUITY

During the period immediately following official enslavement and until
the Brown decision of 1954, the number of African-Americans seeking
the presumed benefits of schooling increased tremendously. It was also
during this period that the White community began conceptualizing
schooling for African-Americans as a "gratuity" rather than a constitutional responsibility of the United States government (see Ogbu 1978;
Weinberg 1977). Nearly all African-Americans wanted to learn to read
and write; hence, they anxiously and relentlessly sought schooling's presumed benefits. Their zeal in this endeavor was unprecedented.

Each of the individual states had its own strategy for educating the
formerly enslaved population. This decentralized system led to a kind of
ad hominem, individualistic approach to Black people's schooling,
clearly manifested, for example, in Holtzclaw's autobiography, *The
Black Man's Burden* (1970). Holtzclaw vividly details how he and his
parents sought to fulfill his dream to "get an education"—the presumed
key to success. To realize that dream required defiance of existing laws
and of the pervasive low expectations for Black people. Indeed, comply-
ing with existing social expectations was guaranteed to abort the dream.

> As I grew older it became more and more difficult for me to
> go to school. When cotton first began to open,—early in the
> fall,—it brought a higher price than at any other time of the
> year. At this time the landlord wanted us all to stop school

and pick cotton. But Mother wanted me to remain in school, so, when the landlord came to the quarters early in the morning to stir up the cotton pickers, she used to outgeneral him by hiding me behind the skillets, ovens, and pots, throwing some old rags over me until he was gone. Then she would slip me off to school through the back way. I can see her now with her hands upon my shoulder shoving me along through the woods and underbrush, in a roundabout way, keeping me all the time out of sight of the great plantation until we reached the point, a mile away from home, where we came to the public road. There my mother would bid me good-bye, whereupon she would return to the plantation and try to make up to the landlord for the work of us both in the field as cotton pickers. (Holtzclaw 1970:30)

Holtzclaw's insatiable desire for schooling intensified as he grew older, leading to greater defiance of existing external rules and norms as well as a heightened sense of "abnormality."

When I was nine years old I began work as a regular field-hand. My mother now devised another plan to keep me in school: I took turns with my brother at the plow and in school; one day I plowed and he went to school, the next day he plowed and I went to school; what he learned on his school day he taught me at night and I did the same for him. In this way we each got a month of schooling during the year, and with that month of school we also acquired the habit of studying at home. (Holtzclaw 1970:31)

Holtzclaw's description of how he and his parents resisted efforts to deny him schooling appears to be typical of both the kinds of obstacles confronting Americans of African ancestry during this period and the varied ways they resisted these externally imposed constraints.

Even when African-Americans were successful in resisting society's constraints and received the schooling they so eagerly sought, education *reinforced* rather than changed their social status (see J. Anderson 1973; Ogbu 1978; Spivey 1978). J. Anderson argues that during the First Emancipation, schooling for African-Americans was the chief mechanism through which White domination was legitimated and perpetuated. The system of "Negro education" that emerged was "deemed necessary for the development and maintenance of a particular form of economic order and white rule" (J. Anderson 1975:18).

Other scholars offer similar analyses. Ogbu (1978), Spivey (1978), and Berry and Blassingame (1982) document how during the First Emancipation "black youngsters clutched at any morsel of education." According to Berry and Blassingame, Black youngsters' newly acquired freedom entitled them, in their view, to the same skills, opportunities to learn, and cultural desiderata that their enslavement had systematically and legally denied them. Many Black people defined schooling as the quintessential commodity to eliminate the differential imposed upon them by the stigmas of slavery and Africanness.

Similarly, Spivey (1978) insists that the schooling made available to African-Americans was intended to reenslave them by providing them "schooling for a . . . new [kind of] slavery." Both the approach and the type of schooling were strongly resisted by people who were either formerly enslaved or were descendants of slaves. Their image of schooling was often on a collision course with the efforts of White Americans to make it available only at their discretion and on their terms:

> [African-Americans'] passion for education in the 1860s was
> equaled by the whites' desire to deny or limit the education
> they received. During the early years of Reconstruction, south-
> ern whites burned schools (thirty-seven in Tennessee in 1869)
> and regularly insulted and whipped white teachers of [African-
> American students]. In a typical case, white college students
> in Lexington, Virginia regularly greeted one white woman as
> that "damned Yankee bitch of a nigger teacher." What south-
> ern whites feared most was that the education of [African-
> Americans] would destroy white supremacy. (Berry and Blas-
> singame 1982:264)

Weinberg's analysis (1977:63) leads to a similar conclusion. He cites Bond's evaluation (1966) of the deplorable conditions in Black schools, including physical plants, books, teaching, and other school-specific materials in Oklahoma; he notes similar, maybe even worse conditions in Mississippi, Georgia, South Carolina, Maryland, Illinois, and New York City. Yet African-American parents and their children persisted in their efforts to overcome the hostility of White Americans, the dilapidated school buildings, the inequitable teachers' salaries, and the lack of books and other supplies. While this insatiable hunger for schooling accurately characterizes African-Americans' general response immediately following the Civil War and the Reconstruction Era, by the turn of the century they had lost "the battle for education" (Berry and Blassingame 1982). Acceptance of differentiated schooling for Black citizens by most Southern White and Northern industrialists resulted in the establishment of what became known as industrial education (see J. Anderson 1973, 1975; Bond 1966; Bullock 1967; Ogbu 1978; Spivey 1978; Weinberg

1977). Industrial education became indelibly linked with Booker T. Washington and Tuskegee Institute. Spivey (1978) insists that the central lessons sanctioned in the curriculum at Tuskegee were not about industrial skills but about "how to behave." According to Berry and Blassingame (1982), the general response of Black students to Tuskegee's system of industrial schooling, coupled with the substitution of behavioral concerns, was to become "morose, disheartened, and [to] pull . . . away from all social life, except the monthly religious meetings at the cabin church" (cited in Berry and Blassingame 1982:264; see also Holtzclaw 1970).

During the first two decades of the twentieth century, the response of Black people to schooling was very different from their response during the decades immediately following the Reconstruction Era. Beginning about 1900 (according to Bond 1966), the gap in quality between Black schooling and White schooling grew larger and larger, and this negative growth in inequality continued until about 1930. In fact, several writers insist that conditions for African-Americans worsened with the *Plessy* v. *Ferguson* case in 1896 (see, for example, Johnson 1934; Mays 1971; McPherson 1982; Murray 1978; Spivey 1978; Michael Wallace 1970–71; Weinberg 1977). Johnson's analyses (1934, 1941) show clearly how a job ceiling for African-Americans undermined Southern Black people's efforts to raise their standard of living. He cites one Black sharecropper's response to the effect of the limitations in the opportunity structure and how these limitations eroded African-Americans' "work ethic" and their desire to change the hopeless, castelike condition in which they were forced to live: "What kills us here is that we jest can't make it 'cause they pay us nothing for what we give them [the white landlords], and they charge us double price when they sell it back to us." (Johnson 1934:126)

Using four of the most prevalent income brackets existing at the time—(1) $200–299; (2) $300–399; (3) $400–499; and (4) $500 and above—Johnson (1934) documented an inverse relationship between the number of years of schooling of African-American males in rural Tuskegee, Alabama, and their earned income. He found that African-American males with the most schooling made less than those males with less; men with eight or more years of schooling made less than those men with five or six years of schooling.

> It appears that the environment is less hostile to men with little education than to men with enough to read and write easily. Practically considered, the most successful families financially are those who are either too illiterate to take advantage of their surroundings nor have more schooling than is de-

manded by their dependent economic situation. They would
be expected to thrive best in an environment that bred few
landowners, tolerated few innovations and placed a penalty
upon too much book learning. (Johnson 1934:143)

Relegated to an occupational role repertoire dominated by sharecropping, African-Americans in the South who were able to obtain skills
and knowledge unrelated to that role learned to disvalue it because of the
accompanying frustrations. Unable to use what they learned in contexts
outside the sharecropping system, most African-Americans opted for ad-
aptations to the existing social reality, choosing to become "safe Negroes," "sycophantic Negroes," or "uppity Negroes" (Bullock 1982:
217; Rohrer and Edmondson 1960).

Bullock maintains that while almost all African-Americans were opposed to their lowly status in the social system and protested against it,
those who chose to adapt to the existing ecological conditions, the "safe
Negroes," were often aggressive in defending it. By contrast, "uppity"[8]
African-Americans challenged the existing caste system, seeking to improve the lot of all African-Americans. Bullock (1982) claims that the
contribution of this small segment of the Black population was often
ignored by other African-Americans and was feared by most White
Americans. Nevertheless, Bullock insists, it was they who would eventually change or at least modify the caste system (see Grier and Cobbs
1968).

For African-Americans in urban and Northern areas, the response
to schooling at the turn of the century was similar in many ways to that
of their Southern and rural counterparts. Initially, Northern Black people
eagerly sought school credentials and skills because they assumed that
these would eliminate racial distinctions and counterbalance the distinct
advantage enjoyed by Whites (see J. Anderson 1973, 1975; Bond 1966;
Bullock 1967, 1982; Drake and Cayton 1970; Liebow 1967; Spivey
1978; Weinberg 1977). However, as they came to realize that schooling
would not lead to greater economic opportunity nor to the elimination
of the job ceiling for Black people, they redirected their energy towards
changing the kind of schooling being made available to them. Many
scholars, including J. Anderson (1973, 1975), Berry and Blassingame
(1982), Bond (1966), Bullock (1967, 1982), Ogbu (1978), Redcay
(1935), Spivey (1978), and Weinberg (1977), acknowledge that the system of public schooling at both the secondary and postsecondary levels
was not intended to prepare Black students to compete with Whites (see
also Holtzclaw 1970; Mays 1971; Murray 1978). Indeed, Ogbu (1982c)
insists that the schooling made available to African-Americans prior to

the Brown decision consistently disqualified them for competition with White students. The cumulative effects of this kind of schooling are evident in the response pattern of Second Emancipation students.

Other writers have also noted the diminishing academic effort of African-Americans during the latter half of the First Emancipation, shaped largely by their response to the instrumental limitations in the opportunity structure. Drake and Cayton's analysis (1970) of the response of African-Americans before 1945 to the job ceiling in Chicago is a typical example:

> [African-Americans] have for so long had a subordinate "place" in American life that many find it hard to conceive of themselves or other [African-Americans] except in that place. The initial reaction of many [African-Americans] to [an African-American] locomotive engineer or [an African-American] streetcar conductor is one of surprise, coupled with expressions of doubt—made jokingly, yet half-serious—as to whether . . . [an African-American] is capable of holding the job. This attitude is soon replaced, ordinarily, by intense pride that "one of our boys made it."
>
> A low [job] ceiling results in low horizons. Social workers and vocational counselors report a real problem in encouraging [African-American] youth to raise their sights. They have to fight always against a legacy of self-doubt and the acceptance of "place." (Drake and Cayton 1970:300–301)

Drake and Cayton show that the greater the distance from the Civil War and the Reconstruction Era, the weaker the faith of Black people in the efficacy of the public school system. These writers indicate that African-Americans' growing disbelief in that system was fueled by a contradictory element in their social reality: competitiveness merged to a fixed social status. According to Ogbu (1982b; see also Drake and Cayton 1970), outside the South, the public schooling made available to Black people "disqualified" them for the most highly valued positions, effectively robbing them of the motivation to continue to seek the presumed benefits of education. Not surprisingly, the "insatiable hunger" that characterized their Reconstruction response was altered, replaced by a less sanguine outlook.

Tyack's analysis (1974) of the system of schooling available to Black Americans after 1930 vividly documents the lack of congruence between Black people's ability to obtain the necessary school credentials and their inability to compete with the dominant White population. He reports that the enrollment of Black students at the high-school level "soared" during this period, and there was increased enrollment in vocational education in the northern, western, and midwestern quadrants of the country: "Literacy among blacks increased from 42.9 percent in 1890 to 90 percent in 1940; [African-American] high school enrollment jumped from 19,242 in 1917–18 to 25,580 in 1939–40 (an increase from 1.6 percent of total black enrollment to 10.5 percent)" (Tyack 1974:222).

These data suggest an unambivalent response to the presumed value of schooling in the years before World War II. Yet, despite this enormous increase in the number of Black high-school enrollees, a Black educator concluded that "the more schooling a black person achieved, the more dissatisfied he was with his job" (Blascoer, cited in Tyack 1974:222). This lack of job satisfaction was intimately linked to the static nature of the Black job repertoire. Indeed, it was (1) the pervasive influence of the omnipresent job ceiling, (2) the racism of employers in white-collar and professional occupations, and (3) widespread discrimination in unions during the "great migration" to northern cities that led to the "'adjust[ment]' [of] the black child to the white middle-class norms educators accepted unquestioningly" (Tyack 1974:220).

In summary, during the period of the First Emancipation, the imagined Black community embodied and camouflaged a process of *resistance* (see Cole 1967:322; Weis 1985; J. Scott 1985:33–34, 1990) that was structured both as conformity and avoidance. Researchers have found that as a "weapon of the weak" (J. Scott 1985:29), Black resistance was invariably a guerilla-type response to an ongoing oppressive reality. It symbolized African-Americans' efforts to compel the American government to fulfill its constitutional responsibility (Ogbu 1978; Spivey 1978), and to make available to the newly freed population the same system of schooling that was made available to the White population. While the depth and intensity of African-Americans' resistance varied, individual Black people consistently found ways to defy the norms that tended to violate and invalidate their self-declared humanness. But defying existing norms invariably suggests abnormality, and learning to behave abnormally is not easy for any social group. It risks accusations of sedition or treason as well as alienation and perceived lawlessness. Behaving abnormally also necessitates breaching existing social conventions and practices. Nevertheless, some members of every social group are willing to risk being identified as outlaws, as abnormal, because they can see their actions as leading to a better life.

Initially, African-Americans resisted their designated low status by displaying what appeared to be an insatiable desire for schooling. They tended to consume academic learning at an alarming rate, quelling their voracious appetites by any means possible.

I never before saw children so eager to learn, although I had
several years' experience in New England schools. Coming to
school is a constant delight and recreation to them. They come
here as other children go to play. The older ones, during the
summer, work in the fields from early morning until eleven or
twelve o'clock, and then come into school, after their hard toil
in the hot sun, as bright and as anxious to learn as ever . . .
The tiniest children are delighted to get a book in their hands.
Many of them already know their letters. The parents are eager to have them learn. They sometimes say to me,—"Do,
Miss, let de chil'en learn eberything dey can. We nebber had
no chance to learn nuttin', but we wants de chil'en to learn."
They [the parents] are willing to make many sacrifices that
their children may attend school. (McPherson 1982:114–118)

This response was typical and was evoked, in part at least, by the
society's structured "uneven exchanges" between Blacks and Whites.
Among African-Americans, schooling was defined as a commodity to be
obtained and then traded for a higher social and economic status. In
striking contrast, Whites defined schooling for African-Americans as a
"gratuity," a gift bestowed at their discretion (Ogbu 1978; Weinberg
1977). Hence, the general resistance of African-Americans to it, its uneven availability, and its elementary level.

The cumulative effects of obtaining schooling which went unre-
warded in terms of employment and social mobility were a growing
resistance manifested as avoidance. This strain of resistance is strikingly
evident in the responses of Black adolescents who were born and
schooled during the Second Emancipation.

THE SECOND EMANCIPATION: A BENCHMARK IN BECOMING HUMAN

Prior to the Second Emancipation, legal documents and other ideological
props both confirmed and denied the existence of inequality in American
society. The Declaration of Independence and the Constitution coexisted
with the "three-fifths clause" in the latter, making five slaves equal to
three free men, and the Supreme Court's decision in *Plessy* v. *Ferguson,*
making "separate but equal"—segregation—the law of the land. Hence,
the changed response in the Black fictive kinship system and in the response of Black adolescents to school-sanctioned learning. Earlier, segregation was legal and was considered by many to be a moral system as
well. Social and economic barriers limiting African-Americans' upward
mobility were rigidly defined and implemented. Black achievement—as
defined by the larger society—was group sanctioned. Assimilation as a

social goal was widely supported in the White and African-American communities (Dizard 1970). This general response was most often aided by group support, clearly affirming the value the Black community attributed to this way of responding to group oppression. The achievement of a member of the community was generally interpreted as a contribution to the advancement of the group, not merely as self-advancement. This was particularly true of achievement in those domains controlled by White Americans or regarded as the prerogatives of White Americans, such as higher education, the legal and medical professions, and banking.

The boundary changes resulting from the Second Emancipation often impelled individual members of the group to feel freer to pursue their own interests, *with* or *without* the approval of the collective. Morrison (1987) describes the effects of this changed perception within the African-American community:

> Now people choose their identities. *Now people choose to be Black* (emphasis added). They used to be *born* Black. That's not true anymore. You can be Black genetically and choose not to be. You just change your mind or your eyes, change anything. It's just a mind-set. (Morrison, quoted in E. Washington 1987:136; see also Carter 1993:55–79)

During the Second Emancipation, there is less certainty that individual achievements or accomplishments are for the good of the collective. Hence, African-American adolescents who wish to pursue academic excellence are confronted with two formidable obstacles: the barriers established by the larger society and implemented in the curricular and structural organization of the school, and *intra*group pressures manifested in the fictive kinship system, which reward or confer prestige on those members of the Black community who foreground their connectedness to the imagined Black community.

Further, African-Americans' fear of the Self being dominated generally evokes an unconscious reaction to efforts to advance made by individual members of the group. First, they question whether these "achievements" are likely to further the advancement of the collective. If they ultimately decide that the achievements of members in the dominant community are likely to result in an improved status for the collective, unconditional group support is offered. But if they conclude that certain individual achievements will likely threaten the collective, they withdraw support, leaving the individual to feel isolated and alienated, consigned, as it were, to a kind of individual purgatory. For most Black people, this response is unbearable; it is tantamount to what Paterson (1982) has labeled "social death."

The fictive kinship system that currently exists in the Black community is rooted in a cultural history that necessitates a suspension of the idea of a separation of a personal and a nonpersonal self. Indeed, some researchers (see, for example, B. Williams 1988; Snead 1984) argue that a striking feature of African-American culture and hence the contemporary fictive kinship system is its participants' almost unilateral focus on density and repetition in their interactions. The existence of these features suggests that a valued component of group life is knowing group members at many levels. In other words, Black people tend to judge each other in "the round" (see Bailey 1971), in terms of the group's norms and standards as well as its anxieties and hostilities. There is also a passion for "texture . . . preference for depth over breadth, an interest in rich, vivid, personal, concrete, tangled detail" (B. Williams 1988:84).

Black Adolescents' Academic Performance and the Second Emancipation

I argue that prestige in the Black community is imagined as sharing and giving rather than accumulating and hoarding. This contrasts sharply with what is expected of students in the school, which fosters an individualist ethos; greater attention to breadth than to depth; and noninvolvement rather than deep, tangled engagements and collaboration (B. Williams 1988).

The fact that virtually everyone in the African-American community understands and is in some way connected to the fictive kinship system does not mean that every Black person marches in lockstep to the imaging of the system described above. They do not. There are contested understandings of the dictates of the fictive kinship system, as well as challenges and disagreements concerning both the value and the advantages of belonging to it and honoring its principles. The critical question is why the fictive kinship system persists in the high school context, why cultural maintenance rather than social change is so central in the academic performance of Black adolescents (see Moore 1981).

The centrality of cultural maintenance poses a real dilemma for Black adolescents. Students view the divergent boundaries of the school and the African-American community as making conflicting demands on them. In school, Black students are asked to relinquish their identity and sense of belonging to the Black community in exchange for academic progress. Out of school, these same students feel pressured to give priority to their identity as people of African ancestry. Consequently, when they move from elementary to secondary school, they find themselves increasingly involved in an institution that rewards behaviors and an interactional style that is essentially an inversion of a preexisting pattern. They are urged to participate in a prestige or reward system in the high school context that promotes behaviors totally unacceptable in the context of the fictive kinship system. In some instances the student's social class and personal sense of identity mask the effects of the resulting conflict. But while lower-income students are more likely to be negatively affected than higher-income students, the desire to remain connected to the fictive kinship system is a relevant factor regulating the academic performance of nearly all Black students.[9] In general, the idealized image of a successful person in the Black community, coupled with the intrusive influence of the individualistic ethos of the dominant social system, subverts the aspirations of Black students and their efforts to achieve academic success.

Privileging Individual Competition: Knowledge over Wisdom

In American society there are two major ways of learning: through experience and acquired wisdom or through lectures, reading, and reasoning. America's system of public schooling tends to sanction knowledge derived from written texts rather than experience.[10] This methodology is almost universal in the Western world, though often challenged. Because the imagined Black community privileges experience over text knowledge, African-American students often find themselves in direct conflict with the dominant society's conceptualizations of knowledge and truth (see Collins 1991:202). The uncritical acceptance of individual competition signals the importance the dominant society attributes to the accumulation of information from multiple written sources as opposed to knowledge obtained from personal or orally transmitted experiences. The privileging of individualism and the acquiring of knowledge from books is generally accepted in the dominant society but is culturally foreign to most African-American adolescents, a learned response that is unevenly grafted onto an existing cultural system in which wisdom is more highly valued than textual knowledge (Collins 1991).

There are strong historical reasons why African-Americans tend to disvalue what is written.[11] While they cannot be fully developed here, suffice it to note that during the entire official enslavement period and most of the First Emancipation, what was officially inscribed in the nation's "public transcripts" (J. Scott 1990:2) was not applicable or only partially applicable to African-Americans. Hence, they repeatedly found themselves having to go to some official and to ask him or her to give an oral interpretation of a particular document: "What does this mean for me and other Black folks?" African-Americans came to understand that an oral interpretation of official documents was essential for their survival because taking literally such statements as "All men are created equal," "Open for business," "Please use the front door" could lead to imprisonment, lynching, rape, and other state-sponsored violence (see Michael Wallace: 1970–71). African-Americans learned the hard way that text knowledge was not sufficient for their survival. They needed more. Hence the saliency of wisdom drawn from experience in African-Americans' evolving cultural system and the widespread use of the epithet "an educated fool" to denote someone who had only book learning.

For most Black people during these historical eras, documents were virtually useless—inapplicable—in structuring their lives. They learned not to trust what was written, to image what was written as useless in the construction of their lives. The dilemma we now face in our schools is how to reverse this predisposition, how to convince Second Emancipation African-American adolescents that understanding and valuing textual knowledge is worthy of their time and effort.

The privileging of individualism and the acquisition of textually derived knowledge overshadow the idea of sharing and giving rather than accumulating and hoarding in the African-American community today; and the hybridity that is inevitable in response to the ongoing controversy over the relative merits of wisdom and textually derived knowledge, competitive individualism and collective giving, is discounted.

As I have already noted, one of the primary goals of the process of schooling is cultural transmission. Another fundamental goal is to build boundaries that structure and excoriate the mind (see Cohen 1970:72–98; Lightfoot 1978:20–42). This knowledge gap between Black and White Americans means that Black adolescents' resistance to schooling is neither understood nor identified as having sociopolitical meaning. It is certainly not interpreted nor interrogated as Black resistance to White domination, especially when Black school officials are the targets of the students' resistance. Rather, the students' reluctance to engage in one-on-one competition for high grades is most often constructed as "laziness," "lack of interest," "lack of intelligence," and so forth. Student responses that resist school-approved ways of learning and behaving are seen as validating a lack of humanness rather than a violation of a valid, preexisting culture or humanness. The issue is thus framed as "What's wrong with the students at this school?" rather than "Should we be demanding that the students reject their specific ways of learning and interacting?" or "Should we make success contingent upon a transformation of the students' racial, cultural, or gendered identities?"

Thus, the commitment of African-American students to the Black fictive kinship system sanctions individual competition only if it compels the individual to give competitively, to use his or her skills to connect or reconnect himself or herself to an imagined Black community. If individuals possess skills and expertise in an area external to what their peers construct as the Black community, the people who have access to them assume that they will be willing to share this "gift" or skill—unconditionally (Haskins 1975). The "gifted" or skilled individual thus becomes human only through the process of helping others. This is the only value or prestige the "gift" or skill has for the individual, *the* one way he or she can become wise, something other than "an educated fool." Thus humanness is constructed and contested as encapsulation and connectedness to the Black community.[12]

I have argued elsewhere (Fordham 1993:1991a) that a central element in the academic performance of Black adolescents is an evolving commitment to a stigmatized identity—what the students label Blackness. Thus, in defiance of the integration ideology, today's Black adolescents seek to validate and affirm a historical Black Self by projecting onto an imaged identityless past their contemporary understandings and meanings of that past. In school, this commitment to identity compels African-American adolescents to behave in ways that are, from their perspective, abnormal or atypical. Given this situation, it is not surprising that significant numbers of contemporary Black adolescents are ambivalent about school-sanctioned learning, because they see it as part of the larger society's efforts to reconstitute their Black identity. While the degree of resistance varies from student to student, a central claim of this analysis is that this sociopolitical opposition negatively affects Black adolescents' academic effort. The critical weapon students use to oppose this identity makeover and to maintain and celebrate the humanness they desire is resistance, either by conforming to or avoiding established school norms and practices.

Imaging Fictive Kinship at Capital High

At Capital High, the influence of the fictive kinship system is clearly evident, though officially negated. As the students' primary way of gaining prestige—that is, of winning approval from other Black people—the fictive kinship system exists both subversively and in juxtaposition with the individualistic system nourished by the core curriculum, school officials, and the larger society. For Capital students, a primary goal is to both avoid and absorb the structure supported by the school while simultaneously engaging in and celebrating the structure and prestige sanctioned by the fictive kinship system. Further, because the official curriculum is what really matters, the students' reluctance to embrace its principles and postulates exacerbates the consequences of their resistance. The negative impact of the society's reward system is evident in the students' propensity to seek the unity centering on a racialized identity and group solidarity rather than on individualism and socioeconomic class.

The influence of African-Americans' hybridized egalitarian ethos is most clearly manifested in the students' articulation of a kind of orientation that makes it unnecessary for everyone to have the same level of expertise in all school subjects. In some ways, there are negative sanctions associated with individuals having the same or similar levels of expertise in arenas that group members have defined, either consciously or unconsciously, as work (see Abrahams and Gay 1972; Gay and Abrahams 1972; Haskins 1975; Delpit 1988). Capital students' general response in such contexts tends to be cooperation and collaboration rather than competition. The central problem is that what they term sharing or collaborating is defined in the dominant community and the school context as cheating, and is therefore inappropriate.

For most Capital High students, it is the act of sharing the unique knowledge or skills he or she possesses that evoke humanness or self-actualization. Sharing as traditionally defined in the Black community is not approved in the American system of schooling.[13] African-American adolescents who engage in the practice therefore not only undermine their individual academic futures but put in jeopardy the futures of those classmates with whom they share. And since cheating as defined by the dominant population is behavior that negates the societal importance associated with individualism, African-Americans' more group-centered cultural frame is stigmatized and relegated to the catalogue of behaviors and norms disapproved by the public and by "official" America.

Among the students at Capital, the meaning of Blackness has evolved, spawning not only the anticipated changes associated with racial stratification but also a process that has actually inverted the meaning of a stigmatized racial identity. What results is an *implosion* of African-Americans' identity where factors usually diametrically opposed are beginning to burst inward, where a phenomenon has changed its expected course of action and is currently functioning in unexpected or unanticipated ways.[14] For the students at Capital, Blackness has been destigmatized, generating an identity implosion within the Black community. The emergence of Blackness as a positive identity force compels contemporary African-American adolescents to struggle with the problem of constructing an identity that fuses assimilation and separatism.

The reluctance of most Capital High students to follow the socially sanctioned pattern of individualistic competition mystifies their teachers and other school officials. Indeed, they watch in hapless consternation as new recruits to the school—ninth- and tenth-graders as well as transfer students—are incorporated into the general group-oriented ethos that dominates the organizational pattern of the student population. The change in the response patterns of Black adolescents was not anticipated by school officials.[15] Like other officials in the dominant community, school officials erroneously assumed that if integration were offered to a formerly stigmatized student population, it would stimulate overwhelming gratitude. It did not. As I have already indicated, a breach in expectations has occurred primarily because race and ethnicity are not static concepts. They are ongoing, contested phenomena, perpetually folding and unfolding, undergoing various kinds of mutations.

The response of the students of the Second Emancipation is a quintessential example of this process. Their response pattern is so unlike what was anticipated that they do not appear to view as sacred whatever has been so labeled in the past.[16] The following example is a case in point.

> Ms. Apropos, an English teacher, and Mr. Artisan (one of the shop teachers) talked freely about the problems at Capital. They both lamented the fact that Black children don't appear to be as concerned about "making it" in school as they once were. Ms. Apropos told me about a young male student in her class a couple of years ago who was able to perform well and did but who had to take a surreptitious route to do it. She said that he lived in one of the federally subsidized housing projects that feed into Capital, a place where it is definitely a no-no for males to be caught with books of any kind. She noticed that when he left her class he always put his books under his jacket, so one day she asked him why he did that. He told her that he would be laughed out of his neighborhood if he were seen with books. (Fieldnotes, September 13, 1982)

On the face of it, this response appears to be phenomenally unhealthy. How could modern Black people, whose history includes enslavement and state-sanctioned denial to book learning, trivialize such knowledge? How could they now seek to avoid school-sanctioned knowledge? No explanation appears sufficient. As noted earlier, our forebears were brutalized, even murdered, for surreptitiously seeking and obtaining knowledge embedded in books.

> Ms. Apropos told me about the students' general unwillingness to do more than what is absolutely required. If she gives an exam to a regular Capital student, the student is as satisfied with a score of 70 as with a score of 100; perhaps even more satisfied with the 70 score than the 100 because it doesn't make him or her seem bookish. When she tries to convey to someone who scored 70 on an exam how close he or she came to not passing, she is thwarted by the student's continual refrain, "I passed, didn't I?" (Fieldnotes, September 13, 1982)

Thus, unlike Holtzclaw's response during the First Emancipation, most Capital students are resisting through avoiding the compulsory nature of assimilation, as it is currently legislated and implemented in America's public school system.

Ironically, even though most school officials and teachers at Capital High share the students' racialized body image and are themselves African-American, their response to these students' unanticipated and "unacceptable" behaviors is either feigned lack of understanding of this culturally mediated process or a scripted reaction mandated by both their personal schooling experience and the structure of state-sponsored schooling to discount this culturally patterned approach to the handling of information and knowledge.[17]

When the school's administrators and teachers juxtapose their First Emancipation high school experiences and responses to those of the students they are currently teaching, they do not see themselves or their cohorts in the racialized bodies at Capital High. As they frame the situation, members of this new generation of Black adolescents are ingrates, unappreciative of the sacrifices of either their parents or their ancestors. Further, as these adults imagine them, these students are in some important ways strangers.

Adults at the school verbalize their recollections of how long and hard our Black ancestors fought to get the right to go to school and how hopelessly frustrated they were by both the legal and extralegal means White Americans used to deny them access to the means that would have enabled them to achieve their personal and professional goals (Ogbu 1978; Spivey 1978). With this background, most adults at the school find particularly galling the way students seem to take access to education for granted.

In response, teachers and other school officials dig in, clinging tenaciously to their perceptions of how students *should* respond to school and schooling and, in particular, how African-American adolescents *should* respond to this institution. This uncompromising stance exacerbates a terribly unhealthy learning situation, further diminishing the students' willingness to travel successfully the academic tightrope of schooling at Capital High.

"What's Wrong With the Students at This School?"

"Why is it that nobody competes with anybody around here?" Administrators and classroom teachers at Capital High School frequently ask this question in utter frustration. While most are baffled by the students' reluctance to engage in the expected competition characteristic of an academic environment, they do not expect an answer; most assume they know why. Curiously, not many Capital students ask this question. Those who do, ask it in bemused bewilderment, unable to fathom why their peers do not respond to school as they think they should.

Mr. McGriff, the principal, has an unalterable motto: "Another day, another A." He badgers the students, trying to motivate them to study more. His constant refrain as he interacts with them while walking the halls or walking the Avenue is: "If I were you, I would be studying. If I were you, I would be studying. If I were you, I would be studying." He never squanders the opportunity to chant advice: "If I were you, I would be studying." His preoccupation with the students' performance on standardized measures of school success is legendary. He repeatedly advises them that on the Scholastic Aptitude Test, for instance, "You get 300 points just for writing your name. You get 300 points just for writing your name." This is his way of telling them that a score of 300 or less is not impressive. Most of Capital's students respond by acting as if they do not hear him. Their silence does not deter him from repeating his pet themes: "If I were you, I would be studying" . . . "You get 300 points just for writing your name."

Every member of the faculty, like every student at the school, is aware of Mr. McGriff's concern for the students and his desire to have them do well. Most people resist him by trying to avoid him. Avoiding the messenger is their way of eschewing the message. Mr. McGriff's perceived obsession with the products of individual effort and what the students generally associate with the Other lead many of them to identify him both as someone who does not value their identity and as someone who hates himself. Students tend to perceive his behavior as indicative of the greater value he attributes to (an) Other, in this case a White Other. Although this perception is not completely accurate, it structures the students' behaviors and interactions with him. The following example is revealing.

Lisa—a high-achieving female—constantly criticizes her peers for refusing to immerse themselves in the academic component of the school. She insists that the biggest problem at Capital High is the almost complete absence of competition coupled with her peers' self-conscious avoidance of school-sanctioned learning. Ironically, however, when she observes this desired competitive spirit in Mr. McGriff, she hates it.

> All he think is work, work, work. I mean, you know, he
> won't give no breaks. You know, I'm sitting at the lunch—I
> mean at the cafeteria, breakfast time, I'm just getting in, he's
> going to say, touching me, "You could be studying there!" I
> think he cares about us, but in a way, you know, he be com-
> paring [us to white folks]. Like he'll say when I was in the li-
> brary, he said, "You all should be in class. That's why you all
> don't know nothing now. You see white folks are already
> ahead of you." I mean, he don't have to throw them in there;

he could just say, "You're already behind." I mean, he don't
have to throw them in there. (Interview, March 10, 1983)

Mr. McGriff's decision to "throw them in there"—that is, "You see
white folks are already ahead of you"—was virtually all Lisa heard.
Comparing Black people to White people at Capital High is totally unacceptable! It is the ultimate faux pas.

Lisa's anger at Mr. McGriff's insensitivity was unbridled. Her facial
features became distorted and her beautiful brown eyes brimmed with
tears as she recalled the pain she experienced during that interaction
more than six months earlier. In a voice thick with emotion, she continued:

> In a way, I mean, but, you know, you already know they're
> ahead. But why rub it in? I mean, he could say—he could
> have left that "white folks already ahead of you" out. He
> could have said, "You're already behind. It's time for us to
> catch up," or something like that. He didn't have to—he
> threw them in. (Interview, March 10, 1983)

Lisa's recollection of how denigrated and dehumanized she felt when
the principal of the school compared Capital students to White people
is typical of how most of the students respond to school officials' efforts
to transform them. In reporting her reaction to what Mr. McGriff said
to her, it was clear that she shared her peers' concerns regarding the
school's efforts to reconstruct them. Furthermore, the intensity of emotions she displayed in recalling the incident suggests a passionate disavowal of this approach to motivating Black adolescents to refocus and
double their academic effort.

Mr. McGriff and many other school administrators appear unaware
of how totally counterproductive this strategy of comparing is. They
frequently resort to unfavorable racial comparison when trying to "peer-
proof" the students' academic performance.[18] Most school officials use
their own First Emancipation high-school experiences as the basis for
evaluating the rightness or wrongness of activities at Capital High. Regrettably, they refuse to acknowledge that the Second Emancipation
teenagers are coming to adulthood in a cultural context that is drastically
different from the one they inherited as young adults.

Among the students who offer comments regarding the lack of competition at the school, several acknowledge that it does not currently
exist and recognize that it is highly desired. Alice, another high-achieving
female, mourns the lack of competition:

> They [school officials] just don't care, ain't nobody—[Black
> students] ain't got no push, nobody pushing them, nobody say-

ing, "I demand such-and-such a thing from you, and I expect you to do it." But it's the parents, they not pushing their kids, like my mother, she *demands* that I not get Cs, so I don't get Cs, I get Bs and As—As and Bs. I can't bring home a C, she gets upset. I think I brought [home] a C first advisory—second advisory, in math. She said, "Third advisory, I don't want this C on this report card." I said, "It won't *be* on there," and it wasn't. I got a B+. (Interview, May 6, 1983)

Later Alice concludes that "everybody wants to be like everybody else . . . Nobody really wants to be themselves, be what they are and do what they *can* do" (interview, May 23, 1983). Her response is not atypical of the high-achieving students.

Lisa made a similar observation when she was asked to identify some of the biggest problems at Capital: "No competition . . . 'cause, you know, nobody study. You know, if you have somebody to compete with, that's what *I* want. I'm serious . . . I mean, you know, they study a little bit. I'm talking about, like, everybody, you know, you're competing real hard" (interview, March 10, 1983).

Capital High students are not known for their willingness to take each other on in one-on-one competition. This is, however, what most officials expect; it is also what some of the high-achieving students assume will happen. Both groups are frustrated and disheartened by the absence of competition as they have learned to define it. The fact that in the school's core curriculum, one-on-one competition does not occur confirms a nonverbalized belief about the low level of academic achievement by African-American adolescents: that these students are mentally defective in some way. Curiously, neither group questions the appropriateness of the demand that the students compete with each other individually.

Black adolescents learn the meaning of fictive kinship from their parents and peers while they are growing up. And it appears that they learn it early enough and well enough so that they more or less unconsciously associate their life chances and potential for success with those of their peers and other members of the Black community in ways that suggest a great sense of mutual dependence. Group membership is essential in Black peer relationships.[19] As a result, when it comes to dealing with White people and White institutions, the unexpressed assumption guiding Black peoples' behavior seems to be that "my brother is my brother regardless of what he does or has done" (Haskins 1975; Sargent 1985) or, as one Black politician has put it, in the Black community a "culture of forgiveness" is the norm.

One of the repeatedly enforced *internal* cultural rules operating at

Capital High calls for concurrently avoiding the existing dominating social structure and limiting the flow of individuals across established group boundaries. Such conduct differs significantly from that of earlier generations of Black people.

Why has this pattern of behavior emerged? Why does it persist, despite widely acknowledged negative sanctions? How are school officials coping with this almost total disregard for the value of one-on-one competition? Why are Alice and Lisa so unhappy with their classmates' lack of competitive effort? What are some of the existing formal and informal constraints limiting the willingness of school officials to incorporate their knowledge of Black life and culture into the core curriculum of the school? What are the effects, if any, of the 1960s' revolutions on the group identity and aspirations of this, the Second Emancipation generation of Black adolescents? If the school's formal constraints were modified or eliminated, would school officials still view the students' preferred way of interacting as illegitimate? Alternatively, are school officials constrained not only by the existing school structure but by what Woodson (1933) has labeled a social mandate to "miseducate the Negro"?

These are the perennial questions confronting school officials and classroom teachers at Capital High School. They loom larger in the minds of such officials today primarily because the unacceptable responses of Capital High students to school-sanctioned learning practices, including one-on-one competition, seem to have emerged and to have grown by leaps and bounds during the Second Emancipation.

Adults' Non-Competitiveness in the White Domain
While in the school context, Capital's administrators and teachers constantly sing the praises of individualism and book learning—the norms and values generally promoted in the larger society. Nevertheless, they too appear to be, at best, ambivalent about their value in both their professional and personal lives.

Some Capital adults openly acknowledge that they find it difficult to compete individually with other African-Americans in contexts that are generally perceived to be characterized by the two w's—"work" and "white." For example, one of the most "proper" teachers at the school concedes her reluctance to compete with other African-Americans in the classroom. She is unusual in that she admits that she does not feel comfortable trying to outperform other African-Americans in such a racially charged social field. She acknowledges that she actively seeks advanced degrees in predominantly white universities. In these settings, she reasons, she is freer to construct her competitors as "the enemy" and is then able to lose all inhibitions regarding the possible negative effects of their loss of self-esteem at being beaten by a person of African ancestry. This was her rationale for preferring to be a student at George-town University rather than at Howard University, even though her most beloved and influential teacher is employed at Howard.

Another adult at the school gave a response that appears to be much more common among African-Americans, vis-à-vis competition with a dominant Other. She made this observation while talking with another adult about the next step on the ladder to full membership in the larger American society.

> Ms. Sampson noted that she is supposed to attend a meeting of her Lutheran church's council, which is largely White, this coming Saturday. At this annual event, each member is asked to get up and regurgitate his or her life history. She does not like to do this, so in the past when she's talked about her family history, she's omitted certain portions of it. (She has consistently omitted discussing miscegenation as it is manifested in her family). She said, "I'm not going to go to that mess this Saturday . . . As the only African-American likely to be in attendance at this gathering, she declared, "I am not going to try to compete with those people." (Fieldnotes, February 4–8, 1983)

In this chapter I have outlined the cultural history of people of African ancestry in America and have reviewed previous theorists' views regarding Black students' academic failure. I have described the emergence and evolution of the Black fictive kinship system and the egalitarian ethos during Black enslavement and the First and Second Emancipations, and I analyzed how these twin phenomena—fictive kinship and egalitarianism—are embodied, reflected, manifested, and privileged at Capital High and within the Capital community. I argued that a contradictory, multilayered process is affecting the academic effort of students at Capital High: first, racism pervades the curriculum and the general academic ambience; second, students tend to display non-competitive behavior in the academic context; and, finally, an idealized prestige system prevails, a fictive kinship system that privileges sharing and giving, wisdom and experience, rather than accumulating and hoarding (see Collins 1991).[20] Further, I argue, such a prestige system rewards and honors group members who seek positive evaluations, respect, and esteem, *first and foremost from other Black people.* Black people who seek to remain in the fictive kinship system are obligated to present an appropriate identity, one which suggests that individual members will remain forever connected to the Black community and give not only what they learn and earn but of themselves unconditionally. Finally, I have argued that much of this cultural knowledge is unconscious, a kind of carbon dioxide of the mind.

The impact of racism, coupled with the coexistence of the situationally-specific noncompetitive process and the mandate to remain connected to the Black community by giving competitively, extends to school professionals and other adults as well. Racism is a serious ongoing component of the lives of Black professionals in Washington, DC. It seems that the noncompetitive ethos within the community is manifested or prevalent in those domains controlled by White people (see Fordham and Ogbu 1986). At the same time, the mandate to remain connected and give competitively is limited primarily to the activities and interactions *within* the African-American community.

THREE

Parenthood, Childrearing, and Female Academic Success

Thirteen years tall, I stood in the living room doorway. My clothes were wet. My hair was mangled. I was in tears, in shock, and in need of my mother's warm arms. Slowly, she looked me up and down, stood up from the couch and walked towards me, her body clenched in criticism. Putting her hands on her hips and planting herself, her shadow falling over my face, she asked in a voice of barely suppressed rage, "What happened?" I flinched as if struck by the unexpected anger and answered, "They put my head in the toilet. They say I can't swim with them." "They" were eight white girls at my high school. I reached out to hold her, but she roughly brushed my hands aside and said, "Like hell! Get your coat. Let's go."

My mother taught me two powerful and enduring lessons that day. She taught me that I would have to fight back against racial and sexual injustice. Striding down Greenfield Avenue and across the Southfield Expressway with me crying and following behind, terrified of how she was going to embarrass me even more, she taught me that my feelings did not matter, that no matter how hurt I was, how ashamed, or how surprised I was, I had to fight back because if I did not, then I would always be somebody's victim. She also taught me a lesson I did not want to learn: She taught me exactly when my private pain had to become a public event that must be dealt with in a public manner. That day my mother offered me no personal comfort for my momentary shame and embarrassment; instead she made me see my pain as not mine. Though she spoke no words directly, she made me realize instinctively that my experience was not some expression of tenth-grade girls' jealousy—not a silly, private adolescent version of "They don't like *me*." My experience, she taught me, was directly related to facts I could not control—my blackness and my womanness. This was her lesson.

I did not know then that my childhood had ended and my initiation into black womanhood had begun. Neither did I know that I had experienced my mother's habit of surviving. I just knew that standing up for myself was what I had to do because it was the way black women had to be. We had to stand up in public for what was right, and stand against what was wrong. That was our role and our achievement. It was as Lena Horne had said in an interview: "If anyone should ask a black woman in America what has been her greatest achievement, the honest answer would be 'I survived.'" (K. Scott 1990:1–2)

A discourse—that is, a way of speaking—based on a "veiled use of power" (Delpit 1988; see also M. Foster 1989) or on indirectness (Tannen 1994) is not the way most parents at Capital High seek to rear their children, although, as Delpit (1988) points out, this is a preferred discourse in childrearing among large segments of middle- and upper-class America and certainly the most widely sanctioned way of speaking in school. Delpit's assertions are supported in Wexler's discussion (1994) of the adjustment of European au pairs in "a strange land": Washington, DC. The reactions of these women to such discourse are captured in the following scenario:

Gillian recounts this story: Her host mother, Annie, bought a new dress for her daughter Maddie, age 4. "And, you know, Annie—I just worship the ground she walks on. But she brought home this dress, and she said"—Gillian pauses for emphasis—"'I hope Maddie likes it.'" Her voice rises. "*What difference does it make whether she likes it or not?* She's only 4 years old! If it had been my mother, she would have said, 'You'll wear this or nothing.'" The others nod. "When I first got here I was so shocked," Susanne says. "I thought, my God, they let the kids jump on the couch, throw the pillows on the floor, put their juice down wherever they want on the table. [Their kids] just control the family." (Wexler 1994:30).

A foreign au pair would not have had this experience in most of the homes in the Capital community because language is generally not used to cloak or mask one's power. In the Capital community, the parental role is constructed as one imbued with power, and the parents' "ways with words" (Heath 1983) generally signal this perception. Hence, issuing a directive in a way that disguises the power differential between the adult and the child by appearing to offer the child more than one way to respond is not, as Delpit (1988) convincingly argues, the preferred way African-American parents interact with their children. Indeed, the most widely used discourse is one that makes clear who has power, who is entitled to make the rules and who is expected to obey them.[1] Familiarity with this direct way of speaking leads many African-American adolescents to misunderstand the "veiled use of power" so prevalent in written and oral school discourse as practiced by teachers and other school officials. More central to this analysis, the prevalence of a veiled use of power discourse at Capital High promotes resistance to it.

Among the parents of female students at Capital, resistance as "the habit of surviving" (K. Scott 1990) is the central element in the childrearing practices and in the discourse embodying those practices. It is clearly manifested in the jugular childrearing dictum: "Don't let them tell you you can't do that; you can do anything anyone else can do." But while resistance is rampant, at the same time it is riddled with contradictions and conflicts. In rearing African-American females, resistance is constructed both as avoidance of the White female body ("Don't you try to act like those White girls") and as conformity ("You can do anything anyone else can do"). The parents seek to rear their daughters to be both survivors and "ladies," the latter embodying those characteristics traditionally affiliated with upper-class White womanhood (see, for example, Ostrander 1984; Paglia 1994; J. F. Scott 1965)—dressage,[2] silence, and passivity, embodied in notions of grace, dignity, and charm and an essentialized aristocratic style. Not surprisingly, these efforts get tangled in a web of survival issues which, as K. Scott (1990) notes, are frequently smothered by the parents' use of a discourse that strongly reflects their desire to ensure their daughters' survival in a world generally hostile to such an outcome.

Among key questions are these: What does it mean to be female and human in the Capital community? How do Black parents there teach their daughters to be human? How do they prepare them to live their lives as citizens in both the Capital community and the larger society? Moreover, how do these parents create themselves while being constructed as racialized bodies? As parents who are so constructed, how do they scramble these constructions in rearing other racialized bodies?

Within the Capital community, culturally appropriate values from both the Black fictive kinship system and the dominant society are idealized. But because the values from the larger society are often dominant and in conflict with those valued in the Black fictive kinship system, being valued as a Black person is often constructed as oxymoronic. Consequently, contemporary African-American parents feel compelled to rear their children, especially their daughters, for dual—though in many ways contradictory—citizenship. The dilemma is compounded by unacknowledged gender-specific problems. Because African-American females are often symbolically constructed as male (see Jewell 1993:55), images of racialized pollution and contamination are entangled with issues of gender—femininity and masculinity (Bullivant 1987). All of this is conveyed most directly in the dominant conflicting manners of speech existing in the Black and the White communities.

In this chapter and the next are accounts, some conflicting, of how Capital High parents both serve as role models and teach their children to become human—accounts given in the voices of the parents, their children, their teachers, and other adults. Included in these accounts are indications of the parents' self-constructions, ways of speaking, relationships with siblings and peers, and images of the Capital community, juxtaposed with their imaging of the dominant society and their perceptions of appropriate and inappropriate gender-specific childrearing practices. I have included descriptions of household or family structure and of the parents' schooling and employment. The childrearing practices include socialization for marriage and family, religious beliefs and practices, and perceptions of the opportunity structure. Described as well are the hopes and dreams of parents for their daughters and for Black people in general.

These data were obtained primarily from the students' parents, through observation and both formal and informal interviews. In addition to the parental data, I have chosen to layer the analysis by structuring and often juxtaposing parental observations and the response of a daughter, a school official, a teacher, another adult, or a friend. These data were extracted from a multiplicity of sources: daily observations; formal and informal interviews; fieldnotes; and documentary data from the school's daily news bulletins, daily attendance sheets, and other official documents, both from within the school and from the central office downtown. Formal interviews were solicited from the parents of all the students who agreed to serve as the study's key informants. The parents of fourteen students (seven female and seven male) were willing and able to participate during the given time frame. Most of the parents I interviewed were rearing underachieving students.

PARENTAL AMBIVALENCE ABOUT THE VALUE OF SCHOOLING

For most of the parents of the female students, resistance is essential to being human. Since being human has at least three possible meanings in this context—(1) being firmly connected to one's family of creation, (2) evincing a sense of belonging and being anchored and grounded in the Black community, and (3) acquiring the socially dictated academic and social skills—resistance surfaced both as conformity and avoidance in these parents' childrearing practices as well as in their perception of how they were compelled to live their own lives. Capital High parents generally taught their daughters—both implicitly and explicitly—to re- sist the constant degradation associated with being Black and female and to survive in a world that not only devalues them but actively seeks to undermine their growth and development. These parents' ambivalence was clearly manifested in their discussions of the value of school and schooling—regardless of the level of their daughter's academic perfor- mance. Dawn's parents, as noted earlier (page 56), exemplify this ambiv- alence: they both respect and reject schooling. I repeat a portion of their argument here.

> *Dawn's Mother:* I think she should get as much education as she can. I want all my children to get as much as they can.
>
> *Dawn's Father:* Well, there's definite disadvantages if you don't have an education. You know. 'Cause the White people been using that so long—you know, that you're not qualified, so—you know, if you don't have it, the way I look at it, if you got to compete with a White, you got to be twice as good as he is. Or else you got two strikes against you to start . . . and they always think all—they think all Black people are dumb.
>
> *Dawn's Mother:* Well, I don't think they're still to that point of thinking everybody's dumb, or uneducated. But they have that feeling that once you come in with a little certain amount of education you have been to school and you can show where you are qualified for certain things, they're seeing the men get jealous . . . and they're trying to hold us back. You know? But then sometime our people bend kind of overboard, when they get a little bit of knowledge. I really think some of them go overboard.
>
> *Dawn's Father:* If you're—you take me, I'm dark . . . And you find a Black guy who's lighter than I am, and he got pretty good hair. Do you feel that he thinks he's better than me? . . . I find that to be true. A lot of them, you know, they like to deal with the Whites. (Interview, June 17, 1983)

While the parents of the female informants want their children to obtain as much schooling as possible, they also admit that there are many ways in which schooling for African-Americans is dysfunctional and should be avoided. Kaela's mother's responses to questions about the value of schooling point to a typical ambivalence. She was the only one of the parents of an underachieving female who had some college training, yet like other parents she is ambivalent about "advanced schooling" for Black people. She indicated that there were many tensions in the Black community between those persons who have obtained schooling beyond the rudimentary level and those who have not.

> I don't think Black people can ever get *too* much schooling. But I think . . . I don't . . . let me see, I don't want to contradict myself—I've known some people that *I* think had too much. They don't know what to do with what they have. But on the whole I don't think you can get too much. It all depends on what you yourself want to make out of yourself, as to how much education you should have. What *you* feel it takes for *you* to get the job that you're suppose to do. But very few—I think, as a whole, Black people go to the expense and everything of getting all this education, and they . . . and they never get the type of jobs that really, you know, that really they're qualified to do. They don't get compensated for doing . . . I really don't see why they put all that money in there when they *know* they're not going to get it. The White person's going to get it over if there's any way possible. They'll fill Blacks—they'll put them in these positions for a while, and then, if there's any way they can *de*mote them, they'll do that. You know, and I . . . I guess there's always . . . I guess Black folks feel there's always a chance that White folks *will* be fair, so be prepared. But to *my* way of thinking, I don't think it's taken place yet. (Interview, June 28, 1983)

As an extremely light-skinned African-American, Kaela's mother's relationships with White Americans as well as other Black Washingtonians are punctuated with conflict and tensions. As a lifelong Washingtonian, she knows how important race (as an external construct) and color (as an internal construct) have been and continue to be in the African-American community.

The color complex as it operates in the Black community (Russell, Wilson, and Hall 1992; see also Morrison 1972; McCall 1994) was the most salient factor (more important than class, for example) in Kaela's family of orientation. In part because of her light color, her mother's sister went to Smith College, which her mother regarded as a "finishing school.[3]" Despite the family's herculean financial efforts to keep her in school until she completed the required course of study, she was not qualified to teach in the public school system when she left Smith. Now knowing that she needed additional courses to qualify, the family was devastated. They had simply misunderstood the meaning of "finishing school."

Kaela's mother described her experiences as a business track student in the District of Columbia Public School System during the late 1940s and the early 1950s.[4] As an undergraduate at Howard, she pursued music as a major in order to please her mother, who held a lower-level government job, a prestigious career path at a time when employment opportunities were very limited for African-Americans.

> Now my mother—you know, I told you she worked for the federal government for 32 years. Well, if you got in the government when . . . at that day and time, you were very exceptional, very exceptional. The average Black person was a domestic or a chauffeur, or worked on the street—street-clean—sweeping the streets . . . It didn't make any difference how much education unless you were a professional, you were a doctor or lawyer or something like that, you had it made as a government worker. 'Cause you were a uppity nigger then, see. [Nervous laughter] That's the way the other Blacks felt about you. (Interview, June 28, 1983)

Like many other African-Americans, Kaela's mother was compelled to conclude that her schooling did not mute the consequences of her race. She found her racial and cultural inheritance extremely burdensome, even though she was "light, bright, and damn near white" and though she benefited from her light complexion. In response to these constraints, she sought to eschew her feelings of powerlessness by rejecting those aspects of her racialized identity that she thought were implicated in her lack of social mobility. As the mother of eight children, she had fulfilled an important component of what is traditionally defined as Black womanhood. She also honored and obeyed the wishes of her father (she followed the business track in high school in order to meet his need for a secretary) and of her mother (she pursued a major in music at Howard University primarily because her mother wanted her to). Yet a critical component of what was important to her was still unfulfilled.

Her daughter Kaela identified this lack of fulfillment as being manifested in an insidious, latent anger at her blocked dreams and aspirations, embodied in her decision to leave college and a potential musical career for marriage and family. In response to a series of questions regarding the likelihood of her mother's supporting her desire to go to college, Kaela admitted that the chances were remote because, in the case of one of her older sisters, her mother had refused to complete the necessary financial aid forms.

My mother wouldn't fill out the forms for her . . . Because—
I don't *know* why. My mother—okay, my mother had a boyfriend. And it's like, he was telling her this stuff, saying that,
"Well, if you fill out those forms, they're going to give that information to the government, and they're going to *do* that,"
and then she's so stupid, she believed everything he said or
something. I don't agree with that. I don't think that. I don't
think that the government, that they're going to give that information to the government. It sounds really stupid to me. . . .
But he's dead now. (Interview, April 22, 1983)

Kaela is angry with her mother for not being sufficiently supportive—in her opinion—of a sibling's desire to go to college.

Yeah, my sister could have gone away to college. And I feel
bad now, because I see her—she's not really trying to progress
or any—I mean, she works in a doctor's office now, and she
make a pretty good salary for her, 'cause she's . . . independent. But she still live at home. And she's still—she got a
baby. And I think that's wrong, I mean that's bad . . . She
would have been gone. And I—it's just bad, because I see her,
and she got a boyfriend, he don't work. I mean, it's bad, you
know, it's a bad situation. (Interview, April 22, 1983)

Later in the interview, Kaela admitted that she was frightened by
her sister's revelation that her mother had been unwilling to help her get
into college; and at times she felt stripped of her dream of going to
college. When I asked Kaela directly if she thought her mother would
now complete the financial aid forms for her to go to college, in light of
the recent death of her boyfriend, she was uncertain:

Well, I don't know. That's why I'm saying, I don't know.
'Cause she's—I don't know. I think she's *scared* for somebody
to succeed or something . . . I think *she* failed, and my father
held *her* back . . . My mother plays piano. She could have
been a concert pianist. And my father was jealous of her skills,
so he wouldn't let her play. But that's her fault, 'cause she
shouldn't have let him have that authority. That's the way *I*
feel. (Interview, April 22, 1983)

Kaela was merciless in her assessment of why her mother was not
as supportive as she could be or should be in the realization of her
daughters', not her sons', varied dreams. She attributed her mother's
indecisiveness to her submission to the two men she had loved, first her
husband and later a long-term "male friend." Kaela blamed her mother's

unacceptable behavior on the religious doctrine of the Catholic Church that mandates honoring the existing patriarchy *at all costs.*

> Okay, you know my family's Catholic, and it's a certain amount of—well, it's—the religion is changing now, but, like, it's like everything would have to be centered around the church. I mean, like, Catholics, good Catholics don't think about birth control. That's taboo, you know, they don't think about abortion or . . . you know, they do, but divorce, stuff like that. I don't agree with that. I don't agree with that at all, because I think that they should do it on the individual situation. Because divorce is sometimes—I think it's *mandatory!* 'Cause I think if I was married to someone, and it wasn't working out, and I was being held to it . . . because of my religion, I think I might end up *killing* somebody! I mean, literally. I think I would kill them, if I couldn't divorce them, if I couldn't get out of that marriage. I'd kill him! He'd be gone. (Interview, April 22, 1983)

Kaela's mother's ambivalence about African-Americans and schooling reflects a perception that had been nurtured in the discordant themes embedded in her childhood in segregated Washington, a perception her daughter too readily dismissed. Kaela's mother insisted that while the form and structure of the discrimination facing people of African ancestry in Washington has changed over the years, racial discrimination is still a major deterrent to social mobility, and schooling comparable to that generally obtained by White Americans is still generally unavailable to Black folks. She thinks that the ongoing subtle discrimination is most evident in the work arena, in African-Americans' exclusion from certain job categories.

As a recently unemployed community worker with some college training, her bitterness was leveled at both the Black and White communities:

> But I know—in my experiences, some Black people are jealous of other Black people—of each other. And, I mean, not saying all of them, 'cause there are always exceptions to every rule, but in general, Black people—if a Black person does well, and is getting along well, there'll be another Black person who says, "Oh, you're doing just fine," with his hand right up on top of his head, trying to hold him down just as fast as he can, you know, and I don't understand that. Blacks just—they continually just push each other down. I don't understand that at all. And I—maybe it's because they were suppressed for so

long, and they endured so much. But look—that would be
more reason to be—you know, supportive of one another.
(Interview, June 28, 1983)

Her subsequent remarks suggested that she was intimately familiar
with the contradictory elements embodied in the hybridized egalitarian
ethos in the Black community. Her comments also intimated that she
was not supportive of these divergent themes, especially as they are manifested in the larger social context, where achievement is strongly aligned
with an individualistic ethos.

> Black people just do that. They don't want to see the other
> one get ahead. If you have as much as I have, that's fine. But
> don't get more than I have. Because then you think you're
> cute, and I know that I'm going to help you come right on
> back down to my level! (Interview, June 28, 1983)

Like most of the parents of the underachieving female students,
Kaela's mother wants her daughter to be both popular and successful,
but her daughter's happiness appears to be more important than any
other factor. For example, she tends to sacrifice Kaela's school attendance to her happiness. When Kaela does not go to school—which happens often—her mother does not push her hard, in part because she
insists that Kaela has been depressed since her grandmother's death.

BECOMING FEMALE AND ACADEMIC SUCCESS

The case of Rita, one of the high-achieving students, provides consider-
able insight into another side of how parents are implicated in the resis-
tance/survival issue. Because she is not a high school graduate, Rita's
mother's perception of how and what she should teach her daughter was
riddled with contradictory messages.

> Well, I'm not a high-school—I'm not even a high-school grad.
> And that's why I . . . a lot of times, I sit back and regret it,
> that I didn't graduate. . . . And I felt like had I had a better ed-
> ucation, I could have done better. You know, working and
> whatever. So, since I didn't, that's why I try to encourage
> them—that's one thing I try to encourage all of them: get that
> high school diploma, even if you can't get no more than that.
> You know, get that. And with Rita, I think she's just—she's
> just smarter than the rest. Or she may not be smarter, but she
> just put forth what she had. See? She's just the type that will
> put forth that extra effort. (Interview, May 5, 1983)

While their own children may or may not be doing well in school, Capital High parents observe that most of their children's friends and the children of their neighbors and of Black people in general are not doing as well in school as they think they should nor as well as their generation did prior to the Civil Rights revolution. These parents are also aware of the heavy media coverage of Black students' "failure" in the school context. They are even more aware of the limited academic effort on the part of Black children who are in school today. And since they construct academic failure as evidence of lack of agency, these perceptions and expectations influence their efforts to teach their children and their children's generation what it means to be human.

It is indeed remarkable that in the Capital community, African-American parents are able to achieve a degree of synergy in their child-rearing practices. This is especially pertinent given that Black parents who were schooled on the cusp of the Civil Rights Movement are members of the "crossover generation," confused and conflicted regarding the predicament of contemporary African-American people. As Berry and Blassingame (1982) note, their "long memory" colors their expectations and perceptions of what is actually occurring in the current social context. They face this dilemma because they are obliged to migrate from the world of segregated and overtly racist America to the unfolding, still emerging, nonlinear world of integration.

WELDING ACCULTURATION TO ISOLATION

All Americans experience acculturation, some more than others. As outsiders to the dominant society and insiders or outsiders to the African-American fictive kinship system, the parents of the Capital community are influenced in their understanding and acceptance of the values of the dominant society by their first learned cultural system.[5] Inevitably they teach their children contradictory messages. In some instances, African-Americans demand that their children become human in the traditional Black sense: in a multi-income and, in some cases, multi-class community, Black middle-income children are taught both to see themselves as indistinguishable from the people in the dominant community and, at the same time, to fuse their identity to that of their lower-income African-American peers. There are also instances, however, when parents seek to impart only those values and beliefs that, in their minds, promote success in the dominant society, including an extreme focus on separation and estrangement from the dominant imaging of the Black Self.

This estrangement is evident in the lifestyles of many of the parents, especially the parents of the high-achieving female students. It is also evident in what they say and what their children report. Maggie's mother's response is a case in point.

Maggie's family has lived in the same house in the same neighborhood for fifteen years, yet neither Maggie nor her mother knows or visits the neighbors. Her mother described her interactions with the people who live on her street, in her block:

> I don't know about my neighbors' education, I don't know what they do. All I know is they live in this community, they say "Good morning, good evening." I say "Good morning, good evening." You know, things like that. But as far as knowing what they do, or in their houses—you can count the houses on your finger that I've been in, and that's limited to one. My next-door neighbor, which is . . . he's great. He's all right. And he's part of an older couple, he's about eighty-something, he's retired. But the other folks, I have *never* been in their houses. . . . And the majority of them has never been in *this* house. I just don't make a habit of being in, 'cause that's where friction and that starts. You're better off being neighborly. You know, when somebody dies on the street, then we have a . . . club or someone come around and collect money. If you need help, they collect money, and this and that, but that's as far as it goes. I just don't really . . . and the children, they don't run in and out of here [my house] either. I don't—I just don't believe in that. (Interview, June 2, 1983)

Maggie confirms her mother's assertion about the family's estrangement from the community in which they live:

> I used to have a lot of friends at school. I mean, they was just . . . they weren't like *close* friends, but I had a lot of friends. I never really got close to anybody . . . My mother always told me, your best friend is your worst enemy so I never did trust anybody *too* much . . . The only person I trust is my mother . . . and my sister and the rest of my family. But never too many outsiders . . . I didn't really consider them as friends. (Interview, January 5, 1983)

It is clear that this interactional pattern differs drastically from what I have hypothesized as the Black fictive kinship system. Maggie's parents are teaching her to separate herself from the community of people who look like her, to see herself as being different from those Black bodies surrounding her. Indeed, they are actively engaged in reconstructing their daughter in the image of the Other.

ENCULTURATION IN MULTIVOICE

In many instances Black parents' efforts to rear their daughters to conform to existing norms, including the norms and values taught in the public school system, are misunderstood or rejected by their children. In other instances when parents try to model those values, the children only partially understand their efforts. For example, in discussing her mother's multivocal language practices, Maggie's response suggests a rejection of her mother's efforts to be bicultural, primarily because, as she sees it, the attempt is at best disingenuous. She acknowledges that her mother often "talks white"—appropriates the linguistic code of the dominant Other—when she is talking on the phone or outside their home.

> She just talks like that on the telephone, I'll put it like that.
> When she talks, she puts on airs, you know, sounds White . . .
> so you can't tell whether she's White or Black. But when she's
> around the house, she talks, you know, regular; but when
> she's out around other people, anywhere out besides the
> house, she talks in a proper ["White"] manner. (Interview, February 25, 1983)

Maggie views her mother's hybridized linguistic practices as evidence of "phoniness" on her part. "When my mother does it [switches codes], it appears that she's trying to be someone she's not." Conversely, Maggie declares that she never participates in such linguistic practices. Indeed, she insists, "I talk the same way all the time" (interview, February 25, 1983). More important, she categorizes her "unchanging" linguistic response as an appropriate, or correct, way to structure an ideal Black life. Maggie believes this to be an accurate statement of how she uses language and, in most instances, it is. At times, however, most often in her interactions with teachers and school officials, she is forced to switch codes in ways paralleling her mother's language practices.

All kinds of evidence exist to show that for many of the students at Capital High, code switching is not a component of their language discourse, even when interacting with their teachers and other school officials. Indeed, their collective avoidance and even downright refusal to display one of the critical symbols of the achievement of power in the school context, is inextricably implicated in their large-scale school failure. This response pattern supports Holt's claim (1972) regarding language usage in the Black community as a kind of "linguistic guerilla-warfare."

FRIENDSHIP, RELIGION, AND PARENTAL ENCOURAGEMENT

The parents of high-achieving females tend to limit their daughters' friendships, sanction their involvement with religion, and give very little encouragement to their academic aspirations, while most parents of underachieving females allow and even encourage their children to have lots of friends and dates, are generally indifferent about religion, and strongly encourage their daughters' academic aspirations.

Friends are vital to Black adolescents, and the childrearing practices of the parents of the female underachievers ground them in the tentacles of the Black fictive kinship system by minimizing their daughters' sense of loss, alienation, and isolation. For example, Sade's father's practice of escorting her and her friends home after Flag Girl practice every week affirms her choice of friends and indicates his approval.

> There have been times when I thought she had lots of friends. Then there have been times where I wondered if she had any friends. But I . . . when she was at . . . where was it? . . . At Carson Junior High or . . . every time I looked up, two, three, four girls'd be coming here—Sade, Sade, you know. Then when she went to Capital—well, it wasn't that many friends *visiting;* I don't know how many she had at school—she never really talks about how many friends she has. But since she been on the Flag Girl team, I've met quite a few of the girls on the team, you know, by transporting them different times. And I've seen them perform in different programs, too, you know. But I don't know how many others that she has. That's about the extent of my knowledge. (Interview, May 17, 1983)

This childrearing pattern is not replicated among the parents of the high-achieving females, who are extremely protective of their daughters, limiting their activities and friendships in order to police their emerging sexuality.

A similar divergence emerges when one looks at religion. It was not nearly as essential to the lives of the parents of underachieving females and their children as it was to the parents of the high-achieving females. In some ways, avoiding religion was perceived as a way of disrupting the existing system of domination. This was most readily apparent in sporadic to nonexistent church attendance, although Judeo-Christian principles still structured the lives of every one of these families.

There also appeared to be less conflict between the parents of the underachieving females and their daughters, with the parent-daughter (especially the mother-daughter) relationship being less fraught with ambiguity, hostility, and misunderstanding. For example, while Kaela was reared as a Catholic and her mother spent most of her non-working time at the neighborhood church, she did not insist on the same level of commitment from her daughter. Her children, including Kaela, perceived her involvement in the church as a social outlet for *her*. It was not a social outlet for the entire family.

Similarly, while Dawn's parents assert that religion is very important, they do not insist that Dawn and her younger siblings attend church every Sunday. Dawn's mother attends church regularly, almost every Sunday; her father does not "go to church that much." Dawn's mother insists that religion is very important and that she had no difficulty getting her older children—who are no longer living at home—to go to church when they were Dawn's age. Dawn, however, is a child in the last group of seven siblings, and her parents, especially her mother, have found that as this last band of children get older, it is a bit more difficult to convince them that they should go to church.

> I didn't have any trouble out of the older kids . . . But these kids will have an argument. . . . When I come back to go in the bathroom, well, they're standing in the line, "I want to get in the bathroom, 'cause I ain't had my bath yet!" They sitting looking at the paper, laughing and talking . . . Then it runs me late when they all mess around and get in *my* way. Sometimes we have an argument before we go. But we'll go . . . Sometimes I don't worry. I just get up and go anyway. But I definitely think they should have religious training. (Interview, June 17, 1983)

Similarly, despite being schooled most of their lives in Catholic schools with their explicit emphasis on religion, neither Kaela nor her mother appears to be particularly religious.

> I don't know about Kaela and religion. I think, when she was going to parochial schools, it played a much larger part in her life than it does now. During this past year, she's said several times, she's made attempts several times to go back to Mass on Sundays. In fact, some Sunday mornings she's the only one that actually goes to Mass. But when she was—when you had it every day—well, when you have religion forced upon you, and you have it every day, it was a large part on her mind, I think, then. But I think everybody likes to get away from that, too. Once you've had it over the years for so long . . . But I

don't think . . . well, in her case, I don't think . . . I don't think she prefers—maybe she hasn't been introduced to any other, but I don't think she prefers any other religion. (Interview, June 28, 1983)

Though Sakay's mother does not attend church regularly and though she does not demand that her children go to church on Sunday, a strong sense of morality permeates the life of her family. Nekia's aunt and uncle do not attend church often and do not insist that Nekia go to church. In fact, Nekia describes her activities on Sunday as self-determined and self-initiated:

Some Sunday mornings I get up and cook breakfast . . . I get up, turn the radio on, listen to WHUR—the gospel show on WHUR. And I help cook dinner, 'cause we cook a big dinner on Sunday, so I help my aunt cook dinner. And then we just sit around the house. And sometimes her friends come over . . . We try to be a little conservative on Sunday. (Interview, March 9, 1983)

The one major exception to this general pattern of nominal commitment to religion and church attendance was recounted by one of the two fathers interviewed. Sade's father declared that religion has always been very important in the life of the family and that his wife and daughters attend church every Sunday. He does not.

Sunday School's at ten, yeah . . . They stay for church services . . . And then they go back in the afternoon, on Sunday afternoon. At six [o'clock], yeah. Most of the time. But my wife, she usually—her and Sade goes practically *every* Sunday, but since [my older daughter] has been in college, sometimes she doesn't go back, 'cause she's got all this homework and stuff . . . getting it together, you know. [Religion] kind of goes together with their education. 'Cause they're getting educated in the Sunday School and in church, and along with the education that the public schools—it kind of goes hand in hand. And I think without that, it might have been a different story. I think religion is *very* important. (Interview, May 17, 1983)

DREAMS OF LEAVING AND THE DEATH OF DAUGHTERS' DREAMS

Among Capital's high-achieving female students, parental control is pervasive. It is the critical tool in teaching the daughters resistance through conformity. Yet parental control is also elusive, and it has strong implications for school success. Four of the six high-achieving girls who participated in the ethnographic component of the study are growing up in two-parent homes, where there are strict controls and varying yet consistent demands for conformity: obedience to parental and school authority. It is with their mothers that the girls appear to have the most intimate, yet contentious, relationship. Alice, for example, performs well in school primarily because she is fearful of her mother's reactions were she to "earn any grade less than a B." What we talked about during our formal and informal interview sessions was as much her mother's values and beliefs as it was her own.

> I'm not going to be like everybody else [at Capital High]. I'm not that kind of person. Just like my mother—my mother, she says she *never* was like—tried to be like everybody else. She [tried] to be her *own* person, and that's what *I* try to do. (Interview, May 23, 1983)

When we talked about the summer job that she had just learned she would have, our conversation went like this:

Alice: Yeah, so I'm going to be working, making some money. My mother just keep hollering, ever since I got the thing, saying, "When you gonna, when you get paid?" [She will] force me to give her all my money.

Anthro: Oh, yeah? Will you?

Alice: Mm-hm.

Anthro: You will?

Alice: Yeah, I'm going to give it to her.

Anthro: Why?

Alice: She gonna give me an allowance.

Anthro: Oh, I see. And what will she do with the rest of it?[6]

Alice: She give me ten dollars every other week. Whenever I get paid, I get ten dollars out of the money. 'Cause I don't need that much money. There ain't nothing I want to buy.

Anthro: You don't? You don't buy clothes?

Alice: Naw. She buys my clothes.

Anthro: She buys your clothes?

Alice: I mean, I'm there, but, you know, she picks them out. She say I ain't got no taste.

Anthro: (Laughter) Do you agree with her?

Alice: Huh?—No! Well, no . . .

Anthro: But wouldn't that, aren't there things you'd like to buy yourself, that you'd like to have, that she perhaps says no to?

Alice: Well, most of the—generally—most nine times out of ten, I get what I want. (Interview, May 23, 1983)

Alice was going to receive five dollars a week out of her salary for an allowance (what most of her peers receive even when they don't have a paid job). She was not pleased about her mother's controlling behavior, but she said what she thought she should say about this issue when answering the questions posed. As a sixteen-year-old urban female in the eighties, she longed to have more control over her life. However, that is not likely to happen, primarily because her mother's goal and the goal of most of the childrearing practices of the parents of the high-achieving females is to inculcate conformity rather than avoidance of authority.

Alice wants to go to dental school in California, but her mother seeks to keep her at home in Washington, both because she does not want her to go to dental school and because she does not want her to go away from home.[7] It is not quite clear why keeping Alice home is so important to her. Certainly, Alice is a very valuable resource at home, and perhaps her mother fears this loss. When Alice was asked if she were experiencing conflict about leaving home, she offered the following ambiguous response:

> Well, not really. I mean, I could leave home. My mother don't really want me to. 'Cause she'll miss me so bad. See, I wanted to go to California, to go to school. . . . I mean, because they got a good dental school in California . . . I forgot the name of it now, but they got a good dental school there. And I wanted to go there. My mother said she ain't want me to, 'cause she'd miss me too much . . . She said, "Why don't you go to Howard? They got a good dental school." But, see, I wanted to go to California . . . I *can* go here, to Howard. And besides, it'd save her a whole bunch of money . . . 'Cause I would [not] have to [rent] an apartment [as I would have to in California]. This way I'll stay home and live with her. She was pointing them facts out so good to me! "You could stay here, and since I got to pay rent anyway, you wouldn't be taking up that much space," and so on, on money, and I said, "Okay, Mom. Okay, Mom, you sold me." . . . 'Cause she'd be lonesome . . . yeah, she love me to death. That's why I wish I . . . [felt differently about her]. (Interview, May 23, 1983)

Alice's use of the past tense to talk about going to dental school in California is the most salient indicator of the death of her dream.

Another high-achieving student, Katrina, has a similar problem. Her mother and father are older than most of the parents of the high-achieving students, and she is the youngest female in her family. She is baffled by what she defines as her parents' lack of trust in her, and she laments the fact that she can never conform enough to please them. She notes, with a mounting sense of frustration, that her life is extremely circumscribed and is becoming even more so.

> If I *want* to go, I want to be *able* to go. But . . . the way
> things are now, I have to get their approval and everything. I
> mean, I remember I had to . . . I remember once, I went to the
> *library*. And it's not near my house, it's—I can just catch one
> bus and I'm there. I *could* walk, but it's several blocks. And I
> went after school, I didn't come home. And I told my sister
> that I may not be home, I was going to the library. Me, Sakay
> and I, were in the library, trying to get this thing together.
> And here comes my sister and my mother, driving up! (Laugh-
> ter) And out she comes—you know, I guess they were check-
> ing up on me—I don't know! And they took me home. I re-
> ally thought that was unnecessary. God! I can't walk to the
> store without my mother—after six, I think—yeah. When it
> gets dark, they don't want me walking *anywhere*—to the cor-
> ner store, *anywhere*. God! It's terrible! And once I went to a
> Math Society meeting. Okay, my sister said . . . Okay, I got
> home a little bit before nine, got into the bed—I didn't say
> anything to anyone, you know. And my sister said my
> mother—okay, it was about eight—that my mother, about
> 8:30, she felt that I should have been home. You know, she
> started to walk up to the bus stop to . . . you know, I guess to
> wait for me when I got off the bus. And my sister, she came
> upstairs about nine and looked in my room. So I was asleep,
> you know, and she told my mother, and my sister said my
> mother was really upset. And once I went to dance practice,
> and I got home about nine o'clock. I got a ride home. My sis-
> ter said she had to give my mother some pills to make her go
> to sleep! And I said, "You're joking!" I said, "No!" And I
> went into her room, she was out of it. She wasn't totally
> asleep. And she said, "Why are you so late?" I said, "They
> had to drop—" Okay, I was in, like, a car pool, so they had
> to drop several people off. Boy! Nine o'clock on a Saturday! I
> feel that is *nothing!* I mean, I'm sure my peers, they can stay
> out till twelve. I mean, God! I'm almost seventeen. (Interview,
> February 8, 1983)

Katrina's parents are concerned about her and want to be supportive of her development as a proper young lady. Hence, they emphasize conformity as the way to resist the low expectations for African-American females. At the same time, they are fearful of her desire to leave—both metaphorically and literally. Most of their fear relates to her developing sexuality. However, she does not read their strict constraints and curfews as evidence of both support and fear; she perceives these unilateral limitations as unmitigated lack of support.

Rita's parents, particularly her mother, emphasize conformity to the larger society's norms and expectations. Although they try to control their daughter's life the way Katrina's parents do, they are less successful because Rita has a much stronger personality. Her relationship with her mother could be accurately characterized as mutually controlling. As the youngest daughter in a family of six, she is extremely bitter about her relationship with her parents, especially her mother:

> Sometimes I used to say, "I want to change my parents!" And sometimes . . . I can get along. . . . It's mostly my mother. . . . Sometimes I hate her. I say, "I hate you, woman. Why can't you leave me alone?" And, see, that makes *me* feel bad, because . . . [When I was younger] she would always . . . it was like an ongoing thing—she would, like, make promises, and she would break them. Every time I would turn around, it was like she kept crying, "Wolf! Wolf!" and you know, there *was* no wolf. And I'd say, "Where is the wolf, woman? Come on!"
>
> My mother always broke promises. And that hurt, it really did. . . . As I grew older, I used to hang around outside a lot, and she was punishing me by making me stay in the house. So I didn't want to be punished any more, so in my subconscious, I realize I did now. . . . I stopped going outside. I did it, and it was like a thing that I no longer did any more. I just stopped going outside and playing around. I would just go outside to do what I *had* to do, then I would come back in, and I would not go back outside. And I don't go outside now. Then I had to have something to compensate for the fact that I didn't go outside, so it was TV. And then she would come and punish me by saying, "No TV." So I said, "Okay." At the *time* I didn't realize I was doing this, but I just cut out TV. So I had her there, right? . . . And then I would get a big thrill out of going around the house, running around the house. "To your room." Now they [my parents and siblings] can't put me *out* of my room, and they hate it because I'm antisocial, as far as they're concerned. "We can't get Rita to go any-

where!" She's going to tell you this when you get ready to talk to her. And *I* want you to understand why. "We can't get her to go anywhere . . . because *I* have developed my own way now. They—she can't punish me anymore. And that's the beautiful thing, she *can't* punish me anymore. . . . She has nothing to punish me with. One time she tried to punish me, she made me wash the dishes for a week. That isn't no punishment! Now, come on, let's be for real—to wash dishes for a week is not a punishment.

I wish I could change *her* in my life. And then sometimes, too, I feel sorry for her, becasue she doesn't understand me. And I'm making her feel guilty for what she did, and every time we bring up anything, I say, "Once you kill a person, you can't say you're sorry, because they're dead." And then that makes me feel really bad, but that's the way *I* feel. And she keeps saying how I hold things against her, what happened years ago, but I'm sorry, because it has led up to this. And that's the way it is. And that's why I'm sorry. What can I do about it? I remember . . . (Interview, May 4, 1983)

Rita resisted her mother by conforming to every demand made of her and by learning not to desire what her mother told her she could not have. Rita's mother describes her tortuous relationship with her daughter as one that makes her feel guilty and unhappy but that she feels compelled to continue because of the strong religious beliefs she attempts to uphold:

Well, basically, Rita has always, you know, very much had a mind of her own, and I just tried to do the things that parents are suppose to do. I mean, I'm not going to say I did them all right all the time, because . . . but basically Rita's had a drive to always do her work, and I mean, you know, she's always been a smart child. See? Sometimes, some things she wanted to do, I wouldn't let her. In school . . . she wanted to get in certain sports and things. I sort . . . sometimes I be wishy-washy, you know, I'll . . . sometimes I say one thing, and then another. That irritates her—a lot. 'Cause she like you to say something and do it. But she's put up with it quite a bit. We've had our struggles and our ups and downs, and we've had a terrible little go-round. (Interview, May 5, 1983)

Unlike the mothers of the other high-achieving females, Rita's mother's efforts to control her daughter have been visibly costly, so deleterious that one might wonder if the control she sought and achieved has resulted in a pyrrhic victory.

Central to the power struggle between Rita and her mother is Rita's refusal to acquiesce to the demands of her mother that she accept the religious teachings which have taken over her mother's life. There is also Rita's willfulness.

> Rita's just a—I don't know what you say—she . . . it's like she's got a mind of her own, and a lot of times she can get real strong-willed, and we've went through some changes, like when I tried to get her to do the religious Meeting and differ-ent things, she said she didn't want it. And we fight, she get beatings, and she put on a performance . . . I mean she can perform, but she's gotten out of some of that. I mean, you know, I be dragging her down the steps, and she be holding the railing, on the side of the door, screaming and hollering and everything. [Laughter] So we've been through some times. But I can look back and see where she's made improvement. (Interview, May 5, 1983)

Rita's mother admits that much of the tension in the family that led to the beatings she regularly administered—especially to Rita—was the result of her inability to do "everything I was suppose to be doing, see?" She insisted that "It's not as, like being a Witness that's so hard" (interview, May 5, 1983). She contends that the reason for the failures in her childrearing practices is her desire to "[conform to the wishes of] other people" at the expense of her own children, especially Rita.

> She feel I didn't give her the time. You know. Because I got along easy with the other two girls, and a lot of times with her, I would just say something and never fulfill it . . . I used to like . . . see, I used to like to go a lot. I would go out and go places and—you know, riding and shopping centers. A lot of times I wasn't here when they got home or something. And I think that made a difference. (Interview, May 5, 1983)

There were so many areas of conflict in this mother's espoused be-liefs, so many contentious principles, that it was difficult to follow her argument. Additionally, there was the enormous pain in her voice and in her eyes. She appeared to be so lonely, so alone in this enormous family, so unsure of how to rear a Black daughter in the uncharted world of the post-Second Emancipation era. She seemed so unhappy with the negative outcomes she associates with most of the strategies and tactics she used in rearing Rita, yet—as she acknowledges—she continues down this no-win path.

Rita's mother acknowledged that her children's father had never "interfered" in her childrearing practices, but, given the higher status of males in her religion, if he objected, his wishes would supersede hers, even though he was not a member of her church.

> He tell the girls they can do what they want to do. He's not a Witness; he don't profess any religion . . . It's just me. My oldest girl is baptized. But my next daughter and Rita and the rest of them isn't. But I'm still holding onto it . . .
>
> The Bible does teach that the man is the head of the household. So, you know, just because I don't approve of it, I let them know it. But if I say "Don't," and he say "Do," then they do what he say, because he is the head of the household. But I have to hold firm to what I believe. (Interview, May 5, 1983)

Rita acknowledged that the ways she interacted with her father and showed respect for him were quite different from the way she treated her mother:

> I don't know my father [even though he has lived with us all of my life]. I . . . I feel like my father's like me; he's the underdog. 'Cause my mother, she always coming *down* on the poor man—everything! It's like . . . and I don't say anything to my father, *he* don't say anything to *me*. If I want something, I'll ask him for it. If *he* wants something from *me*, then *he'll* ask *me* for it. And I—this sounds sort of stupid, but I'm afraid to ask people for things. And some way—in his own way, he's afraid to ask *me* to do things *for* him. I can tell by the way he goes about doing it. And it's really dumb, because—because here I am, I'm trying to tell myself, I have no reason because I know he's like me. (Interview, May 4, 1983)

Rita's response regarding her father's lack of involvement in the family system reveals how most of the fathers of the students at Capital—high-achieving and underachieving—are both present and absent, concurrently, in the lives of their families. Their presence in the home is hardly distinguishable from their absence, and their silence and seeming lack of involvement suggests to their children that the fathers share the status of victims. This leads the female students either to reject or to overidentify and long to protect and rescue. This reaction is not necessarily the result of a conspiracy, conscious or unconscious, on the part of either the children or the male parent.

Like Rita, Maggie acknowledges her father's "absence" from the family, but unlike Rita, she does not long for his greater involvement.

She concedes that she does not know whether her father is a high-school graduate, and the only thing she knows about his work is that he is an electrician employed by the federal government. He never goes with his wife and children—his family of procreation—on their annual summer vacation, choosing instead to spend it with his family of orientation in North Carolina. (Every year Maggie's mother takes her and her younger brother to a new part of the United States, hoping to expand their knowledge and understanding of their country. She feels that she should make this a regular component of her childrearing practices). Maggie's description of her father's lack of interaction with the family he created while he maintains inordinately close ties to his family of orientation, suggests a kind of bigamy—marriage to both families, concurrently.

UNLIMITED FREEDOM AND THE DEATH OF PARENTS' DREAMS

Control is not central to the childrearing practices of the parents of the underachieving females. By comparison with their high-achieving female cohorts, the underachieving females are amazingly free to make final decisions regarding the configuration of their school schedules, dating, working after school, and general problems and policies. Their parents allow them to plan their individual futures without considering their limitations. Essentially, the underachieving females are free to contemplate leaving their parents' homes and fulfilling their individual dreams in ways that their high-achieving female cohorts do not dare. Not that the parents of the underachieving females allow their daughters to run wild. Rather, they are very supportive of their daughters and encourage them to live a life distinctly different from what they themselves lived as the teenagers of extremely authoritarian parents.

Three of the six underachieving females were living with their biological mother and father: Dawn, Shelvy, and Sade. Nekia lived with a maternal aunt and uncle. Of the other two informants, Sakay and Kaela, their mothers were each the single head of the household. Sakay was living with her mother as a result of her parents' divorce; Kaela's father had died when she was two years old.

Most of the underachieving young women had their parents' unconditional support for their expressed dreams and aspirations. Indeed, in some instances, these parents wished their daughters would dream more ambitious dreams. Sakay's mother was disappointed by the modest post–high school goals her daughter aspired to:

> I was *very* disappointed in her at one point, because two years
> ago she wanted to be a hairdresser . . . Seventh or eighth
> grade, she told me she was going to settle for being that, and I

said, "Oh, my goodness!" But I didn't, didn't let *her* know this, you know. I said, "I hope she comes off of that because they never say what they want to until, you know, actually— sometimes they don't even know when they *get* into college . . . That wasn't what I—I think I would *really* like for her to be one of the professionals, I really do. (Interview, June 28, 1983)

The degree to which the parents supported their daughters' dreams was the most salient difference in the childrearing formulas of the parents of the high-achieving and underachieving females. Typically, the parents of the underachieving females appeared to want more for their daughters than their daughters wanted for themselves.

Sakay's mother's description of her approach to rearing Sakay, the youngest of her three children, is typical of the responses the parents gave when talking about how they approached childrearing.

I think one of the things that I did—and what was *not* a conscious effort—a lot of my child-raising was sheer luck! I kid you not! But I think that one of the things—and I have to go back to saying that—I firmly believe that if you give children a sense of themselves and give them at least the desire to think for themselves . . . 'Cause when they're little, you gotta control them, you gotta tell them a lot of the things that they need to know and show them how to do things. But if you let them learn to think for themselves, and that, I think, is what has helped Sakay, 'cause she's a very strong little girl. (Interview, May 3, 1983)

Not surprisingly, this mother asserts that she is not now nor has she ever been strict with her children.

I'm not a strict disciplinarian, and I think if you give your kids enough . . . if you teach them how to think for themselves when they're little, it works better for you. Now, a lot of their decisions I don't agree with. Yes, some of Sakay's I don't agree with. But they do have the right to make their own decisions, and they all three seem to be doing pretty good with it. Pretty good. Sakay's a good kid. She's a good one. I think the worst problem that I've had with her is her problem with telling time. And she can come home very late. She's doing better with it, though. Very good—oh, she's very good with it now. She gets home on time, or if she's not going to be home, she'll call and she'll let me know that she's going to be late and tell me where she is. But for a while her finger didn't fit in any of

those little holes in the telephone. She couldn't call. Or if she
called, it was super-late. And she was letting me know, "I am
on my way home right now." . . . But that's about the worst,
that's about the worst. (Interview, May 3, 1983)

Sakay's parents were divorced when she was in elementary school.
Her father remarried but is currently separated from his wife. Sakay has
maintained a good relationship with him over the years, and she often
spends weekends with him in his "bachelor" apartment.

Both of her parents are high-school graduates. They have lived most
of their adult lives in Washington, where her father was born and reared.
He is a police officer. Sakay's mother grew up in Richmond, Virginia,
and was an excellent student. She is now working part-time in a computer store while looking for a better job. She sees her own parents as
having been too strict, and she has consciously sought not to replicate
their childrearing practices.

Kaela's mother had seven children before Kaela, and she says that
her childrearing energies had "burned out" by the time Kaela arrived.
Kaela's father, an alcoholic, died when the child was two. His death
made it absolutely essential for her mother to work and take care of the
family of ten. Kaela's paternal grandmother, who lived with them in a
grand old house in the Capital community, was primarily responsible
for rearing Kaela. The close bond between the two was abruptly ended
two years ago when the grandmother died.

Kaela's grandmother and several of her older brothers and sisters
prepared her for school every day and helped her with her homework.
In fact, Kaela's mother is absolutely certain that her mother-in-law had
the greatest influence on her youngest daughter.

Mm-hm. I'm sure of that . . . 'Cause I didn't have the time to
spend with her that I would *like* to have had . . . 'Cause I've
been home so seldom. I'm in and out *all* the time. They say,
"Momma, you're never home." And for this last six months,
I've been home more in this period than I've been home in the
fifteen years that I, you know, what I worked . . . I had to
work. Sometimes I had to work more than one job. In fact,
most of the time . . . And her grandmother used to listen to
her lessons, help her with them, and everything, so I'm sure
she was the person that motivated her the most. (Interview,
June 28, 1983)

As devout Catholics, all the children in this family, including Kaela,
went to Catholic schools in the community and the surrounding suburbs.
However, unlike her older siblings, who completed all their secondary

schooling in the Catholic schools, Kaela is having to attend Capital because Kaela's mother lost her job. For several years she had worked in an organization funded by the United Givers' Fund, but she is currently working part-time and receiving unemployment benefits.

This is Kaela's first year at Capital and the change of schools has caused her a lot of stress. Her mother feels that it is the change of school that is the primary reason why she is not doing well at Capital.

> The reason *I* feel she did not do well at Capital is because she didn't want to go there to start with. After she had gotten in there (it was something new to her when she started), then after she got in there and found out there were all those people in there, and—I mean, there was such *bedlam* in there, poor Kaela was just like she was—I mean, she was confused, you know? And she said, I guess she thought, "Well, gee whiz, I'm just one of all these people. I can't do any better than anybody else here," you know—could not excel there. I think that's why. (Interview, June 28, 1983)

The primary factor negatively affecting Kaela's underachievement at Capital is avoidance; she simply refuses to go to school. Everyone acknowledges that her refusal to go is due, in part at least, to the depression she is still experiencing as a result of her grandmother's death. She is absent from school more than she is present, and her mother does not appear to be able to stop this absenteeism.

> She can't go to school most of the time because she . . . And half the time, she can't get up! . . . I don't press her . . . I can't say I didn't at all, 'cause sometimes I'd say, "Well, you just get up. If you're late, I don't care if you're late. . . . you're going in there today, 'cause I'm carrying [driving] you." And I would carry [drive] her up to the school. And I did that a couple of times, and turned around, and she beat me home, almost . . . I would get here and be in there getting my coffee mug, and "Momma, I'm sorry. Momma, I'm going tomorrow. I'm going tomorrow, Momma. I just can't go today. I don't have this," and "I don't have that," and "I don't have this prepared," and "I don't have that prepared." . . . I'd drive her *to* school, and come back and get my coffee, and Kaela would be here a few minutes after I got back. (Interview, June 28, 1983)

Kaela's mother is sensitive to the charges frequently made about Black parents not caring about their children's school attendance. While she is not a "spring chicken," she is very much in tune with the contemporary world and realizes that if her daughter does not get the credentials sanctioned by the larger society, she will not be the independent, self-supportive person she must become in order to "make it" in America. Nor will she be able to get a job that will make her financially capable of supporting herself and any children she might have. But juxtaposed to this practical view is the strong desire of Kaela's mother for her daughter's happiness. She is keenly aware of Kaela's depression, which contributes to her reluctance to go to school, and she fears that her own employment problem may be adding to her daughter's troubles. Kaela's mother acknowledges that initially she did not know that Kaela was skipping school. When she became aware of her behavior, she described her reaction:

> I went up there to talk to her counselor *and* to the assistant principal, you know, to see about getting her back in there. I think that was when I first discovered she'd been out of school five weeks. (Interview, June 28, 1983)

Despite her mother's intervention, Kaela still attends school only intermittently. Her daughter's unhappiness and lack of funds for tuition made Kaela's mother reluctant to quarrel with Kaela about returning to Catholic school.

> Truthfully, I didn't want Kaela to go back to the Catholic high school because I felt that—I don't know, something just happened there that last year that she was there. There wasn't that closeness, that you felt and all, and I began to have serious doubts about the system. Mm-hm, I really did. She came home repeatedly almost in tears, and, she was—you know, she came in, she would tell me, "I *hate* this person, I *hate* that. . . ." I said, "Kaela, you don't hate anybody." "But I hate *her*," she'd say. And she would tell me all the little incidents where she thought they were being partial, you know, towards other [non-Black] students. (Interview, June 28, 1983)

Sade also has a very stable family and home environment, and it is clear that both of her parents love her very much. They are financially more secure than the parents of any other female students in the sample, high- or underachieving. Her father has worked since 1973 as a refrigeration repairman at one of the major hospitals in the city, and he is satisfied with his job. He is a high-school graduate. Sade's mother, also a high-school graduate, works as a secretary in one of the numerous federal agencies.

Sade's parents bought the house they live in in 1968. It is in a small enclave of well-maintained townhouses not far from Capital High, squeaky clean and tastefully decorated. Like many of the parents, they invited me to dinner and later took me to a midweek prayer service at their predominantly White church in suburban Maryland.

Sade, a shy, well-behaved girl, is the younger of two female siblings. Her father offered the following assessment of how he and his wife reared her:

> I don't know, really—unless she just take after Dad and try to
> do the best she can in whatever she do—in whatever she does.
> [Laugh] . . . Well, I try—seriously, I try to teach them [Sade
> and her older sister], you know, to do the best they can.
> 'Cause after you do the best you can, there's no more you can
> do . . . (Interview, May 17, 1983)

Sade's father admits that he is the more available parent and therefore the more influential. He is home from about eight in the morning until close to midnight, when he leaves for work. He is the parent Sade and her older sister call in case of an emergency, and he is also the person who sets and enforces most of the rules and regulations regarding homework, visiting with friends, and so forth.

> Well, we don't like the darkness to catch up with her. You
> know. We try to emphasize, you know, being home before
> dark. And there have been times where she would call here,
> and most of the time I would go pick her up. But, no, other
> than that, we didn't limit no time. Because she didn't, she
> didn't visit friends that often. She didn't visit friends that
> often . . .
>   I don't want them to be coming home in the dark, you
> know. Especially riding the bus, cause she rides the bus, you
> know. It's bad enough coming home in the day, really! But
> when it gets night, now you know, if you know anything
> about Washington—well, most areas nowadays—with all this
> drugs and everything going on, somebody'll hit you in the
> head in a minute. And then they had a series of rapes in this
> area—I imagine you heard about that. And that's one of the
> reasons I don't want the darkness to catch up with them. But
> it hasn't been that often where she has been—you know, do-
> ing that much visiting, where we had to be concerned about it.
> (Interview, May 17, 1983)

Sade's father's response differs from that of the other parents of the underachieving females, who appear to place greater importance on their daughters' ability to have strong connections with their peers than they do to controlling the girls' activities with rigid curfews and other rules limiting extrafamilial interactions. Unlike most of the parents of the underachieving females, Sade's father admits that they do not encourage their daughters to seek out friendships.

> Well, she—in elementary school, she had—I guess three or four little *close* friends, and all of them was very nice . . . But now, going to Capital, she picks her own friends, and I don't have any qualms about her friends. She seems to get along good with them, as far as *I* know. But I don't know too much *about* her friends at Capital, except—well, some of the girls on the Flag team 'cause sometime I take her up there, and I pick up some of the—a couple of her girlfriends. On days that they have—they perform, I may have to pick them, pick a couple of the other girlfriends up and drop them off at their house, and then bring *her* on home . . . She had . . . one or two times that they've spent the night here with her, and I believe she went and spent the night with—who?—Jackie, once, too, didn't you? Yeah . . . I've never known her to have any friends that we didn't like or approve of. (Interview, May 17, 1983)

Despite the greater control Sade's parents exert, it is less than that of most of the parents of the high-achieving females. For example, Sade is free to decide to participate in an after-school activity. Neither Rita nor Katrina, two high-achieving females, were able to make such a choice, even though they wanted to participate after school in some of these activities. Sade decides to be a member of the Flag Girls' Marching Team. She can also expect the support of her parents; she knows that she can depend on her father to give her and her friends a ride home, if they want one. None of the high-achieving females is so lucky. In fact, several of them did not participate in any of the after-school activities because their parents disapproved, fearing both that their daughters might be guided by unacceptable norms and standards of their friends and that they would not be supervised by a responsible adult.

DATING AND WAITING

There is virtually no time during the day when the mothers of the high-achieving girls do not know where their daughters are. Most of the girls, who are either seventeen or just short of that age, are not allowed to date or their dating is relentlessly controlled. Maggie is just beginning to date, but her parents have imposed severe restrictions. Her mother takes her and her date to the movies and returns to pick them up. She insists that if Maggie were to disobey her, she would be subjected to the same discipline she received when she was younger:

If [she does something that is] bad, [I would punish her] the
same way I did when she was little. She got the spanking. But,
you know, as I said, it wasn't . . . break her arms or anything,
it was on the hips, and I tried not to whip too many clothes.
Now she gets them—you know, she hasn't had one in a while,
but if she does something wrong, she will definitely know
she's getting a whipping. And her daddy will get her, too.
And—but sometimes she get—little minor thing, no
phone—we'll take away TV, because it's . . . most of the time,
basically she's a good child. Basically, but, you know, every
now and then, it's phone privileges, and that's for snapping
back, or a attitude thing, basically. But if she would do anything really bad, she knows she will get a whipping . . . That's
right. She will never get too old for me to whip her if she's doing something wrong. (Interview, June 2, 1983)

When I responded by indicating disbelief that she would actually
whip her seventeen-year-old daughter, she assured me that she would:

Yes, I would, too! I sure would! If she did something wrong,
or disrespect me in some way, I will reach and grab her right
here, and whip her. She knows that, too. I'm not—it's not to
make her afraid, but she knows to do right. She knows right
and wrong. And she thinks about that, I think, a lot of times
before she do things. And, 'cause like I say, her father very seldom whip her, but if she does something wrong, he will get
her! So—and even when she was going to school, if she did
something wrong in elementary school and got a spanking for
it, when she got home she got another spanking. Of course
she got another one. Of course. She didn't . . . when she . . .
on her way home, she knew, she started crying before she got
in the door, 'cause she knew she was going to get another one.
So you don't do it, 'cause you got double on you. And if you
lie about it, you're going to get another one . . . she thinks
twice before she does anything wrong, knowing what she's going to get. And that makes her think, make her brain work,
you know.
    I demand respect, and I get it. And I think most parents
should get respect from their children. You know, a lot of
kids, they don't respect their parents, they just say anything
around them: "You don't tell me what to do." I say I brought
you into the world, and I deserve respect for that. (Interview,
June 2, 1983)

While Maggie's mother was talking, the passion with which she sought to determine whether her daughter should be involved in this study of school success flashed through my mind, giving her present assertions a chilling ring of truth. I remembered how fearful Maggie was that her mother would not permit her to participate in the study and how I had to call her several times to reassure her that I was neither from the FBI nor on its "most wanted" list.

Katrina would not dare broach the subject of dating with her parents. Fortunately, she does not want to date yet. She would like to go out with her peers in group gatherings, but her parents will have no part of that either.

Similarly, Alice's mother does not encourage her to date, although her reasoning, as summarized by Alice, is riddled with ambivalence.

> *Alice:* Hm-mm, not yet. I mean I can, I'm sixteen, I *can*. But . . . Nobody I met yet, that I would want to spend some time with . . . [My mother] said the longer I wait, the better *she* feel about it . . . She don't really *want* me to, but I mean, I can. But she prefer that I wait so I can check out men, so they can't put me in a trick.
>
> *Anthro:* What would be putting you "in a trick"?
>
> *Alice:* Like trying to get me to their house or apartment. (Interview, May 23, 1983)

Like most of the mothers of the high-achieving females, Rita's mother did not allow her to date, even though she was seventeen. One element in Rita's situation made it different from that of most of her peers: the religious prohibition. Rita has two older female siblings, who are high-school graduates and employed in semiskilled jobs. As young adults, they could date now but choose not to. Their mother agreed that her two older daughters could date "if they wanted to do it against my will—but I'm thankful that they haven't." (Interview, May 4, 1983)

> I don't mean that they can't, but like the Bible say, when you start it, you should have marriage in view . . . See? And because—I mean, you can just look around the world today, and look at the problems that comes from young people being intimate, and going places and things unchaperoned. And see, so then you have a lot of illegitimate children, and diseases and things are just running wild. And . . . so, like I said, they meet someone that they feel like they want to—that's in the organization. Rita says she is not in the organization, but I still hold the same rules for her, also. And . . . it's the teaching of the Bible. Right. And even as far back—when the Bible shows

when God created Adam and Eve, it says He blessed them,
then He told them to be fruitful and fill the earth. So that's
what I basically believe. (Interview, May 5, 1983)

Lisa is probably freer to live her life as a separate and distinct person
than any of the other high-achieving females. Her mother appears to
trust her judgment and allows her more freedom than any of the other
high-achieving girls enjoy. Unlike most of the other parents, Lisa's
mother and father are divorced. She lives with her mother, her maternal
grandparents, and four siblings in a rundown three-bedroom apartment.

Being deserted by her father when he divorced her mother several
years ago has made Lisa very distrustful of men, especially Black men.
"You know, I don't really, like, trust in—you know, Black males, I
mean, they *tell* you one thing and—*I* think it's trust. It all boils down
to lack of trusting each other" (interview, March 10, 1983). Hence, she
is extremely wary of getting emotionally involved with men her own
age. Like most of the female students at Capital High, she prefers to
date males who are older and who are not students at Capital. She has
an "older" boyfriend who comes to "court" for a few minutes most
evenings. She also goes out with him on weekends, with her mother's
blessing and consent.

I just don't care too much for going with boys in the same
school I go to. I never really—I don't know, I think *I'*d feel
awkward. It seem like your business get out—you know, a
roach in her house—you know, just *something*—you know
. . . They just never attract my attention. Let's put it that way.
I mean, I like to joke with them and stuff, but not to go with.
It just never entered my mind, 'cause I like *older* dudes. I
don't know why. (Interview, March 28, 1983)

The mere fact that Lisa is openly allowed to date makes her an
exception among the high-achieving female students.

DATING WITH RELUCTANT APPROVAL

In stark contrast to the "high-achieving" parents, most of whom were
extremely concerned about the kind of people in their daughters' lives,
the parents of the underachieving girls actively maintained a connection
with the Black community through advocacy of culturally approved dating practices. Among the students at Capital, dating is a factor in being
perceived as a well-rounded person. They derive pleasure from being
socially connected to their peers. As was noted earlier, Sakay has a

loosely enforced curfew. When her mother was asked at what age she allowed Sakay to begin dating, her response was illuminating:

> I didn't . . . I didn't. She just . . . [sort of slipped into it] . . . Yeah. She would say things like, "Katrina and I are going to the movies, and this little fellow is going." . . . At any rate, she kind of *eased* into it . . . And she just kind of—she *eased* me into her dating. Yeah . . . She checked first to see if she could go. Now, she didn't come in and ask, "May I?" She would say, "I'm going to go to the movies with so-and-so," or "I'm going to go this place. Is that all right?" (Interview, May 3, 1983)

Interestingly, Sakay's mother's response was not one of sadness; rather, her tone of voice, as well as the loving looks she gave her daughter as she gave this account, signaled admiration and support, suggesting that her daughter did the right thing.

Kaela's mother makes a similar claim. She implied that when Kaela went from an all-girls' Catholic high school to a coed public school, she confronted the issue of male interest for the first time. As her mother described it, this male interest was both very intense and unavoidable.

> And then too, you have the little boys to contend with, and what have you, up here [at Capital], and they didn't have that there [at the Catholic school]. It was a all-girls' school. Kaela got to be quite popular here at Capital—too popular. [Laugh] . . . Too popular, according to all the telephone calls that she receives. But I think I . . . I don't have any problem with Kaela. (Interview, June 28, 1983)

As eleventh-grade students, most of the females in the underachieving sample are seventeen or soon will be and most of them are dating. Most are also actively discovering and exploring their evolving sexuality.[8] Even Sade, whose father wants her to be home before dark, is dating for the first time this year. However, unlike Sakay and Kaela, she has a definite curfew: midnight. And she is not allowed to date during the week.

Dawn's parents put no restrictions on her dating; her problem is that she has not been asked for a date. She is a tall woman—six feet two inches—and a basketball player. She has a good many male friends, but no special male friend. Both the male and female track members value Dawn's friendship and welcome the lack of tensions her presence provides. Like most other members of the track team, she ridicules many of the behaviors and activities generally associated with girls and femininity. In one of my many observations of Dawn's pattern of interaction with males, I noticed that she competed with them. The competition was not malicious, intent upon destroying her competitor. Rather, it appeared to be designed to minimize gender differences, to show her male peers that—at least in her case—gender distinction was a useless cultural construct. For example, she would often join the track players at lunch and proceed to "eat them under the table." As a result, many of them had become promoters of the claim that "Dawn is better."

While her male peers seemed to be more amused than threatened, they clearly did not see her as someone they would like to date or marry. They did not seek to imitate her; rather, the emphasis was always on having her imitate them. Dawn was thus not viewed as a sexual object, distracting her male peers from the achievement of their athletic goals, nor was she unequivocally defined as "one of the boys." Indeed, her liminal status made her an anomaly, a kind of neutered Other (L. Cary 1991).

Dawn's mother and father are keenly aware of her unspoken concerns regarding both her weight and her height. Since both parents are tall, they strongly empathize with her problem.

> *Dawn's Father:* I think she's a little self-conscious . . . I do, 'cause . . . other kids will call her a lot of names and . . . I know *I* had problems when *I* was going to school, 'cause I got burnt when I was a baby. And kids'd laugh at me, they'll pick at me, you know, call me names and all that.
>
> *Dawn's Mother:* We all are not made alike, and we not from the same people. So everybody can't be small, everybody can't be short, everybody can't be tall. So this is the way I feel. You know? When I hear people criticizing other people about certain things, you know, I know there comes a time that people overindulge into eating and drinking and—you know. And I feel that if she slow down on her eating and drinking, she can lose weight. But there have been times when I'll tell her, I'll say, "Okay now, watch yourself now with those calories." And she gets insulted! Sometimes. Then when I go upstairs, she'll slip and eat and drink . . . I come down, I say, "Who drink the sodas?" I go up in her room, she's got two or three cups up there. (Interview, June 17, 1983)

DENYING RACE AND THE PRIVILEGED OTHER

Curiously, most of the parents of the high-achieving females taught their daughters that race was neither a social privilege nor a social stigma. In other words, they verbally denied the saliency of racialized bodies. Most of them taught their daughters that they were "equal" to all other peoples in the world. Yet, in the context of their own lives, especially in the world of work, the parents of the high-achieving females were constantly struggling with the limitations forced upon them because of the stigma of their race.

Race as a cultural category and racial differences are the two topics most avoided by the parents of the high-achieving females. All of them appeared to be made uncomfortable by implications of racial discrimination for their children's lives.

Dawn's father's experience of racial discrimination as a young child made him extremely receptive to the claims of the integration ideology.

> I can now—listen to people fight busing. They talk about "busing is this" and "busing is that." My birthday, I was sixty-one years old . . . Yes ma'am. I was sixty-one the tenth of June . . . And they've been busing ever since *I* was a kid. Those white kids used to come by us and holler, "Nigger!" You know . . . They were riding the bus, and we were walking. And now you hear plenty of people get out there and talk against busing. If busing—if you don't have any [other] method for any—solving desegregation, why not use it? I'm not against busing. You know what I mean? 'Cause they been busing all my life. But now, just as soon as these Black kids started going to school with the White kids this . . . all of a sudden, it's busing that's the problem. (Interview, June 17, 1983)

Dawn's father acknowledges that "[working] conditions now has changed in all walks of life." At the same time, he observes not only the persistence of racism and its debilitating effects on African-Americans but also the growing magnitude of the problem.

> I guess since President Reagan . . ., I mean, you can see it's getting worse and worse. I mean every time they'll say that they're not hiring nobody, but every time you look, there's a new face. And he's all White. (Interview, June 17, 1983)

Dawn's mother supported her husband's observation concerning the devastating effects of racism in the lives of Black Washingtonians. Like her husband, she noted that positions like her custodial job are being appropriated by White Americans.

> We're doing the type of work that we're doing [janitorial, custodial, etc.], and you know what they're bringing in? Young White girls. I'm not kidding. You think they're coming from

the office.[9] And [yet] they're working [the custodial jobs] just like we're working. They come from way down in Maryland and Virginia, where they can't find work, 'cause employers down there are not paying that much money. And they will come up here and work—up here in them offices like we [Black people] work and go on back in the morning. And you think they come from the office. I'm not kidding—you [should] come down there and see the folks! (Interview, June 17, 1983)

Rita's mother looks to her religion for evidence that race and religion are "mixed," or inextricably linked, and therefore the work of a benevolent, all-loving God.

I know race and racism exist. Definitely. You know, I'm not that naive—I know discrimination exists, but I would just teach my children—you know, just like I would just tell them from the Bible that people are going to be this way. And it's nothing that—the person themselves would have to change. And when a race of people have been taught all of their lives that they are superior and they are the best, it's nothing that you can do to change it. So you're just going to have to learn to live with it. You know, just be what you're going to be, and deal with it. (Interview, May 5, 1983)

Because her religion essentially posits the claim that life after death is more important than the "earthly world," Rita's mother feels constrained to urge her children to adjust to life here on earth. She never allowed any of her children to wear their hair natural during the Civil Rights Movement, because her religion would not condone such practices.

It—okay, say had I been in the world, had I not been a Witness, yes, I would have allowed it. But at the time that [Afro hair style] came out, it was, from what I understood, a sign to let people know that we're Black and we're coming out, we're getting our chance. . . . I probably would have went for the Afro and whatever. But, see, the Bible teaches that we're not part of the world. Just like Jesus was no part of the world when He was on earth. He taught his followers that. . . . (Interview, May 5, 1983)

When she was asked to talk about how she prepared Rita to face the racial hostility many African-Americans face in the work arena, she admitted that she was uncertain about what to tell her children, especially Rita. Part of this ambivalence is related to her lack of experience and involvement in the world she envisions her daughter(s) inheriting.

> I don't—I truthfully don't know, because, you know, from the things I've heard about the working world, you've got to be exceptionally good if you're reaching for a position. And if you're Black, you've got to have exceptional qualifications. And so maybe if she had the right qualifications, it might not be, but I couldn't say for sure. The only thing I have to tell her, just to try to do the best she can . . . (Interview, May 5, 1983)

When I asked her to share with me how she reacted to Rita's questions regarding race and skin color, she responded by claiming that they "never basically was into that." This she said was especially true for Rita. She went on to tell of her oldest daughter's initiation of a conversation about skin color and its meaning:

> My oldest daughter, she thought she was White. [Laughter] She came to me one time because her other sister [not Rita] said she was "colored," and she came—no, her sister called her "Black," I think, and she came and told me her sister called her a bad word. I said, "So what did she call you?" She said, "She told me I was Black." I said, "Well, you are." I said, "You are of the Black race." I said, "But you are a light-skinned Black person," I said, "because the Black race has all colors of people. And you just happen to be a light-skinned Black person, just like I am light-skinned." And I said, "And that comes from my grandmother's mother and her grand-mother being White and half Indian and all that mixed up together, it comes down through the . . . And my father's mother is a Indian. And so I say, "And so that's what it is." I say, "Rita's not as light as you, your other sister is not as light as—you know, all of you." But I had sisters that is as dark as my middle daughter's complexion. And then I have a sister that's [my complexion]. 'Cause my father is dark and my mother is light. See? So I told them, "That's it. But we're all colored." (Interview, May 5, 1983)

According to Rita's mother, this was the extent of her daughters' interest in race and skin color and their one and only conversation on the subject. Moreover, she insisted that her husband had not talked with "the girls" about race and skin color:

> See, basically, my husband, he's not the talker—you know, the children usually talk to me. 'Cause I talk to them. And

that's the way my husband is, because when he was growing
up, his mother was the one that did everything. So he's a person of habit. So he felt like that I should be the one—you
know [to talk to them about such things]. (Interview, May 5,
1983)

Like Rita's mother, Maggie's mother denied the importance of
Blackness as a barrier to social mobility in her life and in the lives of
her daughters. Hence she taught them nothing about race and race consciousness.

I couldn't say, "Maggie, don't play with that little White kid
over there, 'cause her mother's racist," or whatever. Let her
find out for herself. I don't—you know, my thing is, love everybody. Treat them right and it comes back to you. So I
never taught racial discrimination. What she's learned, she's
learned by dealing with them themselves, seeing on her own.
I never taught her, you know, my thing is, she'll know—she'll
know what to do. If somebody walks up and calls her a name,
she knows how to walk away. And the same thing with fights
or anything, name calling—walk away. It takes two. And if
you don't say anything, nine times out of ten, they'll get tired,
it'll go away. And if you say something, it blows it all out of
proportion. If it happens to her, I feel she can deal with it. . . .
'Cause me, I've never had any problem, even though I was
raised in the South—not really South, but Virginia is South.
I, in the little town, in a sense, I never was, they never ran
into discrimination. 'Cause we lived up under Whites. But we
couldn't go to school [with them] though. But basically I never
was—they never what they call, "You Black this, you do, you
that." I never ran into burning crosses or anything. I didn't
know anything about that. But . . . you just learn. You just
learn . . . [Maggie] didn't never approach me. 'Cause I know
they had essays and all, they wrote on it, she did research
work. And they wrote essays and things on race. But basically,
coming to me to ask me about race, no. (Interview, June 2, 1983)

The responses of these parents of these high-achieving girls with
respect to race in their childrearing practices and in their philosophy of
life make clear what the girls learned about race from their parents: it
is a taboo subject. This conveyed to the girls two notions: that race is
inconsequential in America and that it is so important that it is banned
in civilized conversation. It was as if a conspiracy of silence existed about

the subject, based on the hope that if no one talked about it, it would go away.

A similar response pattern is evident among the parents of the underachieving females, including the eager acknowledgment that their work lives are riddled with racism. For example, Dawn's mother and father admit the continued existence of racial discrimination in their lives. In recalling his experiences in South Carolina, Dawn's father described the debilitating effects of racism on his educational opportunities:

> Well, I can tell you myself: I experienced discrimination. I was born and raised in the South, and me and my oldest sister—the one that live down in Columbia now—we used to have to walk about five miles to school . . . I can remember we was walking from school, and we stopped at the White school to get a drink of water. The teacher would come to the door and run us away from the pump. I can remember that, walking from the school. They had a pump outside. *We* didn't have a pump outside. And we would stop by to get a drink of water. I don't know how much noise . . . to tell you exactly how much noise we made, or where something was being done that we shouldn't have done, but . . . she would be in there, and she'd come to the door and run us away. (Interview, June 17, 1983)

Likewise, the father of Sade, one of the underachieving students in the sample, notes the widespread racism on his job in a federal agency in Washington.

> Yeah, we [Black people] *have* made a lot of progress. And—but I think we have a long way to go. Because I see so much, or hear about so many things happening on my job today that shows me, and is *proof* that they're still trying to hold the Blacks down, you know. Because I've seen them deny well-qualified Blacks jobs and give them to the Whites. My supervisor, for instance: he was . . . he had three different positions within about a six-month period that was denied him and given to White people, and he was *much* more qualified than the people they gave it to . . . Oh, yes. Well, the thing is, he's one of the top mechanics out there—he *is* the top mechanic out there, and they were relying on him, and they don't want to *lose* him, but they don't want to *give* him anything either, see? And it just seems like he just can't get anywhere, 'cause those White people are holding him down, you know. And,

oh!, it's, oh, numerous incidents that happen like that, out there where I work. And well, I hear talk of it in other agencies, in other jobs, too. (Interview May 17, 1983)

This father went on to observe that his wife, who works for another federal agency in the city, also encounters and observes racist practices that deny African-Americans the opportunity to compete with their white counterparts. Yet he insists that he never talked to Sade and her older sister about the damaging effects of racism:

No, I really—never considered talking about racism with my child. It really never crossed my mind. I never thought about it before. No, I never thought about it. Like I was saying earlier, some of the things that you [the anthropologist] asked me, it just never dawned on me, I never gave it a thought. And particularly about having any problem with Sade or [her sister] we just haven't *had* any [racial] problems, so I never had to think about these kind of things . . . And I imagine in school that they're talking about the Blacks now, and Black history and all. But I haven't personally really found it necessary to talk about it. Maybe I should have. But . . . (Interview, May 17, 1983)

The willful denial of race as an issue while rearing their children was not limited to the fathers in the study. Sakay's mother offered a similar response when asked to describe what she taught her daughter that would help her cope with racism either in school or later life.

(Sigh) Not a lot. Not a lot. I—I'm *not* racially motivated. I don't see race as an issue. I *know* it's an issue, I just don't *see* it as an issue. I think that whatever I do, I do because I am me, and not because I'm Black. And if I excel, it's because *I* want to excel, and not because I'm excelling for a race. I just—I'm not into the Black-White issue. I've never been in— maybe I should be, but I'm not . . . Be proud of who you are and that's about it. I—I can't even think of anybody in my family who is racially motivated. We just—we're not really deeply into causes, except for children. We're very *baby-conscious* in my family . . . Yeah, children are the best thing since shoes . . . We're just not . . . The biggest cause that we can have is children. We're not into race, and we're not into all the other things. We're just kind of into children. And I think my children are too. I've not heard Sakay discuss race a lot; in fact, I can't think of when she *has* discussed race with me. It's just not a big thing for me. (Interview, May 3, 1983)

When I asked if Sakay's father's response was similar to hers, she said:

> Yeah. In fact, it was more true for him, because—well (sigh), why I don't know. He came from—he came from a background—oh, I guess you'd say servitude. His family has always worked for Whites—rich ones. But they've always had everything they wanted. And I think my former husband sees the race issue as being foolish, because it has never *been* an issue for him. That's really never been an issue for him. He's lived around Blacks, and he's lived around Whites, and he was accepted by both, and he had no problem with any of it. So with him race is something out in left field, and it's . . . Anybody who is saying anything about the racial issue is probably some Black who doesn't want to excel, and he doesn't want to do anything. That's probably the way Sakay's father sees it. And with him being a cop, he sees a *lot* of it, more so—he sees the destitute Black, or the criminal Black. So the race issue is nothing for him . . . Bless his heart! (Interview, May 3, 1983)

These adults' approach to the race issue had some devastatingly unanticipated consequences. Maggie's perception of her racial identity is a case in point. Regrettably, as these young women—both high- and underachieving—are "find[ing] out for [themselves]," Blackness is a stigmatized racial feature, one that is limiting their ability to have the kinds of futures they hope for.

NURTURING THROUGH CONTROLLING AND LIMITING EXPECTATIONS

Most of the parents of the high-achieving females interact with their daughters in ways that suggest, at least superficially, great ambivalence about the daughters' lofty academic aspirations. This is perhaps best seen in Alice's description of her mother's seeming lack of support for her desire to attend dental school in California.

Maggie's mother does not limit her encouragement to accepting college as a possibility after graduation from high school. What she does instead is to urge her to "get a job," broadly defined.

> I'm very concerned. If I can just [get her] to be grown—eighteen, twenty-one at the most, with a job. If she wants to go to school [college], that's fine. If she . . . Right now she's talking about . . . she doesn't really want to go to college, she wants to go to computer school, 'cause she's interested in com-

puter. And I said, "Well, that's up to you." She feels that four
years of college won't help her right now, unless she [goes] in
a specialized field. I said, "Well, that's the way you feel, if you
go to a computer school and specialize, and you get a job, and
then get more on-the-job training, that's fine, you know, but
at least you'll be able to do something to help yourself. Don't
be dependent on others to do it for you . . . I don't know
which direction she's going, and I don't push her. Because I believe if you push her into going to the college or whatever, because *you* want her to go, that's wrong. Because they're going
to foul up somewhere along the line. So this will be her—this
is *her* life now, she has to make the decision . . . I mean, you
kind of guide them a little bit—"Look at this area, look at
this area." But you don't say, "I want you to be a doctor. I
want you to be a nurse." And they feel like they're obligated
to do that. And they are not really happy. I figure, let them
make the decision on their own. (Interview, June 2, 1983)

Maggie's mother's view of how she sought to influence her daughter's academic and job aspirations differed drastically from how her
daughter perceived it. To Maggie, her mother's desires for her after high
school were the pivotal factors in her decision not to seek a college
education, despite her high academic performance.

[My goal is to] go to a training school and specialize in com-
puters . . . [Become a] computer programmer . . . I'm taking
computer programming now. I took COBOL last year . . . I
got to do COBOL. I did pretty well. I made Bs the whole time
I was in there . . . COBOL is . . . (Interview, January 5, 1983)

It would be wrong to conclude that Maggie does not want to go to
college. She does. But her mother's practical concerns about getting her
daughter established and her conviction that she has successfully accomplished what she is supposed to do as a parent—give her children
wings—compel Maggie to conclude that there are sensible alternatives
to college attendance.

It's not that I don't want to go to college—I mean, you know,
it's a lot of people out here with college degrees and they not,
you know, gettin' jobs, so my mother said if I wanted to specialize in one thing, I should go to a specialized school, you
know, that specializes in one thing . . . Instead of taking all
those different classes, paying money for nothing. (Interview,
January 5, 1983)

Another typical parental response to a daughter's high academic achievement is that of Rita's mother, who, like Maggie's mother, is ambivalent about Rita's going to college. Indeed, it is probably more accurate to say that she is fearful of her daughter's school achievement and what it means in terms of options for Rita.

> I'm going to tell you like this, Ms. Fordham: I am really happy that Rita's doing what she's doing, and I'm not going to be hypocritical about it. But if Rita didn't go to college, it would not make me a bit of difference . . . No, it would not. Because, like I said, you know, education is good. And I think that Rita—she says that she wants to go into neurology, or something to that effect. And from studying the Bible and looking at the events the way that they are today, the Bible shows that this system is not going to be here that long. Whenever it is that it's going to come to an end—well, not the system—it's not going to end, but the end of wickedness, we don't know. See, the Bible say there's going to be people that's going to survive the destruction of the system of things. But from looking at the way that things are going on the world scene, and looking at your colleges and things today, I mean—for the right purpose, but a lot of things happen in college. See? And . . . I mean kids that get hung up with drugs, and these sororities and things now, the things that they . . . I was reading some article in the paper about these sororities initiating these young guys, and they died from drinking all this—drinking too much and stuff like that, the things they make them do. And, basically, I just . . . you know, I'm just not that enthused. (Interview, May 5, 1983)

When I asked her mother if she would be happier if her Rita did *not* go to college, she responded:

> I think I would . . . Yeah. Because I'm not looking forward to a future, you see, because the system is crumbling, basically. I'm not against learning, now, don't misunderstand me. I'm not against learning. I'm happy that Rita has the qualifications and things to go to college. I mean, were things different, and we were living at a different period of time, I mean, it would be all right. Now her father's all for it, you know, and I'm not totally against it, but I'm saying, looking at . . . for people now to plan a career . . . mean, I've seen people [Black people] with college degrees and everything, they cannot even get a job. (Interview, May 5, 1983)

The sources of this mother's ambivalence were quite varied. There was her religion, which mandated that unmarried women remain in their parents' home until they marry. There was her verbalized fear of crime and drugs and other social problems. Still further, there was the unspoken fear of how success would change and perhaps further alienate her daughter from her family and the Black community.

A common, relentless goal in the childrearing practices of virtually all of the mothers of the high-achieving females is *control* of their daughter's lives and even of the options they seriously consider. The central lesson the mothers of the high-achieving females taught them was the value of behaving in socially appropriate ways (conformity)—most important, *not* bringing shame on the family by acting on their developing sexuality. The mothers of the high-achieving girls do not overtly praise their daughters for their school accomplishments, but they are both proud of and fearful of these school accomplishments. What the daughters sensed most keenly was the fear. Indeed, the lack of praise for the daughters, particularly when sons were applauded, was a source of familial conflict between the high-achieving daughters and their mothers.

The mothers of the high-achieving females perceived their lack of verbal praise as a necessary leveling agent, a necessary "evil" designed to keep their daughters grounded in the norms and values of the imagined Black community as well as to reinforce their ability to survive. Regrettably, their daughters read their lack of praise and constant restraints as signs of a lack of pride and support. The hurt caused by this practice was exacerbated by their mothers' tendency to be generally much more overtly supportive of their sons' school achievements.

FAMILY STABILITY AND UNCONDITIONAL LOVE

Curiously, as a group the parents of the underachieving females have the most stable, long-term marriages. Their family patterns closely approximate those of the high-achieving sample: mother and father present in the home, or mother as only parent. For example, during the first year of the research project, Dawn's parents had been married for thirty-nine years; Shelvy's mother and father were still legally married though estranged. Sade's parents were married in the 1960s and were still very much a family unit. Nekia's aunt and uncle, her guardians, had a long-term marriage. Kaela's father died when she was only two, but she had seven siblings, and her parents had a long history together before his death. Sakay's parents were the only divorced couple among the parents in the underachieving female sample. Thus, family stability for the female underachievers—as in long-term marriages between mother and father—does not appear to promote school success.

FOUR

Parenthood, Childrearing, and Male Academic Success

Dummy in the blue shirt. Dummy in the blue shirt. Dummy in the blue shirt, they were saying, and I knew they were talking about me, even though I was wearing not a blue shirt but a blue sweater . . . "Hey, Dummy, turn around." "Yeah, look at us, Dummy!" . . . "Were you too dumb to take a bath this morning, Dummy?" "Yeah, you sure are dirty." "Phew! I can smell you from here . . ."

I said nothing to my family about this, that day, but the following morning I told my mother about the incident while she was knocking a few naps out of my hair with a very small-toothed comb. It wasn't till I was about three quarters of the way through the story that I realized I'd made a mistake. In the first place, my mother has never been a "morning person," and she went about all her morning tasks with great flame and fury even when things were running smoothly. But as my story unfolded I noted she began combing my hair with increasing vehemence. It felt as though some great bird were swooping down on me, clutching my head with its blade-sharp talons, and by degrees, plucking the bone away to get to the meat. Quite honestly, I had expected her to lay the comb aside, set me on her lap, and coo rather than caw. But Mama said, "What were you doing? Were you acting like a dummy?" And I said, "No, ma'am, I was just walking." "Well," she said, combing with still greater heat, "you must've been doing something, boy." I was pretty sure my scalp had begun bleeding. "Hold still, boy," she said. Then, "I tell you *what*—if I *ever* catch you acting the fool at school or anywhere else, I'll skin you alive—you hear me?" And I said, "Yes, ma'am, I did, but I didn't do a thing except walk home from school." "I said hold still, boy! You better not be lying to me, Reginald." I was in tears by this time and all I could manage to say was what I'd already said before, that I'd just been walking, so forth. Then, in a last-ditch effort for sympathy, I mentioned the rock they'd chucked, and that it had just barely missed hitting me smack on the head. "Well, why didn't you throw one back?" Mama said, and then she said she'd be dammed if she was going to raise anybody's sissy. But I heard something catch in her throat, and she laid the comb on the rim of the basin, then rested her hands on my shoulders. I was too ashamed of my tears to look up into the mirror and at her reflection. She turned me about, drew me into her warm bosom, held me, talked about how ignorant some people were, that I shouldn't let a bunch of stupid boys upset me, that the world could sometimes be a tough, mean, petty place and I was just going to have to toughen up right along with it. She said a few more things, which I can no longer remember, but I do remember that her warmth and the sounds that issued from her throat, dozy, lugubrious, made my belly heat up and glow, made my legs tremble, made me want to sleep. But Mama said, "Come on now, son, you got to be strong." She took me by the shoulders again, turned me back around, and resumed working on my hair.

I think I was about eight then. (McKnight 1993:97–99)

Like the parents of the female students, the parents of male students at Capital High use a discourse—that is, a way of speaking—that clearly conveys the power differential between adult and child. They, too, are impaled on a fulcrum of resistance. Consciously and unconsciously, they teach their sons through the use of a particular linguistic code to survive by resisting claims regarding the Black Self; they teach them to both conform to and avoid socially defined race and gender roles.

The dicta for successfully rearing African-American males are more complex and complicated than those used by the parents of females. One reason for the difference is that parents of males are compelled to take into consideration not only the racialized nature of America as a nation but also the patriarchal principles that exist in both the larger society and the imagined Black community.

African-American parents are thus compelled to teach their sons to embrace a twofold contradictory formula: to concurrently accept subordination and the attendant humiliation (for survival in the larger society) and preserve gender domination (for survival in the Black community).[1]

At Capital High, adult parental identity roles are split at the intersection of race and gender issues, with most parents struggling to maintain a balance that will ensure their sons' survival. Ruptures at this intersection are indicative of these parents' efforts to rear their sons to be both nondominating and successful in a racialized patriarchy. The irony embodied in such a stance should not be overlooked: The meaning of maleness in hierarchical and/or racialized patriarchies is embedded in notions of power and domination, yet these parents are compelled to raise children who are male but whose systematic denial of what is socially symptomatic of maleness—power and domination—negates this biological designation.

Rearing such a child is an extremely challenging task, one in which the childrearing practices must create a skillful blending of conformity and avoidance, a tightrope dance that empowers the male child both to survive (an absolute prerequisite) and then to inconspicuously work to transform his racialized sense of entitlement into power and domination. Hence, for the parents of Capital High males, childrearing practices are always in flux, because they are forever trying to find effective and productive ways of teaching their sons to avoid an assigned sense of place by concurrently accepting and rejecting existing socially constructed realities.

The relatively stable family patterns (mother and father present in the home, and mother as only parent) observed for virtually all the female students in the study were duplicated only among the families of the high-achieving male students. The family pattern for the underachieving males was strikingly different. Five of the six high-achieving male students who participated in the ethnographic sample are growing up in homes with two parents or guardians; Adam, Martin, Kent, and Norris live with their biological mother and father, and Paul with his aunt and uncle. Wendell lives with his mother and younger sister in public housing; his mother receives Aid to Families with Dependent Children. In contrast, four of the six underachieving males are being reared primarily by their mothers: their fathers are not and have not been an integral part of their lives. Korey's mother and father were never married; Manley does not know what his father looks like and, in fact, doubts that he was ever married to his mother. Karl's father has been dead for several years. Art's mother and father were divorced when he was about eight years old. He knows where his father lives and is free to visit, but he chooses not to have a strong relationship with him. Only Sidney and Max have parents who are currently married and living together.

ALLOWING INDEPENDENCE

Paul is an eleventh-grade student and, at age fourteen, the youngest person in the study. Nevertheless, he is taller than most of his classmates and makes better grades than nearly all of them. He earned accelerated promotions in elementary school and had the highest overall score of anyone in his class on the PSAT.

Paul lives with his aunt and uncle in a big single-family house in the Capital community. He acknowledges that his aunt provides a strong image for him and is the most influential person in his life. For years she was a high-ranking official in the District of Columbia Public School System, and when Paul attended the schools where his aunt worked, she arranged his class schedule to include the best teachers. Additionally, his male guardian—his aunt's husband—is a professional person and much respected by Paul. It is not so much what his aunt and uncle say to him as it is his sense of their status in the community that impels him to be as close to perfect as possible. During his childhood years, an eccentric grandmother taught Paul the alphabet, numbers, and spelling. She motivated him to learn by catering to him and taking him to the Washington museums, monuments, and libraries. He credits both her and his aunt with making him the excellent student he is.

Despite his gratitude for his aunt's mentorship and his respect for his uncle, Paul is resentful of what he perceives to be their total domination of his life. He considers them to be unduly strict. He is allowed to go to all class-sponsored activities. Though they encourage him to go to the library, he is expected to be home shortly after the 10 p.m. closing hour. Consequently, when he wants to join his friends in Georgetown or take part in any activity unrelated to school, he tells his guardians that he is going to the Martin Luther King Library in downtown Washington. This means that he actually does have to make an appearance at the library and check out at least one book. But as soon as that is done, he goes off with his friends. If they go to Georgetown, they must bring him back home by the witching hour because, at fourteen, he does not have a driver's permit. At sixteen, most of his friends have permits and can borrow their family's cars.

Paul claims that because of such restrictions he often stays home, despite his friends' pleas. His social life is further limited by his age, and he attributes his voracious reading habits to these barriers. He laments, "I don't have anything else to do." Since both his aunt and uncle are employed, he spends a lot of his after-school time at home, alone. To escape the loneliness, he reads and reads and reads.

Interestingly, while Paul perceives his guardians as imposing unnecessarily strict limits, his aunt maintains that they cannot get him out of the house:

> We worried about him for a while, because . . . that is, my
> husband and I . . . because he does not go out in the evening.

Okay? And my husband felt, and I too, that he was not going to be broad enough, okay? . . . Because he didn't go out and hang around with the boys and things. Then my husband went upstairs one week, and we keep forgetting that this . . . this—I'm sorry, I have to tell her [Paul was present]. We keep forgetting that this is just a kid. My husband went upstairs one day, and he [Paul] was on the telephone and had his stuffed animal up in his arms. And can you imagine somebody almost six feel tall with a stuffed animal? So my husband came downstairs and said, "Niki, we're going to have to talk to Paul. That boy's up there with a stuffed animal." Then my husband said, "Oh, my God! You know, I forget that's just a—still a baby." So anyway, we stopped trying to push him out in the street. Because we said, at *14*, he could be hanging out there. Okay? But we should be grateful that he spends his time in books and that he's interested in the better things in life, by whatever definition we want to use.

But he hasn't been a problem. We never, ever have to worry about where he is. We become upset because he does not go out. So therefore when he goes out and stays out beyond the ungodly hour of eight, then, you see, we . . . really, we get very, very upset. Like my husband let him go one time down to the library, the Martin Luther King Library. And I had gone to a PTA meeting or something, and when I came, Paul wasn't here. My husband was just upset 'cause it had gotten dark. But he had those fears because he had never let him go. And because it was after dark, my husband became very upset and of course thought all the strangest things, and unfortunately something did happen to him that night. He rode the subway home, and a guy snatched his gold chain off of his neck and threatened to kill him. You see? Now, of course, when my husband—but Paul went to the police, you see? Now, an irrational person would not have thought to do that. But—so we worry about him, but we're proud of him. (Interview, April 26, 1983)

Paul gets many covert messages that he must be "a good boy." He rebels by rejecting what he defines as his aunt's insincere suggestions that he spend more time away from home. He interprets her overtures as "small tests" to verify his loyalty to the ideas she and her husband espouse.

Other high-achieving male students also remarked on the presence of a strong parental influence. Adam identified his father as the most influential person in his life, while all the other high-achieving males identified their mother or a female adult relative as the most influential. For them, the most significant person was the one who took time to be intimately involved in their lives.

When Adam was very young, his father had major surgery which kept him home for a while. As a result, he spent a lot of time teaching his son, and he is still very much involved in the family's life. He does most of the cooking, and it is he who is likely to call and tell Adam what to take out of the freezer for dinner.

Adam graduated valedictorian of his junior high class. He is on the honor roll and was inducted into the National Honor Society at Capital while in eleventh grade. As the youngest of three children, he feels pressure to do as well as his brother and sister, both of whom graduated from high school and obtained at least some college education. His father maintains that his earlier experiences with the two older children have helped him immensely in rearing Adam.

> Well, Adam is five years behind the child previous. And I got a lot of experience with the first two. I don't think I did anything special with Adam, other than when he came out of elementary school, I changed his school. He went to a different high school than the two kids before him. Because I noticed something in that school . . . I participated real fully with that school, I'm not going to call a name or whatever, but I sent him to a different junior high school, because I thought it was much better. And it definitely paid off. There was a variety, a bigger variety, or better variety, or curriculum. Adam adapted to it nicely. It was a longer distance from home, whatever, but he adapted to it nicely. And with the experience from the first two—well, boy, girl, boy, that's the way the kids were born, I think Adam and I have a better rapport, as far as communication. You know, like I say, he can almost read my mind . . . knowing what he should do and what he should not do, 'cause if he does not do what he should he knows that he will suffer some way or another. Not physically—you know, with beating or anything like that. You can discipline a child without beatings. If beatings are necessary, oh, he'll get that. But Adam is almost six feet tall, and I'm about five feet nine. See? But at his age, I don't think beating is necessary. But Adam knows right from wrong. And I think it all stems from early in life. (Interview, May 9, 1983)

Like all of the other male high-achievers except Paul, Adam is now free to make decisions about where he is going and when he will return.

He doesn't ask his parents' permission; he simply informs them. When he comes home in the afternoon, he calls his mother, or (more likely) she calls him to see if he is okay, to ask him to do an errand, and to learn what his plans are for the afternoon. If he wants to play ball or practice with the rap band, he tells her that is what he will be doing. She does not automatically assume that she has veto power over his plans. She listens and advises him to be careful.

At an earlier age, his father asserts, there were limits on his outside activities:

> We had . . . always had curfews. As far as his friends, we
> never had any problem with that. The people he would associ-
> ate with were okay, as far as I was concerned . . . We had
> that trouble with the two older ones, because they came
> through a phase where "Black Power" this and "Black Power"
> that, and this and that. But Adam missed all of that. So he
> didn't have that type of influence. We had to curb the two
> older ones' association with certain people, but with Adam, it
> is a lot different. And I don't think he has ever been so aggres-
> sive that if he's out on the front, say out in front of the apart-
> ment, and certain people would come up . . . Hey! he'd leave.
> But we didn't have to worry about that, because Adam's usu-
> ally in one of four places: next door, downstairs, on the bas-
> ketball court, or down to his . . . brother's. Other than that, if
> he was somewhere else, he'd be driving . . . He'd come home
> in the evening and, of course, the fact that he's the only child
> in the house, he would call his mother. 'Cause he knows call-
> ing me at work, it's a little harder, you know. And he'd call
> her and say, "I'm home." (Interview, May 9, 1983)

Like many of the parents of the high-achieving students, Adam's parents—especially his father—are ambivalent about the value of school and schooling, and that may be why they are not pushing him to attend college.

> *Mother:* [Adam] wants to go to trade school.
> *Father:* He wants to go to trade school. But he's not really in-
> terested in going to college . . .
> *Anthro:* How do you feel about that?
> *Father:* I'm not complaining about it, because I think when he
> gets out there and find out what he needs, if he needs to go to
> college, he'll change his mind. If he comes out with an educa-
> tion in a trade—I'm thinking about his drafting, he's real inter-
> ested in that, and that's what he wants to go into—if he can

come out of high school and find a job in that trade, that's
fine with me, as long as he continues his education. And
there's a lot of schools that you can go to continue his education in that field, without having to go to college. Or a major
college. So if he can come out and find a job in that, fine. As
long as he continues to study along that line . . .

Mother: Oh. I agree with him as far as furthering his schooling. Like I said, we aren't going to push too far and say, "You
have to go to college. You must go to college," and all this—
let him make his own decision once he get out there. Find out
what it's like out there in the world. If he figure he can survive
off of $3.35 an hour minimum wage, you know, go ahead,
and he'll find out that he can't. But let him make that decision
once he, you know, get out there and experience what it's all
about. But I feel before he leaves school, he'll find that he
needs to do something to further his education, he can't just
make it on just a high school education unless he has something else to back him up. (Interview, May 9, 1983)

Another factor involved in the ambivalence of Adam's parents regarding the value of school and schooling may be their own experience.
They migrated to Washington from Norfolk, Virginia, as a young married couple in 1957. Adam's mother is a high-school graduate with one
year of postsecondary schooling; his father is a high-school graduate
with two years of college. As a biology major, he eagerly sought the
presumed benefits of schooling but had to leave school because of health
problems. He has been employed in a semiprofessional job with the
federal government since 1957. Adam's mother has worked at the same
company for sixteen years. Both insist that the most important attribute
one can possess is "home training."

Kent's parents are also ambivalent about the putative value of
schools and schooling. They want him to do well in school, but they do
not put a lot of pressure on him. They provide a stable home environment and allow him to take advantage of the opportunities that present
themselves. This appears to be their nonverbalized position because to
them it is far more important that he become human in the traditional
African-American sense—generous, respectful, and honest—than that
he become the most successful person in America.

Like Adam's parents, Kent's exert minimal direct control over his
decisions. Indeed, it is quite clear that they trust he will make wise
decisions and that he will advise them of his plans prior to acting on
them. He is not expected to consult with them before making decisions,
but as the oldest of six children, he feels pressure to set an example for

his younger brothers and sisters. His mother insists that while they taught him appropriate values—to be nondominating while seeking success, and to show respect for adults—they also taught him to be cautious and even distrustful. They have continually warned him that if he gets into trouble with the legal system, they will not bail him out.

Kent's perceptions of what and how his parents taught him are very similar to theirs. As an extremely self-directed individual who does not appear to need his peers' approval for school success, he tends to make school-related decisions without being preoccupied with the pervasive self-policing so common at the school. In this regard, he is one of the most unusual male students at Capital High. It is the one way in which he drastically differs from his peers.

Kent appears to be both adult-oriented and goal-oriented. He was on the honor roll during the last semester of his sophomore year and consistently makes good grades. He never cuts class, nor has he missed a day in school since seventh grade. He was selected male valedictorian of his junior high school class. He loves track and could probably earn a track scholarship were he to participate at Capital. He recently resigned from the track team, however, because he said that practice interfered with his completing his math homework. His track coach was devastated! He could not believe that Kent would just walk away from what might possibly be his ticket out of poverty.

Kent lives with his mother and father and four younger siblings in an extremely dilapidated apartment building within walking distance of Capital High. Kent claims that his father is an engineer, which is, as I infer from my perusal of his cumulative folder, a glorified term for custodian or maintenance man. Both his parents were born and attended school in Washington. His father served in the army after graduating from high school. His mother does not work full-time outside the home, but periodically she obtains part-time employment, which often involves marketing by telephone. During our formal interview sessions, she indicated that she and her husband were both somewhat frustrated by the fact that their status as high school graduates did not make their lives easier.

Kent claims that his mother is the most influential person in his life because, unlike his father, she is intimately involved in it, is extremely supportive, and does not criticize him much. During my visits to his home, his father was not there. I was told that he worked from 4:30 P.M. until about 1:00 A.M.

Kent's mother readily admits that Kent is not just an unusual child but *an extremely unusual child* who appeared, at a very early age, to be oblivious to peer pressure and to be inner-directed and goal-oriented. She is unable to identify exactly what it is that made him the way he is but notes that because he was her first child and she was employed, he spent a lot of time with a baby-sitter. She thinks that perhaps this experience was influential in making him so goal-directed and eager to be successful in life. She speculates that since this is the only obvious way in which their parenting practices differed from those used with his siblings (she was at home and intimately involved in the parenting of all her other children), perhaps it was the centrality of this experience that propelled him to be the kind of person he has become. She denies that either she or other members of the family gave her firstborn child anything special.

> Yeah, we've given him support, but he seems . . . he
> doesn't . . . he strikes out on his own a lot. He does a lot of
> things on his own—a lot of positive things that sometimes
> we're not even aware of. . . . And I like the fact that he shows
> a lot of respect for the teachers and all at school. So I like
> that. You know, a lot of kids are scholarly, but they're still
> not as respectful as they should be. You know. And I've heard
> that—well, I have never had that problem with little Kent.
> Never. (Interview, June 14, 1983)

Kent's respectfulness—people's description of him as a good person—was as important or perhaps more important to his mother than the high grades he earns in school. Being a good person is an extremely valued characteristic in the Capital community.

> One of his teachers wrote me a letter one time, when he was
> in elementary school—his sixth-grade teacher or his fifth-grade
> teacher—she wrote a letter and she told me, she said she
> wished that she had twenty kids like him in her class. Because
> she said he was from the *old* school. You know, she said he
> was a gentleman . . . And I know . . . when he graduated
> from Valley Garden Junior High, the principal gave an award
> to the—an out . . . a unique award for an outstanding stu-
> dent; only one student could get this award. And when he
> said, "This student is a gentleman and a scholar," I knew it
> was him. I mean, I didn't—I had no—you know, I knew that
> it was him. So we're very proud of Kent, you know. (Inter-
> view, June 14, 1983)

Kent's mother was the only parent of a high-achieving or underachieving male who shared with me the observation that her son loved to read.

> . . . He likes to read. He reads a lot. And I think that helps,
> too . . . Yeah. Ever since he started, I think, in elementary

school, he started—he started liking—yeah, he liked to read, you know. And he likes science, so he likes reading a lot of—he has a lot of books here, a closetful of books on science. So he, he's very thorough. Very thorough. (Interview, June 14, 1983)

Kent's resistance to socially defined race and gender roles, manifested as conformity to criteria of success that have been defined by both the larger society and the imagined Black community, may also be influenced by the fact that he was retained in first grade for two years. Apparently the experience of repeating was so searingly negative that he can never forget it, and the memory continues to undergird his academic behavior. Kent and his mother acknowledge that she attempts to slow him down, urging him to take a day off from school every now and then. He never takes her advice, insisting that he must go to school every day in order to do well in life.

Norris is another high-achieving student whose mother does not put strict limitations on where he can go, when he should return, or with whom he should spend his time. That is not to suggest, in any way, that she is not concerned about his activities outside of school. It is just that at this level of his development, she apparently assumes that he knows right from wrong and will remember her earlier teachings.

Norris claims that his mother taught him and his older brother what they needed to know about how to behave, what is and is not appropriate behavior, and, generally, everything a Black child needs to know in order both to conform to social expectations and to avoid the overwhelmingly disfiguring sense of place prescribed for African-American males. He also identifies his mother as the most influential person in his life, the one constant, unwavering beacon that has constantly reassured him. In his construction, his mother appears to be perfect, with one exception: she made the ghastly mistake of living with his father for seventeen years. Norris unequivocally credits his mother with shaping his humanness. Both he and his older brother Kai learned from their mother how to become a person through other people. She is not soft with Norris; she believes in corporal punishment, and she used it in rearing her children:

One time Norris said this boy was really acting up in class, and Norris said he sat there and he thought to himself, "If *I* did that, my mother would *kill* me!" I said, "You know I wouldn't kill you." He said, "No, *but* I would know that I was wrong, and I would get a beating for it. Okay?" . . . So I didn't have to threaten a lot. And I didn't have to do very much spanking . . . As Norris say[s], "When Momma give you that look, you know what that means, don't you?" I would give him a look, and that was either "You're on the verge of dying" or "You'd better move." You know. (Interview, April 28, 1983)

Her ability to skillfully mix the ways of becoming human in the larger social system and in the Black community is clearly illustrated in the way she taught them to be human as prescribed by the Black community: to develop and maintain a generous nature buffered by a commitment to an idealized egalitarian ethos fused to a belief in the uniqueness of each individual.

Norris's mother admits that when he and his older brother were younger, she was very strict with them about schoolwork and out-of-school activities. She structured their lives so that she could be as helpful to them as possible, given her full-time job and the lack of support—financial or emotional—from her spouse. She details how she structured her sons' lives when they began school:

> So when they got ready to start school, I just told them that when you go into the classroom, the teacher more or less is your mother for that period of time that you are there . . . If you feel that you want to be a clown, I will take you out of school now, take you to Florida, and let you stay in the Ringling Brothers Circus where they winter in Florida. I feel that your education is something that no one can take away from you once you get it in your head. And I used to tell them, it's hard out there. And the White man will try to do whatever he can to you. But once you get that knowledge, you've got it made. Because you may have a house, you may have a car, you may have money, and that can be taken away from you at any time. But once you get the knowledge in your head, you can make enough money to buy another house, to buy another car. But you've got to start with the basics. If you don't have the basics, you're not hitting on anything. So I think they kind of got that across. I don't know if you would say that I was hard on them about their studies, I tried not to make it as hard as possible by saying, "If you don't do this," you know, and stuff like that. Kind of tried to help them along, and let them see for themselves. And they just kind of—sort of grasped things as they went along . . . So that's basically how I did it. (Interview, April 28, 1983)

Norris graduated valedictorian of his junior high school class. He was also doing very well at Capital. Not surprisingly, he gave most of the credit for his high academic performance to his mother. When I asked her about her influence on his school performance, she replied:

> Well, let me put it this way: Adolph Eichmann had nothing on me. Neither did Hitler. Let's put it this way. Like I said, I was demanding as far as getting their lessons done. If it wasn't to my satisfaction, it was not right. I didn't care what the teacher said. *I* was right. Okay? So—and then I tried not to be *too* hard on them and say, "Well, I expect for you to make straight As and Bs on your report card." *But* I'm not going to tolerate Ds and Fs. Because Ds and Fs stand for dummies and flunkies. And I did not make two dummies and a flunky—or two—a flunky and a dummy, whichever. I said. And so I figured, well, if you bring me Bs and Cs, hey, that's pretty good. So they knew what my expectations were. (Interview, April 28, 1983)

Norris's mother was obviously a successful single parent. Both Norris and his brother Kai loved and respected her, primarily because she was strong and unwavering in her demands for excellence in school and in life in general. She appeared ideally suited for Norris as a Black mother. She apparently knew him well and knew when to rescue, praise, support, and protect him. I remember her response when I noted that Norris had the highest math score on the PSAT at Capital High School that year:

> *Anthro:* Your son had the highest score on the math section of the PSAT.
>
> *Mother:* Mm-hm. He told me.
>
> *Anthro:* He told you?
>
> *Mother:* Yes. He tells me everything.
>
> *Anthro:* How do you feel about that?
>
> *Mother:* I feel pretty good about it. But I didn't make a big issue out of it with him . . . Because I don't want him to get swellheaded. Keep a little humility about yourself at all times. Because sometimes when you get swell-headed, you can be quite obnoxious. And I do not like obnoxious people. (Interview, April 28, 1983)

For this mother, becoming human means living a life that suggests the commonality of people in the community, a connectedness to other people that is not contingent upon one's academic performance. She was absolutely thrilled that her son had performed so well on what she saw as a prestigious exam, yet she hid most of her pride from him, hoping that he would maintain the communal balance so central in the community members' essentialized constructions of the Black Self.

Even though Norris's parents had lived together as husband and wife all of Norris's life, his mother constructed her husband as a remote entity: although present, he was an absentee father. When asked if she thought he had any influence on Norris's high performance in school, she was blunt and to the point: "No. None." Norris has ambivalent feelings about his father, feelings which at times border on hatred.[2] This was clear in his description of his feelings about his father's refusal to work during the seventeen years he lived with them:

> It made me not like him too much. 'Cause he wasn't contributing to my mother and helping my brother and me, bringing in something and supporting us and everything. He was just around to say we had a father, that's all. And we really didn't need him. (Interview, February 9, 1983)

His striking physical resemblance to his father makes him fearful that he might become the image of him. When asked to talk about his father and his feelings toward him, he refused to discuss him in any great detail.

Martin is another high-achieving male student whose mother has been and remains the most influential person in his life. He is the youngest of five children. Since his birth, he has lived with his mother and father in the Capital Community's "projects."

Martin's father is a parking-lot attendant. Apparently, he is extremely bitter and disappointed with his life and soothes the pain by drinking. Martin describes him as being a virtual nonentity in his life, not involved in the family he has created. He sees his father as finding escape from home in his work:

> He says he enjoy work. He say he'd rather do that than to sit home. 'Cause he don't do nothing at home. He don't clean up, he don't dry dishes, he don't wash dishes, he don't cook, nothing. He just come home, eat, sleep, get back up the next morning and go to work, come home and sleep, eat . . . (Interview, February 28, 1983).

Martin's mother has broader insights, more deeply rooted in the history of Black/White relationships in America. She concedes that everybody in the family has been somewhat disfigured by her husband's lack of participation: "None of them ask their Daddy for anything, *none* of them . . . Well, like I said, he drinks—which he's trying to kick the habit. But that's all. 'Cause, I mean, you know, he's not a fighter, but he's a agitator—he agitates, you know" (interview, June 7, 1983).

Martin's mother is almost totally responsible for teaching their children how to become human through other people. She has also single-handedly taught them resistance, both as conformity and as avoidance. She sees life as an endless struggle, punctuated with moments of bliss when all the members of the family are together. Nothing is more satisfying, to her mind, than family and family-related activities. Though she currently works as a custodian for the government, she would not hesitate to leave her job if one of her children showed signs of becoming involved in illicit activities. She has always considered rearing her children her principal responsibility and her duty in life. Indeed, motherhood is the cornerstone in her perception of who she is.

> No! No! I've always been home with *my* babies. Mm-hm. That's right. I've *always* been. I don't want nobody watching my children. No, Lord! *Nobody!* That's right! My mother would have watched them, but otherwise, no. Hm-mm . . . She's dead now, but she did live [with us briefly].
> Believe me, I was just talking with my daughter, I tell my daughter, "Don't get a job." It's good to have a trade. But, see, I had four years of typing, but I didn't finish it up; you know, I haven't really kept with it. But if a mother can get by without having to work—that was a long time ago—if you can, do it.[3] But, see, I figure, still, if I had gotten a job, I wouldn't be living where I am now [in the projects]. But a baby-sitter would have hurt me too. So . . . my husband never said nothing about me going to work, really, until my mother had to come to live with us. And when she left, he shut up. (Interview, June 7, 1983)

The extent to which the parents of both the high- and the underachieving students were concerned about their children surpassed even my expectations. For example, Martin's mother indicated that nothing—not wealth, not status—was nearly as important as her children's *safety*. She was very anxious and pleased to have her children present in the home, primarily because it indicated that they were safe, not in danger.

> I *love* to hear him play the drums! . . . Yes . . . Anything to keep the children in the house. Yeah. Anything, uh-huh. I mean, you know, just to have them in the house all together. (Interview, June 27, 1983)

> So they stay *home,* and *I* can *sleep!* That's why I wouldn't—okay, I'm going to put it to you this way: if they were bad children, I would not be working. I'd be running up and down the street behind *them!* So . . . basically, I will—I'll continue to work until I get tired. I had one . . . I did quit a job be-

cause of [Martin]. He going out there and learn to slow drag.
I quit! That's right! I was working from six to ten, and he out
there in the street trying to learn how to dance. I quit! Just to
get him straight. And I watched him. And when I felt like I
was ready to go back, I had him walk with me again to put in
for that job application . . . I *definitely* don't want them in the
street. I'm not saying little girls are—some of the girls are a
good example for boys, and I'd rather for them to have little
girls to date than hanging around with some of these guys out
there. (Interview, June 7, 1983)

Her desire for her children's safety motivated her, making her both
fiercely protective and unyielding in her insistence on their loyalty and
obedience.

All he can do now is go to school—right now, and he just
gotta . . . he just has to . . . really plan. He doesn't sass—you
see how some kids sass? He might look at you or something
like that, like I told . . . made a suggestion to him about getting a haircut: "I don't have no hair on my head now!" I
made another suggestion about the shirt for him to wear and
have his school picture taken: "But you can't *see* the stripes!"
See, that's coming out of his mouth now, you know. And to
me, you know what it sound like? You're sassing. That's
right, that's right. You know. All he has to do is say, "Okay,
Mama." But "So-and-so, so-and-so" goes better, you know.
So . . . basically, most of the time—you know, *all* the time, he
will listen to me. (Interview, June 7, 1983)

Martin's mother shared with me some of the strategies she used to
control the behavior of Martin and her other children:

Punish him. I used to lock them all outdoors, except for Martin 'cause he was the baby . . . They make me mad, I'd lock
the door, and my husband drove all of them outside, until I
feel better. But I kept him inside . . . I'm trying to remember . . . I don't—I used to beat them. I'll tell you, I'll get that
stick behind them. But now in junior high and high—what he
do wrong? I know he do some things wrongs, I get after him.
I shouldn't have to punish him. (Interview, June 7, 1983)

She has been somewhat compulsive about her children's schooling:

They come home in the evening at three o'clock, they change
their clothes, they have to sit down at this table . . . Uh-huh,
they have to do their homework. And the homework should

have been done before dinner. And they know better than to go outside . . . They never did. They would go outside sometimes. But they know they had to do their homework . . . So all of them would do their homework together—just about. I had two—I think it was Martin and my second child—I had to stay on them a little bit. But Martin just probably had the knack for it, and maybe Martin had his little friends that was on the Honor Society. Maybe he—I don't know, really, it's just something *he* wanted to do. And to be, you know. If he can keep it up, I appreciate that. (Interview, June 7, 1983)

Martin's mother describes her son in these words:

He's basically a quiet child, as long as he can tinker with something—you know, mess around with something in his hands, that's what he is. Mm-hm. Like, he's up there with the drums right now . . . I know when he's upstairs, he's messing with those drums. And the stereo set used to be upstairs. But most of the times, he's with his music or the drums.

Martin has never given me too much trouble. He's a good child. He's pretty good. I—he gets kind of stubborn—he acts kinda stubborn and young—you know, younger age. But maybe by him being the youngest one, the kids get on him. Other than that, he's basically got what he's always wanted. I kept him busy with toys, they had a Show-and-Tell, so—like we keep them occupied. I guess that's the reason why the children are the way they are. And I'm hoping it'll continue that way. If I can keep this year busy for him, and let him . . . you know, keep himself going until he get established, 'cause he has one more year to go. If I keep him busy this last school year, I will have made it. I will have made it. (Interview, June 7, 1983)

She describes him as "too free-hearted": "He got his license. But . . . he let his girlfriend drive the car. My car! Now, you know, I don't let him—he just got it, and so now he's grounded." The claim that Martin is too free-hearted rang a bell, suggesting that he embraces the norms and values strongly identified with the Capital community and African-Americans. It led me to ask her what she expected of Martin. Her initial response was "Nothing." Later, however, she summed up her creed: "That's what I would mainly expect out of him in life, to stand on his own two feet and tell people no" (interview, June 7, 1983).

Like most of the other parents of the high-achieving males, Martin's mother and father are supportive of his postsecondary goals, whatever they happen to be.

> As for what I wanted him to be, really, was up to him what he wanted to be. Martin said one time he wanted to go in the Air Force. He's changed his mind. He said he wanted to go to the TESST school, and so I'm going to have to go along with that if he wants to go in there. But he know he's going to have to do *something* . . . I believe . . . he want to consider going to . . . college. 'Cause one time I thought he was going into the service and then take up a trade. He's changed his mind . . . He has less than that year, less than a year. At least by December he's going to have to make his mind up about what he want out of life. [I'll be happy with whatever he chooses to do.] . . . No preference, as long as he do the best he can in whatever he chooses. I'm sure he *will*, you know. And don't get discouraged, as not to—you know, go the other way. But the most thing is, make sure he doesn't get upset and get with the wrong crowd. You know. (Interview, June 7, 1983)

Martin's parents neither sought to restructure his academic plans nor tried to annul them. They did not convey to him that he was disloyal to the family or selfish for dreaming his dreams. Like the parents of most of the other students, they do not pressure him about his future.

The Underachieving Males

The parents of the underachieving males acknowledge that teaching their sons what it means to be human—to become a person through other people—is the most challenging task they have ever faced. If they have daughters, they readily admit that the challenge confronting them is strikingly different. One of the difficulties they face in rearing their sons is their uncertainty as to what it means to be Black and male in contemporary America.

This is a very important consideration in a rigid, racially stratified patriarchy, since patriarchy implies male domination (Friedl 1975; Goldberg 1973; Reiter 1975; Rosaldo and Lamphere 1974; Segal 1990). It also implies teaching males who are not socially defined as members of the highest social stratum acceptance of a secondary status. The question thus becomes, How do parents or classroom teachers prepare males to accept a status that denies them the dominant position of White males in a stratified patriarchy, especially if they belong to a lower-status group (Gibbs 1988; Larson 1988; Majors 1990, 1987, 1986)? This is the dilemma confronting the parents and teachers of African-American males at Capital High.

The confusion of the parents of male students at Capital is clearly manifested in their attempts to teach their male children how to survive and endure in a society that favors maleness but debases Blackness. What makes this process particularly troublesome for these parents is their sons' outright rejection of a subservient place in the extant gender hierarchy, as well as their sons' outright rejection of a subservient place in the extant gender hierarchy, and their appropriation of an alternative definition of maleness that is centered in "the construction of unique, expressive, and conspicuous styles of demeanor, speech, gesture, clothing, hairstyle, walk, stance, and handshake" (Majors 1990:111; McCall 1994). African-American males often resist their assigned "place" in the male hierarchy both by conforming to and avoiding the dominant norms and values (E. Anderson 1990). Their resistance, of course, further stigmatizes them, reproducing the patriarchy and their consignment to secondary domination.[4]

In their efforts to teach their sons to live by the rules in both the Black and the White communities, the married parents of Sidney and Max are as frustrated as are the single parents of Korey, Karl, Art, and Manley. Sidney is one of only two underachieving males who are official members of the advanced placement program at the school.[5] Sidney's mother is a housewife who does not seek employment. His father is a bus driver in the city and a deeply religious man. Sidney is the only one of the underachieving males who goes to church with his parents *every* Sunday.

> Surprisingly, Sidney described his father as being more heavily into religion than his mother. They belong to a Holiness church in Maryland, and every Sunday they all go there. Sidney told me that he has lived in the Capital community all his life. His mother was born and reared in this section of the city as well. While he does not know his father's relatives, his mother's family of orientation also lives in the community, one in the same apartment building. There are so many of his mother's relatives . . . that they frequently get on his nerves. (Fieldnotes, March 17, 1983)

Sidney, as the oldest of three children, plays guitar in the gospel band his father created.

Max's mother is the only parent of an underachieving student—male or female—who is a college graduate. She is a teacher in one of the local school systems. Art's mother, a nurse, has an associate degree and is currently working to complete a bachelor's degree. None of the other mothers of the underachieving males have schooling beyond high school; most did not graduate. None of the fathers of these underachieving males completed high school. I made the following observations regarding Max's grades, including his counselor's assessment of his potential:

> As noted by Ms. Yanmon, Max's grades are quite poor. His deportment evaluation ranges from Excellent to Satisfactory, with Good predominating. He was in school 169 days in ninth grade, with only three unexcused absences; he was in school 178 days in tenth grade, with only one unexcused absence. When I told Ms. Yanmon that I was interested in Max as an informant in the underachieving category, she said she would talk with him, that he is an easygoing child who is too attached to his mother. She claims that he is an only child (actually he has an older brother) and that his mother is too protective. Ms. Yanmon thinks he will agree to participate in the study. (Fieldnotes, November 8, 1982)

Ms. Yanmon's assessment of the source of Max's academic problem—that his mother is too protective—was widely shared by his teachers and other school officials. The response of his homeroom teacher, Ms. Murdock, was typical:

> Ms. Murdock says that Max's mom tends to want him to have special treatment and, she insists, that is impossible in a classroom of forty students. Moreover, he does not help himself but is usually daydreaming or something else—anything but concentrating on the "mundane" task at hand. For example, he loves to discuss rockets and spaceships. She urged me to talk with him and verify this claim. She noted that he has built such ships in his mind and can give minute details. His focus on these things, she believes, is largely responsible for his poor performance in school: he does not have time for such trivial matters as studying. (Fieldnotes, November 9, 1982)

As an elementary-school teacher, Max's mother has worked extremely hard to prepare him for the growing complexity of the learning process in the academy. Both she and her husband strongly value schooling. During elementary school, she enrolled him in the schools where she taught, carefully selecting his teachers in order to give him the best there was available. His only sibling, an older brother, has two college degrees—a bachelor's and a master's—but is currently unemployed. Perhaps his brother's inability to find work has had a greater impact on

Max's school performance than anyone cares to acknowledge. Nevertheless, he is still in school and appears to have bought the school achievement ideology completely, with one minor caveat: he does not practice what he preaches.

Max's mother deliberately chose to send him to Capital because she thought that participating in the advanced placement program would enable him to obtain vital academic skills. Because he failed English in both the ninth and tenth grades, Max's mother carefully selected his English teacher during his eleventh-grade year—the year this study began.

I remember the day I called Max's mother, asking her permission to have him participate in the study. She was more than happy to have him do so, as she thought it would help her to understand his deliberate underachievement. The following excerpt from my fieldnotes reveals what happened.

> When I asked Max if he thought he might be interested in participating, he responded with one word, yes. When I asked if he thought I should call his parents, he said yes. When I asked whom I should speak with, he said, "My mother. She is more familiar with these kinds of things."
>
> I asked when I should call. He said his mother was home around 3:30. I must admit that as I dialed her number shortly after 6:15 I began to feel a heightened sense of anxiety. What if she says no? What if she asks questions I cannot answer to her satisfaction? Boy, was I in for a surprise! She answered the phone. I told her who I was, what I was trying to do, and why I was seeking her son's participation. She said, "Of course." Her voice betrayed her anxiety about her son's performance and her perception of his capabilities. She said she too was seeking answers to the question of low performance because she could not understand how her son could perform so well on the CTBS (Comprehensive Test of Basic Skills) every year and get Fs in English. (Fieldnotes, November 10, 1982)

Max's parents—especially his mother—are burdened and baffled by his underachievement at Capital High. They see themselves as providing all the external supports necessary for him to do well: a loving, stable home environment, adequate food and nutrition, and support for his voiced dreams and aspirations. Any school-related goal he voices, they support. Whatever he says he wants, they make every effort to provide. They do not understand why he performs so much better on standardized examinations than he does in the daily work of the classroom. Nor do they understand why the various strategies they have used to get him to put forth greater effort have failed. They have tried everything, including buying him a used car that he drives to school every day.

Art's mother presents still another case of an African-American mother whose great concern and nurturing behaviors are producing undesired outcomes. Her son is failing in school. And, like Max's parents, she is unable to come up with any solution. She is baffled by his lack of academic effort and achievement.

Art's mother is currently attending college. She has an associate of arts degree. Unlike Max's mother, she has been separated from her husband for many years and is rearing Art without the help of his father. Like Max, Art is the youngest child in his family. Curiously, all of her children are still living in their mother's home, even though they range in age from seventeen to twenty-four. The only female sibling is next to Art in the birth order; she is nineteen.

Art's mother's description of how she reared her children and her influence and impact in their school life is typical of how the underachieving parental sample teaches its children—perhaps unwittingly—to practice avoidance. Art's mother admits that she makes very few demands on her children, especially Art. In fact, when they were younger, her primary preoccupation was their safety; she was obsessed with making sure they stayed out of harm's way and had enough food to eat.

> When they were younger, my main purpose then was to keep them in the house and keep them out of trouble—buy the food and cook and stuff, so they didn't really have to do nothing. And *now* that they're big, they *don't* do nothing! [Laughter] And so . . . because, see, I had to work, so they had to mind themselves. So they [the older siblings] would do, go downstairs—the bus would blow, and they'd go downstairs and get Art and bring him upstairs, and . . . something like that. So then they would mind him—see, I had to be at work at three, so the bus wouldn't bring him [home] till like six, so they would mind him, and I'd cook everything [and leave it] on the stove so they could fix it. So anyway, they—that's the way they were raised, or I raised them. They mind themselves while I went to work—they went to school, and then I would cook and wash clothes at night when I come home. And then at night—not every night, but, like, when I'd have to wash clothes, it was a laundromat open on New York Avenue and 17th Street, down in front of the five-and-ten; it was open all night, and I had a piece of car, so I would put the clothes in

plastic bags and take them to the laundromat while the kids sleep—you know, wash them, dry—like that. Then I'd get about two or three hours' sleep or something, so I could iron the clothes so they'd be ready for school. And stuff like that. So, anyway, I made it. And they didn't give me any trouble . . . And that's all they did—they stayed in the house. So they've never been in trouble, or jail, or stealing, or dope or nothing, yet . . . I hope they don't, but anyway . . . (Interview, June 15, 1983)

Art's mother's preoccupation with her children's safety when they were younger led her to make a pact with the devil, so to speak. If they obeyed her primary command that they stay in the apartment during the time she was at work, she was willing to do everything and anything for them. Her concern for their safety took precedence over every other consideration. She assumed that they would notice how difficult her parenting role was and that they would seek to reciprocate by helping her in every way they could. Her expectations were not realized. They did not and still do not seek to make her parenting role less difficult. Rather, they tend to see her herculean efforts as what parents are *supposed* to do; they see nothing extraordinary in what she does for them and thus nothing for which they should be especially grateful.

Art's mother acknowledges that her martyrdom has had a negative effect on all her children, especially on Art, the youngest.

Art was smart in elementary school. But now, as he got older, he got lazier, I guess. He's still smart; he almost know most of the things that you ask him, or something. But he just won't do anything—any work. So he tells me—you can make a— you can pass on a D, but you make like a F and a D on the first part, and you can make Bs and Cs and still pass on the last grade. So why should you work all year? [Laughter] So he got an answer to it: Why should you work all year? So anyway . . . I don't know what I'm going to do with Art [said indulgently, with laughter]. But he draws good—he can draw *anything*, almost. He does very good with that. And he'll do what you ask him, or what I ask him, but he's not going to volunteer to do too much at home . . . (Interview, June 15, 1983)

Art's mother admits that she continues to indulge her children, especially Art, making virtually no demands of them. She works two full-time jobs in order to meet their requests for the latest clothes, toys, stereo equipment, and foods that take little time to prepare. Last summer she bought Art a secondhand dirt bike that cost $500.

> I guess my children still think they're not supposed to do any-thing. But they *do* know that you have to work to live . . . Art think he suppose to be getting a summer job. Last summer he got a motorcycle—a dirt bike. And he had it all figured out: one [of my other sons] . . . was to give a hundred dollars, the oldest one . . . give a hundred dollars, Art was to save two hundred, and I was going to give the other hundred. 'Cause it was five hundred dollars; he looked in the paper for it, a boy was selling it. So he got his dirt bike.
>   And he got in trouble with that, too; I had to go to school with that. I didn't even know that he . . . 'cause, I told him, I said—'cause he live right near the school, right? So I said, "You don't ride the bike to school." Went to school one day, [they] threw him out, I had to go—the teacher said Art had the dirt bike in the evening time, had the motorcycle on the—I think, the playground or something, and he was racing, you know, running around. So they threw him off—he and Mr. McGriff can't get along! [Laughter] So they threw him out of there. And I said, "Art, I thought I told you not to ride the bike to school." "Oh!" he said, "I didn't ride it to school," he said. "That was in the evening." After school close, then they're up there in that field, whatever they're doing, I guess the gym class, I don't know what they were doing. Anyway, he would come home and get the bike and go up there. [Laughter] So now it's on the back porch—he asked me yester-day—just yesterday, "Ma, you gonna fix my bike?" I said no. (Interview, June 15, 1983)

Art's mother is one of the hardest-working mothers in the sample. She has used her divorce from her children's father to motivate her to achieve what she would never have dared to dream had she remained married to him. By working extremely hard, overcoming many obstacles, and generally impersonating the lifestyle of middle-class America, she has been able to buy her family a house. She also owns a late-model, expensive car. But, as will become clear, in exchange for these symbols of success, she has paid an extremely high price.

The worst problems the parents of the underachieving males appear to have in rearing their sons are putting limitations on their behaviors, motivating them to raise their academic effort and expectations, and convincing them that avoidance is counterproductive in transforming their status as African-Americans. The apprehensions and uncertainties of these parents—especially the mothers—are conveyed to their sons and are used by their sons to manipulate and control them.

In their responses the mothers of the underachieving males are virtually indistinguishable from the mothers of the high-achieving males. The real difference is that a majority of the mothers of the high-achieving males are coparenting their sons with their husbands or some other adult male. In those few instances when this is not the case, the mothers of the high-achieving males are both willing and able to synthesize the mother-father roles. This is not generally true of the mothers of the underachieving males, who are often solely responsible for rearing their sons and who are also unable to commingle or merge the roles of mother and father.

The mothers of the underachieving males are more willing than the other mothers to appropriate the childrearing practices long associated with the dominant community. In addition, they tend to be more child-like in their interactions with their sons, who feign adult male status. This is not how these mothers interacted with their sons when they were in elementary school, and in some instances in junior high school; at least this was not the only way they interacted with them. But as these young males reached puberty and entered high school, their mothers appear to have adopted a relationship style that closely approximates that which they have with adult males who are objects of their love and affection. They appear to seek the approval of these males by not criticizing them, not setting limitations, and not demanding a relationship based on mutual respect.

Manley and his mother are a case in point. He is the adult male; his mother allows him to treat her as if she were a child or his female cohort. Manley acknowledges that he is in control of the relationship with his mother and that they do not "get along that good." He claims that this is the case because he always tells her what he wants her to know, regardless of how offensive or hurtful it might be.

> I mean, I let her know she can't *stop* me from doing nothing
> I'm going to do anyway. And if she think she going to stop
> me, and she think she gonna put a end to it, I'll just get out
> and pack my bags and go. Then she won't have to worry
> about me, that'll be one less mouth to feed. Besides, I don't
> eat anyway. Not in that house. (Interview, May 13, 1983)

Manley is often well aware of the rightness of what his mother is proposing or suggesting; but he will frequently oppose her simply because he wants to be in control of their relationship. He does this, he says, because it enables him to "feel like a man." For example, when he was asked how he envisions becoming the multimillionaire he fantasizes being, his vague answers typify the responses of the other underachieving males: "I don't know—own my own business . . . A variety of business[es]. I guess I'd open up a department store in one place, and a skating rink in another place, a sports shop another place . . . just spread it around in different things" (interview, May 13, 1983).

Even more revealing was his response when he was asked how the courses he was currently taking were propelling him toward his future goal:

> *Anthro:* What business courses are you taking to prepare you for this?
> *Manley:* Nothing now. I'm just taking regular—some high school courses, and College-bound English.
> *Anthro:* Why are you taking College-bound English?
> *Manley:* That's the class they gave me. (Interview, May 13, 1983)

Manley's responses make him appear to be sleepwalking through life and his schooling experience. Like his underachieving cohorts, he tends to have big dreams that are unrelated to his academic performance. For him, whether or not he is "successful" in the pursuit of his announced dreams is a great "crap shoot," totally unrelated to school achievement. His desire to capture what he perceives to be the essence of maleness—control and domination—coupled with his mother's rather timid approach to disciplining him has led him to exaggerate what he identifies as "manly" behaviors, including taking orders from no one either at home or in school.

One of the dominant parenting practices of the mothers of the underachieving males includes being their most ardent cheerleader, point guard, and rescuer. This parenting practice appears to reassure the sons that they are unconditionally loved. At the same time, an unintended consequence of the cheerleader strategy is the suppression and undermining of respect. These mothers' sons love them but they do not show respect for them.

The undesired consequences of this dominant parenting practice are everywhere apparent, especially in the school context. They are also discernible in the responses, actions, and behaviors of the males outside of school. For example, Karl's mother's unconditional support of her son is widely believed to be implicated in his rapidly growing drug problem.

Another common practice negatively affecting the academic performance of the underachieving males is the tendency of parents to assign their sons adult status before they are mature enough to handle that role. For most of the young men, their father's absence from their lives means that there is no one to balance their mother's unconditional love. Karl appears to be particularly victimized by his father's absence and the smothering, overwhelming expectations of his mother and other family members. The following gives evidence of Karl's growing addiction and his all-consuming fear, yet secret desire, that someone would tell his mother.

> At about 3:15, Karl arrived. As soon as he entered the room he told me that he could stay only fifteen minutes. He appeared very uptight, hyper. He told me once more that he had to get his hair cut. That seemed highly unlikely unless the barber planned to scalp him. Feeling a bit more than annoyed at his rather infantile behavior, I told him that if we were going to do the scheduled interview, it would not end in fifteen minutes. I was rather firm in my statement. He told me that he was afraid that if he did not come I would call Ms. Raye and she would call his mother. This comment is indicative of the young man's dependence on external limitations; the rightness or wrongness of a situation does not appear to be the issue. Rather, Karl's actions and reactions are determined by whether or not he can "get away with it." When I tried to pursue the conversation to get at why he no longer wanted to be involved in the research study, he became quite impatient and insisted that we get on with the interview since he had only fifteen minutes that he could give me. (Fieldnotes, March 15, 1983)

There is no way to adequately convey the level of frustration I experienced as this "child in pain" established the rules regarding our meeting that day. It was clear that he desperately needed guidance, but, unfortunately, no one was offering him any. I was so constrained by my primary role in his life—that of the anthropologist—that I, too, was unable to give him guidance. The following excerpt from my fieldnotes suggests the depth of the dilemma we both faced:

> My attempt to "interview" Karl was awful; he answered the questions I asked curtly and without explanation. Indeed, while I tried to talk with him, he did his math homework. Finally, I *asked* him to leave, and I assured him that he didn't have to worry because I would not be seeking any further interviews with him. Surprisingly (but not so surprisingly), he now did not want to leave, but again he was only reacting to the possibility that I would tell Ms. Raye of his behavior and she would tell his mother. I assured him that I would not seek out Ms. Raye . . . to tell her about his behavior. On the other

hand, if she *asked* me, I would have to be honest in my response.

As Karl left, I felt quite unhappy about the whole situation. If I were his mother and he was behaving as Karl has been behaving recently, I'd want to know about it. If I were his homeroom teacher, I would advise his parent of his school behavior and activities. (Ms. Raye insists that he is "on those drugs.") But as a researcher whose ability to obtain information is heavily dependent on trust in my ability to protect my sources, I can't do anything. Moreover, since I am just learning what signs to look for in detecting whether a student is "smoking," I am not exactly sure I know the signals. Karl left, and I got my things together to leave the building. (Fieldnotes, March 15, 1983)

Karl's ambiguous response following inappropriate behavior is quite typical among the underachieving males. Art and Manley offer other examples.

When I asked Art why he is expelled from school so often, he said Mr. McGriff and the other administrators were "picking on" him. He noted that when they expel him, his mother has to come to the school to get him back in. He's been expelled twice this year (at least I am aware of two expulsions), and in each instance his mother had to come see Mr. McGriff and get the expulsion overturned. (Fieldnotes, March 15, 1983)

As his mother perceived it, Art was just not likely to do what was asked or demanded of him. Manley's mother was unable to offer an explanation for her son's refusal to follow school and family rules.

DATING AND RITUALIZED PLAYING

While the parents of the high-achieving girls were constantly monitoring their daughters' lives, trying to limit extrafamilial influences while suppressing their sexuality, the parents of the high-achieving males are far less involved in their sons' lives. Indeed, they appear to be eager for their sons to validate and affirm their maleness. The limits they set for their sons are not nearly as stringent as those imposed on their female counterparts. For example, Martin's mother admits that she does not want her children to leave home—ever. At the same time, she insists that if they live at home, they have to obey her house rules.

He ain't going to go—can't go nowhere Saturday night. If he goes anywhere, he has got to be home about—at least by eleven or eleven-thirty. I'm going to tell you: I mean, you can't stand at the bus stop! You know, anywhere! Without somebody picking after you. Now, Martin's little friend that live on Georgia Avenue, I have gotten out of my bed to take that little girl home. And Martin has gone there to see her, and I be worried to death. I will tell him, I said, "Well Martin, you have to leave early in order to be home by ten-thirty or eleven o'clock. He comes in this door at twelve o'clock, I'm mad. 'Cause it is dangerous. Even though he's got to do this when he gets older. So that's the reason why I let him get his license. He can get hurt either way—he can get hurt driving; he going to get hurt waiting at the bus stop. But I would prefer him to be driving, so he get home quicker, you know. I don't want him doing any wrong. But you know, that's the way my makeup is. I'm not . . . I don't want to kiss his feet. I want to protect my kids. To the fullest of my ability, you know. So that's the way I feel about it, right now. (Interview, June 7, 1983)

Parents of the high-achieving males encourage their sons to date. They allow them a great deal of latitude in this area, with most of the parents jokingly and sometimes not so jokingly acknowledging that their son has a "little girlfriend." This popular term implies it is not serious and won't have long-term consequences. It suggests the "sowing of wild oats," nothing more. Having a steady girlfriend is important to most of the high-achieving males. This is admitted and acknowledged. Some painfully confess that they do not have a girlfriend, but most appear to have a strong monogamous relationship. This is one of the ways in which the dating practices of the high-achieving males differ from those reported by the underachieving males. Wendell is "madly in love" with a girl at Capital High; Norris has a very strong relationship with one of his classmates; Martin also has a strong relationship with an eleventh-grade female. The parents of all these males know the girls their sons are dating.

Though the parents may not approve of a son's current relationship, they do not demand that he discontinue it. Norris's mother is extremely concerned about the level of commitment he appears to have with the young woman he is dating, and Wendell's mother is anxious about the amount of time he is devoting to his current girlfriend. But Martin's mother does not appear to object to her son's relationship, even though he has told her about the girl's baby.

On the other hand, Paul is not allowed to date because of his age, though he says one of his female classmates is "an item." Kent does not have a girlfriend and that seems appropriate for him; his preoccupation with his classwork takes precedence in his life—for now. Adam is still flirting with the idea of dating, but he has not yet made a "commitment" to any one girl.

More than his high-achieving counterparts, the underachieving male student seeks to avoid emotional entanglements by establishing a reputation as an aloof, distant "ladies' man." A quintessential symbol of maleness, this "cool pose" (Majors 1990, 1986, 1987; Majors and Billson 1992) also seems to be related to the great emphasis on physicality among these young males. And the parents help perpetuate this male mythology. For example, the mothers of the underachieving males frequently refer to their sons' link to a bevy of girls, none of whom has individual importance. Sons are expected to sow wild oats in the process of becoming men. Sidney's response and his parents' tacit approval are a case in point.

> Sidney takes all the advanced placement classes, but is not doing as well as he could be. He is a football player, and that seems to be more important than anything else. A short male (about 5′5″) with light-brown skin, a close haircut, and a quick smile that exposes well-formed white teeth, Sidney proved to be a very insightful and open interviewee. Despite the fact that he is jokingly referred to as "Mr. Advanced Placement," his greater loyalty is to his self-defined peer group: students who are *not* in the special academic program. When asked why he is not doing better in school, he was unable to offer a reasonable explanation. In fact, he felt awful that he could not become more serious about his work. He acknowledges that he spends too much time playing and practicing football, talking on the telephone, listening to the radio, and interacting with "the girls," but he does not seem to be able to stop himself. He admits that he spends very little time at home during the week . . . Most days he has football practice after school until 5:30, but on the days when he does not, he goes to some girl's house and stays until well after dinner. When he does come home, he spends most of his time talking on the telephone. (Interview, March 17, 1983)

Sidney's mother and father jokingly referred to his concentration on "the women." At no time did they indicate that they thought he spent too much time engaged in the pursuit of "mating, dating, and ritualized playing."

A question to Art about dating produced a striking response.

When I asked Art if he dated, he laughed heartily. When he regained control, he assured me that "dating is what old people do." Boy! Did that take me for a loop! I used to date and still do date, and I had not thought of myself as a senior citizen until Art made his remark. He went on to say that he does not take girls out, if that's what I meant. If he meets one while he is at an arcade, for instance, he'll talk to her and maybe even spend some time with her, but he never pays her way to the movie or anywhere else. She pays her own way. He usually goes to the arcade on Friday and Saturday nights and talks to and interacts with anyone available. (Fieldnotes, March 15, 1983)

Korey denies having a "real" girlfriend, and he too denies that he dates: "No, I don't really say it's a date. We just . . . [he gives me a knowing look that is intended to suggest that they have sex but he does not care about her] . . . Naw. I just be—I just talk to girls . . ." (interview, June 15, 1983).

Sidney is more direct. As he sees it, one of the primary ways of becoming a real man is to achieve a reputation as a "ladies' man." In his mind, this route to maleness enhances one's reputation more than being an athlete. It should not go unnoticed that this approach to "dating and mating" is also a kind of "practice game" that appears to be appropriate for a patriarchal order that does not promote monogamy.

> *Anthro:* How are *you* seeking—what is the major way *you're* seeking to become a male? I know you're an athlete . . .
>
> *Sidney:* A man?
>
> *Anthro:* . . . I'm sorry, a man. [Laughter] Sorry!
>
> *Sidney:* Well . . . it just happened so fast. One moment I was playing around with my buddies, next minute I'm in a house with someone's daughter. Well, it's like this: I [feel] that I became a man being around the ladies more.
>
> *Anthro:* Would you say you're a ladies' man?
>
> *Sidney:* No. You know, some people try to call me that; they say that about me. (Interview, March 22, 1983)

Sidney went on to tell me that being a playboy or "ladies' man" is also critically important to being known as a man, the quintessential evidence of manhood.

> Well, okay, a playboy goes around talking to every girl that he sees . . . As far as athletics, you do *not* have to be successful

as an athlete to be recognized as a real man. Yes, you could be sorry [weak] on the basketball team, sit on the bench, and still be recognized [as a real man]. Yes. Because of the fact that you're on the basketball team. Establish yourself as being a role player, have your reputation just for being on the basketball team . . . In a way, I've changed [from "the goody-goody type"]—abruptly, yes . . . It just happened so fast, right? One minute I was quiet, shy . . . next minute I'm one of the loudest people in the school. Number two, people try to call me a ladies' man. Number three, I'm an athlete [and that's equivalent to being a playboy] . . . Four, they say I talk to—try to talk to older women instead of women my age and younger. (Interview, March 22, 1983)

Sidney's parents and most of the other parents of the underachieving males recognize their sons' drastically changed behavior, but they do not openly seek to either abort or transform the observed change. In fact, they appear to sanction it, believing it is a critical ritual of maleness. Their indulgent responses and reluctance to become involved in the redirection of their sons' behaviors and actions are read by their sons as approval.

One of the common themes in each of the responses of the parents of the high-achieving males was their assertion that if their son got into trouble with the law, they were not going to rescue him. The interviews with the mothers of Norris, Wendell, and Martin include clear statements to this effect and provide a striking contrast to the statements made by mothers of underachieving students. While the latter appeared to ask nothing of their sons except their presence, the mothers of the high-achievers constantly advised their sons that involvement in legal troubles meant they were on their own. Norris's mother told of her warning:

I have never been a person to choose other people's friends. *I* feel that Kai and Norris have to be with those other kids. I just tried to tell them, you know, you can't be a friend to everybody, because everybody will not allow you to be their friend. Now, number one, you know perfectly well the things that I *will* tolerate and the things that I will *not* tolerate. Now if you're outside with a group, and they decide that they're going to do something that you know I will kill you for, then I would advise you to depart the premises and either come in the house or move away from whatever they're getting ready to do. Because more than likely it's going to be something destructive, and you know *you* don't want anybody destroying

your property, so you better not be out there destroying anybody else's property. You see? Or it's going to be something
that's going to be harmful to one in the group, because what
they are planning may backfire, and one of you might get hurt
by accident. So the best thing for you to do is, whenever . . .
they're *your* friends, I'm not picking them for you, but if you
feel that they are up to no good, and you know what's right,
and you know what's wrong. And that's it. (Interview, April
28, 1983)

Wendell's mother encouraged her son to behave. As a single mother,
she did not have even the semblance of a backup should her efforts fail.
So she gave an explicit warning:

He knew—he knew who to associate with, and who not to associate with. Even now, I don't [limit his friends]. Because,
you know, I—my aunt did that—my cousin couldn't associate
with this or that [person]. Honey, he ain't turned out to be
nothing . . . You can't do a child like that. And it really hurt
me to see how he used to be. Now he nothing but a drunken
alcoholic. And he young. You don't do a child like that.

I feel like this: everybody knows, like women got instincts,
I don't know what it is men got, or boys—but you know who
to associate with and who not to. I don't think you should
take and put a tag on a certain person. Don't you do that. Let
them find out for themselves. 'Cause you can't always—I ain't
gonna always be with him. And I told Wendell, "I done
taught you right from wrong, and you go out there and get in
trouble, don't you call me, I mean that! Don't you call me.
I'm not going to get you out of no mess, you go out there and
get yourself in trouble . . . I *sure* did [tell him that]! I *mean*
that! I'm not going to—if I done warned you against something, and you're going to go with your eyes wide open . . .
Now, if you are not responsible, that's a different thing. Now,
if I—if you done gone out there [with] somebody, and you
know they steal and stuff, and you out there with them, and
they get caught, you going to jail! You tell the man, "I'm
sorry, [but my mother ain't coming] when it's visiting hours."
I mean that! You're going to jail. (Interview June 13, 1983)

Martin's mother had an answer that is virtually indistinguishable
from the one offered by Wendell's mother.

Living in this community, [my children] see—they see crime.
They're *living* in crime, in other words. And they know the

penalty for doing wrong. I've told them, too, that if they do wrong, I'm not going to get them out of it. You get them out of it *one* time, they know better when they do it that one time; number two, they're going to do it again. They're going to come right back out here and do it again! So why should I help get them out of that first one? I'm not going to do it! But Martin has never given me too much trouble. He's a good child. He's pretty good. (Interview, June 7, 1983)

There is far less participation in organized sports among the high-achieving males than among their lower-achieving counterparts. Indeed, two of them, Kent and Norris, have recently abandoned their interest in track in order to devote more time to their school work. Their parents were neither critical nor applauding; they allowed their sons the space to make these decisions on their own.

Wendell and Martin are members of the band. Their parents' response to their participation in this and other after-school activities is drastically different from that of the parents of the high-achieving females. Rita's parents insisted she discontinue her involvement in track; Katrina's, that she quit a dance group. Kent's mother—who is concerned about her son's apparent preoccupation with classwork—did not object to his leaving the track team. When he told her he was absolutely certain that was what he wanted to do, she immediately withdrew from the decision-making process.

For an underachieving student like Max, organized play has many positives. Both he and his parents hope he will earn a football scholarship to college. When he was asked what his after-school plans were, he made the following statement:

After high school, I'd like to go to college, hopefully on scholarship, but that's not really—I'm trying to get—just basically going on my grades. So, you know, I like to participate in sports, but I'm not going to let it exceed my interest in the courses I want to pass. (Interview, March 7, 1983)

Max's parents, particularly his mother, nurture his postsecondary dreams. This is not difficult for them to do, because his dreams are mirror reflections of their dreams for him. They are not wealthy people, so enrolling him in a private school has not been a real option. Nevertheless, they have sought to maximize the opportunities that are available to him, including sending him to the public schools where his mother was employed, providing him with a more controlled learning environment, and carefully selecting his teachers.

PLAYING IT SAFE AND DENYING THE REALITY OF RACE

With the exception of Paul's guardians, none of the parents of the high-achieving males acknowledged having ongoing open, frank discussions of the privileging and stigmatizing of race in America. They admit that they deny the reality of race when interacting with their children, though they are forced to confront it on a daily basis in their personal and work lives. Kent's mother offers an example:

> I've told my children that we're equal, and they shouldn't—
> you know, the White man and Blacks, we're all the same. You
> know, and I told them there are going to be some White peo-
> ple that just *do not like* Black people, period. You know,
> there's some Black people that just do not like White people.
> You know, they just don't like each other. Just you—know,
> period. And because I've wondered about the—some of—
> about the Klan . . . I just taught them that they're going to
> meet White people that do not like Blacks. (Interview, June
> 14, 1983)

Since African-Americans and Capital community residents have limited contact with real, live White Americans, the widely reported fratricide is often against those group members who are perceived as "acting white." Since obtaining schooling is the only obligatory "acting white" feature of the lives of people of African ancestry, African-Americans with more than rudimentary schooling are primary targets of this latent fury. Adam's father frames it this way:

> I hate to say this—I have more problems getting along with
> my own family, the ones that are educated. For some reason. I
> can't deal in that circle. Because to me it's phony. In some re-
> spects, because, hey, you're blood relatives. You know . . . I
> still go back to that home—if you've got good common sense,
> even without an education. Or a diploma—well, now, the rea-
> son you can't make it nowadays is because of the education re-
> quirement. You know, there's very few places you can go to
> even get a job without a high school diploma. But to get a
> high school diploma, if you've got good common sense and a
> good brain . . . head on your shoulders, you can deal with the
> world. And I don't see where—in other words, the people that
> I associate with, nobody's talking about their education, or
> saying, "I got this degree, and I got that degree." We're just
> out enjoying each other's company, and I think if you can talk
> to someone intelligently, you'll get along. That has to do with

education too. So I'm not taking anything away from education. No way. (Interview, May 9, 1983)

The response of Adam's father was not atypical. His ambivalence
about the centrality of race and the value of schooling as the way for
Americans of African ancestry to get out of poverty and enjoy its subsequent, transformative powers are captured in the following statements:

> I don't really think that his education made Martin Luther
> King what he is. Martin Luther King was just a born leader. A
> lot of your rock-and-roll singers out there, they are idols for
> the younger generation. But a lot of them have never finished
> college. I'd like the ones that have done something with their
> education sort of like to return it to the community—to the
> race. Now, those are the ones that I really admire. Those are
> the ones I really admire. Good. That's education. You're doing
> something to help your fellowman. And I don't like to say just
> Blacks. I really don't like to put it in a racial thing. I've just
> never been racial. I don't know why, I've just never been ra-
> cial. I can look out and see things that we are not getting
> what the other races are getting, but I still say, hey, don't put
> your tail between your legs and whine about it. Go out and
> *do* something about it. Get your education. And then go out
> and make something of yourself, and then come back and help
> your fellowman. And I see a lot of them that don't do this.
> And that's the part that makes me angry. (Interview, May 9,
> 1983)

Curiously, while Adam's father acknowledges that he is fully conscious of the existence of racial discrimination in America, his first incli-
nation is to dismiss it, to define it as an insignificant factor in the life of
Black people, and to teach Adam—as he taught the older siblings—to
persevere in spite of its existence. According to Adam's father, the anti-
dote to racism is education. What he urged his children to do, including
his youngest son, Adam, was to "Go out and *do* something about [rac-
ism]. Get your education" (interview May 9, 1983).

Wendell's mother asserted that the race problem in America is primarily a problem of Black people discriminating against other Black
people rather than White people discriminating against Black people.

> It's just *some* White people. It's—it's some of them, the
> White, the way they been taught. Then after they really get to
> *know* a Black person, they find out they're not like that. It's
> how you program a child when they little. You will be sur-
> prised how you can hurt a child when they little! You can

turn them against a lot of things—even make them think certain things about yourself. 'Cause I know certain things my
mother taught *me*. And . . . since I got old enough, I found
out it wasn't like that . . . You can really do *damage* to a
child by what you . . . you think that child forget, the child
don't forget. A child just like a elephant—they don't forget
nothing. (Interview, June 13, 1983)

Her greatest anger is directed at Black folks whose school credentials
are generally beyond the reach of most other African-Americans. She
insisted that they are the "biggest fools" because they do not know how
to treat other nonschooled Black folks.

[They're fools] because they hold . . . they hold each other
down! . . . They've forgotten where they came from. And then
they . . . when you go to talk to them, they ain't got time. But
look who took time out for *them*. And you think they'd say,
"Well, okay, since I see you trying to help . . . I might help
you." They don't do that! Oh, honey, you can't touch them
with a ten-foot pole! You know? Lord have mercy, they walk
around there like they're God's gift to mankind. And they're
something else. They do. They do . . . They do. They forget
where they got to—where they got to . . . Just because you
might be educated, you don't down somebody that's not educated, you know? Because we can always help somebody else.
Then a lot of time, I sit in the midst of people that were
highly educated. But honey . . . when you start talking about
this common sense—some of them ain't got *common* sense!
They're right simple. They is—they're simple! They is! And
there's some that I've told, "Honey, I might not be educated,
but I [got] better sense than to . . ." They don't know how to
talk to nobody. They're conceited, they're selfish, and any
other word they got in [the] vocabulary that you can use,
that's them. (Interview, June 13, 1983)

Wendell's mother's lament at the lack of "common sense" among
schooled African-Americans suggests that the specific (some would label
it essentialized and inappropriate) knowledge of this segment of the
Black community is lost or was never mastered during the process of
schooling. The absence of "common sense" suggests a lack of what
enabled the imagined Black community to survive when schooling and
school credentials were forbidden. Her fury is heightened by her perception that these schooled Black Americans deliberately put limitations on
what they can learn and need to learn from the community.

Kent's mother's observations lend support to those of Wendell's mother.

> . . . I told my children, I said, Black people restrict themselves
> so much. They restrict themselves from doing this and from
> doing that. And White people have never been restricted. So,
> like I was telling my son Kent, I said, "You see a little White
> person walking down the street barefoot, nobody pays any at-
> tention to that. That's normal." I mean, you know, you
> don't . . . but then you see a Black person, the *Black* person is
> going to say something about it. "Oh, that nigger must not
> have any shoes" . . . They don't say nothing about the White
> person. So why do they say that about the Black person? Why
> can't *we* walk around when it's hot, without—you know, bare-
> foot. The little White kids do it. But see, that's because they've
> always been free. They had no limitations, no restrictions. But
> we've always been told, "Put some shoes on," you know, "Do
> this, do that." And when *we* go barefoot, "They must not—
> you know, they don't have no shoes. Look at that coon! He
> don't have no [business] in there." And I just don't—I don't
> understand [Black people holding each other down]. That's in
> here [pointing to her head] . . . in here. So why do we . . .
> we're putting *ourselves* down! (Interview, June 14, 1983)

While Kent's mother claims that people of African ancestry restrict *themselves,* her assertion that "White people have never been restricted" suggests that Black people in America indeed differ from White people in America: White Americans have never been restricted; African-Americans have always been restricted. Moreover, according to Wendell's mother, since that has been their constant reality, African-Americans continue to actively seek restrictions, imposing them on themselves when they are not externally imposed. But while today's restrictions, in her view, are self-imposed, externally imposed restrictions have been endemic in the historical experience of African people in America (Woodson 1933).

For her part, Martin's mother claims that she is unlikely to get promoted where she works, not because of racial discrimination but because of the "jealousy" of her fellow Black workers.

> I don't think [Black people are discriminated against]—hmm.
> Huh-uh, because Black people discriminate against each
> other . . . Well . . . I'm going to—you know, like where I
> work [as a custodian], right? We have a—how can I put
> it?—it's no chance for advancement because it's jealousy

there, in our ranks. And I see it. And it hurts *me* to see that, how our Blacks *are*. Do *not* care to see [another Black] man get up. And the supervisor could make more preparations and getting something done, if [we] only work together. Yeah. I don't like it. That's why I'm saying . . . Jealousy. I could put it down to jealousy, or no heart, or whatever. You know. That's about all *I* can see . . . It upsets me because it's no togetherness. And you will find that, in our work force, it could be all racists—Blacks or Whites or anyone. But, you know, I don't see too much racism, you know, because I don't work 'round that kind. But I see it within the Blacks . . . To *me* it's stabbing in the back. It's blacklisting, talking about each other. That's what *I* would say. As far as racism is concerned. I'd say Blacks among Blacks. (Interview, June 7, 1983)

Norris's mother makes an even stronger allegation, claiming that during the Second Emancipation era, those African-Americans who initially got promoted were "not qualified for those jobs." When asked why she thought they were not qualified, she offered the following reason:

I worked in the government prior to going into private industry. And there were quite a few Black people in relatively responsible positions who were not qualified for [those jobs] . . . I didn't feel that they were qualified for those jobs . . . [They lacked] intelligence. Pure and simple. Because a lot of them at that time were still Uncle Tomming.[6] They didn't have enough pride in themselves, in their mental capabilities, to say, "Well, I think this should be done this way." (Interview, April 28, 1983)

However, when describing how she came to have the midlevel management position she presently occupies, she concedes that she was repeatedly overlooked, not because she could not do the job but because she had the wrong racial heritage.

I—well, let's put it this way: When I first went to Southern, it implied just what it says—Southuhn—Southuhn Railway, y'all, with a heavy accent. One of them type places, okay? And the Black people who were employed there, you could count on your hand. But as time went along, you saw more and more Black faces coming in. So when *I* went there, which was in '69, they probably were trying at that time to fill quotas. Okay? So I got my foot in the door with them trying to fill a quota. And I filled two recommendations at one time, or criteria: I was Black, and I was a woman. So that's all—

because I understand, for a long time Southern had no female stenographers, just men. (Interview, April 28, 1983)

She worked as a stenographer at Southern from 1969 to 1973, under several male bosses. Each time the position of real estate specialist that she currently occupies became available, she was never considered, never asked to apply.

So the last person I worked for [as a stenographer] was the assistant director of the department. So when the vacancy became available for a real estate specialist [one more time], he told the director, "Why do you keep going outside, bringing in people, when we have a very qualified person right here in this office?" They wondered who he was talking about. And he told them, *me*. Because a lot of times when I—when he would give me dictation, and stacks and stacks of filing and everything, I would get there and I would do it . . . you know, and still have time to do crossword puzzles. And he never could understand how I could do that, you know. But it was just a matter of absorbing what I was doing, comprehending what I was doing, and being able to put it together so that I could stay ahead of him. So he was my biggest backer in that respect. So therefore, when [the real estate specialist] position became available [for the umpteenth time], I had to go upstairs, take this little stupid test—*I* thought it was really stupid, and anybody could have passed it, but a lot of people didn't pass it. And that was just to make it look good. And I got the job. So I've been a real estate specialist since then. (Interview, April 28, 1983)

Unlike the parents of all other high-achieving students, both of Paul's guardians are college-educated and have consciously taught him the positiveness of being Black. His uncle has an extensive library that celebrates the contributions of Black people to America, and his aunt has devoted her life to helping Black children. She never understates the problems associated with being a Black person in this country. What she pins her hope on is the younger generation of Whites, which tends not to see color:

This has nothing to do with Paul, but maybe it can help explain. I was an official . . . in the District of Columbia Public School System for 27 years. And I only dealt with all-Black students. I applied for this job in Virginia that deals with a White population. And the parents, of course, I know, were kind of upset and curious when I was chosen, because I had a big bush [natural hair style] on my head, bigger than this—that I'm not going to cut—and there was standing room only because they were curious about me. But I have found that the White kids would care less what color I am. They don't even see my color. You understand? And what happens is, it's the parents who do it to them, the adults. If we could take all grown people and flush them down the toilet . . . I'm serious. Then we would eliminate all of that. Serious. Because it is the parents. For instance, who would say to Paul and . . . the Jewish guy that sits next to him, "Why is it that nigger got the A?" Now, seriously, it would be the adult. (Interview, April 26, 1983)

Paul's guardians are aware of his ambivalence about being Black and his need to resist the limitations imposed on Black people, by both comforming to and avoiding the larger society's expectations. Their college training and middle-class status appear to have broadened their understanding of the structural limitations confronting people of African ancestry, even after the Civil Rights Movement and the Second Emancipation. They recognize the continued existence of cultural and racial discrimination in American society and unhappily watch Paul being conditioned by it, even as he begins to learn a little about Black writers. For example, their concern about his preoccupation with the Euramerican experience as taught at Capital, as well as their disillusionment with the "integration ethos," led them to encourage Paul to get what they describe as the Black experience.

The reason we became upset, because I'll never forget, he was home in the Virgin Islands with his mom, and his mom called and told me that Paul was going to the library to find out all he could about—who was it that got married? . . . Prince Charles. And she said, "When are you going to read about some Black folks?" You see? But everything he was getting at school had nothing to do with his own heritage and his own people. You see? And that's the reason why I have those kinds of feelings about him going to an all-White college. 'Cause he hasn't had that experience. He's *not* had that Black experience [despite the fact that he's attended predominantly Black schools all his life] . . . My argument with him is that I don't think *he* understands at this point how being Black can [and will] be a handicap. Okay? If you care to call it a handicap. That is why I have some problems with him, as I said to you earlier, about being fifteen at this point—just becoming fifteen, and thinking about going to an all-White institution. I think he needs to first—and especially when he's talking going into medicine—I think he needs to, for his *own* enlightenment, spend his premed years in a Black institution . . . Being so young, he needs to be, *I* feel, with folks who are feeling people. And Black folks are feeling people. And he needs to be where I *know* folks will—and maybe that's my own insecurity, but I think he needs to be where *I* know folks will watch out for him . . . We know he is a genius. *I* know it, *Capital* knows it, all of the community knows it. But going to an all-White institution, being Black, they aren't going to accept him as being that genius. If he would go, let's say, to an all-White institution, he *knows* he's an A student. And the guy sitting beside him is White. The mere fact that *he* is Black, he will get the C and the White guy will get the A, who does not have the intelligence that *he* has. That's what I . . . you know . . . [he needs in order to be able] to handle it. (Interview, April 26, 1983)

Paul's guardians want him to attend his uncle's alma mater, a predominantly Black college in the South. He wants to attend a predominantly White, Ivy League college in the Northeast.

Well, I definitely want to get away from Washington for a while. And MIT, they—even though they're an engineering-based school, the people in the medical school, they get more individualized attention, so that they're more ready for the . . . And Johns Hopkins—well, everybody knows about Johns Hopkins. And then . . . my uncle's school, he's an alumnus . . . that's got to be one of my choices. It's a pretty nice school. I love the labs. It's a nice school. (Interview, January 10, 1983)

This is what he told me about his college choices while the tape recorder was on. In private conversations, his perception of his uncle's alma mater was far less impressive. Indeed, his perception of predominantly Black colleges is so distorted that he constantly referred to his uncle's alma mater as "the thirteenth grade."

Although his guardians do not know it, Paul is absolutely determined that he is not going to get "the Black experience" at a predominantly Black college. He has been a model child and has done everything they have asked him to do, in school and out of it. He is obedient, loyal, and respectful of their image in the community. But in terms of the collegiate experience he is planning, he is defiant. He relishes the opportunity to resist the low expectations for African-Americans by going to a prestigious college and doing better than most of the White elite students with whom he would have to compete. He believes his grades at Capital and his scores on the PSAT have set him apart from his peers and that he should be allowed to play in the big league in order to increase his chances for success in spite of his Blackness. He is remarkably clear-sighted:

Being Black in a White society means that you have a lot of things hard for you. It means that you are not meant to succeed; that if you are going to succeed, you are going to have to do it by yourself; you're going to have to work hard and you are going to have to succeed [on your own] no matter what. (Interview, February 3, 1983)

FIVE

Teachers and School Officials as Foreign Sages

Learning how to not-learn is an intellectual and social challenge; sometimes you have to work very hard at it. It consists of an active, often ingenious, willful rejection of even the most compassionate and well-designed teaching. It subverts attempts at remediation as much as it rejects learning in the first place. It was through insight into my own not-learning that I began to understand the inner world of students who chose to not-learn what I wanted to teach . . .

I cannot speak Yiddish, though I have had opportunities to learn from the time I was born. My father's parents spoke Yiddish most of the time, and since my family lived downstairs from them in a two-family house for fourteen of my first seventeen years, my failure to learn wasn't from lack of exposure. My father speaks both Yiddish and English and never indicated that he wouldn't teach me Yiddish. Nor did he ever try to coerce me to learn the language, so I never had educational traumas associated with learning Yiddish. My mother and her family had everything to do with it. They didn't speak Yiddish at all. Learning Yiddish meant being party to conversations that excluded my mother. I didn't reject my grandparents and their language. It's just that I didn't want to be included in conversations unless my mother was also included. In solidarity with her I learned how to not-learn Yiddish . . .

Deciding to actively not-learn something involves closing off part of oneself and limiting one's experience. It can require actively refusing to pay attention, acting dumb, scrambling one's thoughts, and overriding curiosity. The balance of gains and losses resulting from such a turning away from experience is difficult to assess. I still can't tell how much I gained or lost by not-learning Yiddish. I know that I lost a language that would have enriched my life, but I gained an understanding of

the psychology of active not-learning that has been very useful
to me as a teacher. (Kohl 1994:2–4)

As documented in the two preceding chapters, the parents of Capital
High students tend to be ambivalent about the value of their children's
academic performance. One of the fundamental issues they confront is
whether they should encourage their children to succeed in the White or
in the Black community. Each decision has enormous consequences. If
these parents instill in their children a strong sense of resistance to Whiteness, through either conformity or avoidance, their children will cast
their lot with the Black community, making it more difficult—but not
impossible—for them to succeed academically. On the other hand, teaching their children to be independent and individualistic will instill a
worldview which closely approximates the one held by members of the
dominant society, and exercising this option will enhance the possibility
of achieving academic success. Those parents who express doubt about
the existence of meaningful rewards for African-Americans who excel in
school often guide their children—perhaps unwittingly—to a marginal
cultural space, where they are forever ambivalent about achieving academic success within an institution dominated by the values of the Other.

Most classroom teachers at Capital High are Black women, with
roles as both teachers and parents. Publicly, teacher-parents at Capital
are not at all ambivalent about the importance of education: they consider academic success and its perceived association with prestige and
an increase of material wealth to be worthy personal and societal goals.
In the course of my study, however, I encountered some teachers who
were in despair because their own children had rejected them as role
models and the purported value of the schooling they provided. The
children of these Capital High teachers are underachievers, and their
mothers do not understand why. They do not understand their biological
children's not-learning, their willful refusal to learn what is taught in
school.

> Ms. Yanmon is very unhappy with her son's poor perfor-
> mance in math. She attributes his weakness to a lack of confi-
> dence. She told Ms. Sampson that she and her husband had a
> big disagreement about how to help him. For example, yester-
> day morning Mr. Yanmon had their son out of bed very early
> in the morning so that he could get his math assignment done.
> Ms. Yanmon noted that her husband's tone of voice was
> rough and unsympathetic. This she did not like, so last night
> "I slept way on my side of the bed." (Fieldnotes, November 9,
> 1982)

It is against this teacher-parent or teacher-as-parent background that I examine how African-American teachers at Capital High attempt to dislodge the students they teach from their commitment to not-learning and to transmit socially approved knowledge and values to African-American adolescents, including their own biological children. I also discuss the consequences of being an African-American teacher in an institution that has been defined by the social and cultural norms of the dominant Other. Finally, I argue that, in their role as public-school teachers, African-American adults are both symbolically transformed into "foreign" sages and confined to the construction of African-American adolescents who display appropriate(d) identities.

CONFORMITY AND THE CHILDREN OF CAPITAL HIGH TEACHERS

As I talked with Ms. Aster, coordinator of the school's advanced placement program, during one of the first few days of the term, we were interrupted by a parent who had come to help his daughter, Wendy, register as a first-time student at Capital. Mr. Tedson talked with Ms. Aster about Wendy's insistence on transferring from private to public school because she despised the regimentation, as well as the emphasis on religion, at the parochial school she had attended the previous year. He also told her that his daughter's desire to transfer out of the private school, which *he* preferred and could afford, bitterly disappointed him.

When Mr. Tedson left, Ms. Aster appeared eager to share with me some information from Wendy's academic record: one official at the parochial school had assessed her as "very poor" in most categories, including academic potential. Ms. Aster pointed out that one of Wendy's teachers had indicated that her lack of academic success was directly related to her decision to not-learn because of her immense dislike of the school and its programs. She went to the school only because her parents, who are middle-income (her father owns a small moving business), did not want her to attend public school. They believe their earned "higher status" entitles them to send their daughter to an exclusive school. According to Ms. Aster, one teacher at that school who wrote a letter of recommendation was convinced that Wendy's grades would improve if she could attend the school of her choice.

Ms. Aster shared this information with me because she strongly identified with the dilemma faced by Wendy's parents. Her empathy and understanding of the parents' heartache were the direct result of having lived through a similar situation with her own daughter.

The discussion of Wendy led Ms. Aster to tell me of her own problems with her oldest daughter Alese. Graduating from high school at sixteen (she had been allowed to skip first grade because, according to the standardized examination scores, she was performing at the 3.2 year level), this very capable Black female refuses to go to college or do anything else that her mother, Ms. Aster, feels will enable her to make it in White America. Like Wendy, Ms. Aster's daughter has had many opportunities that are not available to other Black teenagers and opportunities that were unheard of for Ms. Aster and her contemporaries. Ms. Aster has close relatives employed at different universities in America who have tried to convince Alese to come to their schools and let them assist her in her efforts to acquire a college degree—all to no avail. (Fieldnotes, September 7, 1982)

Ms. Aster confided that her daughter's recalcitrant behavior so upset her that she has been taking the sedative Valium for several years. She does not see how she will be able to get off this addictive medication.

Her facial expressions suggested the depth of her pain and disappointment, her longing to give her offspring opportunities that, as a Black female growing up in Georgia before the Second Emancipation, she never had. "I don't like to take this stuff," she said, showing me the Valium container, "but I was so upset with her the other day that I think that if they had not given me this stuff, I would have killed her." (Fieldnotes, September 7, 1982)

As coordinator of the advanced placement program at the school, Ms. Aster is considered to have a fairly prestigious position in the school hierarchy. Her job consists of coordinating the courses in the program, clearing students for admission and dismissal, meeting with parents, interacting with officials at other schools, and so forth. She has served in this capacity for four years. She sees her daughter's refusal to go to college as the ultimate rejection and insult. She has done virtually everything she can think of to persuade Alese to do what her mother thinks is good for her, cajoling, manipulating, and forcing her into two or three courses at a local community college. She secretly hopes that such courses will inspire or motivate her to go to a four-year college.

Meanwhile, Ms. Aster acknowledges that she has two more "little ones" at home who are also "overachievers."[1] She hopes that they will not end up being the problem she thinks her eldest daughter is. Looking back on Alese's years of schooling, she wishes that she had not allowed her to skip a grade when she began school. She thinks that part of Alese's problem results from having to work with students who were older than she is. If she had it to do again, Ms. Aster says, she would not permit her child to advance beyond her chronological age and grade level.

Ms. Aster's rage and frustration tore at my heart. She could not understand why her daughter did not want the prestige symbols she wanted for her. To add insult to injury, Alese is currently working at a fast-food restaurant and dating a young man whom her mother despises.

Like many Black middle-income parents, Ms. Aster clings to a belief that equality of opportunity for all requires a willingness and an ability to conform to the rules and norms of the dominant society.[2] Her reluctance to acknowledge the discrepancies inherent in the policies and practices of integration has made her life with her oldest daughter extremely confrontational, emotionally disabling, and a living nightmare for both of them. As she tells it, her daughter has rejected every smidgen of her value system. What makes this even more painful for Ms. Aster is that Alese can handle school-sanctioned learning with ease: she can speak, write, and think in the school-sanctioned discourse without difficulty. Her confrontation with her mother centers around her own efforts to avoid this discourse and to create a safe space in which the Self is not conquered (Kadi 1993). While her mother believes that she is resisting racial stigmatization by conforming to the norms of the dominant culture, Alese is unconvinced and avoids behavior that could be viewed as conforming.

While Wendy's and Alese's responses to schooling are not uncommon among contemporary African-American teenagers, their parents perceive their actions as deliberate rejection of academic success, success that they can easily achieve if they are willing to do so. Instead, the daughters perceive success in school-sanctioned learning as physical and mental separation from the Black community.

As the above examples suggest, the problem of some Black teenagers' seeming disdain for school norms is not limited to African-Americans in the lower-income bracket, or what some social scientists are labeling the Black underclass (Glasgow 1980; Wilson 1978, 1987). Like Ms. Aster, the teacher-parents at Capital High want their own children to attend private schools or, at the very least, a suburban public school system; this is a much-desired social goal. Because most Capital teachers and administrators live in the suburbs—a small number live in Strawberry Hill—their children do not attend school in the District of Columbia Public School System. Those few teachers who live in Washington and have school-age children most often feel compelled to send them to private school.

In some instances, even the teachers who live in the surrounding suburbs send their children to private school. Ms. Yanmon's son is a student at one of the most expensive private schools in the area. His mother is sending him there because she envisions his attending a small, predominantly White college in New England.

Ms. Yanmon acknowledges that her son's life is fairly regimented and that he does not have very much input into the decisions that are made concerning him. And, like the students at Capital, he makes use of one of the primary "weapons of the weak": resistance (J. Scott 1985). "Ms. Yanmon told me about the problems she had trying to get her son to memorize a passage from Shakespeare, last night's homework assignment. She noted that though the passage was not long, he had extreme difficulty in memorizing it and this baffled her" (fieldnotes, March 8, 1983).

Of the more than a hundred teachers at Capital High, the child of only one—Ms. Costen—is enrolled at the school. A physics teacher, she is the mother of two children who are socially defined as African-American. One of her children is a high-achieving student in the advanced placement program.

Although riddled with contradictions and ambivalence, Ms. Costen is a socially conscious woman practicing what A. Epstein (1978) describes as "situational ethnicity" in a context where the "effects of the multiple negative" (C. Epstein 1973) of being Black and female are virtually insurmountable. While at Capital, she is a committed African-American; in other contexts she is from one of the Caribbean countries and identifies herself as a South American Indian. "Were it not for her affected British accent, one would not be able to distinguish her from any of the other Black Americans at the school" (fieldnotes, January 5, 1983).

As one of the few teachers at the school who self-consciously celebrate their dual ethnicity, she is frequently criticized for her pungent ideas and opinions. She is also frequently criticized for being a know-it-all. Translated, that means she is frequently and incontrovertibly guilty of acting white. At times Ms. Costen appears to be in contradiction with her declared Self. For example, before one faculty meeting, as her colleagues were entering the room, she gave each of them a copy of her program for enhancing their math skills. The program read as follows:

Dear Colleague:
It is well-known that some people are inclined to forget content areas they do not constantly use (especially basic algebra). It is also well-known that many people suffer from fear of and anxiety over mathematics. Should you fall into either of these two categories, you may be interested in joining the weekly

meetings for teachers in subject areas other than math. Besides decreasing your fear and/or anxiety, there will be review and discussion of the following topics:

1) EQUATIONS AND THEIR USES
2) POLYNOMIALS AND FACTORING
3) LINEAR AND QUADRATIC SYSTEMS
4) BINOMIAL DISTRIBUTIONS
5) BASIC NOTIONS IN PROB. AND STATISTICS
6) RADICALS, EXPONENTS, AND LOGARITHMS
7) REAL AND IMAGINARY NUMBERS
8) DIRECT AND INDIRECT RATIOS MATRICES
9) GREAT MATHEMATICIANS AND THEIR CONTRIBUTIONS
10) MATHEMATICS IN ART

Meetings will begin in March should there be sufficient interest and will be replete with handouts, guest lecturers, and a field trip. Kindly tear off bottom portion and return to me.

[Ms. Costen, Room 459]

....

Tear here _____

_____ I am interested in Survival Algebra Skills for non-Math Teachers.

_____ I am not interested at this time.

_____ I would prefer to attend anxiety seminars *only*.

Name _____ Dept. _____

Room No. _____

When Mr. McGriff acknowledged her desire to speak about her proposal later in the meeting, she announced that teachers from a neighboring junior high school were also being invited to join the classes. She ended her presentation by asking if there were any questions or comments. The silence that followed could be heard throughout Washington. Not a single person indicated that he or she had the slightest interest in what she was proposing. Nevertheless, the silence was pregnant with meaning, which apparently escaped her. When she gave her colleagues the announcement as they entered the room, their primary response—just before their eyes glazed over—might be decoded as, "Where did this crazy woman come from?"

The announcements were discarded or were hidden from view, as if removing them from one's sight expelled them from one's consciousness. A male substitute teacher who sat near me during the meeting asked in an incredulous voice: "Who is that loose cannon? Does she teach here?"

Ms. Costen's uniqueness among Capital High teachers is evident also in her approach to parenting. Her daughter, an early admission student at Capital, is a tenth-grade student at fourteen. Like two of the high-achieving students in my sample, Paul and Katrina, she won first place in her chosen category at the science fair. Ms. Costen had worked hard to help her daughter achieve the prize. On a daily basis for more than a month, she had taken her to Georgetown University during Capital's lunch hour so that she could obtain one-on-one instruction from professors at that university. Other teachers at Capital were generally not supportive of Ms. Costen's efforts:

> Ms. Costen talked about the problems she encountered ob-
> taining excuses from her daughter's German teacher during
> the last week in order to work on her science project. Her Ger-
> man teacher, Ms. O'Brian, demanded that before she could be
> readmitted to class after having been absent the previous day,
> she had to obtain a signed excuse. Ms. Costen wrote Ms.
> O'Brian a note telling her why her daughter had been absent
> from class: she was working on her science project. This did
> not satisfy Ms. O'Brian; she wanted an excuse from Ms.
> Aster, the teacher-sponsor of the fair at Capital. Ms. O'Brian's
> behavior annoyed Ms. Costen because, as she saw it, her
> daughter had one of the best averages in [her] German class.
> Ms. Costen perceived Ms. O'Brian's behavior as harassment of
> her daughter, and she is determined to see that Ms. O'Brian
> teach "my child" well. Her daughter does extremely well in
> the [German] class. "My child" has an A average in the class
> and that annoys Ms. O'Brian. One day when the class took an
> exam, "my child" finished well in advance of the other stu-
> dents, put her pencil down, laid her head on her desk, and
> closed her eyes as if she were asleep. Ms. O'Brian (who appar-
> ently read her behavior to mean that she found the test too
> easy and was bored) was not amused; she insisted that the
> young lady sit up. She did.
>   Ms. Costen went to talk with her about the incident and
> told her that she was going to have to "teach 'my child'" be-
> cause she was going to be on Ms. O'Brian's case like "white
> on rice." (Fieldnotes, March 8, 1983)

On another occasion, Ms. Costen took issue with an administrative policy. March 17 is St. Patrick's Day, the first holiday following Black History Month. When I entered the building that day, shamrocks were everywhere—in the upper right-hand corner of every copy of the daily school bulletin, on the walls outside the main office, in teachers' lapels, on students' cheeks, on the bathroom doors, and so on ad infinitum. People whom I had never seen wearing green had on something green. The whole building was a sea of green. Ms. Costen placed the following note in every teacher's mailbox:

> Recognizing the right of the leprechauns to sponsor today's ac-
> tivities in celebration of St. Patrick's Day, I wonder why there
> was no such effort to sponsor a party, fun, and merriment to
> celebrate Black History Month! That was month, not day. Oh
> yes, there was the assembly that almost did not take place, to
> which only selected teachers were invited to take their classes.
> A few individuals did make bulletin boards. But there was no
> cake, no school-wide merriment, no leadership to *celebrate* the
> accomplishments of Black heroes. The birthday of Martin Lu-
> ther King, Jr. was properly ignored by all but a few. As you
> take a bite into that piece of green cake today, I want you to
> feel GUILTY, especially if you are Black. During February, you
> were not Black and proud, you were Black and hiding, or
> Black and ashamed. Today you are pretending to be Irish! It's
> not the leprechaun that will get you the real pot of gold, it's
> more Black pride and the dedication that accompanies that
> pride.
>
> Y.B.C.
> Your Black Conscience

Almost as soon as I entered the building on March 17, one of Ms. Costen's colleagues thrust a copy of her unsigned Y.B.C. note into my hand. No one knew why she was responding as she was to established school norms and practices. One of three teachers—the other two were White females—who took the PSAT at the school that fall, Ms. Costen passed the exam with flying colors—99th percentile—and, according to some of her colleagues, was "feeling her oats." Some attributed her new assertiveness to her approaching divorce from an abusive husband. Still others declared it reflective of the fact that she is near completion of a doctorate in physics. My fieldnotes on that day capture my reaction:

> As I stood there with my mouth open, in shock after reading
> Ms. Costen's Y.B.C. note, unable to believe that someone at
> this school was really that . . . bold, one of Ms. Costen's col-
> leagues showed me an invitation from Ms. Ritter, the chair of
> the Home Economics Department, inviting most teachers to
> come to the Home Economics Suite at fourth period for green
> cake and door prizes. Apparently, it was this note and the
> green shamrock on today's bulletin that provoked the writing

of the Y.B.C. note. Her colleague, who had a small green shamrock on her jacket lapel, said that she was wearing it because both her sons had Irish names. I was dumbfounded at her reasoning. (Fieldnotes, March 17, 1983)

In a formal interview a few days later, Ms. Costen acknowledged that she was the author of the Y.B.C. note, and that her identity had been discovered by at least two of her colleagues, both of Irish descent and both female. One of these two Irish women is her daughter's German teacher: Ms. O'Brian. Each woman felt personally attacked by Ms. Costen's note. Each was intimately involved in planning the luncheon activities on St. Patrick's Day.

It was impossible not to be sympathetic with Ms. Costen's outrage. It was also impossible not to be absolutely baffled and appalled by her total misreading of what was and was not even remotely likely to be acceptable to her colleagues. Her actions and her colleagues' responses to them strongly suggested that she was culturally illiterate in many meaningful, nonacademic ways. It was transparently clear that she "knew" the subject matter of her discipline, but lacked the requisite wisdom central to survival in the imagined Black community (Hill Collins 1991). Despite her "certified competence," she was totally and unequivocally ineffective in working with her colleagues and almost as ineffective in teaching the students. The harder she "revved her engine," the stronger and more deadly her colleagues' resistance. The war between her and her colleagues, as well as between her and the students, was primarily silent, punctuated with nonviolent verbal breaches of this tacit agreement.

Many other teachers and administrators at Capital High showed more subtle signs of resistance to existing school norms, values, and practices. Even though the resistance as conformity practiced by teachers and other school officials is largely unconscious and virtually wordless, its silence does not soften its forceful and dynamic impact. It ricochets in classrooms, especially in the content and subject matter of the courses offered; in the several faculty lounges, in teachers' interactions, in faculty and PTA meetings; and between parents and other school officials. Resistance in order to prove adequacy and avoid inadequacy is their burden as they wade through texts and other documents that not only have no meaning or context in their lives but that also undermine and devalue who they are. It also manifests itself in school officials' attempts to both build a power base and establish psychological control of those they teach.

School officials, including teachers, feel compelled to create and maintain boundaries minimizing penetration of the physical plant by outsiders. They are also obliged to invent and sustain psychological barriers to unwelcome external forces. For example, all things identified as having their origins in the African-American and Capital communities are constructed negatively and disallowed in the classroom or school context. The celebration of Black History Month and the offering of an elective Black History course during the spring of the first year of this study were exceptions to this rule.

> For the first time this month (February 22—twenty-two days after the beginning of Black History Month) an assembly in celebration of Black History Month was held. This assembly was planned and carried out by Mr. Zack. As a former social studies teacher, including Black History, he is very concerned about what he sees as Black students' lack of understanding of the problems confronting Black people. He invited Lt. Clarence D. "Lucky" Lester to speak to the students. Lester was one of the "Black Eagles" in the U.S. Air Force during World War II. (Fieldnotes, February 22, 1983)

Ironically, the school's *official* celebration of Black History Month did not take place until the second day of March—two days after Black History Month had ended.

> The assembly was well attended but, as I have noted elsewhere, the auditorium at this school is very small. Ms. Mentor and one of her students and I went to the auditorium at 9:30 and remained there until 11:05, when the assembly finally ended. It was a rather mundane program. Various students, including four in my study, acted the parts of widely known Black Americans. Dawn was Barbara Jordan; Sidney was Dr. J.; Nekia assisted with the master-of-ceremonies activities. All of the student participants made a significant statement about the life and contribution of the Black American he/she portrayed. Each of them announced who she/he was. The monotony was punctuated by songs (for example, the student portraying Mahalia Jackson sang a few bars of a song she was famous for) from individual students, the school chorus, and the band. (Fieldnotes, March 2, 1983)

Some members of the Capital High community said that the inclusion of a course in Black History in the spring schedule was in honor of the upcoming celebration of Black History Month; others insisted that its inclusion had nothing to do with Black pride, nationalism, identity, or anything remotely related to Black solidarity and cohesion. Mr. Mylan, the teacher assigned to teach the course, noted that offering a new course in midyear is quite unusual. The Black History course replaces the formerly required World History course. Mr. Mylan insisted that "the decision to no longer make World History a requirement meant its certain demise because if such a course is not required, the students don't take it" (fieldnotes, February 22, 1983).

The Black History class was an elective rather than a required course. Yet student interest was so high that a second section was offered. A third section would also have been fully subscribed, but the administration would not schedule it.

The efforts of students and teachers to remain linked to the Black community—despite their involvement in an institution of the dominant culture—are an underground process that also enables African-American teachers and school officials to retain their sense of Self by separating, defining, and maintaining personal boundary space while at the same time *appearing* to be unabashedly committed to the values propagated by the larger society and the school system. Although they see value in the rules and values of the larger society, many of them are also equally committed to the ideological claims promoted in the Black community.

At Capital High most African-American adults are constrained— often unconsciously—by the raw material that is created, maintained, changed, charged, and manipulated by their daily human activities as African-Americans. The processing of this material at Capital is neither recognized nor legitimated. It is therefore a contested, subversive process that minimizes the widely feared specter of "contamination" (Bullivant 1987). Because its existence corrupts and defiles the socially approved mechanism for separating African-Americans from the Self, it is intrinsically implicated in the creation of the "book-black Black." Such a person embodies what Kadi (1993) describes as a "conquered Self"; he or she struggles to maintain a personal cultural space that is unevenly and often haphazardly bounded by the individuality that each classroom teacher and school administrator is compelled to practice. The asymmetrical nature of the relationship is graphically illustrated in the response of Mr. Zack, an assistant principal, to the request to buy new books for the library:

> Mr. Zack is in his office this morning because he has been assigned the task of selecting serial and book titles for the library. (Somebody has to do it, and remember there is no librarian at the school). He has been given a $1,500 budget and cannot exceed that amount. He told me that he was not going to order any more titles about minorities. I wondered why that was his position, but because his assistant was there, I did not ask him to explain. (Fieldnotes, March 23, 1983)

The practice of excluding from the curriculum everything that might be linked to the Black community is pervasive. Many members of the African-American community have internalized the cultural rules of the dominant society because they are forced to obey them. At the very least, they exercise resistance (as conformity) in order to become "acceptable" professionals. The endorsement of this cultural hegemony is gnarled and uneven, running the gamut from total internalization by some teacher-parents and parent-teachers to complete but silent resistance from the others. Their varied responses paralleled but were not analogous to the students' acceptance of the prevailing dominant definition of the Black Self.

Although subversive, retaining and maintaining one's African-American identity is highly valued by most adults at Capital High. Unlike the students, most adults at the school do not equate conformity with loss of identity. As adults who are both what Denton and Sussman (1981) identify as the "crossover generation" and a critical mass of contemporary Black intelligentsia, school officials at Capital High are lacerated by contesting loyalties: those emanating from the African-American community in the form of the fictive kinship system and those dominating the school and the larger society in the form of rugged individualism. Historically, African-Americans are the only people in the United States who have not engaged in the assertion of individuality or the socially sanctioned process of "makin' it" in America. As an enslaved people and as people of African ancestry, they were not allowed to distinguish themselves from each other (Blassingame 1979; Rawick 1972). More important, in the most prestigious work arenas they have not been allowed to compete with other Americans. Schools and schooling in contemporary America have emphasized the production of "unhyphenated" African-Americans (Peshkin 1991) in which the African part of the identity of Black students is purely symbolic.[3] This is a fairly recent inversion of the long-standing process of not allowing Americans of African ancestry to become detribalized, that is, become the fabled individual American.

As representatives of the crossover generation, however, Capital school officials are struggling with an internal group dynamic in which the "African" component of their hyphenated identity has emerged as the unvoiced epicenter of their lives, fulminating in the wake of the convergence of the Civil Rights and Black Nationalist movements. The unfolding centrality of the African component of their identity has created an emotional cul-de-sac, leading to an identity implosion rather than a dissipation of those cultural features that link them directly to their imagined African origins.[4] Continuing an uneven but nonetheless continuous process which had its genesis in the Civil Rights revolution, this imagined past (see Friedman 1993) is generally more often evoked today than it has been since Kunta Kinte and the first generation of slaves arrived on these shores (Haley 1976).

At the same time, powerful forces are operating outside the Black community to stifle this imagined community (B. Anderson 1991). These varied responses are coupled with the general resistance-as-conformity mandate with which most Capital adults are extremely conversant. It is the coexistence of these diametrically opposed ideas and impulses, as well as their interminable shifting and collapsing meanings in the psyches of the adults at Capital High and the society at large, that is at the center of the descriptions presented in this chapter.

BUYING AND DENYING THE INADEQUACY MYTH

Among the teachers and other school officials, resistance to dominant representations of the Black Self in order to avoid the appearance of inadequacy is rampant. Ironically, the very best protection is available as conformity. Avoidance of inadequacy is evident in the unacknowledged apprehensions of teachers and other school officials about the value of schools and schooling and in their efforts to transform the traditional downward course of the collective future of African-Americans. As avoidance, it is also apparent in the unwillingness or inability of these educators to comprehend why so many contemporary African-American adolescents are, in their view, sacrificing their futures by not working hard in school. They are convinced that if Capital students would work in ways that parallel the pedagogical claims postulated in their teacher-training courses, they would become something other than victims in an oppressive social system.

School officials readily acknowledge and welcome the academic excellence of a small segment of the student population; student conformity to the norms of the dominant society is constructed as resistance. On the other hand, these same officials generally construct the avoidance and underachievement of the largest segment of the student population as betrayal of the imagined Black community. The academic excellence of the high achievers provides positive proof of the academic adequacy of African-American adolescents. For example, when Capital High's "It's Academic" team defeated a team of all-White students from a private all-girls' school in the metropolitan Washington area, clear evidence was established for Capital educators that three of their students possessed the central markers of an educated mind:

> [Members of the faculty] had not seen the televised "It's Academic" program when it was originally shown at 9:00 a.m.

the preceding Sunday. When the video was shown at the faculty meeting March 30, they were proud of the accomplishments of the students—Paul, one of my key informants, and
two senior students. A common theme heard in the public
and private comments of the teachers at the meeting was that,
since one of the teams was composed of White students from
a private all-girls' school in the metro area, there was special
glee in their happiness. Black students in Washington and even
the surrounding suburbs are so totally maligned by the press
and other agencies of the dominant society (they tend to view
Black children and the institutions they attend as being characterized by lack) that to beat White students at something they
are supposed to be better at made many of the teachers raise
their chins higher. (Fieldnotes, March 30, 1983)

At the same time, the small number of Capital students who pursue
academic excellence leads many school officials to define the children
they teach as deficient and inadequate in some vital ways: academically,
socially, and even morally, with the unvoiced subtext being their failure
to conform.[5]

Two business teachers seemed to agree that the students at
Capital are terribly deficient in the needed social graces. Ms.
Lortie described how she has to "tell them everything." When
a student leaned back in his chair and yawned and stretched,
she had to tell him that such behavior was inappropriate. Another instance given was about teaching students to clean the
typewriters they were using; if they do not keep their typewriters and office space clean, she told them, no one else will. She
described their general unwillingness to participate in such
mundane activities and noted that those who refuse to, despite
repeated attempts to get their cooperation, are given Fs for the
day. They resent this cleanup activity because they see this
task, according to her, as being in the domain of the custodial
staff.
    Ms. Backin agreed that her experiences with students par-
alleled Ms. Lortie's. A final example of the lack of social readi-
ness for the work world was their tendency to take their chewing gum out of their mouths (in response to her demand that
they remove all chewing gum) and stick it on their wrists or
the back of their hands. All of this suggests to these two teachers that the students are not ready for the dominant work
world and that their parents are not teaching them what they
should be teaching them. (Fieldnotes, October 22, 1982)

Other school officials are also seen as consuming and representing the Other and Otherness. This was made crystal clear one day as I sat in Ms. Sampson's office, waiting for her to return from a brief errand in the main office. As one of the counselors at the school, she is responsible for developing students' course schedules and making sure academic integrity is not in jeopardy.

> Shortly after the beginning of the third period, the telephone intercom in Ms. Sampson's office rang. It was Ms. Monet, one of the assistant principals. She apparently told Ms. Sampson, "I have a nice young lady I want you to work with." Ms. Sampson told me about this conversation as soon as she hung up the phone. She said, "I'll bet you that the 'nice young lady' she wants me to work with is either White or a very fair-skinned Black girl." When I responded by saying "Maybe not," she became even more certain. When I asked how she would know, she simply said, *"I know Ms. Monet."*
> Ms. Sampson was right. Shortly after the beginning of the third period, Rachael (one of the four White students in the school) came into Ms. Sampson's office with another White girl, whose behavior suggested a lack of familiarity with the school. Ms. Sampson was not at her desk at the time, so I invited them in and asked them to have a seat. Rachael said she could not stay. The young woman with her said, "Ms. Monet called Ms. Sampson earlier about me." Shortly thereafter, Ms. Sampson returned to her office and worked with the young woman, to get the morning-only schedule she wanted. She lives with her aunt and uncle and plans to get a job as a secretary at the FBI Building with the help of her aunt, who is the military person in the family. (Fieldnotes, October 29, 1982)

I did not fully appreciate how widely the teachers shared this perception of their students' inadequacy until I witnessed the response to a former student's request for a letter of recommendation:

> Someone knocked on the door of the teachers' lounge; however, no one responded. A young man who was identified as a graduate, or at least a former student, came in. Ms. Blumberg said in a very stern voice, "Young man, you cannot come in here." When he started to protest by saying, "Ms. Blumberg, don't you remember me?" she cut him off: "This is the teachers' lounge and you cannot come in here." No one said anything. Indeed, there was a deathly silence. After he left the room, Ms. Blumberg and Ms. Floret carried on a very intense

discussion of the young man, who had left Capital in 1979. Ms. Blumberg remembered that he was in her English IV class back then. Ms. Apropos also admitted knowing him, but she did not feel that she could help him with his request for assistance in completing some employment papers. (Fieldnotes, October 26, 1982)

When he finally left the room, the silence was deafening. I tried not to make eye contact with any of the teachers because I felt I would telegraph my sense of horror and disbelief. I wrestled with my internal confusion. My immediate goal was to absorb what had just transpired. Apparently, the teachers either sensed my revulsion or some internal mechanism told them that they had behaved inappropriately for committed teachers, especially in the presence of an "outsider." Suddenly, as if trying to explain or excuse their avoidance of the student, they began sharing with me "insider" secrets of students' inadequacy.

Ms. Floret told me about a student she had in one of her English IV classes who wanted to graduate in order to be able to live with her boyfriend. When she did not pass her class, the young woman's boyfriend came to the school to "beat her up." Luckily Ms. Floret was not at the school that afternoon. Ms. Floret described an incident involving Ms. Apropos, another English teacher. A parent followed her for weeks after school because he was unhappy with her assessment of his child.

Ms. DeWitt described her current unhappiness with all her tenth-grade English classes, especially the advanced placement class. They make her so angry, she declared.

The bell rang and they were forced to end their conversation, but they assured me that they had just begun. There were things they could tell me, they said, that would make my hair stand straight up on my head. (After what I had just witnessed, I was not sure I wanted to know.) (Fieldnotes, October 26, 1982)

Two school officials offered an explanation for why Capital High students do not do well in school.

Ms. Yanmon maintained that it is the gene factor. If one has parents who have good genes, then the chances are good that the child will also have good genes (depending on whether or not the child gets most of his or her intellectual potential from the parent with the greater intellect). At first I thought she was kidding. However, I learned that she was deadly serious. She and Ms. Sampson identified previous and current students, most of whom I don't know, and their "gene factor." For example, an advanced placement student whose parents are very active in the political activities in the Capital community was thought by Ms. Yanmon to have gotten her genes from her father, who is not as gene smart as her mother. (Fieldnotes, October 28, 1982)

Sadly, many of the teachers equated low performance with low intellect rather than viewing low performance as evidence of a "willful refusal" to learn, or resistance.

I saw Ms. Rathway for the first time several months later. She'd been out of school because of illness the first semester. She is a very short, dark-skinned Black woman with a short, salt-and-pepper bush. She was standing at the table flipping through the newspaper—either the *Washington Post* or the *Washington Times*. In an effort to be friendly, I told her that I had heard that she was sick. She quickly corrected me: she'd been out for "mental health" reasons.[6] I then went on to tell her why I was at Capital. I asked her if she might be willing to talk with me about her perceptions of the problems at the school and the reason she believed Black students were not doing as well as they could academically. She told me that the students didn't do any better than they did because they are lazy, don't care, are not motivated, and because their parents don't care, except at certain times. I sensed extreme unhappiness and defensiveness, which led me to conclude that this woman would never tell me anything about the school in a one-on-one interview. She was too bitter. (Fieldnotes, March 7, 1983)

In the opinion of one of my informants, the tragedy of Ms. Rathway's perspective is compounded in that these already low expectations for students are continuing to fall. As time passes, Capital students will probably display even fewer academic skills.

Mr. Hardy teaches a variety of math courses. He is quite annoyed with the increasingly low expectations of students' capabilities that are reflected in the courses students are [required] to take. For example, there is Algebra I, or Elementary Algebra, and General Math. He argues that General Math is really arithmetic, which all students take for nine years (from first through ninth grade). Nevertheless, when they come to tenth grade at Capital, they are once again required to take a "glorified" arithmetic course.

When students enrolled in Algebra I, or Elementary Algebra, come to his class, afraid and uncertain about their ability to master the subject matter, he asks them a standard question: "How long did it take you to learn arithmetic?" They generally answer ever since they've been in school. He then asks them to tell him how long the class they are taking from him—Algebra I—is scheduled to last. They answer one year. He then asks them to tell him which is more difficult, based on length of time offered.

What bothers him even more is the inclusion in the curriculum of weaker and weaker math and science courses. The newly created "Lab Skills" course, he maintains, is evidence. He believes that at the base of this problem is the fact that very few Black people pursue majors in the physical sciences, while many more pursue degrees in the biological sciences. Hence, the teachers in the public-school system in the natural science area are much more likely to be biologists than physical scientists. Biology, he claims, has its own unique set of problems, leading to such illogical curriculum inclusions as the current Lab Skills course. Lab Skills, he believes, represents a corruption of what the biological and physical sciences are. Moreover, it represents a reduction of what is expected of students. He feels that Black children can achieve at the appropriate level if they are given the opportunity and adequate encouragement. He is sick to death of the lower expectation syndrome. (Fieldnotes, October 14, 1982)

At the same time, it must be acknowledged that even when teachers and other school officials seek to place students in components of the school curriculum that historically were not offered at predominantly Black schools (higher-level math courses, physics and other upper-level natural science courses, advanced literature courses, and so forth) the students resist, seeking to avoid these courses. Most of the counselors are baffled by the students' resistance to their efforts to get them to take courses outside the established racial and gender domains. Mr. Wesylan was constantly demanding that his advisees go beyond these boundaries. In one incident, he tried to convince a young man to take typing rather than an arts and crafts class. Finally, in exasperation, Mr. Wesylan asked him what his after-school plans were. The student said he was going to join the U.S. Army.

> Mr. Wesylan's response was that the military used men who could type well, but the student was still unconvinced. Frustrated, Mr. Wesylan resorted to a focus on how the lack of skills hampers employability. "You leave here with no skills and then you'll claim that the reason Whitey won't hire you is because of discrimination. What are you going to do with arts and crafts?" The young man was unyielding. Mr. Wesylan "caved in." (Fieldnotes, September 13, 1983)

Resistance as conformity has weakened many teachers, and the effect is evident in their facial appearance and body movements, and in their frequently unsuccessful attempts to disguise their anger and growing alienation. Often their eyes are dull, devoid of hope and energy. Many of them walk slowly and loosely, their postures suggesting a lack of control over their environment. Their facial expressions reveal stress and anxiety. This "battle fatigue" is also manifested in hostility and in both denigration and sanctification of school-approved norms and values.

Virtually none of the teachers appears delighted to be at Capital High. While most of them admit that they would fight to remain there, they also concede that the fight would not be indicative of a love for their current work site. Rather, they would fight to remain at Capital in order to retain building seniority, a highly valued perk in the District of Columbia School System.[7]

A LOVE-HATE RELATIONSHIP: EGALITARIANISM FUSED WITH CAPITALISM

Job dissatisfaction reinscribed as conformity at the school is so pervasive that anyone who claims to really enjoy teaching at Capital will not be believed. Ms. Burgess's declaration of a love of teaching at Capital is an example par excellence of the "What's wrong with you?" syndrome operating at the school.

Ms. Burgess teaches only in the advanced placement program. Her limited interaction with students in the other operative tracks may influence her perceptions. Nevertheless, when the tape of a segment on the advanced placement program that had been televised by the local ABC affiliate was played back, her colleagues laughed at her assertion that she "loved her job" at Capital.

> While the Channel 7 news team talked to quite a few teachers
> in the advanced placement program, only two or three actu-
> ally appeared on TV. One was a biology teacher, Ms. Burgess,
> who declared, on TV, that she loved her job and wanted to re-
> main at Capital for the rest of her life. When she said that on
> the tape, her colleagues laughed heartily because they did not
> believe her; they assumed that she was just making a public re-
> lations statement. (Fieldnotes, March 30, 1983)

A look around the room showed everyone laughing. They found Ms. Burgess's strong declaration of loyalty and commitment to Capital High absolutely incredible! Interestingly, all of them appeared to accept J. Scott's (1990) claims regarding the lies inherent in "public transcripts."

Later, Ms. Mentor asserted that she was quite annoyed with her colleagues for laughing at Ms. Burgess's honest statement of her feelings. She believed that Ms. Burgess was being totally sincere when she talked with the television crew and that she is unconditionally committed to the education of African-American adolescents.

It is widely accepted that most people remain in teaching and at Capital for reasons that are only obliquely related to the joy of teaching Capital students. Some are at the school because teaching is imagined to be primarily a symbol of success. For others, being a teacher or an administrator is one way of earning a middle-class income. Still others view teaching as a way to resist, through conformity, the hegemonic claims of the dominating population.

The economic needs of the teachers at the school are also a major issue. Solving their personal financial problems is a major concern of a large number of the teachers. It is such a salient motivator that one might begin to think that an implicit goal of Capital High School was to give contemporary African-American adults some way to increase their incomes.

This is not to suggest that the money-making efforts of the adults at Capital are limited to the school building. A large number of the teachers, as well as some of the administrators, work part-time driving taxis, selling real estate, selling stocks and bonds and life insurance, selling furniture, serving as reservists in the military, and teaching night school both at Capital and elsewhere in the city.

Not every teacher who practices secondary capitalism at Capital High is African-American. Some of the White teachers engage in this practice as well. The crucial difference is that these White teachers do not have a history like that of Black people in this country.[8] Further, their relatively greater success with so much less effort reinforces African-Americans' perceptions of the importance of race in deterring or promoting success: race as a stigma versus race as a privilege complicates the problem of resistance as avoidance of inadequacy. The following examples are cases in point.

> Mr. Levy peddles various stocks to [other] teachers at the school. As a part-time stockbroker, he advises teachers of the value of having a diversified investment portfolio. To that end, he regularly places memos in their mailboxes reporting how the stock market has changed since September. (Fieldnotes, November 18, 1982, and January 31, 1983)

During his unscheduled class time—at least two periods in the morning—Mr. Levy hawks these stocks and bonds to his less sophisticated colleagues. While not many of them invest in the stock market, they frequently listen to his advice regarding the value of retirement annuities, insurance policies—especially the whole-life variety—and mutual funds.

Ms. Albaney, another White teacher, sells real estate part-time. She loves that aspect of her life. To the degree that she loves selling real estate, she despises teaching at Capital, primarily because she thinks it is beneath her. She does not respect the other teachers, administrators, or students. For example, during a meeting of the "lunch bunch,"[9] one of the Black teachers mentioned that she was taking a course for certification at the land-grant institution in the city of Washington, which has a predominantly Black faculty and student body. The professor had assigned the class a research paper requiring that each participant submit a proposed title and bibliography. As the teacher moaned and groaned about the difficulty of getting to the library to locate book titles and so forth, most members of the lunch group accurately read her complaints as obligatory graduate student behavior. Ms. Albaney did not. She supported Ms. Dressler's shorthand approach to the class assignment. She even suggested that Ms. Dressler make up book titles because, in her view, the instructor was "probably so dumb that he'll never be able to tell anyway" (fieldnotes, March 30, 1983).

Ms. Albaney was scathingly critical of the professor of the course, whom she did not know and whose requirements she apparently did not understand. Her suggestion that her colleague fabricate a bibliography for the professor because, as she put it, "What would he know?" went beyond even what is generally considered acceptable by this group. Nervous laughter ensued. Nevertheless, there was more than a hint of the same old nagging question: Is this because she assumes the professor is Black?

Ms. Albaney is married to a Black man and constantly tells the "lunch bunch" how wonderful her husband is to her. (See Adams's discussion [1994] of "the white wife" and B. Staples's admitted preference

[1989] for "the white girl"). She either misses or dismisses the choreographed silence of her Black female listeners and its attendant, pungent
hostility: the gnashing and grinding of their teeth, the fire in their eyes,
and the flush of their multihued skins as they listen to this non-Black
woman wax eloquently about her *woooon-derful* Black husband. Their
sense of indignation and betrayal is quite obvious, yet she appears to be
totally oblivious to it. Some of the teachers find her bravado and behavior so offensive that when she comes to lunch (which is virtually every
day), they do not. Typically, two members of the group would walk into
the room, see her, and leave. Some days, they say, they just can't take
Ms. Albaney's braggadocio or her self-righteous behavior.

Ms. Albaney offered her Black female colleagues counsel on how to
make a marriage "heavenly." Her unsolicited advice was tendered in
response to Ms. Mentor's "harmless" complaint about feeling overwhelmed with family and spousal responsibilities.

> Ms. Albaney described how her marriage bordered on the
> "ideal." She and her husband share every task. She says they
> are so close that, despite the fact that she may be hungry
> when she gets home from the real estate office after she leaves
> Capital, she does not eat until her husband gets home from his
> night-school job at King High at 9:15. Fifteen minutes later,
> she serves dinner (she has a microwave oven). They then share
> the task of cleaning up the kitchen and putting the food away.
> While she hires maids to come and clean her house once a
> week, for $40, the little things necessary to keep the house live-
> able are done by the two of them. Interestingly, Ms. Albaney
> appeared to be totally oblivious to the seething resentment of
> the women in the room as she described how helpful her
> *Black* man was and the other two married women, whose hus-
> bands are also Black, noted how little help they get from their
> husbands. (Fieldnotes, February 10, 1982)

Ms. Albaney's celebratory comments about her personal life and
how little effort it took to make a Black man happy had the deadly,
though probably unintentional, consequence of documenting one of
these women's worse fears: empirical evidence that they were inadequate
as wives and lovers. They both wanted to hear how she managed her
relationship with her husband and, at the same time, dreaded that what
she would tell them would remove all doubts about their adequacy as
wives and lovers. While they realized that hers was not the last word
and testament on the subject, they also knew that she shared a perspective with a great number of the Other. Even those members who refused
to join the lunch group when she was present were eager to learn what

she told the group about her personal life. They would invariably seek out Ms. Mentor or some other member of the group later in the day and ask what Ms. Albaney's specific comments had been. Hence, these women were lacerated by two conflicting motives: their resistance to established societal norms regarding male-female relationships and their desire to know how they measured up against these established norms.

African-American teachers at Capital tend to view their White colleagues' capitalistic efforts in contradictory ways. First, their part-time hustle is taken as carte blanche evidence that they really do not have the teaching of African-American adolescents as a top priority, regardless of whether or not this is true. Most of the women who knew that Ms. Albaney worked as a real estate agent decried her involvement in that profession because they perceived it as confirmation of her lack of real commitment to the first-rate schooling of Black students. Second, the activities in which White teachers are engaged—either as a result of the part-time job or as the part-time job—are frequently seen as prima facie evidence of success and as what they, the African-American teachers, could be doing, were it not for the baggage of their race.

Many of Ms. Albaney's Black colleagues secretly wanted to be able to do what she does in terms of streamlining their household chores. In general, they tend to see their White colleagues as being able to live the American Dream in spite of their involvement with African-American students at Capital High. Most of the African-American teachers conclude, though, that there are very few parallels between their lives and the lives of the White men and women in Washington, DC. They see themselves as struggling to make ends meet, living from paycheck to paycheck. Financial exigencies make it impossible for them to live the kind of carefree life they most often attribute to their White colleagues. Generally, these perceptions reinforce their unfolding beliefs about the lack of racial parity during the Second Emancipation. These perceptions eat away at their commitment to the idea of the "declining significance of race" (Wilson 1978, 1987), as well as the conviction that school is an institution that neutralizes the privileges associated with race.

EMBRACING THE AMERICAN DREAM AND COMPETITIVE GIVING

Owning a home, an expensive car, and good clothes, and obtaining the best possible schooling for one's children are labeled prestigious goals and associated with imagining the American Dream.[10] These symbols of success are also frequently associated with conformity. Most school officials desire them, but at the same time they want to maintain a distance from the Other—that is, they do not want to be carbon copies of White Americans. This, the epicenter of their dilemma as the "educated Other," often leads them to display their connectedness to the Black community through competitive giving[11] (Benedict 1934; Harris 1974, 1989) and other "weapons of the weak."

Of these four symbols of success, home ownership is the most highly coveted and anxiously sought.

> Ms. Yanmon pointed out that Mr. Madison appears to be absent from school even more than usual this year. She and Ms. Sampson gave me the "lowdown" on Mr. Madison's new home in Virginia, an hour-and-a-half to two-hour drive from Capital. Mr. Madison lived in the nearby Maryland suburbs until this year, in a home he purchased several years ago. Desiring to move up in the world, he rented his old home to Mr. McGriff shortly after the latter became the principal of Capital. Mr. Madison then moved his wife and three children to a new, larger, and more ostentatious home, with a three-car garage. (Fieldnotes, November 22, 1982)

> I was surprised at the size of Ms. Aldine's house . . . It was very large and, since neither she nor her husband has children, seemed too big for two people . . . As I stood in line for the buffet, I observed the huge sunken living room with its oriental rugs, custom-made draperies, and original art work. The house had been custom built by the previous owner, and he had not cut corners. The picture window looks out on a beautiful green forest. In the rear of the house is a swimming pool. Ms. Mentor told me that Ms. Aldine and her husband own the house next door as well. Later Ms. Aldine showed me the bedroom section of the house. The whole house was tastefully decorated, with expensive whatnots and vacation souvenirs scattered throughout. [T]here were only three bedrooms on the main floor, but there were four baths—one each for two bedrooms and two in the master bedroom. (Fieldnotes, March 31, 1983)

There were many conversations about home ownership and living on the edge or even beyond one's financial means in order to own a home.[12]

Despite the many hardships that might be associated with home ownership, its desirability remains disproportionate to any other symbol of success. A really nice home was something to be shared with one's colleagues, to validate one's success as defined by the larger society. Some teachers argued that having a well-furnished, "important" house had its roots in the slave experience, where the kind of home one lived in signaled one's social status—master or slave. Not to own a home made an undesired admission: I have not quite arrived. Doubts about Mr. McGriff's appropriateness as the symbol of Capital High based not only on his lack of his own home were intensified by his decision to lease a house from Mr. Madison, his subordinate.

Not every teacher and administrator at the school displays an equal desire for material wealth, nor does that desire manifest itself in the same way. Some teachers love clothes and cars and expend an inordinate amount of energy seeking to obtain them. Others are preoccupied with the image projected by the home they own. Still others do not care much for any of these symbols.

Holidays offered Capital's teachers and administrators critical opportunities to celebrate their achievement of the American Dream. At the same time, however, they smothered the individual's subversive involvement in the world created by African-Americans. Holidays were therefore both stressful and exciting, fraught with tensions and exhilaration that vividly revealed the ambivalence that is central to their lives. On the edge of both the Black and White communities, they are forced to be endlessly vigilant regarding the shifting and in many ways conflicting nuances associated with divergent rituals. For example, for many of them it was necessary to be observant of both Christmas—as their children were taught to observe it in school—and Kwaanza, the middle-class African-Americans' form of Christmas. Unfortunately, the celebration of one often led to accusations of a lack of reverence for the other. Holidays became a time of heightened tension in which the norms and values in each community were threatened with violation and pollution. In addition, they represented opportunities both to display one's achievement and success as defined by the larger society and, conversely, to invert the adopted hoarding practices of the dominant community by embracing the Black community's fictive kinship system and sharing, sharing, sharing. Norm violation, then, was inevitable.

While the level of sharing varied with the individual, it was a common response of the African-American adults at the school. In many ways, sharing—that is, a form of competitive giving—is a cultural imperative *within* the African-American community. One is not fully accepted by the community unless one publicly displays evidence of one's success through sharing or returning to the community some of what the individual has achieved.

Ms. Josey had prepared food as if there were no tomorrow.
We all trooped upstairs through her beautifully carpeted den,
through the spacious kitchen with the microwave oven built
into the wall and the gorgeous plants, to the dining room,
where a smorgasbord of homemade dishes awaited us in heat-

controlled containers. Faculty members loaded their plates (not paper plates but real, inordinately expensive dinnerware and china) with the various meats (chicken, Swiss meatballs, chicken liver pâtés), salads, rice, and potatoes, vegetables, and rolls that she had baked. (Fieldnotes, March 31, 1983)

For some contemporary middle-income African-Americans in Washington, DC, sharing food and hearth are among the most popular ways of showing continued connectedness to the African-American community. It is also one of the major ways of obtaining prestige in the community. But sharing and competitive giving are not limited to food or to money or other material symbols. Many African-Americans who make very little money and have very little wealth are warmly embraced by the Black community because they give of themselves, becoming engaged in church-related activities and supporting national and local Black organizations such as the NAACP, the National Urban League, and the United Negro College Fund. A prime example of sharing in ways that suggest one's materialistic success *and* connectedness to the dominant community is the Christmas party for Capital High's faculty and staff.

One of the male teachers, Mr. Fabre, invited his colleagues to have the school's Christmas party at the country club in his well-heeled suburban community. More than a third of the teachers and administrators paid $25 apiece for the buffet luncheon. The day of the party, everyone was "dressed fit to kill" in Christmas finery. Food was both plentiful and varied. Liquor was served at a cash bar. A kind of talent show was a part of the day's activities. Members of the Capital community temporarily put aside their personal animosities and hostilities in order to enjoy the festive occasion. There was dancing and drinking and much merriment. Once the official lunch ended, most of the group accepted Mr. and Ms. Fabre's invitation to their handsome home for an after-party that continued well into the evening.

BOOK-BLACK BLACKS AND THE EDUCATED OTHER

In the Capital community, book-black Blacks are those persons who have not been successful in avoiding the dreaded imposter image. They are the group members whose Black identity is uncertain. The most acrimonious conversations revolve around the appropriation of Otherness because representing the Other embodies issues of "contamination and assimilation." For example, do African-Americans who actively seek assimilation *become* White Americans? Or, alternatively, do African-Americans who only behave and talk like White Americans while interacting with White Americans unwittingly *become* White Americans?

Conversely, do African-Americans *remain* African and American regardless of their "White" facade or their honorary White status? More important, are African-Americans who become academically successful condemned to a life in which they must dominate others, including other Black people?

The conflicts surrounding these issues are manifested in the pendulum-like existence of African-American school officials. For them, migrating from the indigenous egalitarian system existing in the African-American community to the individualism of the dominant cultural system operating in the school context involves becoming nonhuman. It entails policing one's racialized identity while highlighting one's commitment to the norms, values, and beliefs of the larger society. Within the Black community, this obligatory, contested migration is culturally choreographed, marked by its artificiality, tautness, and lack of rhythm and spontaneity.

This pendulum-like process, however, entails much more than mere migration. A mental transmutation is also mandatory. It requires expunging one's perception of a Black Self, leaching one's racialized identity and all that is stereotypically associated with the Black fictive kinship system. Hence, for African-American school officials, a contested cultural metamorphosis is ordered. The individual must make an ethnic choice, renouncing what is familiar and known for what is distant and alien or finding ways to oppose marginality in both communities. Resistance as conformity appeared to be the weapon of choice among adults at the school.

African-Americans who teach in public schools are in no position to make an ethnic or cultural choice, at least not openly. Teachers who are of African ancestry are expected to teach and even praise the mandated curriculum, norms, and values of the state-mandated school system. The messy, entangled, incomplete, haphazard, yet obligatory nature of this process suggests that what appears to be the existing social reality may not be. Consequently, school officials who are African-American are likely to be in a transient state, endlessly attempting to become the distanced or educated Other. The fragmentary nature of mandatory Self-alienation lends itself easily to an internal and external perception widely held among contemporary African-American teachers. Something essential is missing.

In seeking to analyze the personal and professional dilemmas and personal angst of Capital High School teachers and administrators, I have become aware of an ethos that simultaneously embraces and opposes school norms and values. A threefold process is involved: creating, destroying, and preserving African-American teachers and other school officials as nonhuman[13] and as the educated "Other." Since sharing and hoarding are mutually exclusive in the Black fictive kinship system, learning to accumulate rather than to share, and concentrating on one's self rather than on others—these are archetypal weapons in the transition from the fictive kinship system to the valorizing of individualism that is characteristic of the larger social system.

Inevitably, the transition is discursive, nonlinear, and incomplete, flawed with messy, disorderly meanderings. Further, the serrated nature of the pendulum-like process is intimately implicated in the acquisition by teachers and other school officials of the undesired status of book-black Blacks—individuals whose appearance is African but whose identity and worldview may not be. Hence book-black Blacks are both honored and scorned, praised and ostracized.

CONTESTING DOUBLE-VISIONED LIVES: FUSING COMMUNALISM AND INDIVIDUALISM

Most of the faculty and staff at Capital are proud to be African-American. Nevertheless, as members of the crossover generation, they are pioneers in having to cope with racial ambivalence and conflict. Like the students they teach, they are trailblazers, without models to help them achieve their goals. Ambivalence toward the world that integration is creating is a common feeling among them because they exist in a value system forged from two contested social realities: the world created by the First Emancipation and the world evolving since the Second Emancipation. Because their sense of Self reflects both the limitations and the advantages of these two worlds, they struggle with the resulting double vision, or what Du Bois (1970[1903]) described as the "double consciousness" that these two realities construct. Also, as Woodson (1933) so poignantly noted, their "double consciousness" is welded to the "miseducation" that accompanies schooling in America. A male teacher contrasts his own experience and his response to his father's expectations with that of Capital students:

> When Mr. Mylan's parents spoke, the children listened. "They made darn sure that we twelve children studied three hours a night." Mr. Mylan grew up in a small Oklahoma town, and his parents supervised nightly their study time. Separate report cards were issued for each subject, and his father checked each child's report. In the tenth grade he received a D in geometry. When he got to him, Mr. Mylan thought he'd withhold the Geometry report card, but his mother noticed and said, "One of them is missing." To further demonstrate the insight and brilliance of his father, he talked about how he spent his sum-

mers. The family lived on a farm, and in the summertime Mr. Mylan read two or three books a day. When he tells his students these stories, they tend to think of his father as sadistic or something. In comparison with his experience, Mr. Mylan thinks that there is a big difference in the attitudes and values of today's Black youth and a comparable group when he was a youngster. He claimed that when he was a youngster, even the slowest kids tried to do well in school. (Fieldnotes, February 22, 1983)

This double vision produces a social group whose members—teachers and school administrators—are committed to their identity as African-Americans but whose attempts to resist by conforming inevitably cause discomfort and confusion. While the vast majority are proud to be African in origin, not many of them openly and self-consciously celebrate Blackness. Indeed, when one of them breaks the unwritten rule against openly attributing the oppressive conditions confronting them and their students to racism, he or she is viewed in ways that suggest the hemorrhaging of a reputation.[14] The case of Ms. Costen and the St. Patrick's Day letter described above is illustrative.

Mr. McGriff, the principal, is the quintessential example of the contradictions and alienation that are the inevitable outcome of attempting to resist by conforming. His unadulterated efforts to conform are fused to the stickiness of his Blackness, producing a persona marred by a nonlinear, nonpristine identity.

As I entered the building today, I met Mr. McGriff. He was carrying a briefcase and that, in my [limited] experience with him, was unusual. We exchanged greetings (he always seems sincere when he asks me "How are things going?") and I asked his destination. He said, "I've got to go to one of those regional meetings." The tone of his voice suggested that was not good news. But, since he is always moving at about twenty miles an hour, one can never be sure that he hears everything one says. I've asked myself since I have been coming to this school why they gave him an office. He is never in it. Rather, it is the place where teachers and other school personnel go to make telephone calls, hold informal and formal meetings, and so on. When I was leaving the building yesterday, a committee of teachers decided they would have their meeting in Mr. McGriff's office. He was not there, so there was no problem. As I was leaving the campus, he was outside on the sidewalk, talking with students and generally trying to see what was going on. (Fieldnotes, September 15, 1982)

Mr. McGriff has a reputation for "walking the Avenue." In his determination to round up students and get them back to Capital to attend their afternoon classes, he has even been known to chase the culprits up and down the Avenue. Mimi described how Mr. McGriff pursued students who were (or whom he suspected were) using drugs near the school's campus. This ritualized behavior was a regular occurrence.

> [The students] all outside and stuff. Mr. McGriff be chasing them and stuff. They be dropping drug things. That's how he catch them. They drop this stuff, and then he have to—he grab them, "Come here!" He take them in the building. He have this little walkie-talkie going in the street: "Went around the corner," people looking as he trapping them students and stuff. If students don't want to come to school, don't chase them. You can't *make* a person learn if they don't *want* to. Arcades, he just walk in the arcade and bomb them out and tell them to get out there. "Go to school. School is not a play— you don't supposed to play in school." (Interview, March 17, 1983)

Mimi also vividly described how Mr. McGriff took her for a Capital student a couple of years ago, when she was still attending a neighboring junior high school, and how he chased her up and down the surrounding streets.

> Oh, when I was down at junior high, and it was lunchtime down there, but it was fifth period here. And he came walking toward—told me to get in the building. And at the time I didn't know he was the principal here, I didn't know *who* he was, walking with a walkie-talkie in his hand. So he started running, and I started running. And I ran down Titan Street, I ran up Hunter Avenue, and he ran up there. I ran, 'cause I saw the little grocery store. And he told me to come on. He was huffing and puffing, and I was too. And then he told me to come on down the school, and took me in the office. And I was trying to tell him, and he was saying that I *was*, I *was*—he have to chase me every day. But he wasn't chasing me every day; he was chasing somebody else. And they called my mother, and my mother had to come get me. And then my mother was laughing, and I was laughing, but I was tired! 'Cause he chased me a long ways. Chased me—them houses there were condemned! And it was frames and stuff. And he just chased me! I was so mad—I was mad! I ran a long—I

said, "Look, I don't go to Capital! I don't go to Capital!"
"Yes, you do! Stop! Look here! Looka here!" And I was so
mad, and I told my mother. She was laughing, my father was
laughing, everybody was laughing. First, I was going to the
lunch truck, and then I was going back to my school. And he
just started running after me. I didn't know who he was! (Interview, March 17, 1983)

Mimi's perception of Mr. McGriff was forever influenced by his
mistaken identification of her and the chase that followed. When she
was asked if she thought his vigilant guarding of the building and the
students made a difference in the achievement levels of students at Capital High, her response differed from that of others.

Not at all, 'cause they don't do nothing but chase him away
again, 'cause [the students] think it's funny. They think it's
fun!—to have the principal chasing them up and down the
street. 'Cause he['s] crazy! [Laughter] He—and he misjudge
people. I was going to my locker one day, 'cause my teacher
let me go there to get my book, and he looked at me, and he
said, "It's a shame! Feel sorry for you! Feel sorry for you, just
feel sorry for you!" I said, but—"I just feel sorry for you!" He
misjudge people, he just chase them—I think he—I think he's
a patient, too! [Laughter] (Interview, March 17, 1983)

Mimi's response to the question regarding the efficacy of Mr.
McGriff's draconian efforts to save the school and its students embodies
the "contradictory unity" so prevalent in Black people's academic resistance: to transform an image of exclusion as failure. Her claim that "he's
a patient, too" implies that he has lost mental stability. Indeed, when
she was asked what she meant by "patient," she was unequivocal in her
answer: "I think he's a patient at St. Elizabeth" (the federal mental
hospital in the city of Washington).

Sometimes I *do,* 'cause he act *wild* sometimes. How many principals do you find that chase you up and down the street?
Now, he's a good principal, he just chase you too much. He *is*
a good principal. He *means* well, but—I'll put it, if *I* was the
principal, if they didn't want to come to school, that's their education. You can't make anybody learn if they—*I* wouldn't
chase them. I'd let them go. (Interview, March 17, 1983)

Mimi's perception of Mr. McGriff's mental health was shared by
Sidney and many other students. Sidney asserted that Mr. McGriff not

only goes into the fast-food restaurants but even goes into his neighborhood:

> *Anthro:* What does he usually say when students are in the
> fast-food restaurants after the time for them to be back on the
> school premises?
> *Sidney:* Well, "It's fifth period, folks. You should be in class!
> Another day, another A! Good books, good grades!" or some-
> thing like that. "You should be in the library," and stuff—
> yeah, he actually says that.[15]
> *Anthro:* He actually says that in the . . .?
> *Sidney:* Even in the street, yes.
> *Anthro:* I mean, even in the fast-food places he's . . .?
> *Sidney:* One day when we was at the McDonald's on Hunter
> Avenue, he told the owner not to serve the students.
> *Anthro:* He did? And what did she do?
> *Sidney:* She served them. They're paying! It's her job to feed
> them. They just looked at him and laughed. (Interview, March
> 17, 1983)

Another indication of the students' perception of Mr. McGriff was
their response to Mr. Gallant's announcement at the Black History assembly that the principal was not in school that day. (Mr. McGriff
was virtually never absent from school, hence the significance of the
announcement.)

> Why Mr. Gallant felt the need to make such an announcement
> was unclear, but when he walked on the stage near the end of
> the program and told the students that Mr. McGriff was ab-
> sent, many of them stood and applauded; virtually all the oth-
> ers at least clapped their hands . . . The consequences were
> not good. Students cut class and stayed in the hall all day be-
> cause they knew the principal was not there. While the assis-
> tant principals attempted to take up the slack, they were un-
> able to because of their other responsibilities and because they
> do not have the same status as Mr. McGriff. The students
> were/are very aware of the difference. (Fieldnotes, March 2,
> 1983)

When the students were asked if there was someone at the school
that they really admired and identified as a role model, Wendell's response was typical:

I know you don't think I'm going to say Mr. McGriff! . . .
'Cause I don't want to be like him or none of these teachers
and school administrators . . . Maybe Mr. Wrightman (a male
biology teacher who has not taught him). They say he got a
lot of money and everything. Money help. And money mess
you up sometime. (Interview, March 29, 1983)

Clearly, the students constructed Mr. McGriff in unflattering ways,
missing his complexity. Most students saw him as an uncritical conformist to the ideology of the larger society. He was a disciplinarian and a
book-black Black. In fact, his primary goal is to have them disprove the
reigning ideological claims regarding African-American academic prowess; he also wants them to be able to escape the stigma, the poverty, and
the degradation that are currently rampant in their lives. The only way
they can accomplish this goal, as he sees it, is through academic excellence in school. He persists in the pursuit of this approach to becoming
human even though he realizes the high cost they will have to pay.

When I mentioned that I had heard that Mr. McGriff "walks
the Avenue," a small group of teachers in one of the lounges
smiled and spoke approvingly of his efforts to keep the school
running smoothly. One of them described his penchant for removing litter. She noted that he does not limit this fetish to
the school but applies it outside on the surrounding streets.
She went on to say that he has been seen straightening the
road signs and generally displaying a real concern for the
school and neighborhood.
    Another teacher in the group was particularly appreciative
of Mr. McGriff's orientation. Having been at Capital since
1972, she feels that the past principals spent too much time in
their offices. She said that when Mr. McGriff came to Capital
three years ago he could not believe the dirt and the rodents in
and around the building. She maintains that he has made a big
difference in the school. When I asked if he ever came to their
rooms unannounced, teachers agreed that "he does it all the
time." (Fieldnotes, September 20, 1982)

Many of the teachers supported him because he made them feel safe
at work. His constant visibility in the halls of the school and on the
nearby streets, as well as his unorthodox practice of going into the fast-
food restaurants in the neighborhood and demanding that Capital students return to school, were critically important to his marginal acceptance by the teachers. On the other hand, his penchant for putting the
safety of the students and staff at the school at the top of a list of

priorities produced many undesired consequences, including a registration process that most members of the school—teachers and students—described as a "nightmare."[16]

Mr. McGriff uses many traditional and some not-so-traditional but socially approved measures to improve the academic performance of Black students at Capital. When I arrived at Capital, a copy of a memo from Mr. McGriff to the superintendent was in my mailbox. In the memo he described the concerns he had raised in the preceding week's faculty meeting about athletic events and other system-wide programs that took students out of their regularly scheduled classes. He reminded the superintendent of his unilateral decision to require a revision of DCPS policy and schedule football games at Capital on Saturday. Nevertheless, he noted, Capital students had to leave school *and* their classes early in order to play at other schools that allowed Friday games. He charged the DCPS with complicity in the poor performance of Black children through its failure to reschedule athletic events that interfered with instructional time:

> I believe that a student should attend class each and every day. Here, at Capital High School, if the student is to go on a trip, this trip must be approved by every classroom teacher and parents. Poor performing students cannot go, they must stay and study . . . The current policy in the DCPS encourages students to get involved in activities [that] enable them to miss portions of their academic programs on a regular basis; this is especially true of students involved in athletics . . . In the D.C.P.S. we must also realize that we are contributing to the failure of our students if we condone, and schedule, time away from the classroom as well as time not directed by the certified instructor. I believe that all D.C.P.S. activities can be planned so that our students begin and complete a *full day of learning*. When this occurs, everyone connected with the D.C.P.S. can join us in stating the [Capital High School] motto, "Res G____ Per Virgutem"—"Achievement Through Excellence."
>
> Mr. McGriff,
> Principal

(Fieldnotes, January 31, 1983)

Mr. McGriff insisted that academics take precedence over *all* other activities. (See Schofield [1989] for a similar response pattern among the teachers at Wexler School.) When he repeatedly postponed the Black History Month assembly, Mr. McGriff claimed that it was not important in assuring the students' mastery of school-sanctioned learning. The activities that counted in the school context, he claimed, were those that celebrated "Otherness" rather than the Black "Self." He argued that none of the activities and learning that emerged from the celebration of Black History Month would be included on standardized examinations and, therefore, they had no value in the school context. Their exclusion from standardized tests led him to define and identify them as "frivolous."

My fieldnotes regarding the cancellation of the proposed Black History Month assembly, scheduled for the second period on March 1, indicate some support for Mr. McGriff's attitude:

> Indeed, some teachers have complained that some of their students are out of class in order to practice for the assembly. When I finally got to Ms. Mentor's classroom, I was startled to learn that the assembly had been canceled. An assortment of reasons were given: (1) one teacher dismissed his first period class and took his students to the auditorium instead; (2) some teachers didn't even bother to go to homeroom this morning but instead went directly to the auditorium or loitered in the halls; (3) Mr. McGriff didn't like the idea of all the pom-pom girls and other band members walking in the halls, wearing only the "skimpy" band uniforms. Ms. Mentor insisted that the students were quite angry, and a lot of teachers were disappointed in that they, like the students, had anticipated going to the assembly rather than remaining in the classrooms today. (Fieldnotes, March 1, 1983)

Whatever his quirks, Mr. McGriff is not a one-dimensional person. He suffers from double vision, which, as with most of the other people at the school, leads to a kind of personal purgatory, in which middle-class White American individualism is soldered to the fictive kinship norms that dominate important aspects of his life and the lives of the students at Capital High.

> Ms. Sampson admitted to me that she had called Ms. Yanmon last night to tell her about meeting Mr. McGriff at one of those thriving thrift shops near her home. She said it was not something that she would want the entire school to know, but as she was taking some old clothing from her home to sell at the thrift shop, she met Mr. McGriff. He was browsing through the store and she could tell that this was not a once-in-a-lifetime venture. Indeed, everyone in the store knew him by name. Mr. McGriff greeted her and said, "If you see me with something different on tomorrow, Ms. Sampson, don't tell anyone." Ms. Sampson thought this was the strangest be-

havior for a principal. She and Ms. Yanmon then talked about the fact that he frequently wore jackets that were too big for him and they concluded that they were probably thrift store items. Further, they noted the inordinate number of whatnots in his office and the library. According to Ms. Sampson, the library houses plastic plants and flowers, stuffed birds, etc., that were obviously bought at the thrift store and put in the library. She also observed that when he got married (again) about a year ago, the items in this category proliferated, probably "because his new wife made him get some of that junk out of their house." Ms. Sampson prodded me about whether or not I had seen the numerous whatnots in the library. She suggested that I go upstairs with her *at that very moment* to see them. When I hesitated, she became more persistent. We walked up to the library. She pointed out the numerous items, including plastic plants and flowers and a stuffed bird on the wall. She then directed me to the hallway near the main office where she pointed out the pictures of Black pioneers in education, religion, politics. I had seen all of these things before, but she wanted me to be sure to know that they were given to the school by Mr. McGriff, who, she insisted, bought them at the thrift shops in the neighborhood. (Fieldnotes, October 29, 1982)

My informants thought Mr. McGriff's tendency to buy used items for the school (as well as clothe himself) at the local thrift shop was one of the strongest signs of his lack of understanding of and perhaps even his lack of qualification for the job of principal at the school. They were embarrassed by his behavior. To think that their principal shopped at the local thrift shop! How could he disregard his status as principal of Capital in this way? Did the students' parents know of this bizarre behavior? Did their colleagues outside Capital see him shopping at the thrift shop? To their minds, reputation was 90 percent of the problem. Preventing the hemorrhaging of one's reputation was something that everyone should work at.

There is also the image of a man who sometimes lords his schooling over them:

Our conversation evolved to a discussion of Mr. McGriff, whom we could see outside the building, making his usual inspections. Ms. Mentor remembered a résumé he had given to the faculty and staff when he had his first faculty meeting at Capital. She located it and shared it with me. Looking at it, I made the idle comment that I was certain such a résumé

would cause the Capital faculty and staff to react negatively—he appeared *too* educated. She denied that. I pushed
the issue, noting that she does not like him. She denied that
her dislike had anything to do with the large number of paper
credentials he possesses. Instead, she claimed, she disliked him
because when he came to Capital, he would refer to his schooling experience in Pennsylvania and how he had always had
White teachers. She despised this attitude in Black people,
largely because she sees it as a slap in the face, since she is a
Black teacher. Nor does she agree with the message implicit in
such a statement (my teachers were White so I got a better education), especially since her comparative experiences suggest
that some of the best teachers for Black children are Black
teachers. (Fieldnotes, February 2, 1982)

Mr. McGriff's seemingly unconditional commitment to the ideological claims of the larger society broadened the teachers' resistance. Many
argued that his administrative approach took the *J* out of joy. His refusal
to allow the students to have pep rallies and after-school dances was
viewed with suspicion and even hostility. One announcement signed by
him read as follows:

1. Students—All students are expected to be preparing for 3rd
Advisory Grades and Final Examinations. There are no more
Talent Shows or Musical Shows planned for the remainder of
the year. It is time to make up work, study and prepare for
good final grades. I make all decisions for students as if you
were my own children. This is important for you to know.

Mr. McGriff

(School Bulletin, March 23)

On the other hand, Mr. McGriff's unilateral decision to hold all
football games at Capital on Saturday rather than Friday won widespread approval. Sports in general were widely perceived as vulgar and
low in status in the social hierarchy of possible activities.

In addition to being ambivalent about the decisions Mr. McGriff
made, many of the teachers, especially those with the most seniority,
were constantly comparing him with the last White principal. My informant, who claims to be fourth in seniority at the school, came to Capital
in 1966, and that, in her mind, was "the best of times."

The administration, she argued, could "administrate." She did
not note any flaws in the principal's character or repertoire of
administrative skills. She claimed that he knew *what* to do,
and if he did not know *how* to do it, he had surrounded him-

self with assistants who did. When I asked her if this competent administrator was Black, she replied, "Unfortunately, he
was White." I then asked if Capital had had anyone since the
last White administrator who was comparable in administrative capabilities. She said, "None, bar none."

Mr. McGriff, she acknowledged, had eliminated many of
the disciplinary problems at the school. Between 1970 and
1980, she claimed, one could not get through the halls at the
school, and, indeed, there had been three or four fights a day.
She asked, "Have you seen or heard about many fights?" I
said no. She grudgingly attributed the improvement to Mr.
McGriff's high visibility in the halls and around the building.
(Fieldnotes, January 3, 1983)

These images of the faculty and staff at Capital, as projected through
the school's principal, must be juxtaposed with an equally powerful
image of this man as Capital High's greatest cheerleader. Personifying
Denton and Sussman's description of the crossover generation (1981),
Mr. McGriff's baggage is loaded with what Bakhtin (1981) calls contradictory unity. Like most African-Americans, Mr. McGriff is a strong
believer in the ideology of integration and equality for all. His commitment to the efficacy of schooling is so strong that for many of the students he is guilty of acting white, thereby alienating himself from them
and from many members of his staff. It is important to note that Mr.
McGriff constructs his conformity efforts as resistance to the dominant
imaging of the intellectual capabilities of Black people.

CELEBRATING AND VIOLATING DOMINANT GENDER NORMS

African-American adults at Capital High are conditioned to embrace the
gender-specific roles traditionally assigned White, Euramerican males
and females. The most gender-specific roles have been appropriated from
the dominant community. As indicated in chapter 4, African-American
males appear to be most visibly victimized by their inability to approximate the dominant society's construction of masculinity. Like Black
males in other contexts, those in the academy, broadly defined, both
celebrate and violate dominant social norms. Their "cool pose" might
well be interpreted as a weapon of the weak. At Capital High this is
manifested in the role-overload of most of the adult males—their constant, although discordant, personas surfacing in ways and contexts that
interrupt and violate existing hegemony.

Similarly, among African-American women at the school, the ongoing low-grade pain associated with the unavoidable violation of the

gender-specific role traditionally assigned women in the dominant society is everywhere apparent. Constructed primarily by what they lack vis-à-vis White females, African-American females are buffeted by the juxtaposition of survival needs and belonging needs (Kadi 1993; Maslow 1954; Tracy 1991). There is Ms. Dressler, for instance, who could accurately be dubbed Ms. Hollywood. (Her only rival for the title is Ms. Albaney, the White Spanish teacher.) Her abandonment of the more traditional womanly role for a working role is necessitated by an economic imperative. She does not work just to "shop until she drops" but to maintain the lifestyle to which she has become accustomed: material symbols are critically important to her self-esteem.

> Ms. Dressler readily admits that she hitched her wagon to an older woman at one of the junior high schools where she was employed, and this woman taught her the ropes. They "hunted" the physicians at Howard University Medical School, playing around in some of the "bad" (i.e., good) homes on upper 16th Street, N.W. (the "Gold Coast"). She asserted that she had had a ball there and made some excellent contacts. As she offered her colleague these gems of wisdom, she powdered her nose, brushed her lips with her lip brush, and combed her hair, noting that today was her day to go to the beauty shop. (Fieldnotes, February 16, 1983)

The impact of Ms. Dressler's values and behaviors are conveyed in the following excerpt from my fieldnotes, detailing my reactions to an interview with Nekia, one of the underachieving female informants.

> Apparently, Nekia is extremely impressed by material goods. Her favorite teacher, Ms. Dressler, is a conspicuous consumer. She drives a late model Mercedes convertible, wears fancy designer-label clothes, and goes to the beauty parlor every week. Nekia wants to be like her. She often calls Ms. Dressler "Mom," I have heard, and Nekia has told me that she goes to church with her some Sundays. (Fieldnotes, March 9, 1983)

In the female teachers' conversations about their conjugal life, the areas of greatest conflict centered around their husbands' and lovers' fears that they make more money, or soon will, or are perceived to be more successful than men. These males' fears of loss of control as symbolized by the amount of money they make vis-à-vis their wives haunt the women constantly. They are trying to be all they can be in their work while at the same time reflecting their husbands' individual definitions of the perfect female body. These competing expectations were at the core of their dilemma and their violation of the dominant gender-specific female role.

Separation and divorce are the norm among female teachers at Capital High. Many have experienced painful divorces in which their former spouses sought to make life without them miserable. For example, Ms. Apropos's husband left her and their three children more than ten years ago. The following excerpt from my fieldnotes records what she told me about the end of her marriage and her response to it.

> Ms. Apropos sees herself as a frugal person. When her husband left her with a large, heavily mortgaged house and three children, he told her that she would not last three months: she'd call him in three months to come back home. That prediction was not realized. She has retained the house with ten rooms and a present mortgage of $525 monthly. She has learned to shop for designer clothes at thrift shops. She had on a beautiful blouse today which she described as an R&D that in a store would have cost, according to her, more than $40. She paid only $1.98 for it. I sat there in disbelief! She went on. All of the fine blouses she loves, she buys at thrift stores, and she has even bought shoes (new ones only) at such stores. She maintains that Black women have always found ways to survive and that they don't need men to do it. When I mentioned that since she had been separated from her husband for so long, she had probably gotten over the pain which is frequently associated with such occurrences, she laughed heartily. "Pain?" she said. "The dissolution of our marriage was the best thing that could have happened to me." (Fieldnotes, October 13, 1982)

Many of the women told stories about their attempts to save their marriages, acknowledging that their husbands were extremely committed to the dominant gender-specific definitions of maleness. Their responses indicated that they attached a stronger value to the notion of relationship than to the traditional definition of femaleness. This orientation led them to focus on negotiation and compromise. But their former spouses' all-consuming efforts to control them, to make them totally dependent, thereby limiting their contacts with nonfamily members and even members of their profession, made it impossible to continue the marriage once they gained a little self-confidence. They also shared with me their "nonlinear, polyrhythmic and . . . nonsymmetrical notions" of their role as wife/mother/woman. Elsa Barkley Brown (1988:15) has described this approach to life as being reflective of African-American culture. She argues that "African-American women have indeed created their own lives, shaped their own meanings, and are the voices of authority on their own experience." Such notions were consistent with the female teachers' willful, yet silent, refusal to accept Euramerican and White male definitions of what is and is not an appropriate female body.

Most of the female teachers assert that conjugal conflict is strongly associated with male efforts to control their lives in ways that parallel White male control of their spouses' lives. Black males' more limited access to and command of economic resources, they repeatedly asserted, tend to make such control more problematic in the conjugal relationships of African-American people. Ms. Apropos described her struggle with her estranged husband to bring an official end to their marriage.

> Her ex-husband constantly contests her divorce attempts. While they've been separated ten years, she has not been able to obtain a divorce because he contests her attempts, making the legal fees more than she can pay. She wants to find a man to marry, but she does not plan to be his "slave" as she was in her first marriage. Having gotten married at nineteen, she was naive about life and men. She did all the wifely things, including preparing a dazzling meal on Sundays, which was what he wanted. She asserted that he has never given the two older children any money for their support since he left; he does give the younger one a little money. (Fieldnotes, March 15, 1983)

The society's structural constraints make it difficult for African-Americans, particularly African-American males, to compete effectively for careers and jobs comparable to those of their white counterparts. Such restrictions mean that both sexes have to find alternative ways of displaying and honoring patriarchy in the Black community.[17] They are compelled to find a way to survive in spite of their inability to live the American ideal of "husband and wife and happy children."

While the majority of African-American women at Capital have been or are currently married, they are forced to violate the traditional cultural norms associated with the role of woman as wife. They do not, however, violate the role of mother except that they must work rather than stay at home during the day.

LIVING THE LIE OF A "WHITE" MIDDLE-CLASS LIFE

High blood pressure and other health problems are rampant among school personnel. Many teachers and administrators are overweight despite constant dieting. Smoking is not uncommon, and rumors of public and private drunkenness are not unusual. There is also gossip regarding drug use among some members of the teaching and administrative staff. Marital and family discord are openly acknowledged and discussed. Nearly everyone has an ex-spouse or will have one shortly. A significant number of the Black female teachers are unmarried.

Conversations are fraught with silent bullets. One-upmanship has been elevated to a fine art. Everybody accuses everybody else of being self-centered and breaching the idealized fictive kinship system. One continuous refrain is that the indigenous Black egalitarian ethos has been corrupted and is being replaced by the self-conscious construction of values that permeate the middle-class, White American value system. Conspicuous traits unanimously deplored are individualism and materialism. Yet virtually everyone reveals some indications of desiring the "good life" and "vulgar materialism" (West 1993). Acceptance of the markers is varied and uneven, but it is there nonetheless.

Battle fatigue is, in part at least, a result of the coerced migration of school officials: a perpetual state of anonymous psychological motion between the world continuously created and recreated by African-Americans and the world formulated and reformulated by White Americans. The lack of relief from this coerced migration and endless world-making is exacerbated by the frequent decision of school officials to live in predominantly White neighborhoods, where one is at least expected to socialize with one's White neighbors. This expectation carries with it the overt denial of both the existence and impact of racism in America. At Capital High, teachers and other school officials are obligated to live in both worlds, even to deny, through conformity, the existence of racism and its negative impact on their lives (M. Foster 1990; Siddle Walker 1993). The penalty for resisting dominant ideology is much higher if one does not also observe the norms and standards sanctioned by the dominant society. African-Americans at Capital would be more successful in the school context were they *more willing* than they apparently are to forswear any connection with a racialized Black identity.

Moreover, because these pendulum-like processes are ongoing and at some levels oppositional and interconnected, teachers and administrators at the school are endlessly at risk, some more than others. Further, despite the roller-coaster nature of their reality, the tensions and pressures which characterize their professional lives remain largely unmitigated. Despite the existence of this "ethnic option" to remain connected to the Black fictive kinship system or to seek membership in the dominant community, the beleaguered nature of their lives depletes their energy, stressing them until they are like taut, brittle rubber bands about to snap.

Mr. McGriff was standing at his regular observation post in the hall near his office in anticipation of the bell signaling the end of the second-period class. I noticed that he did not look as optimistic as he usually does. His face looked tense and tired. I stopped and said hello and told him of my concern regarding what looked like stress. I had some clear indication that he was under a lot of pressure this week because Ms. Raye, a math teacher, told me that he used the word "stress" when trying to resolve the problem between her and Ms. Largon, one of the assistant principals, on Tuesday. I had also been told of another incident between Mr. Madison, an assistant principal, and Mr. Fuston yesterday afternoon. Ms. Raye, whose room is across the hall from Mr. Fuston's (he's a history teacher), described the shouting match between Mr. Madison and Mr. Fuston as "near-violent." She did not know what precipitated it, but both men were very angry. I was not sure that Mr. McGriff knew about this altercation, but I guessed that he did and that he had probably been asked to serve as a mediator to resolve their feuding. I was right. He responded to my inquiry by noting that there are bad days and good days, that everything does not always work out as we might hope. He then said that he had to throw two professional adults out of his office this morning. (Fieldnotes, October 14, 1982)

A poignant example of "White" middle-class life was described by Ms. Yanmon, who lives in a predominantly White neighborhood in Bethesda. If there are other people of African ancestry on her block, she has not mentioned them. She has indicated that she is friendly with only one family on her street. She is constantly lamenting the fact that she has no one to go with her to the local Y, nor would any other Black person be there if she went alone. When it was suggested that she go alone and mix with the other people once she got there, she quickly and unequivocally nixed that idea. She pointed out that she is loath to be in another situation where she is forced to engage in what she described as "small talk." She declared, "I do that at church and in my neighborhood; I don't want no more of that" (fieldnotes, February 17, 1983).

Ms. Yanmon went on to indicate that the problems facing middle-class Black people are different from those confronting middle-class Whites, despite their comparable socioeconomic status. To support her claim, she noted that middle-class White parents frequently demand that their children earn money to obtain the clothes, the toys, the cars, and so on that they want. Further, she argued, while they may not make them earn every penny of the cost of whatever it is they want, the parents often insist that they contribute a portion, maybe half, and then they (the parents) will contribute the remainder. A middle-class Black family living in a predominantly middle-class neighborhood of either Black or White people is always suspected of not having enough money to live the life they are trying to live. To put a child out on the street selling newspapers, for example, suggests that his parents "ain't what they pretend to be," So Black children in such neighborhoods do not work outside the home.

This was the problem confronting Ms. Yanmon and her husband when it was their son's turn to deliver the county weekly advertising paper. All the White families in their neighborhood whose sons were older than theirs had delivered "The Advertiser," and their son was looking forward to doing it. But his father would not let him. Though it was a chance for him to earn money on his own, Mr. Yanmon saw it as a chance for the neighbors to see them as being unable to provide for their child, and he was adamant in his refusal to let him earn the money. Like many other Black families in their socioeconomic class, the Yanmons give their child every penny for everything he wants. Ms. Yanmon was not unmindful of the possible unintended consequences of rearing their child in this manner: he might internalize this lack of responsibility and come to take it for granted. Nevertheless, she mused, this is the reality for Black middle-income Americans.

In summary, then, practically every Capital teacher knows that his or her schooling has separated him or her, in some way, from the Black community—spatially or psychologically. Nevertheless, this is one of the best-kept secrets at the school, in that virtually no one publicly acknowledges his or her alienation and isolation from the vast majority of the students they teach.

SIX

School Success and the Construction of "Otherness"

One day, after Hargrave had won a [Scrabble] game and left the room, Jim said, "Hey, man, we can't let this white boy beat us on the Scrabble board." Initially, I didn't get it. "What's the problem?" "Don't you know this cracker thinks he's smarter than us because he's white and we're black? Can't you tell that? He's always trying to bluff us with medical words he thinks we don't know." I knew what Jim meant. I got the same feeling when I played whites at chess. I got the feeling that white boys automatically assumed they could beat me on the board because chess was a thinking person's game. I was black and they were white, therefore they were better thinkers. They never came out and said it, but I could tell by their confident body language and their smug analyses of moves made during games that they assumed they were superior. That's why, whenever I played whites at chess, the fun went completely out of the game. It was war disguised as a game. Every nerve in my body stood on end and my mind focused sharply on every piece on the board; I was like a boxer, eyeing an opponent's every feint and move, ready to use sharply honed reflexes to make him pay dearly for the slightest mistake. (McCall 1994:199–200)

For the high-achieving students at Capital High, pursuing academic success is a kind of warfare, a calculated conformity intended both to minimize a perception of "lack" and to achieve a higher social status. African-American students who opt to live beyond society's limited expectations for Black people feel compelled to "pass" by taking on the identity of (an)Other.

For high-achieving African-American adolescents at Capital High *warfare* is the appropriate term for academic achievement because they are resisting two competing yet similarly debilitating forces: the dominant society's minimal academic expectations for Black students and

235

their classmates' internal policing for group solidarity. Among the high-achieving students, resistance was manifested as conformity. They resisted dominant expectations by imagining schooling as a kind of warfare they were fighting not only for themselves but for the larger, imagined Black community as well, each "a young soldier for the revolution" (Davis, quoted in hooks 1989:10). They were aided in this effort by their parents and other family members who shielded them from any distraction from this goal.

Among the high achievers, resistance is manifested by selectively masquerading as the Other and subsequently using this feigned identity to elevate and transform the extant meaning of African-American humanness. Ideally, I argue, the high-achieving students seek to validate African-Americans' humanness by demonstrating the ability to perform academically in ways that parallel and even surpass those of their White American counterparts. Hence, they often eagerly seek to become indistinguishable from their dominant group counterparts in behavior, worldview, language usage, and so forth. Regrettably, as this analysis documents, *some* of those students are subsequently incarcerated in this dialectic, unable and unwilling to distinguish the imagined Self from the imagined Other and, more important, rejecting extant images of the Self while literally attempting to appropriate the identity of the Other (see Gates 1994: xiii). The dominance of the imagined Other in this struggle for the mind of the Self leads to the emergence of a raceless Self, or, as Said (1989) describes it, the creation of a subversive Self. This subversive or raceless Self obtains legitimacy and acceptance through denying connectedness to other Black Americans, their African ancestry, and all things black (Gates 1994: xiii). Each student group, high- and underachieving, is aware of how the other group perceives, defines, and reflects or deflects Otherness. Each group rejects the strategies the other uses to reclaim the appropriated identity of African-Americans.

Achievers who are uncertain about the efficacy of schools and schooling respond in ways that camouflage their efforts to achieve. Conflict and ambivalence regarding possible accusations of acting white intensifies their uncertainty, which is further exacerbated by their conscious and unconscious efforts to enact hybridity. Like the majority of the students at the school, they are convinced by the very texture of their lives and the lives of their parents and other Black adults in the Capital community that their efforts to achieve upward mobility through school performance very probably will not outweigh the import of their racialized identity. Consequently, the academic performance of these high-achieving students is characterized by conformity as resistance, ambivalence, and stress. Nevertheless, their desire to reclaim what they imagine as the humanness of their ancestors and their lingering belief in the

American Dream frequently overcome their doubts and fears, inspiring them to keep trying to do well in school despite the growing evidence around them that, for Black people, public life in America is not based on the existence of a meritocracy, as they have repeatedly been taught.

This small kernel of hope, coupled with the critical approval of their parents, other Black and White adults, their teachers and other school officials, as well as their conscious and unconscious commitment to the reclamation[1] of Black America's appropriated humanness, lies behind the willingness of the high-achieving students to resist and to persevere in a belief in the power of schooling to transform their lives. It is undoubtedly this small kernel of hope that propels their academic effort and mires their lives in a swamp of contestations.

CONSTRUCTING "OTHERNESS" AT CAPITAL HIGH

At Capital High, academic success embodies the construction of "Otherness," the production of an image that is not "equated with 'lack' in a pejorative sense" (Chow 1993:48). Because the perception of becoming (an)Other inevitably involves liquidating the Black Self at some level, the process is often avoided or, when engaged in, left hyphenated and incomplete. At the center of the construction is a mandate to "cope with the burden of 'acting white'" (see Fordham 1988, 1991a, 1991b; Fordham and Ogbu 1986). "Acting white" implies both Gramsci's (1971) notion of hegemony plus impersonation, the power and ability to act buttressed by the assumption of an image external to the Black Self, an image that is not bloated by a perception of "lack." The construction of Otherness is an open secret at Capital High. It governs much of what is defined as success. Students who seek academic success risk being accused of acting white, of seeking to become the dominant "Other."

The high-achieving students at the school realize that they are likely to be identified in this way. In anticipation of this accusation, many of them have self-consciously developed strategies that enable them to minimize the alienation associated with academic excellence. A few in this group readily admit that they are *acting* in defiance of both existing group norms and the expectations of the larger society. Their general response to these expectations is to insist that race and cultural differences do not seriously alter one's perceptions or worldview, for there is only one way to be human. Thus, for many of them, humanness is a cultural universal, undifferentiated by the individual histories and cultures of the world's varied population groups.

As noted earlier, teachers and administrators at Capital High embrace the norms and values promoted and promulgated by the larger society. These norms are manifested in cumulative grade point averages, elementary and junior high school grades, school and classroom behavior, performance on standardized tests, extracurricular activities, and so forth. These are the only official criteria that are supposed to count in determining who "makes it" at Capital High. Even when other "official" criteria are included, the formal criteria weigh most heavily in the evaluation process.

Cumulative Grade Point Average

For the purposes of my study, I chose six males and six females who were identified by teachers, counselors, and administrators as being among the highest-achieving eleventh-grade students at Capital High. School records confirmed the assessments. Thus all twelve of the high-achieving key informants began the academic year with a cumulative grade point average of B or higher, and all but two of them—one male and one female—had been inducted into the National Honor Society by the end of their junior year.

Teachers and other school personnel who recommended these students generally evaluated them "in the round" (Bailey 1977). That is, they tended to evaluate the whole person, with GPA being only one of the features of academic achievement. For example, one student in the high-achieving category—Adam—had a cumulative GPA of B, but his name, more than any other, surfaced among responses of school personnel when they were asked to identify "successful students." Adam was considered one of the students "most likely to succeed," with GPA being only one of the reasons.

Elementary and Junior High School Grades

All of the high-achieving students in the research sample made consistently good grades in elementary and junior high school. In fact, three of the six high-achieving males were valedictorians of their junior high classes, and the other three graduated in the top ten percent. Only one of the female students graduated from junior high school with honors; all of the others graduated in the top ten percent of their classes.

Rita is the only exception to this composite image. Unlike most of the other high-achieving students, she has not received consistently good grades—even in elementary and junior high school. Her approach is pragmatic: if she needs to do well in order to keep from failing, she will. She thus draws the line at failure, insisting that such a grade is not an option for her, in part because she is an African-American. During elementary and junior high school, her grades vacillated from very good—even excellent—to failing. Rita constructed her academic image in this way partly because she periodically chose to "put brakes" on her academic effort and partly because of poor health. At the time she lost the sight in one eye, she also suffered from an ear infection and was out of school for an extended period. Hence, Rita is the only female high achiever in the group who is not a member of the National Honor Society. Nevertheless, her overall performance on standardized examinations, for example, the PSAT, exceeds that of all other members of the high-achieving female sample. And she is the only member of the high-achieving sample to be nominated to receive a National Merit Scholarship for Outstanding Negro Students.

Behavior
Research shows that in assessments and evaluations by teachers, in-school behavior of African-American students is given much greater weight than the conduct of White students (see W. Cary 1976; Leacock 1969, 1970, 1982; Lightfoot 1973; Rist 1970, 1973). Findings suggest that African-American students often earn good grades at least as much for displaying appropriately deferential behaviors as for doing well on tests, classwork, homework, and other assignments, thus documenting Ogbu's (1981a) claim regarding the patron-client nature of African-American school performance.

High-achieving Rita, though not known as a "bad kid," was not regarded as a "nice kid" either. Baffled peers and teachers were apt to call her "crazy Rita." All of the other high-achieving key informants were widely known as "nice kids"—well-behaved, polite, helpful, and respectful. They were generally very quiet and inconspicuous when in school, so quiet that they were virtually invisible. They came to class regularly and punctually, and they generally did what they were told to do without regard for their personal feelings vis-à-vis the tasks assigned. An exception occurred when one of the high-achieving females— Katrina—balked at appearing on television in "It's Academic," the most "intellectual" high school contest in Washington. When her counselor insisted that she compete, she made it quite clear to the sponsor that, while she was obligated to take part in the preliminaries, she refused to be put in the position of being forced to participate in the actual TV contest. As her counselor anticipated, she scored higher than any of the other students competing for the one remaining position, but she was spared the awful fate of appearing on TV only because the club's sponsor chose to respect her feelings.

The high-achieving students are never involved in fighting or any other actions that could be described as violations of school norms. All of them insist that they are not into drinking, smoking, or drugs. All of the females insist that they are not sexually active; indeed, half of them are not permitted to date. Several of the male high achievers, on the other hand, have begun dating.

Performance on Standardized Tests

Though a first-rate performance on standardized academic tests is usually equated with the ability to get good grades in school, the equation did not always hold for participants in this study. Several of the high-achieving students scored below the national norm on the CTBS and the PSAT, even though they have cumulative GPAs of at least a B. In this particular sample of high-achieving students, excellent behavior and industriousness would seem to have more bearing on obtaining good grades than what can be measured by the standardized tests administered at Capital High. Good students apparently respond to tough courses.

It also seems significant that all eight of the high-achieving students who take most of their classes from the regular curriculum program scored lower on standardized measures of school success than the four students who take all of their courses from the advanced placement offerings. Perhaps what is most informative about the test results of those students who take the regular course offerings, however, is the seemingly inverse relationship between the high GPAs of the students and their performance on standardized measures of school success. One might speculate that these students would do well in the easier courses of the regular curriculum, and teachers would reward their accomplishments.

Studying and Homework

Among their classmates, students appear to gain respect and recognition if they give the impression that they earn good grades without studying or completing assigned homework. Giving that impression seems to be particularly important for male students, whose identity as males may be jeopardized by working for good grades. For example, Norris, who attended a local elementary school, has always been able to perform well in school without much effort. Indeed, he considers his apparent lack of effort as being critically important to his acceptance by his peers despite his high performance in school. Because he did not study in their presence in elementary and junior high school, he appeared to have a "talent" or special gift, and was therefore not thought to be a brainiac or, worse, a "pervert" brainiac.[2]

Of the twelve high-achieving students, only four would admit that they devote some time to studying—a sharp contrast to the ten who readily acknowledge that they complete most written homework assignments. In fact, most do study, although surreptitiously. For instance,

Katrina rises as early as 5:00 most school days in order to prepare for class. The only one of her peers who knows about Katrina's early morning sessions is her best friend, Sakay, who keeps Katrina's secret.

Extracurricular Activities
Nine of the high-achieving students are engaged in least one extracurricular activity. Athletic activities are primarily a male domain among the high-achieving students, with only two of the high-achieving females— Rita and Celesa—participating in sports events. Three of the students are members of JETS—the engineering club; ten were members of the National Honor Society by the end of the base year of the research; one belongs to the Chess Club, which has a membership of two. Three students are members of the math club; three students participate in the band; two—Katrina and Paul—participate in "It's Academic" activities. One student is a member of the Student Government Association; one is in the Future Teachers of America; and one is in Future Business Leaders.

RECONSTRUCTING "OTHERNESS" AS BLACK RESISTANCE

Compliance as Resistance: The Female Students
Contemporary African-American adolescents are tormented by a history of systematic exclusion from the academy. Regrettably, this has been socially reconstructed to mean lack of academic capability. Most of the high-achieving and underachieving students at Capital are conscious of this odious stereotype. Their response is to resist.

In general, the high-achieving students' resistance is manifested in their determination to outdo society's limited expectations of them. In the school context they actively construct an image that invalidates such expectations. Their central problem is that, in doing so, some of them internalize the identity of the Other. For instance, Rita has accepted uncritically, while at some levels rejecting unequivocally, the dominant ethos that emerged in the wake of the Civil Rights Movement: integration. She constantly struggles with the coexistence in her mind of two contradictory beliefs in her identity-fractured body. The first of these beliefs—that race is still a powerful deterrent to success in America—is more or less suppressed; the second—that each African-American is responsible for his or her social status and must bear the blame if he or she has not achieved success—structures her conscious belief system and is embodied in her verbal responses.

While both beliefs structure Rita's behavior, she does not want to see or hear anything that might suggest that Blackness is a persistent stigma.[3] Therefore, when Middlebury College in Vermont sent her a

brochure indicating that the school had a club that welcomed Black
students, she was incensed.

> I mean—okay, this college sent me a Third World . . . I mean,
> they said, "We have a Third World Club." A place for Blacks!
> I mean, the audacity! To even think that I would go to a col-
> lege that has a club for Blacks! I was . . . Okay, Middlebury
> —I went to the college—but they sent me this little pamphlet
> that said, "Minorities at Middlebury"—like, "Do they exist?"
> or something like that . . . I mean, it's like—"Well, we put
> them aside in some other place," or something—I don't care.
> I say, well, I mean, I suppose minorities go there—I mean, I
> guess at least a few of them—there were only twenty-five
> there, out of the whole school. But nevertheless, I *know*
> they're there by you sending me this pamphlet. I don't appreci-
> ate it! (Interview, May 4, 1983)

Presumably the intention of school officials at Middlebury was simply to assure her that she would not be alone—racially—if she chose
their school. They did not realize that she would read their response as
the perpetuation of a "spoiled identity" (Goffman 1963) and would be
totally offended by their action.

Essentially, Rita's commitment to the ideals of the larger society
leads her to actively internalize the construction and celebration of Otherness embodied in academic success. It also encourages her not only to
try to "conceal" (Granfield 1991:338–343) her identification with and
connectedness to the African-American community but also to attempt
to become the Other (see Fordham 1993). Unlike some of the other
high-achieving females who mask their African-American identity beneath a facade of Otherness—"making it by faking it," as Granfield
says—Rita and several others seek to construct an identity that highlights
their commitment to Otherness.

This commitment is manifested in their responses to questions about
Black people and White people—these responses are invariably normative in nature—and to the ideals espoused in textbooks and set forth in
such documents as the Declaration of Independence and the Constitution, which they tend to interpret literally. They want desperately to
believe in the democratic ideals and therefore deny that there is a lack
of congruence between the ideal reality they are taught in school and
the socially constructed reality they are compelled to create. They claim
that their parents never taught them anything about race and racial
matters (see chapter 4), and they tend to argue that their views on racial
issues are grounded in biblical teachings. Hence, they are constantly
struggling with the dialectics embodied in the self-conscious construction

of an image of what they want to be, on the one hand, and who they really are, on the other hand, never quite becoming the Other they seek to become. A striking example is seen in the students' embracing of the terminology preferred by the dominant White population:

> Mr. Mylan was quite surprised to learn how the students [in his Black History class] self-identified during the first [meeting of the] class. He told me that he began by noting that there are quite a few labels used in referring to Black people. He put some of them on the board (Black American, Afro-American, Negro, Colored, Nigger, etc.). He then asked them which they preferred. To his chagrin, the majority said they preferred the label "Negro." While he refers to them as Black Americans, he felt obligated to respect their wishes and call them by the preferred term. This was the label he used until February 8, when a female student in the advanced placement program came to class for the first time. She would have no part of the "Negro" label. She was adamant in her insistence that her classmates identify themselves as Black Americans or she was going to have to leave the class. (Fieldnotes, February 22, 1983)

Katrina also highlights and celebrates the construction of Otherness. Like Rita, she vilifies Black music and several other predominantly Black cultural forms. She insists that she does not like Black music and that her musical tastes are more likely to be fulfilled on radio stations that play "crossover" music, a euphemism for music that is identifiably neither Black nor White. As for movies, she prefers musical comedies starring performers like Doris Day and Fred Astaire.

Like Rita, Katrina is a high-achieving eleventh-grade student at Capital. In fact, her academic performance was superior to that of any of her peers, enabling her to graduate valedictorian of her class in the second year of the study. Like Rita, Katrina seeks to avoid being identified with *and only with* the Black community. As a Black child born and schooled after the Second Emancipation, she is convinced that America is indeed the land of unparalleled opportunities and that those members of the Black community who do not make it have only themselves to blame. She puts responsibility for the socioeconomic deprivation in the Black community solely on the individual members of that community, absolving the larger society of any responsibility. I do not mean to suggest that Katrina and the other students who are the most vocal in their construction of Otherness do not also acknowledge that the history of African-Americans in this country predisposed earlier generations to poverty, but the focus of their analyses is contemporary America. Most of them believe that the problems of the past are no longer salient issues for African-Americans. If African-Americans are experiencing unemployment and other social ills, they say it is because they have opted not to pursue integration.

Katrina described neighborhoods in the Capital community as follows:

> Most of the people around my way don't care about a career or anything, they just . . . I think *they* want it on a silver platter, you know. I mean, they don't try hard enough, you know. Like, one girl I know, my sister's best friend—she's in the same place she's always been. She is working in the government, but she's getting welfare too. And she has three, going on four, children. Not married. And sometimes she doesn't go to work all the time. I remember my sister used to baby-sit for her, and she couldn't pay her because she wouldn't go to work. And sometimes she wouldn't even have the fare to *get* to work. I don't know [what she does with her money]. She has all these kids, and the guy she's with is a loafer, I think. (Interview, February 22, 1983)

In their responses, Rita and Katrina typify a group of the high-achieving students who experience inner struggle, tension, and conflict. Typical also is a nonverbalized effort to become more than or not only Black, to *resist* the prevalent stereotypes of what it means to be of African ancestry in America. In the process these students pay an enormously high price in that their individual psyches are riddled with ambivalence and uncertainties.

Rita and Katrina and this segment of the high-achieving student population have chosen to exercise the putative ethnic option that has become available to African-Americans during the Second Emancipation. The majority of African-American youths, however, are wary of the prevailing ideology that being Black in America is no longer to be equated with limitations, that African-Americans are now free to "choose" not to be Black (Morrison, quoted in E. Washington 1987; Carter 1993).

Lisa, for one, insists that the problems of African-Americans are both external and internal to the group, though heavily weighted toward the internal. Still, she asserts, if she were looking for a job today, she would have more difficulty getting one than a White person, simply "because I'm Black." In addition, she argues:

> Blackness is one strike against you. And having a certain level of education is *another* strike. White people sort of, like, stand out more. It seem like they really do know more, but—

because, I don't know if it's because the Black people are
scared to go out there and get what they want, or just feel
they are not capable of getting it. (Interview, March 17, 1983)

Similarly, Alice regards her mother's lack of a much-deserved job
promotion and her subsequent unemployment as evidence of the un-
fairness of the opportunity structure for African-Americans.

She worked at the Government Printing Office about ten
years, and then . . . then they fired her, 'cause she kept staying
off 'cause she got real sick. 'Cause she got a bad stomach.
And then . . . I think in 1979, she worked at Loyola Federal
Bank in Maryland. They fired her there 'cause they said she
wasn't doing her job right, but she *was*. She says she think it's
because she was Black. She was the only Black woman there.
Of about five women, she was the only Black woman there.
So she think it was because she was Black. (Interview, May 6,
1983)

Despite these widely shared perceptions, life histories, and experiences among high-achieving students, the females in particular persevere
in their quest for academic excellence, resisting contextual evidence and
popular assumptions about the limitations of Blackness. Though Alice
is forced to admit, based on her mother's experience, that racial discrimination is a reality in America, she is able to discount such evidence by
referring to her own experience: "It hasn't affected *me*—me personally,
I haven't come across no prejudice. There ain't no White person ever
looked down on me" (interview, May 6, 1983).

These students' convictions can be read as resistance to the larger
society's limited expectations, the negative connotations for education
associated with Blackness, and the pervasive poverty that is at the center
of their lives.[4] It is ironic that resistance is the weapon of choice among
the high-achieving students at Capital. The irony is centered in the way
they structure resistance: they defy the prevailing contentions that African-Americans cannot successfully compete with their White American
cohorts. Paradoxically, as they resist the popular stereotypes regarding
African-Americans' intellectual capabilities, they must also confront the
insidious process of their own internalization of the dominant Other and
must nullify peer resistance to what the peers interpret as the co-optation
of the bodies and identities of their schoolmates.

Resistance is the secret weapon in their arsenal that enables the
high-achieving students to internalize the component of the Other that
will enable them to transcend their present self-image, to both embrace
the Other and to attempt to liquidate the unacceptable Black Self. Their

resistance also embraces a long-standing tradition in the African-American community: the maintenance of hope in the face of dire conditions. Like their underachieving cohorts, they resist having African-Americans assigned a stigmatized social space. However, unlike the underachieving students, their resistance takes a form that conveys the following unambiguous message to the dominant Other: "Whatever you can do, I can do as well or better." Hence, they resist powerful evidence suggesting that Blackness is a deterrent to academic success.

The students in the newly introduced Black History class were primarily members of the advanced placement program. Because enrollment in the elective course was much greater than expected, officials had to offer an additional section. Mr. Mylan explained the heavy enrollment by insisting that "young people desire to understand their history." Curiously, this primarily subversive wish—"to understand their history"—exists in juxtaposition with an equally powerful mechanism that silently yet continually undermines the reluctant efforts of African-Americans to become assimilated by and identified with the dominant community.

Another example of the high-achieving students' dilemma is seen in Norris, who used his less successful friends to keep himself connected to the Black community while pursuing academic success. At Berkeley Elementary, which was, in Norris's terms, filled with "hoodlums, thugs, and the dregs of society," he had been academically ahead of most of the students in his class and in the school. At the same time, however, realizing that he had to live with those students, he planned a course of action that would minimize any obstacles to his academic development. Since fighting was a favorite pastime at Berkeley, Norris had deliberately chosen for friends individuals who would act as protectors in exchange for his help on homework assignments and tests. He had not been picky about who they were. He had simply wanted them to keep the other kids from beating him up or verbally harassing him so that he would be free to pursue his dream of academic excellence.

> I didn't want to—you know—be with anybody that was like me 'cause I didn't want to get beat up. The school I went to, Berkeley, was really rough, see? It was really rough. So I had to hang with people that were tough, you know? Lived in the projects and everything, and known tough and everything. So I used to hang with them. If anybody ever came in my face and wanted to pick on me, they'd always be there to help me. So I always made sure I had at least two or three bullies to be my friends. Even though if it does mean I have to give up answers in class, I was willing to give up a little to get a lot. So I did that for elementary school. (Interview, January 11, 1983)

Norris's alliance with the bullies and hoodlums in elementary school was a successful survival strategy. In junior high school, however, he chose a different one. He began to develop the "clown" or "comedic" personality that is still a part of his school persona:

> I had to act crazy then . . . you know, nutty, kind of loony. They say . . . "He's crazy"—not a *class* clown to get on the teachers' nerves, I never did that to the . . . around *them*. I'd be crazy. But as soon as I hit the classroom door, it was serious business . . . Only the people who knew me knew my crazy side; when they found out I was smart, they wouldn't believe it. And the people that knew that I was smart, they wouldn't believe it if they were told that I was crazy. So I went through [school] like that. I'm still like that *now*, though. (Interview, January 11, 1983)

Interestingly, as Norris talked to me about how he handled peer resistance to his efforts to achieve academic success, he began to realize that he was *acting* and had been for some time. What seemed to surprise him was that he was still doing it. Among peers whom he identifies as friends, he *acts* as if he is crazy; conversely, among peers who are not so much friends as classmates seeking to obtain the same academic goals he is seeking, he pulls off the mask and displays his academic abilities. The stranger status of his peers empowers him, making it possible to compete with them. On the other hand, the familiarity of peers who are perceived to be friends undermines his willingness to display his academic capabilities but encourages him to clown.

In junior high, he also had the added complication of sexual interest, facing the dilemma unique to his status as a Black man in America's stratified patriarchy: How does a man in a subordinate social position do what men in male-dominated societies do—both dominate and resist domination? His growing acceptance as an athlete in the mold of his older brother, Kai, tended to minimize the complications males sometimes get into as a result of their relationships with females. His athletic prowess in track also helped to lessen the impact of the brainiac sobriquet and to validate and affirm his manhood.

These are just some of the internal "How do I live with my peers?" issues Norris and the other male students confront in school. As this case study shows, with a little ingenuity, peer resistance can easily be overcome. It is the larger social issues, like stigmatized race and gender that are endemic barriers to Capital students' willingness to pursue academic excellence. These intangible barriers are ubiquitous, both within and outside the school. Regrettably, their impact is frequently underestimated.

Capital students who "choose" to pursue academic success must resist a powerful and pervasive yet rarely verbalized dictim of the larger society: "You cannot meet the demands and expectations of school and the larger society." Hence, while Norris was able to subvert his peers' efforts to limit his academic achievement, he was and still is far less capable of overcoming the social barriers embodied in his membership in a stigmatized racial and gender group.

Like the adults discussed in chapter 5, the high-achieving students find that commitment to the achievement ideology is contested, opposed, and frequently thwarted by the limitations endemic to membership in the Black community. Resistance thus becomes the high-achieving students' method of overcoming the barriers that are externally and internally imposed. But not all of them succeed. As the following ethnographic data suggest, the attempts of some high-achieving students are riddled with self-imposed conflict and friction. Their resistance implodes, riddling their psyches with self-doubt.

These high-achieving students' attempts to escape the blackout generally associated with being accused of "acting white" are frequently totally ineffective and even counterproductive. Their use of resistance as a weapon more closely approximates that of their underachieving classmates. They fake the internalization of the larger society's norms in order both to oppose the social forces dictating spatial and psychological separation from the Black community and, at the same time, to reject the claim from a "blacker-than-thou" identity (Napper 1973:37) by denying that in order to be successful in school (and subsequently in life) one has to shun his or her Blackness (Crosby 1970:273; Fordham 1988; Granfield 1991). Clearly, the high-achieving students' construction of Otherness epitomizes the African-American tradition of subtle sociopolitical resistance.

Compliance as Resistance: The Male Students

The academic response of the high-achieving males is marked with the conflict embodied in subtle resistance to normalized expectations for African-Americans. Indeed, the high-achieving males are probably the most conflict-laden segment of the sample, for among them issues of gender take precedence over issues normally associated with race.[5] These high-achieving males were the only segment of the student population to rate gender as more important than race in their definitions of who they are. The high-achieving males are the most ambivalent and uncertain about their "chosen" route to adult status; they are also more equivocal about their academic decisions and less certain about the truthfulness of what they are being taught in school. They are torn between a really strong desire to remain connected to the African-American community and a yearning for academic success and the inevitable separation that ensues.

Paul personifies this dilemma. As the youngest student in the sample, he has less freedom than his classmates enjoy. He has been phenomenally successful in school. While he attributes that success to his ability and willingness to read—an enthusiasm that violates the existing stereotype of men of African ancestry—he admits to feeling terribly inadequate in an arena that is considered one of the unique domains of African-American manhood: athletics. In response to my questions regarding his interest in sports, he admitted:

> I swim occasionally. I was on the swim team, but . . . I developed a permanent allergy to chlorinated water. (Laughter) . . . I was just joking. It's just that I really didn't think I was benefiting the team, considering that I would be disqualified as soon as I dived off the diving board. I don't know how to dive. In order to swim in the swim meets, you have to be able to dive, and you get disqualified if you don't dive in properly. And I'm not one of the best athletes; I mean I'm not into athletics. School . . . I'm trying to explore other areas, and find out—I want to be good at *something*. Everybody's good at *something*, and I hate to think that *my* best thing is school. (Interview, January 13, 1983)

Paul's assertion that he hates to think that his best thing is school is riveting in its import. Why would a young African-American male minimize the importance of his academic achievements? Why does he appear to abhor his academic acumen? His self-analysis suggests that, at least among his peers, being good at school is not the best way to make it. His assertion that "everybody's good at *something*" implies that there are more meaningful goals than good grades. These alternative goals are unlikely to celebrate the appropriation and consumption of Otherness, and they are more likely to be extraneous to the school's core curriculum. More important, since he has failed so miserably at swimming and is not otherwise athletic, Paul is feeling a great need to show that he is good at *"something"* other than school. His statements suggest that in order to make a contribution to what Capital and perhaps African-American students in general have come to define as important, he has to become something more than and even other than a "scholarship boy" (Rodriguez 1982).

Paul's guardians are aware of his ambivalence. Like Paul, they realize that at some level his academic success implies representing Otherness. They claim it is most clearly manifested in his uncertainty about being Black and about the threat Blackness represents for his status as a male.

He therefore shares with his high-achieving male cohorts an inordinate preoccupation with what it means to be male. Only half in jest, he shared with me his bafflement at being considered a "degenerate":

> And it seems that somewhere during my tenth and eleventh grade year, I got this reputation as a degenerate, as a pervert . . . Now where these ideas come from, I *don't* know. Maybe it's because I tell jokes about Sandpaper Sally and dead baby jokes and all sorts of perverse little jokes like that. But I don't know where they come from; I don't know how they could have gotten this idea, when—as nice a person as I am. As nice and kind and upstanding citizen that I am—I don't know where they could have gotten this idea. Just because I seem to find a sexual implication in everything they say, I mean—I don't know where they get this idea from. But anyway. (Interview, January 10, 1983)

Paul was not alone in this preoccupation. Most of his high-achieving male cohorts appeared to have a similar concern. One of the most important markers of male affirmation and perhaps even domination among this group of students is association with women. As noted above, I sometimes went to a sex shop with the high-achieving male students. Paul was one of those who insisted that going to the sex shop was "typical" for him. It was not. Like his high-achieving peers, he felt compelled to present such an image. The fact that he lied about this emerging part of his life is not the issue.

Both the formal and informal interviews and conversations with the male high achievers were littered with discussions of male desires and sexual conquests. The high-achieving males' decision to celebrate Otherness either by internalizing or "faking it" presents them with an overwhelming sense of loss, loss of identity and loss of maleness.

In attempting to minimize the sense of loss associated with the decision to become a scholarship boy, as well as to diminish the limitations they invariably face as a consequence of being Black in America, these students struggle to deal with issues related to gender verification. Their academic achievement compels them to repeatedly resist the almost automatic assumption that they will succumb to the gender-specific academic expectations proclaimed by the larger society.

For the most part, the peers of the high-achieving males perceive their decision to embrace school norms and values as a rejection of the Black community. This perception persists despite the fact that among the male students, regardless of level of achievement, *behavioral* denial of affiliation with the Black community is rare, even when these students *verbally* proclaim disaffiliation.

Regardless of the option they choose, however, African-American males are invariably in conflict; their evolving, nonlinear worldview is contested and opposed. They are also denied what is often defined as a prerogative of maleness in male-dominated societies: the right to dominate and to resist domination. The response of Wendell, a high-achieving male who is struggling with his earlier decision to pursue academic excellence, is typical. His teachers had tried to recruit him for advanced placement:

> They kept on. They almost was trying to *make* me get in the advanced placement program. I would have got in, too. Like, when I was doing my grades, they looked, and my grades checked. They said, "Put him down for advanced placement," they was *telling* me I was going to be in advanced placement. I was in junior high. And they was *telling* me. All through the summer, they kept calling, "You want to be in advanced placement?" "No, that's all right." So that's why I didn't get in advanced placement. And they . . . some things they don't let you do in advanced placement, either. You know, like sportswise and stuff. I don't like that. They almost run your life. (Interview, March 24, 1983)

Wendell graduated from junior high school as class valedictorian. At Capital, he earned honor roll grades both semesters of his sophomore year. But this year his grades have plummeted, a fact that he attributes to his growing awareness of the limitations in the opportunity structure. He has suddenly become sick of attending school. He makes virtually no effort to complete asssignments or do his homework, and he has even begun to cut classes. He appears to be deliberately rejecting the norms and values strongly identified with school success and general social mobility. Even his way of selecting friends reflects the conflict he is experiencing.

> I pick my friends like this: I pick the lower-class people. If a lot of people don't like them, and they come in the class, people talk about them and everything, I'll want to be their friend 'cause I'll feel sorry for them. (Interview, March 19, 1983)

When he told me that his friends are likely to be those who are unacceptable to their teachers and other adults, I asked if their grades are important in his selection of them as friends.

> Nope. I don't care if they dumb or not. They ain't really—I'm gonna say it like this: People . . . you go to school, people classify you as dumb, smart, or average. If I get bad grades now,

they think I'm dumb. But if you look at my other grades, they
say I'm smart. So I don't think school prove anything. (Interview, March 29, 1983)

Wendell's current response represents a drastic change from the way
he once constructed his school persona and behavior. His earlier belief
in the efficacy of schooling as a social "equalizer" has dissipated, and in
its place is a growing yet uneven racial awareness and an equally variable
commitment to group affiliation. This new racial awareness is accompa-
nied by a lessening of academic effort and performance.

The diversity of perspectives and strategies among the high-achieving
students is often overshadowed by the commonality of their primary
goal: disproving the widely held societal stereotype that "Black" and
"smart" are mutually exclusive. Further, the within-group nuances are
frequently ignored, misunderstood, or overlooked. Consequently, the
precipice on which these students' identity is teetering is either disparaged or discounted. The primary issue for them is the duality of their
goal: success as defined by the school and larger society *and* continuing
membership in the Black fictive kinship system.

Achievement as Resistance to the Dominance of Whiteness

The response of high-achieving students to the existing dominance of
Whiteness as a powerful cultural symbol is fraught with conflict and
confusion. Unlike those in the high-achieving sample who are fairly certain that acting white and constructing Otherness are at least necessary
evils, the high-achieving students who are trying to be both successful
and Black are essentially denying the reality of life in America. They are
attempting to invert or at least modify the dominant cultural meanings
of Blackness and Whiteness whereby, for example, black is a symbol of
evil and white represents virtue.[6] The ambivalence embodied in these
students' academic choices is chronic.

One such choice is the decision whether or not to participate in the
advanced placement program. For a good many students at Capital, the
decision to become a member of the program marks the individual as
acting white, compelling him or her to confront the dilemma of a dual
identity in one human body (E. Martin 1987). Many members of the
program are involuntary participants whose parents have insisted that
they participate in it. Many other Capital students refuse to become
official members yet take most of the advanced placement courses available to students at their grade level.

Lisa is a case in point. Although she refuses—unequivocally—to
become a member of the program, nevertheless she takes virtually all of
her courses in it. She is using this route to academic success with the

collusion of her counselors and teachers, who officially ignore the fact that she is taking these courses. Her counselor gently pesters her in private about the benefits of becoming an official member but never gives her an ultimatum because she knows that would make Lisa drop the rigorous course sequence. Nevertheless, Lisa's tactics are an outright violation of the official rules, which demand that everyone taking these courses, with the possible exception of English,[7] be officially enrolled in the advanced placement program.

Lisa's counselor not only allows her to break the rules but actually enables her to do so. Lisa's "success" in acting white is, in fact, contingent upon the collusion of key school officials and some of her significant peers, who help Lisa convey the impression that she is a member of the regular curriculum program rather than the advanced placement program. They join with her in acting as if she is not doing what she is doing.

> Lisa is a highly motivated student. She wants to leave her poor neighborhood, so she studies religiously in order to earn the grades perceived to be her ticket out of the Black community. She keeps repeating that she wants to "make it." She laments her inability to speak standard English readily and her limited academic vocabulary. Every time I used a word she had not heard or did not know the meaning of, she asked me to tell her what it meant as she wrote it down. When she gets home in the afternoon, she spends most of her time studying both be- fore and after dinner. Her mother does not demand that she cook or wash dishes. She has even taken it upon herself to go to classes offered at either Georgetown or George Washington on Saturday mornings that focus on vocabulary building and accounting. (Fieldnotes, February 9, 1983)

Lisa's successful use of this strategy to resist the hegemonic claims of the dominant Other or to escape rejection by the Black community stands in stark contrast to the strategy school officials used to persuade Wendell to become a member of the advanced placement program. His junior high school counselor and Ms. Aster, the director of the program at Capital, badgered him both privately and publicly. As Wendell recalls it, they would not allow him to negotiate entry on his own terms.

Wendell's response was typical. He was neither amused nor per- suaded, and the public nature of the adults' efforts made it impossible for him to use Lisa's strategy.[8] He refused to join the program and denied having any regrets about his decision.

> *Anthro:* Have you any regrets now that you are at Capital and see the people who are in the advanced placement program?

Wendell: Nope.

Anthro: You don't?

Wendell: [No.] 'Cause I take some classes with them.

Anthro: And?

Wendell: Most of them no different from me.

Anthro: There's no difference?

Wendell: Nope. They're kind of smart. But I think that advanced placement won't make you no smarter. Classes—you just take a little harder classes. All *my* classes hard! Don't make no difference what I'm in. (Interview, March 23, 1983)

Wendell's response reflects the collective group orientation characteristic of the cultural orientation embedded in the Black fictive kinship pattern. He was accustomed, in evaluating the worth of an individual, to use other criteria than those related to grades. He did not invariably equate high academic performance with "goodness" and positive self-worth. He insisted that the "official" members of the advanced placement program were no smarter than he. Part of his assessment is based on the perception that in order for his peers to become successful participants in the program at Capital, they were going to have to liquidate the Black Self, an idea with which he was still struggling.

Lisa and Wendell, both members of the high-achieving student sample, are working to achieve academic success and, for the most part, they do so because they resist by conforming. However, unlike several of their high-achieving peers, they conform not by enrolling in the advanced placement program but by remaining in the regular curriculum and unofficially appropriating aspects of the advanced curriculum.

One of the ways the high-achieving students are accused of acting white is by being called "brainiacs." Individuals so labeled snap to attention and disavow its accuracy. Alice's response is more complex than the standard denial.

Anthro: Have you ever heard the term *brainiac* used?

Alice: Yeah. That's what they call *me*—brainiac, "Alice the brainiac" . . .

Anthro: Is that considered to be a positive or a negative term?

Alice: It's positive. Well, I guess they *use* it as a negative, I *take* it as a positive . . . "Brainiac" means like, a computer mind—know all the answers. Call me "computer," "computer-head," and "brainiac." I think it's a . . . you know, I don't—I used to say, "No, I'm not," and now I say, "Sure, I am. Don't you want to be one?" They try to say it as a *nega-*

tive thing . . . They say I'm a brainiac 'cause I'm smart. I can't argue with that, 'cause I *am* smart. But like, I don't show off, "I'm smart, you're dumb," I don't *do* that. If I'm smart, I'm smart. If you think I'm smart, I guess I am. But I don't consider myself smart. I'm good in school, but smart—no, not really. (Interview, March 14, 1983; May 23, 1983)

Most of the students in the sample seek to alter their school performance and behavior if they are identified as brainiacs. Because Martin, for example, values being known as a brainiac but fears being called one, he puts brakes on his academic effort, doing just enough to impress his teachers and to challenge the stereotype frequently associated with the academic performance of Black students.

The high-achieving students understand that their fellow students know the dominant and most widely used meaning of the term *brainiac*. They also know that their classmates often use the term in ways that subvert its formal, purported meaning.

> *Adam:* Brainiac? Oh, brainiac is a person who knows—I guess the way they figure, brainiac is a person who knows everything. Or if they don't know it, they're hitting them books to learn, you know. *I* don't do that! [Laugh] I learn it as I go. I learn it as I go. But . . . 'Cause, see, I don't consider myself smart, but I just consider myself doing the work, and if I do the work, that's how I got my good grades. So I do the work.
>
> *Anthro:* Is that considered a positive or a negative term . . . if someone calls you that, is it a compliment, or is it a negative?
>
> *Adam:* They—some people—yeah, some . . . most people do it as a put-down, like, you know, people think they're bad, they'll do it as a put-down. See, that brainiac, then they're just born with it, or they just—like Kent, you know he's a good friend, you know, they might call *him* a brainiac, but he is *smart!* That boy is smart, you know. I call him a brainiac for a compliment! He is smart! He's smart. (Interview, January 6, 1983)

Privately, everyone would love to be able to master schoolwork as easily as brainiacs supposedly do. But no one wants to be publicly identified as a brainiac with implications of conforming and acting white. Most high-achieving students seek both to be brainiacs and to avoid being identified as such.

Most of the students at Capital High are keenly aware of the symbolic meaning of "blackness" and "whiteness" in American society (Szasz 1970:68). They realize that, despite the Civil Rights Movement and its efforts to modify these meanings, whiteness is still the most highly valued cultural symbol in our society. Its perceived linkage to virtue and success makes it difficult for these Black students to be both Black and academically successful. The limiting nature of blackness as a cultural symbol hovers over their academic effort and their futures, diminishing their hopes of achieving the American Dream.

Because accepting the prevailing cultural definitions of "blackness" and "whiteness" would render the high-achieving students impotent, many of them seek to deny the evidence before them. Fortunately, they have institutional support for their efforts. The following case studies are intended to illuminate how high-achieving students cope with the conflicts endemic to their lives as African-Americans. These same case studies are also intended to document the resiliency of the human spirit at Capital High. The first examples are those from high-achieving students who decided to heed the warning from the larger society: learn to "act white" or fail in school. Following are case studies from among the high-achieving students who were ambivalent about avoiding the perception of being Black.

Rita: "People Are People. Black, White, Spanish, Red, White or Blue, We're All the Same."

If Rita were willing to disguise her academic effort and, at the same time, let go of her comedic persona, she would easily outperform everyone in her class. She takes most of the advanced placement courses available to eleventh-graders. She loves going to school and her test scores show it. She earned high scores on the verbal and math components of the PSAT, which she took during the base year of the study, scoring at the 96th percentile on the verbal component and at the 62d percentile on the math component. She had the highest verbal score at Capital. Her lower math score reflects her tendency to cut her math classes and to put forth only minimal effort when she attends. She does not like math much, but her major reason for not attending her math class this year is the teacher she was assigned.

Rita's performance on standardized measures of school success surpasses that of most of the high-achieving students, male or female, in the study, particularly in areas other than math. Her performance on the Comprehensive Tests of Basic Skills (CTBS) was equally outstanding: she scored at the college level on all subsections of the exam except spelling. She also made an impressive score on the Life Skills examination.[9]

Rita is best described as intelligent, creative, hostile, sarcastic, assertive, garrulous, funny, and manipulative. She is also kind, caring, complex, clever, confused, and troubled. At times she can be inconsistent.

She demands total adherence to the values and rules of the school by teachers and other administrators, but feels free to challenge these same values and rules. Although she can give the impression of being thoughtless and unfeeling, it is altogether likely that this is only a mask, giving the appearance of callousness and shielding the insecurities and sensitivities of a very vulnerable young Black female. She is also extremely angry and unclear about who she is and why she is.

In school, Rita is seen as a clown and is often described by friends, peers, and classmates as "that crazy Rita," even though it is widely known that her academic skills exceed those of other members of the student body, male and female. She is, however, judged primarily by her interactions with peers and classmates and by her behavioral interaction with her teachers. Unfortunately, Rita feels a greater need to be a comedian when in the presence of her peers and her teachers; consequently, the comedic persona is reinforced among these people. Silliness enables her to cope with the pressure of school authorities for achievement and the pressure of her peers against academic excellence. Admittedly, comedians are rare among female students at Capital, but adopting that public persona serves the same purpose for Rita as it does for Norris: it tends to enable her to do what she wants to do in school with the support of her peers.

The dysfunctional nature of Rita's family, combined with the low-status housing in which they live and the general conditions of her community, plays a significant role in her decision to seek academic success. Media images suggest to her that the conditions of her family and her community are not racially determined but are instead evidence of missed opportunities on the part of her family and their neighbors. This perception guides her response to school and schooling. She is convinced that by leaving Capital High with an excellent record and strong recommendations, she will be able to overcome any lingering effects of race and racism in America. She believes absolutely in the efficacy of schools and schooling to produce a meritocratic society. In Rita's view, if her mother relents and allows her to continue her education beyond high school, personal success will be within her grasp.

Rita is unequivocal in her assertion that if she and other Black students are able to perform well in school, they will find equality of opportunity. Yet she is extremely confused and troubled about the issue of race. Like most of the other high-achieving students, she is convinced that although "sometimes it's a situation where it can't be helped," Black Americans are primarily responsible, through their own lack, for the impoverished conditions under which they live. She argues that what they have to do to eliminate the oppression they suffer is to get together and "pull themselves up by their bootstraps":

I feel like Black people have to get together. They're not together. I mean, they turn around—they say, "Hey, brother!
What's up, what's up?" And then they turn around and stab
you in the back. Then there's no unity as far as Blacks are concerned. They can do anything, but they have to get together
first. And if I could do anything, I would want my race together. (Interview, May 4, 1983)

Rita is uncertain about what it takes for Black Americans to view
themselves as successful, but she is certain that one of the factors responsible for their present condition is what she describes as laziness, their
reluctance to become more than what they are. She maintains that they
tend to set their sights too low. While she recognizes that they were
terribly victimized by the historical experience of slavery, nevertheless
she feels that they have allowed that experience and all subsequent acts
of degradation and humiliation to have too great an impact on their
view of themselves individually and of their group collectively. She insists
that, despite the nature of the social structure and despite individual acts
of racial discrimination, anyone can make it with appropriate effort. She
is disgusted with what she views as Black Americans' lack of resilience
in the face of adversity. They tend to give up too easily, she says, and
are much too willing to settle for less than what is needed to progress.

Rita is even more incensed about the society's limited expectations
for African-American students. One of the factors fueling her academic
effort is her desire to disprove the widely held perception that African-
American adolescents do not have the intellectual capabilities of their
White counterparts. As is true for most of the students in the sample,
regardless of achievement level, she responds to schooling with resistance.
Her anger at a system that forces her to prove her humanness robs her of
the stamina to perform consistently at the highest academic level.

At the same time, Rita does not feel a real sense of kinship with
Black Americans at either the verbal or the behavioral level. Despite her
claims that she views blackness and whiteness through the same social
lens, her tendency to disparage constantly activities and events generally
associated with Americans of African descent suggests a preference for
activities her family and some of her friends view as "white."

They [my family] go to all the shows, go out to the Capital
Center and all that crap, and listen to all that trash—as far as
I am concerned. But I don't really like going out there, you
know; but if I ask them to go see the Washington Philharmon-
ics with me, they won't go. "Is that opera?" they want to
know . . . And they don't go to the museum with me either,
'cause they don't think . . . they'd go crazy. They'd rather go

to the movies to see Eddie Murphy in "48 Hours" than to go see "To Fly" at the Air and Space Museum.

Black music is meaningless to me . . . The lyrics. I mean, they . . . "Oh, it's got a nice beat, so it must be good," you know, but that's not always, you know, like that. And so . . . oh, well . . . it's just meaningless, you know. You listen to the lyrics sometime, and Black artists, you know, must [be] into meaningless music. And I think I listen to Stevie Wonder because, you know, all of his records usually have, you know, some sort of meaning, like his "Hotter Than July" album, you know, like, what is it?—"Happy Birthday," "Hotter Than July" . . . it's meaningful. But Vanity 6, "Nasty Girls," I mean, what's that, really? It's not—it's just trash . . . as far as I'm concerned . . . So I start listening to WPGC [a contemporary non-Black music format] . . . instead of OK-100 [a station that plays music sung primarily by Black artists]. (Interview, January 12, 1983)

Ironically, Rita's efforts to minimize her connectedness to the Black community are largely unproductive. Because she is comfortable with most aspects of the larger society, she does not experience the dissonance created by many of the students at Capital High, including some who participated in this study.

In summary, Rita is aware of the endemic limitations of being Black even in the latter years of the twentieth century. It is in response to that knowledge that she seeks to avoid being identified totally as a Black person. While she does not view being Black as a negative factor, she also knows the value of being White or, in the case of today's Black population, the value of acting white.

Katrina: "My Mother's Only Comment Was: 'I See You Changed the Bs to As.'"

Like virtually every other high-achieving female in the study, Katrina doesn't see herself as getting much parental support for her academic achievements, despite her 4.0 average in the tenth grade and her excellent performance on the PSAT (95th percentile in math, 75th percentile on the verbal component). Her parents' failure to offer praise and support pains this academically gifted student.[10] Her relationship with her parents, particularly her mother, is riddled with tension. They appear to take her performance in school for granted, and she feels that she can never do well enough in school to warrant their support.

Katrina lamented the fact that *her mother and father never praise her for her work in school*. When she showed her mother her report card last advisory, she said her mother's only comment was, "I see you changed the Bs to As" (she received two Bs the first advisory). When I suggested that perhaps her mother was also behaving as she (Katrina) claims she is behaving (trying to minimize the disappointment associated with the inability to keep up the track record as well as the negative consequences associated with boasting), she noted how differently her mother reacted to her brother's grade improvement last advisory. She said her mother gave him lots of compliments, telling him how proud she was of him, etc. I suggested that perhaps it was because he was younger. That, too, did not go over very well. She refused to believe anything other than that her parents were not proud of her performance. (Fieldnotes, February 22, 1983)

Katrina and Sakay, one of the underachievers in this study, are best friends. Sakay and her mother believe that if Katrina had the enthusiastic support of her parents, her academic performance would probably be even higher.

The lack of support of Katrina's parents for her academic achievement is not atypical. Most of the female high achievers affirm that while their parents, particularly their mothers, demand that they get good grades, they appear to take their academic excellence for granted. In short, their parents expect them to do well in school, but seem to show no faith in their ability to do what they want to do after high school, and appear to offer no support of their goals and aspirations.

Katrina's personal view of success includes graduating from college with the highest possible ranking, finding a steady job, earning a moderate income, working, making friends, and traveling. She emphasizes the work ethic in her responses, implying that this is not a characteristic of Black Americans' response to their low-status jobs. She does not see marriage in her immediate future, nor does she want to have children; hence, she thinks a moderate income will be sufficient.

Katrina acknowledges that she has put brakes on her school achievement both because her parents do not seem to care and because she fears alienating her peers. This threat has led to a sense of alienation or "affective dissonance" between her and the larger Black community. She has come to view most Black Americans as not desiring to "make it"—as being too lazy to pursue upward mobility. Her limited background reinforces this perception, in part because she sees Black females as being dependent upon Black men for their sense of identity, a position she seeks to avoid. While she considers being female a burden, she does not make the same judgment of Blackness, attributing the massive poverty in the Black community, for example, to Black people's lack of desire to change their social and economic conditions and not necessarily the result of a racist social system.

While at some level all the female students consider Black Americans responsible for their impoverished social status, it is the high-achieving females like Rita and Katrina who dissociate themselves from the Black community, deliberately avoiding Black music, rock concerts by Black stars, and TV programs that focus on the "life ways of Black people." Their knowledge of Black life and culture is rudimentary at best.

The other female informants appear to be much more involved in Black life and culture. They belong to predominantly Black churches, or at least the congregation of their particular church is Black; and they enjoy Black music and other forms of Black entertainment. Indeed, in many ways they tend to avoid activities and entertainment forms that could conceivably be described as non-Black activities, activities that might put one at risk of being described as acting white.

Maggie: "All This Time I Thought I Was Yellow. And Now I'm Black."

Maggie is a seventeen-year-old student with a high GPA whose courses at Capital come primarily from the regular curriculum. She is a quiet—as opposed to a shy—student about 5'4" tall. Maggie lives with her mother and father and younger brother in a single-family, semi-detached house not far from Capital High School. She admits that she does not have a close relationship with her parents, especially her father, with whom she rarely interacts.

Her mother is the most influential person in the family, and, to date, her mother's approval has been tremendously important in Maggie's life. That is changing, however, as the following excerpt from my fieldnotes indicates:

> Maggie did not show for our lunchtime appointment. Since lunch begins at 11:40 and I waited for her until 12:15, I assumed that she forgot . . . or she was too anxious to spend time with her boyfriend . . . to take our appointment seriously. The relationship with her boyfriend is extremely complicated. According to Ms. Mentor, Maggie's mother is not too anxious to have her date, so most of what she does with him at school is done surreptitiously. They are constantly together. In those classes that they take together, e.g. Ms. Mentor's, Maggie does all the work for both of them. According to Ms. Mentor, if she has a written assignment on the board, Maggie copies it for both of them; he spends the time set aside for

copying work from the board bantering with Ms. Mentor. If
she gives the class an assignment, Ms. Mentor claims that
Maggie actually does the work and he copies it from her . . .
She also does any tedious and mundane tasks he assigns her,
which she gladly does for him. In return, he gives her most of
his time at school. (Fieldnotes, March 22, 1983)

As I have indicated, the parents of the high-achieving females are
extremely watchful of their daughters' evolving sexuality. Maggie's
mother enforces tight limits on her daughter's extrafamilial activities.
She has no idea that when Maggie is at school, she is spending most of
her time with her boyfriend. Maggie's hard work in the classroom has
enabled her to earn good grades. But she has remained inconspicuous.
She does what she is asked to do without question, and she completes
all assignments. This practice has been reinforced by her mother, who
demands that she spend two hours every day of the week on assigned
homework and preparation.

The most difficult struggle in Maggie's life appears to be her effort
to come to grips with being Black in a country where being Black is
disvalued. Like Rita and Katrina, she seeks to dissociate herself from the
existing Black fictive kinship system.

> *Maggie:* I consider myself as a Mongoloid.
>
> *Anthro:* You do! Why?
>
> *Maggie:* When I was small, people used to say I was yellow,
> right? So I really thought—I thought, I really thought I was
> yellow. I didn't think I was Black. I thought I was a Mongol-
> oid. So all these . . . all this time I've been—well, not *re-
> cently*—I thought I was yellow until I got into . . . maybe
> around the sixth, seventh grade. Then my mother told me I
> wasn't yellow, 'cause on the papers when we used to fill out, I
> used to put "Yellow" on it, you know, for "Black, White, or
> Other"? I would either put "Other" or put "Yellow" on it,
> 'cause people used to call me "yellow." And my mother told
> me that I was Black.
>
> *Anthro:* And what did that do to you?
>
> *Maggie:* I kind of felt different. I felt like a different person. I
> said, "All this time I thought I was yellow. And now I'm
> Black."
>
> *Anthro:* [Do] you still have problems with coming to grips
> with that?
>
> *Maggie:* No, not really. I can—yeah, I can consider myself as

a . . . not a Negro, I wouldn't call myself a Negro—as a Black.

Anthro: As a Black?

Maggie: Mm-hm.

Anthro: But you had . . . for a long time, you *didn't* identify that way?

Maggie: Uh-huh. (Interview, February 25, 1983)

Her response to the realization that she is a Black American is interesting. As a child, she chose to see herself as a non-Black person, despite the fact that her mother is obviously Black and her little brother is also Black. (I did not meet or see her father when I visited her parents' home; he was upstairs and did not come down to meet me.) Maggie did not see herself as a Black person because her skin was and is lighter than that of the other members of her family and because other people, particularly her peers, jokingly identified her as a non-Black person. The residual effect of this misidentification is still a part of her identity structure, aiding and abetting her self-perception that she is different from most Black people.

Maggie identifies Black culture as "the ways of Black people" (interview, February 25, 1983). Included in the ways of Black people, according to Maggie, are their way of life, their religion, their customs, and so forth. She notes that Black people have a language system different from that of White Americans, but not special. This language system, in her view, is used by most Black Americans when they are in the privacy of their homes, in school, and other predominantly Black contexts. She insists that when Black people use the standard language pattern in communicating with each other or with other non-Black people, they are often perceived by their peers and other Black people as "putting on airs and everything" (interview, February 25, 1983). This way of talking is also identified by other Black people as "talking proper" or an attempt on the part of Black people to "talk white." She acknowledges that her mother often "talks white" when she is talking on the phone or is outside their home.

Maggie views her mother's choosing to talk white in certain circumstances as evidence of "inauthenticity" or "phoniness" and criticizes her for trying to avoid being identified as a Black person when talking with strangers on the phone. She does not perceive any connection between this behavior and her own refusal to be recognized as a Black American during elementary school and ambivalence about her racial identity today. She describes her mother's use of language as an attempt to minimize the negative consequences associated with being Black in America, a strategy she deplores. "I talk the same way all the time," she says.

Another interesting characteristic of this student is her response to the question, "Why do you think so many Black people are poor?" She responded that they were "lazy," "don't care" (fieldnotes, March 22, 1983). The pronoun *they* is significant.

Maggie's behavior at school is another example of how the high-achieving students use avoidance to minimize the negative consequences associated with being Black. Her behavior has been exemplary. In elementary and junior high school, she says she was usually the "teacher's pet." No doubt this special status plus her lighter skin color led her to view herself as neither Black nor White but somewhere in between—Mongolian—and may have led her to see herself as being non-Black or raceless.

The special treatment also led her to the habit of avoiding classmates who might cause her to lose face in the eyes of her teachers and has probably influenced her tendency to spend most of her time alone or with a very limited number of friends, whom she identifies as "acquaintances." Like most of the other high-achieving female students, she acknowledges that she does not trust many people and is in fact quite suspicious of most. In Maggie's case, this attitude is most actively encouraged by her mother, who does not allow her to associate with the other children in her neighborhood. Despite the fact that her family has lived in the same single-family home for over twelve years, she does not know any of the teenagers in the community.

Alice: "She Will Force Me to Give Her All My Money."

Alice is a sixteen-year-old high-achieving female student in the regular curriculum program whose academic performance results from a combination of self-motivation and fear of her mother's wrath. She is a quiet, slim young woman, about 5'7" tall, light-complexioned, with a skin that is covered with pimples.

Alice was inducted into the school's chapter of the National Honor Society that spring, a tribute to her consistent effort in school. Her teachers' assessments of her follow a pattern that began in elementary school. Alice reports that in elementary school she, like Maggie, was frequently "teacher's pet," a status she enjoyed immensely. Throughout elementary school she made excellent grades, and she continued to perform well at the junior high school level. At Capital she made the honor roll both semesters of her tenth-grade year and again the first semester of her junior year.

Alice's plans for after graduation are vague. Her parents are not able to send her to college, and, in any case, her mother wants her to stay at home. Alice, however, expresses an interest in attending a state university in California which has been advertised on TV as having an excellent school of dentistry. She would even go into the military in order to get the training necessary to become a dentist. She is not able to make any definite plans, however, because her mother is not providing any encouragement. Her mother's wishes are extremely important to her, both because her mother would, as she says, "kill me" if she acted against her wishes and because her mother is skilled at making her feel guilty when she disobeys.

Alice lives with her mother, stepfather, and younger sister. Her parents were divorced when she was about two years old. Her contact with her biological father is sporadic and stressful, and she claims to dislike him very much. She has bonded with her stepfather, whom she views as her real father. She loves him because he is emotionally supportive.

Like virtually all the high-achieving females in the sample, Alice is growing up in a home where there are strict controls and demands for obedience. There is also the problem of family responsibility. At sixteen, she does all the cooking at home, despite the fact that her mother is home every day, all day, suffering from some unspecified illness. Alice has been performing such family responsibilities since she was thirteen. She also does all the ironing and half the housecleaning, sharing that chore with her younger sister. She is not encouraged to date, even though she will be seventeen in June. She has very few friends. While she knows a good many people and gets along well with them, she describes them as acquaintances rather than friends.

Alice performs well in school primarily because she believes that by earning good grades she can overcome the devastating socioeconomic conditions that characterize her life. She also performs well because she is fearful of her mother's reaction were she to earn any grade less than a B. Her mother's strong, authoritarian childrearing practices are evident in all aspects of Alice's life. Her impact on Alice's life is so pervasive that many of the interview sessions were as much about her mother's life, achievements, and defeats as they were about Alice herself. Beneath Alice's declarations of love for her mother were strong indications of resentment and anger. The latter were exposed in a discussion of a summer job which Alice had just obtained. It was her first job, and she perceived it as her personal, individual achievement. She insisted that she would not be annoyed by the fact that her mother would take her paycheck and give her only a ten-dollar allowance every two weeks. Yet when she told me about it, she said: "She will force me to give her all my money."

If one were not attuned to the nuances and nonverbal expressions in the Black community, one might easily miss the conflict and ambivalence in Alice's reaction to her mother's wishes. Most—not all—of her oral statements are restatements of her mother's values and rules. Her nonverbal language and a few of her verbal statements are clear indicators of her own thoughts and aspirations.

Effort and perseverance are the critical terms to describe Alice's school performance; she works hard to do well in school. At the same time, she makes her effort as inconspicuous as possible. This is hard to do because she has so many chores and responsibilities at home that it is almost impossible for her to complete all her class assignments before coming to school in the morning. Still, her social life is so severely limited by her mother that she is able to camouflage or disguise the small amount of schoolwork she must complete on the premises. Her appropriately deferential and in some sense servile interaction style with her mother serves her well at school, especially with her teachers. They generally concur that she is a "very nice girl."

As Alice views it, a brainiac is someone with a "computer mind— know all the answers" (interview, May 23, 1983). She notes that most students do not want to be labeled brainiacs. When asked why, she responded:

> 'Cause it's lonely at the top, that's just it. It's lonely at the top. I find that the definition of that is . . . If you're really smart—like, I wouldn't want to be a genius, 'cause it's lonely. 'Cause nobody up to your level. It's like saying, "You're distant. You ain't like everybody else." I guess they saying, "You just odd. Everybody dumb, so you should be dumb, too." So I guess that's how they take that. I don't mean dumb as really dumb, but not to your level, let's put it like that. Not really— don't have high averages. (Interview, March 14, 1983)

Alice went on to describe the herd mentality at Capital, a mind-set that tends to value "sameness" rather than differentiation among the student population. In her view, this was clearly evident in the effort of students to "keep a low profile, be like everybody else here at Capital."

> Everybody want to be like everybody else. But, see, nobody really want to be themselves, be what they are and do what they *can* do. But they just want to be like everybody else. Everybody else dumb, so they want to be dumb too . . . Now if everybody was smart, we'd have some good business over here [at Capital]. Everybody would try to be smart. (Interview, May 23, 1983)

While Alice is not given many opportunities to grow and develop as a free-thinking person, she is very conscious of the need to avoid appearing to be a brainiac. She knows the influence and impact of the collective ethos that dominates the school context.

Several of the high-achieving females are negatively affected by the conflict and ambiguity evoked by the "othering" process. They struggle with their decision to act white while in school, including, as I have noted, the effort to minimize their connectedness to the Black community.[11] The male students, too, experience this conflict, because they are trying to retain their identity as Black Americans while struggling with the issue of "acting white" in school.

In a society where being male is synonymous with domination, African-American males embody and reflect the imperative to resist uninvited authority. They recognize that their lives are limited by their inability to dominate the group of males that has historically dominated them. Their lack of power vis-à-vis White American males often compels them to express maleness in ways that defy and negate White males' pervasive domination. The following case histories of the male high achievers are typical of the kind of resistance operating in this population.

Norris: "[Black People] Think 'Makin' It' Is Getting a Big-Time,
Fancy Job . . . and Hav[ing] a Year's Supply of Fried Chicken."
Like nearly all the high-achieving males in the sample, Norris has conflicting feelings about the value of academic excellence. Apparently he understands that it is critically important for Americans of African descent to live their lives in "black-and-white." He is worried, too, about how his peers tend to see him. Norris is one of only two high-achieving male students in the sample group who are taking all the advanced placement courses offered to eleventh-graders at Capital. He is very sure that he will be going to college when he graduates from high school, because he knows he will receive an academic scholarship. His cumulative grade average is A. He took the PSAT during the fall semester and scored at the 96th percentile on the math component and at the 85th percentile on the verbal component. His performance on the CTBS was similarly impressive, with college-level scores on each of the subsections.

Norris is a brilliant student, but he has learned to camouflage his academic achievement so that his peers do not feel threatened by him and do not shut him out. Because of the way he interacts with students who are underachieving, as well as those who are performing in a manner comparable with his, he is able to pursue his social goals without interference.

Norris has a quick, bright smile and a deliberately developed comedic personality that puts everyone at ease. Like his father, he is very fair in skin color, and he wears his curly hair short. Until four months ago, he lived with both parents and his older brother in a multiunit apartment building that he describes as "the ghetto," a euphemism for "the projects," or publicly subsidized housing. At present, he is living with his mother and his brother in a two-bedroom apartment in an upgraded section of the Capital community. He takes the Metrobus at 7:30 every morning and is in the school building in time for his 8:00 class.

Norris attributes all of his positive characteristics to his mother and his brother. He speaks of his mother as the most influential person in his life. She appears unable to do any wrong, except for making the mistake of living with his father for seventeen years. Norris's striking physical resemblance to his father makes him fear the possibility of becoming like him, a fate which, in his view, would be worse than death.

Norris is quite clear about his plans after graduation. Because his academic performance is so good, he will probably be able to go to the college of his choice. His dilemma is what to pursue as a lifelong profession. He "hates" science yet wants to be a physician. His counselor and other school personnel want him to pursue engineering or one of the natural sciences as a career option. When asked specifically about his career goals and what he wants to accomplish in life, he responded as follows:

> Well, first I'd like to graduate from high school with top honors, and probably get a scholarship for track—full scholarship to a good medical school or medical college. And I'd go there, work for a Master's or Ph.D. or whatever you get . . . Then I'd get my degree . . . well, first I'd go through all of that. Then I'd like to be a doctor—a well-noted doctor. But I don't want to be a surgeon . . . I don't know. I just—ever since I've been able to think, I've been thinking about that [becoming a medical doctor]. And then I started liking computers. Then I wanted to go into computers. See? And a lot of people getting discouraged with me. I really don't know, they keep telling me to go ahead and be the doctor. And now I'm lost; I'm trapped between which one to go. I'm just not sure. See, I want to decide now, so when I go to college I'll know. 'Cause I don't want to go there and say I want to major in computer science, then discover I don't like it and go into medicine. I'd waste a whole year. (Interview, February 23, 1983)

Norris adds, perhaps only half in jest: "If all else fails, I want to be a pimp."

His inability to make up his mind reflects his dependence on adults and his implicit belief that whatever they are advising him to do is in his best interest. Because he trusts his counselor completely, he has found himself in courses that he would not have chosen for himself (French, for instance). He is currently taking a physics course that he claims he "hates" for a variety of reasons, including the fact that the teacher is very dull. It is probably good for him in some ways that he is not allowed total freedom in this regard because he would most likely take all math courses. More important, the fact that someone else makes decisions for him at school is consistent with what is practiced at home and in the Capital community.

Although his career goals are muddled, Norris's view of success is quite clear. He will consider himself a success when "I've accomplished everything I want to accomplish. To me success means that you are what you want to be, and you are happy with what you want to be, and you're the best of what you want to be, to the best of your ability" (interview, February 23, 1983).

Acknowledging that for most African-Americans success means "becoming more than what they are," Norris recognizes that an imagery of "Otherness" pervades the community. When asked what he thinks success means to most Black people in Washington, he says, only half in jest: "They think 'makin' it' is getting a big-time, fancy job that pays a lot of money so they can drive a Cadillac, wear a bunch of jewelry on [their] finger and [their] neck and everything, have a big old house, and have a year's supply of fried chicken" (interview, February 23, 1983).

While he prefers to be identified as a Black American, he reports that most of the students at the school prefer to be identified as "Negroes." Norris sees features of the Black reality as distinguishing African-Americans from the dominant population and hence suggesting the existence of a cultural system in the Black community, separate and distinct from that of the intrusive dominant culture of the school and the larger society. Among these cultural features, in his view, are "their clothing style, the style they wear their hair, the way they act in public and around their friends, the average household, and their performance in school, the food they eat—that's all I can think of" (interview, February 18, 1983).

Norris appears to consciously understand the interactional and behavioral style of Black Americans. He notes the pervasiveness of "cultural inversion" (see Fordham 1982; Ogbu 1983a, 1983b, 1984) in the way they interact:

> Black people treat each other like—as if they were enemies.
> And you know, you can be good friends, but you treat them
> like an enemy. Well, another person [a non-Black person]
> would consider it as treating them as an enemy, but we call it
> friendship. Like we tease each other and hit on each other and
> talk about each other all the time, that's considered friendship.

And that's what you [the dominant society] call abnormal. But
that's the way most Black people I know who are friends *are*.
They say, if you can talk about their mother and get away
with it, you *must* be their friend, so . . . (Interview, February
18, 1983)

Norris acknowledges the continuing existence of racism and discrimination and its effect on the academic performance and behavior of his
classmates and peers and on the lived reality of Black Americans in
Washington and the nation at large. When asked why he thinks so many
Black people in America are poor, he says it is because they give up;
"they don't try." He argues that their failure to put forth the necessary
effort to become the Other is related to their perception that they will
not make it anyway, primarily because of discrimination based on race.
He believes that the stiff educational and schooling requirements for
most prestigious jobs discourage Black people from seeking them because
they fear they will be denied an equal chance to compete. And they are
further discouraged by a lack of concrete evidence that Black Americans
who take on what seems to many an enormously time-consuming task
are actually able to get the desired jobs and/or social positions: "They
say, 'I don't want to do it, besides there's no such thing as a Black
whatever-they-want-to-be . . . Or not *many* Black whatever-they-want-
to-be.' So they'll say, 'Forget it'" (interview, February 18, 1983).

In summary, Norris sees his future as being fairly well charted. He
is performing well in school, and realizes that he has to continue to do
that in order to go to college. His academic success has not been free of
conflict and compromise. In elementary school he resorted to alliances
with the bullies and hoodlums in his classes to protect himself from the
fights he would otherwise have experienced as a high-achieving student.
It was in junior high that he developed the comedic personality he currently presents in a deliberate effort to avoid being identified as a brainiac. This persona helps him thwart the hostility of classmates that is
generally associated with academic achievement and apartness in high
school. It also misleads his schoolmates because clowns and comedians
are generally stereotyped as people who are *not* intellectually gifted. The
strategy is successful for Norris because it permits him to continue to be
the loquacious, talkative person he is and meanwhile demonstrate his
continued allegiance to the Black community in spite of his success in
school.

Based on the analyses generally offered by social scientists, Norris's
home environment and family structure would suggest that he would
not "make it." His father, who lived with his mother until a few months
ago, was habitually unemployed; the family lived in the projects, and

his mother was solely responsible for providing food and shelter and rearing him and his brother. She appears to have found the appropriate mix of a mother's unconditional love and her clearly defined expectations for her male children (R. Staples 1984). Norris's accomplishments in school also support the accuracy of Clark's argument (1983) regarding the relationship between school achievement and family structure. The structure of the family is not the critical factor; it is, instead, the actual processes occurring within the family that either enhance or diminish the academic achievement of poor Black children.

Wendell: "It Seem Like I Have Two Personalities—Three Really: One for School, One for When I Go Out for Jobs and Everything, and One When I'm at Home."

Wendell is the only male high achiever who is growing up in a home without the constant presence of an adult, male role model. His mother is rearing him and his younger sister alone. She is also rearing them in publicly subsidized housing with a source of income that is stigmatized: public welfare.

In elementary school and until graduation from junior high school, Wendell actively engaged in the construction of Otherness, discounting the impact his personal circumstances might have on his schooling. He convinced himself that if he worked hard in school and made good grades, the fact that he was reared in a single-parent household and that his mother received Aid for Dependent Children would be inconsequential.

> My junior high, I used to *love* to go to school. If I'm sick, my mother wake me up, it's almost quarter to nine, I get up and go to school; I don't care [how late it is]. But now that I got at Capital this year, it seem like I'm losing interest in school . . . Really, if I had my way, I'd rather get out *this* year . . . 'Cause I'm getting—I'm going to tell you, in life, you get tired of certain things, and I'm just getting tired of going to school. But I'm not going to drop out . . . School just don't interest me no more . . . I guess that [now] I'm getting up in age [18] that I can do things on my own and everything, I don't want to just take time and sit down and listen to no-body talk for forty-five minutes, and write work and every-thing. I'd rather go and *make* some money. (Interview, March 23, 1983)

Wendell's words capture only part of what he means. He did not have to work hard to earn good grades in elementary and junior high school. It was easy for him to maintain his relationships with his friends and for him to commit himself to the construction of success. Recently, however, he has found that he needs to put forth more effort in order to maintain his previous level of achievement. That would not be too difficult were it not for the fact that some powerfully negative experiences have been associated with his academic accomplishments.

> But the thing I didn't like about [my junior high school], they didn't even give me *nothing*. They should have given me something for being valedictorian . . . You know, some kind of award or something. Money, or something. This man off the ice cream truck, he said whoever had the highest grades, who graduate, he was going to give something to. So I kept telling him, "I'm going to be that person." He ain't believe me. I came to him, and I said, "I got the highest grades, I'm valedictorian, you gonna give me that TV. I get that TV." So he gave me the TV. He was serious . . . he was serious. (Interview, March 23, 1983)

The disregard of school officials for his accomplishments as the top-ranked student in his junior high school class disabused him of a strongly held belief that one is adequately rewarded for academic achievements. Wendell's view of the American social system was forever changed by what happened to him during the several weeks before he graduated from junior high. Both he and his mother are convinced that "they" treated him shabbily because of his family background and living conditions. His mother is convinced that he did not get a reward for earning the title valedictorian because he lives in the "projects" and she gets "welfare." She asserts:

> Because when Wendell graduated, what made me mad—I was listening to the radio one day, and I listened to how they did the other schools, like the junior high *I* used to go to, how they honored the kids and stuff. But over here, they didn't do nothing. Here some man didn't even know Wendell, took and bought him a gift. And bought the salutatorian some stuff . . . If a child . . . it's not so much you paying the child, but letting the child know you appreciate what they did. That's for their school. You know? And I said, every time I turned around, Wendell was the head of everything his junior high school had. Everything—and I used to help support that stuff . . . I didn't think it was fair. I even called the newspaper. I sure did . . . I sure did . . . And [there was] a good big write-up in the paper. And this White lady, she said, "Well, I know how you feel." It was this newswoman I talked to. I told her I

didn't think it was fair . . . And I even went to [the council-person]—this [person], I don't know who she was, but she been knowing Wendell ever since Wendell was in elementary . . . You always want the Black kids to do so much, and they're always there waiting for the kids in [the Capital community]—it's a lot of kids over here, and they not dumb. You know? But they're always talking [about kids in other sections of the city], but nothing over here. They don't honor the kids over here, and I don't think it's fair. (Interview, June 13, 1983)

Wendell's mother went on to tell me how outraged she became when she saw her child and the children in the Capital community referred to as "the kids over here in the ghetto." With the help of a female college student who lived next door, "I wrote [a] letter . . . and I sent it to the [*Washington Post*], but they never put it in the paper . . . They never put it in the paper. I *sure* let them know! I wrote them a four-page letter, I said, honey, don't you be classing *me* as this and that 'cause I live in National Capital Housing. I said, I don't live in no ghetto. I says, some things in my house, honey, I paid more than you did. You know?" (interview, June 13, 1983)

This experience changed Wendell's perception of the nature and function of schooling in America. For the first time in his life, he is feeling ambivalent about school and its value. He now argues that just because a student does not do well in school does not mean that he is unintelligent—a revolutionary insight.

Well, you know, just about everybody know that I was kind of smart. But I don't like them to say I'm real . . . I'm smart; I like them to say that I know some things. When you say they smart, that's the main thing—that's why I think that I lost my interest in school. Because everybody say, "He's smart," and if you're smart, every advisory, "Oh, you get the honor roll?" So this year if they ask me did I get the honor roll, I say, "I really can't say," 'cause I know I didn't get the honor roll, and as soon as I would have said, "No I didn't get the honor roll"—"Oh man, what wrong with you, man? What's wrong with you?" and everything. They looked up to me. That's what I think messed me up the worst. If they would have treated me like everybody else, I think I would have continued my grades here at Capital right. (Interview, March 23, 1983)

The conflict Wendell is experiencing regarding the relationship between academic success and recognition and reward is having a very negative impact on his school performance. His experience as he graduated from junior high has convinced him that there is no value in trying to differentiate himself from his peers and the negative things generally associated with African-Americans. This experience has made him so bitter that he refused to show up for the ceremony inducting him into the National Honor Society. This is how I described his evolving transformation in my fieldnotes:

> For the first time in his life, Wendell wants to shed [the brainiac] image. The image he seems to want to have instead is that of a ladies' man. He has only one girlfriend, with whom he spends an inordinate amount of time. He is also cutting class a lot this year, a totally new thing for him.
>
> Like most of the other male students I have interviewed to date, Wendell noted his paramount desire to be accepted by his male peer group, especially the more macho males. He seems to identify with the guys most of the eleventh-grade girls describe as handsome. He had nothing but praise for Clyde, whose tall, slender frame made him the choice for the "groom" in the junior class's talent show. All the girls think Clyde is absolutely gorgeous. This female response to a male is admired by Wendell, who is just the opposite in physical characteristics . . . Wendell is a short, thin male with big teeth and horn-rimmed glasses. He is generally thought of as a "smart boy" as opposed to Clyde's reputation as a "lady killer." While both males are members of the school band, Wendell plays the drum while Clyde is the drum major and gets to hog the spotlight as well as the females' attention. His long legs prancing up and down the football field or down the street are observed by everyone. Moreover, as drum major he gets to control the action; his whistle is constantly in use. Wendell admires all of these things. He thinks Clyde is the greatest thing since sliced bread. (Fieldnotes, March 29, 1983)

Wendell's desire to be more than what he is, is also reflected in his wish to be more like Clyde and less like himself. Not surprisingly, his inability to "consume" or become either Clyde or the Other is diminishing his academic effort. Like most of the other males at Capital, Wendell views success in monetary terms. Indeed, money is so central to his notion of success that when I asked which male administrator he admired and would like to be like at Capital, he was hard pressed for an answer:

> I know you don't think I'm going to say Mr. McGriff! . . . I don't know [if there is anyone here I admire] . . . None of them . . . 'Cause I wouldn't want to be like none of them . . .

Maybe Mr. Mooney. They say he got a lot of money and everything. Money help . . . (Interview, March 29, 1983)

Wendell and most of the other male students at Capital do not want
to be like Mr. McGriff or the other male faculty members because, in
their view, these men are so much like the Other that they have crossed
over and are guilty of passing for Black. Mr. McGriff does not share
their perceptions of his behavior. Like the high-achieving students, Mr.
McGriff sees his actions as a form of resistance to the low expectations
proclaimed for African-American people. But, as Wendell's response suggests, most of the students—both high- and underachieving—interpret
his behavior as evidence that he overidentifies with "Otherness," aban-
doning the "Self" in the process. They point to his preoccupation with
their school performance and to the fact that he owns a Cadillac.[12] As
Wendell and many of the other high-achieving males view him, Mr.
McGriff is a book-black Black.

Wendell and his peers want to be successful, but they do not want
to become the Other. They want wealth, power, and fame. At the same
time, Wendell declares unequivocally that the most important step for
African-American school success is to rid oneself of Blackness: "Don't
be looked on as Black. Seem like it change a lot of things sometimes"
(interview, May 20, 1983).

Because he thought it imperative that he have his own money—and
because he could no longer tolerate asking his mother for money which
she did not have—Wendell obtained a part-time job. According to his
mother, his French teacher helped him to get it. As Wendell and his
mother perceived it, this is tangible evidence of the fictive kinship system
at work.

Wendell works for a man whose income-tax business generates a
good deal of money. While Wendell is supposed to have set hours from
5 to 9, for example, he often works late if he has not finished the tasks
assigned him. As an all-purpose office boy during the second semester
of his junior year, he is spending a lot of time away from home and
away from his schoolwork. He has no choice but to be at the office,
because federal and state income tax forms are due, and he must get
them mailed as soon as possible.

Achieving academic distinction among African-American males is an
extremely disconcerting process. Wendell talks about his embarrassment
when his French teacher identified him as the class's brainiac and by
extension a much ballyhooed role model.

Like, my French teacher was saying that, was saying that I'm
good and everything, right?—in class, around her, want everybody to act like me. I tried to say, "No! Don't say *that*!" you

know, 'cause I know people get mad at me and stuff. So—it seem like sometime you want to have your friends. (Interview, March 29, 1983)

Wendell was extremely conscious of the strong sanctions against becoming the Other. He realized that if his public persona became linked to the image of the Other, his humanness would be questioned, and he would lose his connectedness to the African-American community. He bluntly summarized it: "Well, they [my friends and schoolmates] say, 'Since he smart, you know, he think he *too* smart. You know, we don't want to deal with him.' Like that . . ." (interview, March 29, 1983).

Martin: "White Ways Are Better than Black Ways."

Perhaps more than any of the other high-achieving males, Martin suffers from conflict emanating from his being an African-American. This conflict and its associated limitations are at the center of his construction of Otherness and undermine his desire for academic success.

Like Wendell, Martin is slight in stature and a member of the school band. As I have already indicated, his academic performance was initially propelled by the absolute insistence of his parents, particularly his mother, on academic accountability. He initially resisted her efforts, but her willingness to punish him, even in the presence of his peers at school, slowly altered his response. His internalization of the views espoused by his mother led him to the following assertion:

> Outside my home . . . really . . . really, the only person that in-
> fluenced me or anything, something like that, is—well, the
> friends that I have—I don't be hanging out with nobody bad,
> that smoke or drink anything, nothing like that. Well, my
> friends, I don't hardly listen to them too much either, because
> some of my friends, *I'm* smarter than *them*. I tell *them* what
> to do. I mean, I [am] the smallest one of the group, and *I* tell
> *them* what to do. And . . . You know, besides the band peo-
> ple, when I hang around them, but before then, everybody
> was about 5'5". I was only about 5, 5'2", something like that.
> And I'd tell *them* what to do. I was the smallest, I was what
> you call the *brains* of the group. They had the muscle. And
> they—but mostly the person that really influence me some-
> times, and [give] me advice, it sometimes be my girlfriend,
> mostly. 'Cause she knows me better than my friends. (Inter-
> view, February 28, 1983)

Martin concedes that he internalizes Otherness in his efforts to obtain school-prescribed humanness. In fact, he asserts that "White ways *are* better than Black ways" (interview, March 23, 1983). And, since "White ways" dominate, even in this predominantly Black high school, he seeks to capture that way of life. At the same time, he acknowledges that choosing such a life is not without conflict and ambivalence. Hence, he migrates between what he describes as the superior "White ways" and "Black ways."

Like Wendell, Martin identifies discrimination and prejudice as being widely practiced by White Americans, who thus limit Black Americans' efforts to improve their economic, political, and social condition. Nevertheless, when asked to explain the horrendous poverty in the Black community, he offers the following response:

> *Martin:* Like I said, they [Black Americans] don't care. That's what I say. They don't care . . . I mean, they'll stand out on the corner, smoke marijuana, and all that. And I think it's—I don't know why nobody . . . you know, they won't get theirself together, but I think that they just don't care.
>
> *Anthro:* You think they're poor because they don't care?
>
> *Martin:* They don't care. They don't *try.* Like the—like welfare, you know. If I was Reagan, I *would* cut it out. 'Cause they should get their butts out there and work. But I know there ain't no jobs out there. But they need to try to get *some* kind of work . . . I mean, okay, around my way, there *are* a lot of people on welfare. And I think that . . . Black people, I don't know why they—they just don't care, that's what *I* say. (Interview, March 23, 1983)

Martin sees himself as being different from most other Black Americans:

> I care. I care what people think of me. I always try to do a good impression on people. I always care, 'cause . . . Mm-hm . . . 'cause most of them—yeah, because most [Black people] don't care. They'll do something, and they'll say, "So? I don't care!" They'll rob and steal—I mean, Whites do rob, too, but the majority is Black. 'Cause I always try to tell, especially the young people that I know, you know, young kids around my way do—they always come to *me* a lot, because I'm known as a brainiac on my street, you know, to little kids. I be talking to them, I tell them stay in school as much as you can, because you *are* going to need it. 'Cause I know when they get up there, it's really going to be hard. (Interview, March 23, 1983)

Martin's view of himself as being different from the masses of Black people deviates from the pattern presented by most of the high-achieving males in the sample. He wants those persons with whom he interacts, including both his peers and his teachers, to think well of him. This desire compels him to adopt a lifestyle and strategies far less harmful than a public stance that brands him a brainiac, preoccupied with individual goals and objectives. Because he both values being known as a brainiac and fears being accused of acting white, he puts brakes on his academic effort. But even though he is propelled in two opposed directions, his commitment to proving that African-Americans can do what the dominant social structure proclaims they cannot do is stronger, fueling his resistance to the pressure his peers apply.

More than any of the other male students, Martin was forthcoming about his personal fear of the loss of maleness and perhaps of his male friends. He asserted that among the male students in the advanced placement program, fear of being looked on as a "pervert brainiac" was omnipresent. Martin feels compelled to delineate the difference between a pervert brainiac and a brainiac:

> Now, a brainiac—okay, you would say, like *me*, right? I'll do my schoolwork and everything, I'll do my homework and everything, but I *will* have *some* fun. I *will*, no matter what. I *will* play around. That is really what a brainiac is. He does the work, but he *will* play around. That's what *I* say a brainiac is, somebody else . . . might call it something else. That's what I say . . . I don't know why, I just don't like [the word "brainiac"] I don't know why, I just do not like the word . . . I haven't heard it in a long—I heard it a couple of times. I [even] be calling people brainiacs. [Laughter] (Interview, March 23, 1983)

Martin goes on to equate a "pervert brainiac" with homosexuality.

> I be calling them ["pervert brainiacs"] gay, too. I be calling—I called this guy, Venny—I said, "Venny, man, you be acting a little gay—gay a little bit, man, you better find a girl, man!" And say, "You want a girl, man, I can hook you up." See, I told that to Venny, right? I know he . . . see, he know he gay, the way he act. You know, him an' his friend, you know? Both of them act gay. I be messing with them and everything. I mean, a guy be sitting all like—I mean, if a guy—okay, you can distinguish a homosexual, I think, by the way he walk, and the way he sit down. 'Cause the way—you know, some

guys sit down, they just do like this. A homosexual sits like that—like that, you know. [Laughter] You know, or put his leg under here like that. I cannot sit like that, you know. I can't do that. I can't do that for nothing. You know, that's what *I* say. A homosexual . . . *I*'d be worried about it if *I* was called [gay]. I'll go to another school, 'cause, you know, you going to have that name on you—homosexual. See, I don't know why—a homosexual can take joning.[13] Somebody call *me* gay, I'm going to bust him, 'cause I'm going to prove to him *I*'m not *gay*. You know . . . (Interview, March 23, 1983)

Martin's admission documents one of the central reasons why the male students at Capital are fearful of the pursuit of academic excellence: they fear being labeled gay. Embodied in the process of becoming the Other is the perception of a loss of gender integrity, a transformation of the gendered Self (Fordham 1989, 1990, 1993).

While none of the other high-achieving males were as explicit as Martin regarding this issue, all of them presented nonverbal as well as verbal signals indicating fear. Like Martin, they noted the importance of being connected to a female. Indeed, most of them have concluded that one of the surest ways of protecting oneself from the charge of being gay is to be sexually involved with women. Hence, the dating practices of the high-achieving males differ drastically from those of the under-achieving males in that the high-achieving male tends to align himself with one female who is then widely and unequivocally known as his "girlfriend."

Paul: "Nobody [at This School] Would Be Caught Dead with a Big Bush [Afro Hairstyle]—Nobody."
As I have already indicated, Paul is ambivalent about his status as a brainiac or a scholarship boy. He is also concerned about how such a status meshes with an identity that is both Black and external to Black-ness. He is not alone.

> To me, Blacks really don't have a culture in America. They do, but it was the sort of things that have developed from be-ing in America. They aren't like Africans or other people of that type. They don't actually have their own culture. I mean, the things that we have in America are really a White culture with maybe, say—let's see, I take sociology—with Black cul-tural survivals, that type of thing. The type of food we eat, it's all culture survivals, I guess you could say. If that's the right term I want to use. Like for instance . . . most Black people like their food well done. And that was because when they

were given meat on the plantation, they always thought something was wrong with it, so they would cook it longer in order
to make sure that it was fit to eat. And so most [Black] people
like their food well done. Except for a few quote-unquote
"bourgeoisie" people, or bougie people who like their meat
medium rare, that sort of thing. But that—most type of
things, like I say, are culture survivals. Maybe rhythm. I kind
of think that some opinions are true, like I think Black people
have a little more rhythm than Whites, myself, personally. (Interview, February 17, 1983)

Paul will not permit himself to believe that people of African ancestry in America developed a culture that is autonomous, not connected
to that of the larger American system.[14] He recognizes that there are
important ways in which Black people differ from White people, but, he
argues, there are areas of overlap, with the American component of
African-Americans' identity being much more visible and more evident
than the African component.

Blacks have a culture all their own, but their culture doesn't
deviate that much from White Western society. They . . . a
Black person could—well, I couldn't really say that—Blacks
have a culture. But it's mostly a White culture. *Blacks judge
other Blacks according to White standards.* And that has
slightly deviated due to certain differences. I mean, the races
are different. Whether some people like to say they aren't. I
don't necessarily—well, yes, I do—I do believe that certain
races are superior. I think Blacks are superior. But then again,
like I said, I'm prejudiced. So anyway . . . I'd say that Black
culture is not only African survivals, but slavery survivals—at
least the east coast, I haven't been west. And I'd say, Southern
ideals, Black Southern ideals, and—well, it all depends on
where you live, too. (Interview, February 17, 1983)

Like many of his classmates, Paul seeks both to embrace and to
distance himself from what is seen as quintessentially Black. This is a
goal because what is identified as totally Black is seen as limiting already
limited opportunities. He wants a future in which race is neither privileged nor stigmatized. Hence, to embrace that which is identified as
distinctively Black sabotages and undermines his upward mobility goals.
According to Paul, while Capital students deplore the thought of mimick-
ing White people, they also want to absorb essential components of that
which is historically associated with White people: the material features
of the idealized life associated with the American Dream.

It's—it's not really like the . . . what do you . . . the Civil
Rights Movement of the '60s and the Black Pride of the '70s.
It's not like that. A lot of people at Capital are *so* conservative. And to us, the things that our parents did were so radical, not that we're not appreciative of the things they did, but
it's so radical, and a lot of people feel it doesn't apply to us,
and so they really—as a matter of fact, everybody's sort of trying to lean toward a Uncle Tom type. They don't—nobody
likes it if you play up to a White person or that sort of thing,
they don't really like that. But they will try and *be* White.
Look at the dress and hair styles and clothes styles. Everything's very conservative now. *Nobody would be caught dead
with a big bush—nobody.* I mean, they would die. And you
hear a lot of people talking about people with big bushes. You
know, my aunt has a big bush. But that's beside the point.
She's very confident in her Blackness, so it doesn't bother her.
But . . . None of my friends, they would *die* if they had a
bush. But . . . that type of thing. And nobody would be
caught with red, green, and black on. You know? They would
say, "Oh, look at him, he's clashing," you know, and all that.
That type of thing. Well, [African-American students have] become very conservative. I think that's sort of the trend. (Interview, February 3, 1983)

In summary, ethnographic data obtained from the Capital High research site show how different segments of the high-achieving student
population seek to enhance their individual futures and, in the process,
alter the dominant negative perceptions regarding African-Americans'
intellectual capabilities. The common theme in the responses of all of
the students is resistance to established, stigmatizing dogma. Their resistance is inextricably linked to the construction of Otherness.

As constructed and manifested by many of the high-achieving students, Otherness is generally perceived to be at variance with maintaining
humanness as it has operated and in some ways still does operate in the
African-American community. But the analysis presented here indicates
that this perception does not capture the diversity, the tensions, and the
fluid nature of the students' lives. Some of the African-American students
at Capital are able to escape accusations associated with the representation of Otherness; others are not. Some students go beyond resistance
to consumption or internalizing Otherness—that is, thinking of themselves as White. It is the group's collective fear of this latter response
that provokes the resistance and unilateral rejection of Otherness.

SEVEN

Retaining Humanness: Underachievement and the Struggle to Affirm the Black Self

Stealing can be a two-edged sword. Apart from increasing the cost of the goods or services to the general public, a less obvious result is that the practice usually acts as a depressant on the employee's own wage level. Owners of small retail establishments and other employers frequently anticipate employee stealing and adjust the wage rate accordingly. Tonk's employer explained why he was paying Tonk $35 for a 55–60 hour workweek. *These men will all steal* (emphasis added), he said. Although he keeps close watch on Tonk, he estimates that Tonk steals from $35 to $40 a week. What he steals, when added to his regular earnings, brings his take-home pay to $70 or $75 per week. The employer said he did not mind this because Tonk is worth that much to the business.

Such a wage-theft system, however, is not as balanced and equitable as it appears. Since the wage level rests on the premise that the employee will steal the unpaid value of his labor, *the man who does not steal on the job is penalized* (emphasis added). And furthermore, even if he does not steal, no one would believe him; the employer and others believe he steals because the system presumes it. (Liebow 1967: 37–38).

Resisting a perceived mandate to appropriate the identity of (an)Other is both an unconscious and a conscious response at Capital High.[1] However, as the extract from Liebow suggests, because both the school and the dominant social system presume inadequacy, or lack, in the Black Other, the system's ongoing practice of raping the Black Self is not appropriately labeled or censured. Capital students who attempt to resist

Self-appropriation often unwittingly reinforce rather than transform the existing social imaging of the Black Other. Their unsuccessful struggle to avoid absorbing the identity of (an)Other is critical to the continuation of the current system of domination (Friedman 1992b).

It is not surprising, therefore, that among the underachieving students at Capital High, schooling is generally constructed as a kind of warfare, an emboldened attempt to reclaim the appropriated Black Self, to avoid being constructed as (an)Other. Unlike the high-achieving students who resist dominant claims of Black people's intellectual inadequacy by consciously conforming to school norms and expectations, underachieving students resist through avoidance. For them, the school experience does not fit that broad category of ceremonies Van Gennep (1960) labels "rites of passage." Instead, it is perhaps best labeled a "rite of survival," where achievement—their merit scholarship—is simply persisting and enduring.

As these students envision their racialized bodies, liquidating the Black Self is vigorously resisted primarily because the existing Black Self, stigmatized by the dominant society, is highly valued by the fictive kinship community. Most of these students view success in school as embodying the construction of Otherness, and they associate such success with an inevitable degree of Self-alienation. Consequently, their psyches are riddled with conflict and tension.

The underachieving students desire validation and affirmation rather than denigration of the Black Self.[2] They want to have Black humanness codified in the White community in the ways it is idealized in the African-American community. They also want their perception of Black humanness linked to—but not embedded in—the affluence and material comforts generally associated with the dominant population.

The dominant ideology postulates that academic achievement is the primary route to success; but to Capital students academic success is the primary route to becoming the Other, the one sure way significant aspects of oneself are remade and the Black Self gets liquidated (Carter 1993:73). The juxtaposition of these conflicting demands, expectations, experiences, and perceptions is at the core of the dilemma undermining academic achievement at Capital High.

Among underachieving students, resistance is used as cultural mortar to reclaim, create, and expand African-American humanness. Their evolving definition of humanness is juxtaposed with the drastically different meaning of resistance as constructed by high-achieving students. These students envision themselves as part of an "imagined community" of diasporic Black people, fighting to regain the appropriated components of their community and their identity. Hence, as I shall document, their school behavior and academic performance reflect their estrangement from the larger society and their encapsulation in this decolonization aesthetic.

Tensions created by the conflict between how Black adolescents *should* respond to schooling, as opposed to how they often actually *do* respond, plague the underachieving students in their efforts to highlight the dignity of their racial and cultural identity. They appear to be severely affected by these tensions in ways comparable to those of their high-achieving counterparts. For both groups of students, anxieties are apparently nourished by their uncompromising efforts to survive, to be both Black and successful in school, which is in many ways a cultural non sequitur.[3]

Since most of the students at Capital High are labeled underachievers, I document in this chapter numerous instances of how underachievers retain a racialized identity as people of African descent. I show how this commitment to a culturally appropriate Self is implicated in their minimal academic effort. The most widely utilized strategy in the underachieving students' preservation of the Self is *avoidance*. As used here, avoidance indicates both a commitment to the survival of a Black Self and the rejection of (an)Other's humanness. It also suggests a not so subtle effort to retain one's existing perception of a Black humanness by refusing to learn what is taught in school.

Avoidance of consuming the Other is everywhere apparent at the school. It is the students' pièce de résistance—their main accomplishment. Outsiders visiting the school often comment on the peaceful atmosphere, on the absence of fighting and other physical violence.[4] But this apparent calm masks the underlying rage and tensions felt by the students. Instead of confronting school officials or constructing an open rebellion or multiple rebellions, they resist the construction of Otherness by avoiding certain courses—World History, for instance, as well as specific school-related activities like the chess club and the math club. This response is most visibly manifested in their concentration in the academic track labeled "regular" and in their wholesale shunning of the advanced placement program, the segment of the school's curriculum that is most likely to lead to academic success at Capital and admission to the nation's elite colleges and universities.

As J. Scott (1985) suggests, avoidance is a "weapon of the weak." The underachieving students appear to understand this intuitively. As they construct their world, becoming (an)Other means not only accepting the accuracy of existing racist labels and definitions such as "These men will all steal" (Liebow 1967:37), but also relinquishing their will to survive, coupled with their humanness as people of African ancestry.

I do not mean to imply that this is a conscious decision on the part of the students; it is for some but not for others. The underachievers generally feel uncomfortable with most of the demands associated with the core curriculum, and they sense a threat to their identity. They are not necessarily aware of why they actively avoid what they are repeatedly told will make life so much easier for them as African-American adults: academic excellence.

AVOIDING "OTHERNESS" AT CAPITAL HIGH

Avoidance among the underachieving students is nearly universal at Capital High, and while males and females develop specific forms and strategies, all resist not only participation in the advanced placement curriculum but also regular and timely school attendance, practices their teachers and other school officials identify as indicators of hostility and violations of established school norms.[5] Still another indicator of avoidance is the students' reluctance to participate in assignments and activities considered absolutely essential to obtaining proficiency in high-level reading and writing skills.

In general, the underachieving students seek to limit their contact with all segments of the school curriculum that might suggest that they are acting white—that is, trying to lessen the perception of lack in the Black Self while avoiding the construction of the Black Self in the image of (an)Other (see Fanon 1967). Although this strategy is psychologically costly and consumes a great deal of time and energy that might otherwise be devoted to schoolwork, it is the strategy of choice among the underachieving students at Capital, and it is the focus of the analysis that follows.

Grade Point Average
Selection of the students in the underachieving sample group was based largely on their teachers' consistent assessments of academic ability, including strong assertions that these students were underperforming in the classroom.[6] I also compared their teachers' oral and written assessments on school measures of their success over time. The single most salient characteristic the sample group shared was a GPA of C− or lower. Like students in the high-achieving sample group, these students were judged "in the round," with subjective and objective assessments merged (Bailey 1977).

Elementary and Junior High School Grades
Although only one of the underachieving males received excellent grades in elementary school, all of them received above-average grades. The picture changed somewhat in junior high school, with most showing a

downward trend. Most of the males insist that studying was not necessary in elementary school; they were able to make good grades simply by completing assigned homework, which they insist was sparse. In junior high school, a little more effort was required, but not enough to warrant a drastic change in behavior. The major cause of the lessened effort and lower grades appears to have been the emerging sense of manhood, which was repeatedly negated by the "master status" (Hughes 1945) of Blackness coupled with a desire for acceptance by the changing peer group.

The underachieving students insist that in order to be accepted by their peers, they had to forgo academic achievement and participate instead in activities such as fighting and "getting into trouble"that indicated a lack of commitment to the ideals and values sanctioned in the school context. For example, Art insists that he "made good grades all in elementary school. In seventh grade, that's where all my trouble started. 'Cause I started getting in fights. I got in a fight the second day of school" (interview, March 14, 1983).

He thinks he was in fights so often during seventh grade because he was publicly seeking school success; indeed, he made the honor roll in both semesters. Art thinks his peers harassed him in seventh grade "'cause they thought I was a sucker." In response, he did not try to make the honor roll in the eighth grade, nor has he made it since.[7]

Sidney, whose grades have skidded downward since junior high school, attributes his low grades in senior high to a lack of willpower and time-on-task. In fact, he appears to be confused by his sudden and drastic change from an honor roll student in junior high to a mediocre performer at Capital. He fails to link that performance to his failure to study. In elementary and junior high he was able to make good grades while spending time-on-task, which is central to success in high school. In general, the effort and grades of the male students were higher in elementary school and have gradually gone downhill, so much so that today their grades are lower than they have been at any other time in their school history.

A somewhat similar picture emerges when one looks at the academic history of the females in this sample. Three of them received grades well above average in elementary school and high enough in junior high to enable each of them to maintain membership in her school's National Honor Society. The other three females maintained a record generally comparable to their present performance.

Sakay's academic achievement was well above that of her classmates in elementary school. She began her schooling in one of the suburban jurisdictions and, as she puts it, "My grades were okay, they were like a C/B average." When she transferred to the elementary school in Washington the next fall, she recalls that she experienced several shocks: all of the students were Black; students in third grade were studying the same things she had mastered in second grade; and her grades "shot up."

> For a long time I sat—for a long time, like *years,* it was like
> I was—I was getting good grades, but I didn't know why,
> because the work that I was doing, it was kind of a rehash.
> And for . . . like two years, I was learning *some* things, but I
> didn't . . . it wasn't really hard on me. It didn't get hard until
> about the eighth grade, because I had real good fifth and sixth
> grade—all my teachers were real good, they taught me some-
> thing. But from third and fourth, it was kind of like, I know
> *that!* (Interview, January 25, 1983)

Sakay's experience in elementary school suggests low expectations and a pattern of not studying that was difficult to change when she began junior high. Somehow she made the necessary adjustment and became a member of the National Honor Society in eighth grade. But she had not been required to exercise self-discipline earlier, and this lack stalked her. Illness took its toll, too, and her grades began to fall in the ninth grade.

Another underachieving female, Dawn, insists that her grades from kindergarten to seventh grade were "great," but since then they have not been comparable in any way. In fact, during the final semester of ninth grade, Dawn earned four Ds and three Cs.

In summary, these high school students attribute their declining grade records chiefly to the low standards and lack of effort called for in the lower grades.

Behavior

Most of the students in this sample group, males and females, have been involved in activities that have brought them to the attention of their classroom teachers and school administrators. While the males, with one exception, acknowledge involvement in forbidden activities, none appears to have been suspended or expelled for any extended period of time.

During elementary and junior high school, all of these students appear to have attended school regularly and punctually. As a group, their greatest problem was their fighting, with most of them claiming that their involvement was defensive rather than offensive. In high school their experience appears to be less traumatic for two reasons: peer group membership is clearly established at this point in their lives, and there is no longer the group impetus to prove one's "manhood" or, in the case of the female students, "sisterhood" by engaging in such activities; and at Capital there are strong, enforced administrative sanctions against fighting.

Several of the male members of the sample admit that they drink moderately, although generally not on the school grounds because of the strong arm of the principal, Mr. McGriff.

> *Anthro:* Is drinking a big problem here? Is it widespread?
>
> *Sidney:* Yes . . . Far as a problem, well, I wouldn't say it's a problem, because they don't drink around the school. They do somewhere else; they wouldn't do it around the school. I *do* give them that much. They *have* discipline enough not to do it around school, yes.
>
> *Anthro:* Do you think that that's the result of the administration, or . . . ?
>
> *Sidney:* Yeah, that's why, I think, the reason why the principal acts the way he does, because the school population, you know . . . He has a job to do, I don't knock that; but sometimes he get out of hand, so—gets carried away. (Interview, March 17, 1983)

Mr. McGriff's apparent ability to appear to be everywhere at once motivates the students to limit their drinking and other banned activities to lunchtime and after school. Sidney made it quite clear that the students curtailed these behaviors while on school grounds *not* because they accepted Mr. McGriff's premise that such activities are morally reprehensible but simply because they did not want to be confronted by Mr. McGriff and forced to listen to his prepackaged lecture on the dominant morality. Off campus they did not hesitate to drink or engage in any of the other activities that Mr. McGriff bans at Capital.

I was fascinated by Sidney's characterization of the students' response to Mr. McGriff's efforts to motivate them to resist by conforming or, as the students generally perceived it, by becoming more like the Other.

> *Sidney:* Well, he figures everyone has to be like him. He's always talking about his university and what he accomplished in life. I say, "People can't be like you. They have to accomplish whatever they want to do in life." If they don't want to accomplish anything, that's them.
>
> *Anthro:* Do you think there's a lot of resentment of him here?
>
> *Sidney:* Yes, very.
>
> *Anthro:* You really think so?
>
> *Sidney:* Yes.

Anthro: You mean people actually resent him?

Sidney: More than half the school population resent him.

Anthro: Why?

Sidney: 'Cause what he talks about. Most of them think he's crazy.

Anthro: And that's not a complimentary "crazy"? I mean, that's not a positive thing?

Sidney: No, that's—they think he's a lunatic.

Anthro: Meaning?

Sidney: He should be over in St. Elizabeth's. He needs mental help.

Anthro: Why do they think that?

Sidney: There would be very many opinions about that. Different views. He walks around, tells students . . . well, he's doing it for their own good, telling them to get out the hallways and go to your class and get good grades and all that, but people think he's crazy 'cause he keeps repeating it, preaching it. (Interview, March 17, 1983)

Only one of the underachieving males appears to have been impaired by involvement with drugs. In fact, Karl's use of marijuana and perhaps other drugs became so extensive that I gave up trying to interview him. Curiously, he was the only student in the underachieving sample who insisted that he did not drink.

In general, the males consider behaviors usually associated with maleness as a part of their preordained role repertoire. Most of them appear to accept Sidney's taxonomy of what it takes to be a real man: alcohol, drugs, athletics, and women, not necessarily in that order.

The female underachievers are widely known at Capital High, most often for behavior that violates school norms or values. Kaela is conspicuous for her lack of attendance; Shelvy is remembered by all of her teachers because she "loves to talk" in class; Sade is known for doing very little schoolwork despite being enrolled in most of the advanced placement classes for her grade level. Nekia is known for her willful refusal to obey school rules, which has led to repeated suspensions.

The only female exception to this pattern of high visibility is Sakay, who received little attention from her teachers and counselors because she did not misbehave in the classroom nor perform well in school. She came to the attention of her counselor this year only after her PSAT results turned out to be well above those of most of her peers, and surpassing all expectations.

Nekia is the most rebellious female student, constantly fighting to preserve her identity as a female African-American in places where such a racialized body is not celebrated. Like Rita, she refuses to be silenced. Unlike Rita, she does not camouflage her resistance by clowning. It is both her unwillingness to become an "honorary male" and her refusal to be silenced that is killing her dreams (Griffin 1981; Pagano 1990:13; Payne 1988:18). Nekia is aware—perhaps not consciously—that the school is actually both anti-female (Lewis and Simon 1986; Pagano 1990; Payne 1988; Rich 1979b) and anti-African-American (Evans 1988; Fordham 1993; Ogbu 1974). Her unwillingness to adopt either the gender or racial identity of the dominant Other makes it very difficult for most adults to determine how to structure their interactions with her (Fordham 1993).

I had several formal interviews with Nekia. Even though I thought I understood why she was responding as she was to the school environment, having an interview with her was like going into a war zone. I dreaded it, primarily because I felt compelled to try to help her clarify her perspective and because, at the same time, I constantly feared that she would misunderstand my intentions.[8]

Nekia was clearly, though again perhaps unconsciously, resisting the school's implicit rejection of her both as an African-American and as a woman.[9] But instead of resisting by becoming pregnant, which Payne (1988:15) asserts is the ultimate effort to feminize the male-dominated school context, Nekia was struggling to demasculinize the school and retain as much of her future as she could without the added responsibility of childrearing.

Performance on Standardized Tests

Underachieving students often perform better on standardized tests than their high-achieving counterparts. For example, during the base year of the study, two of the underachieving males—Max and Sidney—scored as well as or higher than four of the high-achieving males. Max and Sidney take most or all of their courses from the advanced placement sequence that is available to eleventh-graders. One other male student— Manley—was placed, in spite of his objections, in an advanced section of the English course required of all eleventh-grade students. None of the underachieving males boasts about his accomplishments or seeks to separate himself from the males whose scores are much lower. Though Sidney and Max scored higher than most of the high-achieving males on the PSAT, nonetheless their response was to avoid learning what their scores were and, once that was no longer possible, to minimize the importance of what they had done. Since their friends are like them— football players and other athletes—they do not want to call attention to themselves in areas other than athletics. Max confesses: "I knew what

I was capable of doing, but sometimes I held back. I just held myself from doing it, to make somebody else happy. That's all I was doing, really" (interview, March 11, 1983).

The other four underachieving males—Korey, Art, Manley, and Karl—scored at about the same level on standardized measures of school success as most of the high-achieving males. Three of the underachieving females—Kaela, Sakay, and Shelvy—scored better on the standardized measures than all but two of their high-achieving counterparts, Katrina and Rita. On the other hand, all of the underachieving females had lower GPAs than their high-achieving female peers. Indeed, there appears to be an inverse correlation between the GPAs of many of the underachieving females and their performance on standardized tests.

Studying and Homework
Perhaps the most striking common feature of the underachieving students is their almost total lack of effort despite the generally low academic expectations at Capital High. These students, especially the males, regularly fail to complete assigned homework and do almost no studying. The males regard all other aspects of life as more important than the need to complete homework or study. Sidney, for example, insists that he spends only fifteen minutes or so doing homework in the morning, just before rushing off to school:

> Okay. I wake up in the morning. About six o'clock, six-thirty. With my radio on I fall out of bed, kick the phone on the floor . . . I just get up—habit. Just fall on the floor, kick the phone off the hook, you know, go to the bathroom, run into the kitchen, say good morning to my mother, get my school clothes ironed, and go take a shower, wait for breakfast, do last night's homework. [Laughter] About fifteen minutes. I just do the math problems I like. And then other problems, right at the school . . . But, anyway, I eat breakfast, then tell my brother that somebody want him on the phone, but there's no one on the phone. And then I'll eat *his* breakfast, and I hurry up and leave before they can say anything. And I walk to school. (Interview, March 17, 1983)

None of the underachieving students has set aside a specific time to study and/or do homework; rather, it is done haphazardly and hurriedly, late at night when they have completed football or basketball or after visiting with their friends at the recreation center, or, as in the case of Sidney, just as they are leaving for school in the morning.

Art probably studies less and does less homework than any other underachiever in the study. It is therefore not surprising to learn that he receives what some teachers describe as "missionary grades"—that is, grades given out of the goodness of the teacher's heart merely because the student is consistently present in class and behaves well. The grade is usually a D. Art's typical school day does not include any time set aside for studying. Like Manley, he spends most of his free time listening to "hard rock" music. He admits that he rarely studies, and he considers it perfectly acceptable to do homework hurriedly at school in class, perhaps copying it from a classmate. He simply hates doing homework at home: "I don't like doing *nothing* for school, when I be at home" (interview, March 15, 1983).

Korey's homework and studying practices have remained essentially unchanged from elementary and junior high school. They can best be described as consistently erratic. He completes most homework assignments most of the time, although he does them hurriedly and sometimes carelessly. He spends most of his after-school time in the recreation center near his home, shooting pool and interacting with friends and neighbors. When he gets home, he watches TV until he falls asleep. When he gets up, he gives short shrift to his school assignments, spending most of the hour watching cartoons and "Good Morning America." He gets to school half an hour before the first period begins and spends that time with his friends.

The female students spend somewhat more time studying and completing assigned homework than their male counterparts—if they have reason to. Dawn wants to go to college and major in broadcast journalism, and this, she realizes, entails learning as much English as she can. Even so, she acknowledges that she spends a minimum amount of time on homework assignments.

> *Anthro:* About how long does it take you to do your homework?
>
> *Dawn:* About an hour and fifteen minutes.
>
> *Anthro:* Do you usually have homework in each class?
>
> *Dawn:* Not usually, but most of the time I'll just sit down and just look over something, like—something. I'll look over mostly the classes that I like. [Laughter] But when it's time for me to have a test or something like that, then I know I have to sit down and read over it.
>
> *Anthro:* What classes do you like?
>
> *Dawn:* None of them! [Laughter] (Interview, March 22, 1983)

In summary, the underachieving students in the sample devote very little time to studying and completing homework assignments. In part at least, they appear to respond in this manner because they want to avoid consumption of the core curriculum and, by extension, emulation of the dominant Other.

Extracurricular Activities

Extracurricular activities appear to be much more important in the lives of the underachieving student sample than in those of the high-achieving students. In fact, for *some* of the students in the sample group, particularly the males, the extracurricular activities appear to be the reason for coming to school.

While only two of the males in this sample are football players, the other four have a strong interest in athletic activities and often skip classes to watch, that is, to participate vicariously in sports. Manley goes further: "I just, like, go down to the game room, go to the arcade, go to the movies, go skating, pick with anybody when I feel like fighting." He prefers fighting to boxing because, he says, "I ain't trying to get my face all messed up; I ain't trying to get nothing on me messed up that ain't already messed up. So I know in boxing, you get messed up decent, but in street fighting you get to do anything you want" (interview, May 13, 1983).

Manley is more energetic than most of his peers. He tries, not always successfully, to contain his energy in ways that are not destructive. It was his high energy level and his ability to endure much more than his peers could that was responsible for his becoming the leader of his peer group in elementary and junior high school: "We [my friends and I] used to hang out and go everyplace, fight all the time, with each other. If one get in a fight, all fight. One get a attitude, all get a attitude" (interview, May 13, 1983).

Manley's preoccupation with competing with his peers in ways that are not necessarily sanctioned by the school is shared with others in this group of students. Sidney outlines his priorities: "It's just that most of my athletic requirements and my women commitments—you know, I have to divide my time according to that. And so I usually study last. Put my athletics first when I shouldn't, but . . . it just happens like that" (interview, March 17, 1983).

He maintains that one of the most important ways to minimize the hostility of one's peers vis-à-vis academic excellence is to be involved in "something extracurricular, by . . . being an athlete, cheerleader squad, in the band—like that . . . something that's *important,* has something to do with—that represents your school" (interview, March 17, 1983).

While the underachieving females are not as involved in sports as the underachieving males, twice as many of them—four—are involved in some sport or an ancillary sports activity. Dawn is a basketball player;

Nekia is a member of the girls' softball team; Sade is a flag girl in the school's band; and Shelvy is a cheerleader. Only Kaela and Sakay are not involved in athletic activities. But the underachieving females as a group do not display as much interest in competitive behavior as do the males. Most of the females have one or two best friends that they spend time with when the organized activity ends, but often these best friends do not share an interest in whatever extracurricular activity they participate in. Apparently, sports activities among the males produce healthy and acceptable competition that enhances the individual student's self-esteem while binding him closer to his peer group. This is not necessarily true for the female students. The problems Shelvy encountered as a cheerleader are a case in point.

Shelvy is currently experiencing an inordinate amount of stress in conjunction with her role as a cheerleader. The members of the ten-member cheering squad have nominated her for the Rookie of the Year Award. Because they view Shelvy as more of a team player, more loyal to the group, and more dependable than another, more skilled student, they have formed a "sisterhood" of conspiracy to deny the latter the title. Shelvy does not relish the idea of being used as an object to punish a fellow cheerleader, but she appears to be unable to do anything about it. She perceives herself as being in a no-win situation: unhappy with the other eight women's decision to use her to make the more skilled rookie learn to live by the norms of the squad, and receiving an award that, on the basis of talent, she does not deserve.

> Well, I guess—okay, I figure like this: they put me up for
> Rookie of the Year . . . Mm-hm. And the way—and I think
> somebody else deserve it. And *they* think she deserve it, but
> they put me up for it, and, you know . . . I don't know. I
> think she resents it, 'cause we *all* feel as though she really de-
> serves it . . . because, for one, she's cheered for a long time,
> and, you know, she's better—I'm not going to say she's not,
> she's better than me—but they look at the fact that I was at
> every game, and, you know, they was . . . I was dependable,
> you know, they depended on me. (Interview, March 8, 1983)

So, unlike the male underachievers, for whom such group activities appear to be a means of cementing their bonds to one another, the female underachievers appear to perpetuate in such activities the traditional interactive process among females: competition manifested as loss—being a good girl is more important than winning (Miner and Longino 1987; Tracy 1991:137–139).[10] In the scripted case studies that follow, brief gender-specific images of several of the underachieving students are presented as a way of documenting the gender-specific implications of resistance as avoidance.

UNCOUPLING RACIALIZED, GENDERIZED BODIES

Colorizing Desire: The "Socialized Penis"
Like White Americans,[11] African-Americans are preoccupied with light skin color. Nowhere in my study was this more apparent than among the underachieving male students at Capital High. The data obtained from these students suggests that a "socialized penis" (Litewka 1977) has evolved, with preference for that which is either white or "light, bright, and damn near white."

I obtained firsthand documentation of this preoccupation with skin color among the underachieving students when I accepted the invitation extended by a social studies teacher to come to her class and record the responses of her students to the current assignment: "Describe the facial characteristics of your ideal woman."

> The teacher first called on a male student. He, as she had predicted to me, listed thin lips, light-to-brown skin, small [thin] nose, and long hair. One male identified the facial characteristics of the woman he wanted to marry as those belonging to a White woman; not one of the other males identified "Black" features as ideal. Clearly, they did not see their future mate as having kinky hair, thick lips and dark skin, and they even called for light brown or hazel eyes. When the instructor asked why they did not mention thick lips, the young man to whom she pointed said that there was "nothing wrong with it (being black or dark brown in skin color); it is just not what I prefer." Another said specifically about thick lips, "Nice thick lips might suck you up."
>
> At my request, the teacher asked the female students to describe the characteristics of the man they would like to marry. Their list was lengthy: (1) tall; (2) skin complexion unimportant ("complexion don't matter"); (3) nice size ("not too skinny"); (4) real smart; (5) intelligent; (6) "in church" (a church member); (7) "can deal with my problems." For none of the twelve females in this class was skin color identified as important in the selection of a potential husband. Indeed, females were frustrated and baffled when the teacher tried to limit their responses to skin color. One student declared, "[What he looks like] does not matter as long as he is working." As the discussion evolved, students talked about the eco-

nomic side of dating and mating. One student noted that, when dating, "If he asked me to go (with him), then he pays." Another noted that she does not want to earn more money than her future husband because "He is going to take care of me." She went on, "If I make more [than he does], he is still going to have to pay the bills, etc. I'll spend my money for whatever I worked to spend it for." In response to this statement a male student declared, "Damn, baby, you'll be paying some bills or something." [Lots of laughter]. Only one young man said he did not want his future wife to work.

Luckily, the bell rang and I could escape from what I perceived to be an appalling situation. (Fieldnotes, November 15, 1982)

As I sat listening to this overwhelmingly chocolate-to-dark-chocolate male (and female) student population describe the physical characteristics they desired in a mate, I was struck by how incongruous their verbalized fantasies were. Among the male respondents, the female Other was favored. Although these are the students who are most adamant in their refusal to become involved in the pursuit of academic excellence, in their voiced preferences for possible dates and mates they did not seek to reclaim or celebrate Blackness or femaleness fused to Blackness. These men verbalized the greatest preference for dating and perhaps mating outside the race.

Virtually no male or female in the class possessed the physical characteristics most highly lauded by these male students. The students' generally dark skin, voluptuous lips, and African hair and features did not reflect Euramerican standards of beauty. I watched closely the female students' predictable responses. Their vibrant brown eyes became muddied with pain; their lips froze in fraudulent, grotesque smiles, and their bodies sagged in shame as their male contemporaries waxed eloquent about the beautiful female Other. As the teacher later noted, while the female students in the class may not have realized it, they were being publicly taught—perhaps for the first time—a lesson that they would learn over and over again: As teenage dates and adult women in the roles of wives and lovers, their lives were destined to be forever riddled with *lack;* they could only serve as poor substitutes for the real objects of Black males' fantasies.

Although the underachieving students resist the herculean efforts of the school officials to induce them to appropriate academic-related Otherness, they nevertheless do assimilate a few critical aspects of what is perceived to be the dominant Other, including images of beauty pertinent to mate selection. Their general internalizing of Euramerican standards of beauty suggests a kind of hyphenated or muddied reclamation. Hence, despite the underachieving students' general aversion to the valorizing of "whiteness," they, too, are mired in the hybridity endemic to the "color complex": hyphenated colorphobia (see Russell, Wilson, and Hall 1992; also McCall 1994) or what Walker (1983) identifies as colorism.[12] Another example emerged during a discussion I had with Ms. Mentor regarding my efforts to get Kaela involved in my study.[13] Ms. Mentor told me how colorphobia, or colorism, is manifested among the students, particularly the underachieving students, at Capital High.

In addition to meeting the requirements of the "sexual auction block" (Holland and Eisenhart 1990; see also McRobbie 1978) in order to be perceived as potentially desirable mates, several of the underachieving male students explicitly argue that a female student should also earn good grades. For example, Max asserted:

> *I* see it this way . . . [she] should be responsible and educated and have a good head on her shoulders. I'm saying, like, well, more that she cares about the way people take her as being. You know, if you go out and make people think that all you want to do is have a lot of fun and play all the time, that's the way people gonna take you to be . . . Guys like girls who are popular—well, sometime that really doesn't interest them as much as I thought it did, but the way they are in their classes, how they do in schoolwork, the way they act around their friends and when they're in everyday situations, the crowd they hang with, sometimes . . . if she keeping her grades up, you know, and have that self-respect for herself, yes . . . and—well, really, that's just about it. (Interview, March 18, 1983)

Wendell makes a similar assertion:

> [Most valedictorians are girls] . . . In every place you should notice that. Mostly girls'll seem like they are . . . smarter than boys . . . Girls—boys try to be—I don't know what you call it, but girls get more into the work than boys . . . It seem like girls catch on faster than boys—most boys. That's what I was trying to get into your mind. (Interview, March 23, 1983)

Given this widely accepted axiom, male high achievers appear to be much more conscious of and sensitive to societal limitations, much less willing to contest the latent and not so latent rules regarding the "whiteness of maleness."[14] Instead of opposing or defying existing dominant group norms, the male high achievers generally adopt a strategy in which conformity and imitation of the Other are central. The clincher is that even though impersonation of the Other is central to Black male academic achievement, at Capital High African-American males impersonate the Other in order to resist and undermine existing dehumanizing stereotypes. Consequently, more than any of the other student groups, the high-achieving males, in their quest for academic success, suffer an overload of conflict. Their decision to reclaim African-American humanness by appropriating the identity of the Other exemplifies a deliberate breach of the low expectations for African-American students, especially the gender-specific limitations imposed on African-American males.

REFUSING TO LEARN

As I have already indicated, I was struck by the importance of gender identity to the high-achieving males. They were the students who repeatedly asserted a relationship between how they performed in school and their identity as male African-Americans. They were the students who insisted that a "typical" school day involved going to the sex shop. They were also the only males who verbalized a concern about being thought of as gay. None of the underachieving males made such assertions. While I am very much cognizant of the fact that the lack of verbalization on the part of the underachieving males does not mean that they had no such concerns, I must admit that I was surprised by the response differential of the high- and underachieving males, both in the ethnographic data and in my preliminary analysis of a small segment of the quantitative data.[15]

The underachieving males' connection to gender issues was clearly displayed in their assertions regarding the nature and configuration of their multiple relationships with females who, most often, were not students at Capital High. As I pointed out earlier in this chapter, Sidney, Art, and Manley were quite vocal in discussing their superficial involvement with females. Each declared that he was not involved with any one special girl, or, if he had a special "squeeze," she was just that—special but not the only woman in his life. Art described dating as "old people stuff."

> *Anthro:* So what do you do if you want to see a girl?
> *Art:* Whoever we feel we want to see, we just go out somewhere and find some.
> *Anthro:* You just go out and find one?
> *Art:* Yup.

Anthro: And what do you do if you find one?

Art: I don't know.

Anthro: You don't have to take her anyplace or buy her anything, or *anything?*

Art: No, I don't want to spend *my* money on nobody.
[Laughter]

Anthro: So, how do you impress her, then?

Art: I *don't* impress her. If she don't like me the way I am, just go to somebody else.

Anthro: Oh, I see. So when you go to a party, you just dance with [girls] or talk to them, but you don't take them out, you don't go to the movie with them, you don't take them to a party or any of that kind of stuff.

Art: No, I don't do all that. No, I don't take them nowhere . . . We'll probably *go* someplace; but I don't *take* them.

Anthro: They pay their own way, in other words.

Art: Yeah.

Anthro: Do you like girls?

Art: Yeah!

Anthro: Do you have a girlfriend?

Art: Nope.

Anthro: When I [asked you if you dated], I meant the same thing as girlfriend. Why don't you have a girlfriend?

Art: I don't never want one.

Anthro: Why?

Art: 'Cause I don't want to get stuck with the same person.

Anthro: Oh, I see, you like variety.

Art: Yup. (Interview, March 15, 1983)

Unlike the high-achieving males who appeared to be connected in some serious ways with particular females, the underachieving males had nothing but disdain for monogamy or semimonogamous relationships. Perhaps this approach to dating and mating influenced the underachieving males' greater verbal concerns about race and race-related issues. The unilateral resistance of underachievers to school achievement seems to insulate them from the accusations triggered by the school performance of their high-achieving male peers. Their academic underachievement appears to validate their identity as real men, while academic achievement appears to undermine that same identity.

As observed in chapter 4, in rearing their sons, African-Americans tend to embrace a contradictory childrearing formula: They concurrently teach acceptance of *subordination* in the larger society and gender *domination* for power and survival in the Black community. What is central to understanding and explaining the underachievement of African-American males at Capital High is their willful avoidance of the first half of this formula, their refusal to accept—even superficially—the subordination component of the formula. The deportment of the male students suggests a deliberate refusal to learn rather than an inability to learn. The following cases are illustrative of this claim.

Korey: "I Don't Do No Book Reports"

Korey's assertion—"I don't do no book reports"—is a typical example of how the underachieving students struggle to avoid the consumption of Otherness, how they strive not to liquidate the Black "Self." By refusing to complete the book report for his English class, Korey sees himself as resisting what is likely to transform his identity. This strategy is widely practiced by Capital students in required courses.

Like the other underachieving students in the ethnographic sample, Korey is struggling with the issues of racial identity and academic success. His main response is to avoid any aspect of the curriculum that might tamper with his perception of who he is as a Black person. For example, English is a required course each year of high school; it is therefore absolutely impossible to avoid.

Korey lives with his mother in a dilapidated apartment. His mother and father were never married; his father lives elsewhere in the city. Korey sees himself as being victimized by numerous ascriptive characteristics, including race and gender. He abhors the devastating poverty that his family and neighborhood suffer. His mother works full time as a short-order cook, a job that will never enable either of them to escape the poverty that is crushing them. The hopelessness of this situation impels Korey to cling to what is familiar and comfortable. Risking behaviors that are not prevalent among the people he knows is definitely out, regardless of personal or academic cost.

At the same time, as the youngest of three children and the only male, Korey is keenly aware of the privileges his sexual identity confers upon him. But he is equally cognizant of the limitations his race imposes on him. Like many of the male students, he appears to be involved in an ongoing struggle with the problem of whether race or gender should have priority in his life.[16] In addition, he is constantly seeking the appropriate response of Black students to different aspects of the school curriculum. His uncertainty about these issues contributes to his underachievement in school.

Korey's definition of success deviates from that promulgated by the dominant society. He maintains that he will be successful if he is able to get a job "working in a store or something . . . if it pay good money. If I make $3.50 an hour, that'd be all right, if I make—if I find a job making $3.50 an hour. And get paid every two weeks" (interview, June 15, 1983).

Korey goes on to note his most important criterion for success: "I'm living. As long as I ain't dead or nothing, in jail or nothing, you know—as long as I'm living average, like regular people, I guess that'd be successful for me" (interview, June 15, 1983).

Korey's notion of success does not include the material symbols usually associated with self-actualization: owning a big house, a big car, and so on. Instead, he thinks he will be successful if he is able to rent an apartment and live a "regular" or normal life. Korey differs from many of the other underachieving males in that his definition of success meshes with his academic effort and performance.

Korey is uncertain about the value of schools and schooling in his future. This lack of certainty is apparent in his ideas about how he should respond to his English teacher's requests regarding certain course requirements. English is one of the required courses that most of the students at the school would avoid were it possible to do so. Since it is not, many of the underachieving students do the next best thing: they avoid specific components of the English curriculum. For Korey, that specific component is the book report.

Korey's negative reaction to the teaching style of his English teacher and her generally low expectations for her students is typical of the avoidance response of the underachieving students, male and female. When I asked Korey what he thought of Ms. Blumberg as a teacher,[17] for example, he responded by assuring me that there are some requirements in her English class that he refuses to do, *regardless of the academic price he must pay*. When I pushed the issue, asking him to tell me what grade he earned in his English class the previous semester, he admitted it was a D.

Korey completes most mechanical homework assignments, such as defining vocabulary words, completing lower-level math assignments, and answering the questions at the end of the chapter in his history text; but he completes them hurriedly and often carelessly. At the same time he prides himself on being a well-behaved student, admitting that if he were not, Ms. Blumberg probably would have given him an F the previous semester, when he opted not to submit a book report. This act alone made him extremely vulnerable to failure. When I probed further, trying to get at the real issues influencing his decision to avoid that component of his English class, I got the following response: "'Cause I didn't do no book report . . . I do my work. I just don't do no book report" (interview, June 15, 1983).

Like Korey, most of the underachieving students refuse, as a matter of principle, to complete assignments of this nature. Teachers report that they are constantly defeated in their efforts to persuade their students to write short answers to questions either on examinations or in other formal settings. Consequently, virtually no teacher gives essay exams, and underachieving students avoid what is officially unavoidable.

Max: "Worrying about What Other People Think of Me"

Max is a seventeen-year-old. Like Korey, he struggles to maintain what he perceives as his Black Self. Unlike Korey, he takes courses exclusively from the advanced placement track. Like many other students in the program, he is a participant only because his parents insist on it.

Max's parents own a beautiful home and a very expensive automobile. The house has all the trappings associated with middle-class status: a car room, expensive furniture, beautiful plants, an expansive green lawn, a veranda, patio furniture, and so on. His mother and father are very much involved in their child's schooling. She is employed in a job category above the "job ceiling"[18]—she is an elementary school teacher. His father is currently on disability but worked for many years as a foreman for one of the major airlines in the country.

Max's older brother—his only sibling—is twenty-seven, ten years older than he. His brother completed high school in the Capital community and went to college, first to Howard as an undergraduate and then to graduate school in Alabama for a master's degree in psychology. He has not been able to find a job in his field and has resorted to taking jobs that allow him to define himself as self-employed. Interestingly, Max, his parents and many other members of the immediate community have responded to these efforts to become a capitalist by ridiculing them as a way to "make a quick buck."[19]

This response to individual entrepreneurial efforts is probably embedded in the "long memory" connected to enslavement.[20] As descendants of these humans who were transformed into chattel under capitalism, African-Americans are much more likely to question seriously any system in which exploitation is manifest. It is not surprising, then, that Capital students and adults in the Capital community respond to capitalist dicta by constantly resisting efforts to transform their attitudes toward the system that is shaping their lives.

> Well, [my brother] can find a job, but it's just that—well, he's lazy. He wants a job, but he likes fast money. He's always thinking of a way to make a quick buck. Not . . . you know,

he's not all into any heavy stuff [hard labor], but he likes to
use his mind, and make quick money. He has the mind for it.
Well, you know, he tried his own business. It was all right for
a while, but it just flopped. (Interview, March 7, 1983)

During the time Max was involved in this study, his brother was unemployed.

In response to the pressure he feels from his parents, especially his
mother, Max underachieves in his daily school performance. He responds in this way in order to minimize his sense of alienation and
isolation from the racialized Self. While deliberate and forthright avoidance is not possible for him, he is still able to subvert the obligatory
components of the school curriculum by failing every course he is compelled to take. Max admits that failing required components of the
school curriculum is an ongoing experience for him.

Well, I could have done better [in all my school experiences],
but—really, it was—well, it was kind of psychological. It's
kind of hard to explain, you know . . . it's just that—
sometimes I felt that I could do the work, but at times I was
very lazy—you know, I just didn't want to do it. But that's
natural, really, but I just didn't want to do it. But I always get
the pushing behind from my mom, and my teachers also. So
that helped me a whole lot. (Interview, March 7, 1983)

Max failed ninth- and tenth-grade English, both of which are required for points toward graduation. He is now in the second semester
of his junior year, after failing the course again during the first semester.
His mother and current English teacher are baffled; they both know that
Max could pass the course if he would only put forth minimal effort.

Max passes only those courses that are *not* required. As he readily
acknowledges, his grades in school have never accurately reflected who
he is or what he is capable of doing. At all grade levels, he has earned
largely Cs, with a small number of Bs and very few As. During his first
year at Capital (tenth grade), he earned two Fs, two Ds, one C, and
one A. Unfortunately, his grades are not improving, and therefore his
graduation date is in serious jeopardy.

Max is a rather passive person of imposing stature: he is tall and
heavy, weighing close to 300 pounds. He is a defensive tackle on the
football team. Probably his mother contributes most to his passive personality structure. She has repeatedly come to his rescue in school, so
often that he describes her as having "spoiled" him and his older brother.

Well, my mother . . . she's always spoiled me, 'cause if anything ever went wrong, she'd come right there, and she never

really blamed me. She'd always point the finger first. And I
kind of felt secure in that. And . . . that I could get away with
some things. And that was in . . . and that started from my
early years, you know . . . in elementary school and junior
high school, because, you know, as I said, I went to the same
school where she taught. And I kind of got—I didn't get *really*
special treatment, but I was . . . I got . . . I was let by, by the
principal. Even though I hung out with the guys, the principal
still let me off the hook a lot. And, you know, the things I
should have been punished for, like cutting class, I wasn't.
And sometime I think *all* of us got away with it because of
me. (Interview, March 11, 1983)

Despite his rather marginal daily performance in schoolwork, Max
performed better than many of the other students on the PSAT. His
mother was ecstatic: she needed something to reaffirm her undaunting
faith in her child's intellectual ability.

Max's future career goals are both tentative and ambivalent. He
loves astronomy, and if he thought he could be successful pursuing a
career as an astronomer, he insists that he would immediately track that
specialization as a lifetime career option. However, the problem is, first,
no one believes in him and, second, he does not think that he would be
able to find a job in that specialty. He has never seen or even heard of a
Black astronomer.[21] Also, because of the cumulative effect of his lowered
academic effort, he is not sure that, even if he started to put forth all
the effort his strong interest and talent suggest, he would be successful
in gaining admittance to a college offering astronomy as a specialty.
Therefore, he has decided to settle on "engineering, constructional work,
or designing, or—you know, just hold down a job in investing—making
wise investments, and . . . yes, financial investments" (interview, March
18, 1983).

Recently, Max's parents bought him a used car. They did this to
encourage him to perform better in school and to help him break away
from his less than middle-income peers. The motivation has not changed
his school performance. Max still seeks to avoid those components of
the school curriculum that might be seen as separating him from his
peers—as choosing Otherness. The car has simply enhanced his relationship with his friends; now that he can furnish unlimited transportation,
he is even more involved with them. His parents' intense interest in his
school life—particularly his mother's—makes it impossible for him to
avoid the more rigorous component of the school curriculum, but he
can and does avoid behaving in ways that would suggest that he has
internalized the desire for Otherness.

Max insists that his friends, whom he sees as being different from himself, are nevertheless critically important to his sense of belonging. Indeed, I was struck by the tenacity with which he seeks to remain a part of the Capital community, in spite of his mother's repeated efforts to shake him free of these self-imposed restraints. She constantly points out to him how debased and debasing his old friends are and urges him to find new, more acceptable friends. He refuses. Since his friends are critically important to him and his sense of identity, he refuses to forgo his relationship with them, even for academic success. His need to belong takes precedence over all other considerations (Kadi 1993; Maslow 1954; Tracy 1991). When he looks back from his position in school today, he observes, with a mounting sense of sadness:

> You know, I just sacrificed a whole lot out of myself, what
> I could do, just to make my friends happy, you know? And
> it never—it just didn't work. They—you know, all of them
> didn't take advantage of me. They really didn't bother . . . it
> bothered me, but it wasn't that they were trying to just take
> advantage of me, it was just that, you know, sometimes when
> I got my mind—you know, I just, I just got . . . I'd get myself
> psyched out, worrying about what other people thought of
> me. But it really doesn't matter all that much, any more. (Inter-
> view, March 11, 1983)

Max's parents admit that they have consistently failed to protect him from his less successful peers. Without the support and sense of belonging that Max has constantly obtained from them, he seems to be unable to function. He acknowledges that he needs them more than they need him. Despite the class difference between him and his friends, his overwhelming sense of inadequacy and his liminal status in both the Black and White communities make him anxious to be affiliated with other Black people—his peers:

> We don't think the same, me and my friends. That's why I
> used to think that I wasn't . . . I used to think that I wasn't—
> I used to always put myself down, *that I wasn't good enough.*
> Because I could—the things they wanted to do, I didn't want
> to do. I didn't want to do it because I knew it was wrong, and
> that I wouldn't get anything out of it. And really, a cheap
> thrill isn't really all that much to me, really it isn't. It's just
> not worth it, you know? Why go through the trouble? So—
> that's just the way I think. I used to try and change it, but it
> didn't work . . . not for me it didn't anyways. (Interview,
> March 11, 1983)

Despite Max's awareness that he thinks in ways that set him apart and that many of these friends' activities are "cheap thrills," he is unable to break away from them.

Like his friends, Max seeks to avoid mastering aspects of the school's core curriculum. This is displayed in his repeated failures in English, even though both his mother and his English teacher know that he has the ability to complete the course successfully. They are baffled by his refusal to do what he obviously can do with very little effort. One of the primary reasons for his failure is his resistance to what is unavoidable. His parents insist that he take advanced placement courses: that's unavoidable. He resists this lack of choice by not completing homework assignments and by not participating in classroom discussions. Instead, he daydreams, pretending that he is an astronomer actively engaged in solving problems that are unique to astronomers.

Unlike Korey and other friends who avoid even the appearance of being a brainiac, Max must struggle to avoid learning what he is taught at school. Because his parents are deeply involved in his schooling, he is less free to avoid those courses and activities his friends would never participate in. Nevertheless, like them, he manages to subvert the effects of such courses by disengaging his sense of Self from any involvement in the classroom. Hence, while he may have to take an advanced placement English class, he can still retain a sense of identity with his friends by ignoring the required assignments and rejecting classroom participation. He thus avoids the perception of Otherness that mastering those courses would encourage. This response requires more work on Max's part because, in addition to avoiding the subject matter of the course, he must also repeatedly assure his classmates that though he has to take courses generally identified with the school's brainiacs, he is still very much one of the "homeboys." It is not Max's friends who are holding him back. It is, rather, his personal sense of marginality, his desire both to avoid the appearance of consuming the Other (Friedman, 1992a) and to maintain his connectedness to the African-American community.

Art: "And I Was Late about Ninety-Something Times—Ninety-six Times."

Art is another of the underachieving male students who is a master at avoiding the celebration of Otherness. To his mind, the essence of Otherness is embodied in acting white, and he abhors acting white. His most visible tactic for avoiding it is to refuse, unconditionally, to complete any assigned classwork in required courses. But unlike the students who choose absence as a way of avoiding what is obligatory, Art has an excellent attendance record. His insistence that he "loves school" gains support from the fact that he rarely cuts any of his classes. Though he rarely gets to school on time, once he is in the building, he is more than willing to attend classes.[22]

Art's mother and father separated when he was only three years of age. Art has been supervised primarily by his older siblings because of his mother's enormously taxing work schedules. She is a nurse and works *two full-time jobs* on back-to-back shifts. After the father deserted the family, she made a decision that their children would not suffer for lack of any of the creature comforts of life. Her success in her work has provided them with the material goods most Americans equate with success. She was able to buy a three-bedroom brick house in an upscale section of the Capital community and to give Art and his siblings the games, stereo equipment, and other "toys" that adolescents crave.

Yet Art's mother's decision has been costly. Of all the children, Art received the least attention from her because he was the youngest, and her absence affected him severely. She is rarely home, and when she is there, she spends most of the time sleeping.

Art knows his father quite well. He visits him from time to time and even lists him as the person to be contacted in case of an emergency. But he does not have an intimate relationship with his father, and, more important, he insists that he does not want one. He sees his mother as his only real parent, and he attributes what he perceives as the good fortune of the family to her hard work and perseverance.

Art loves his mother immensely and admires her strength. But her draconian efforts to provide for her family have resulted in a tendency on the part of her children to forswear any effort to provide for themselves. Art is no exception. In fact, his dependence is so great that in many ways she has become his "rescuer," much as Max's mother has. Art was expelled from Capital twice during the base year of this study and was suspended twice. Each time his mother rescued him. Essentially, her role in the lives of her children has evolved to one in which she is a "rescuer" as well as the provider.

Art takes very little responsibility for his actions, apparently because he knows his mother loves him *unconditionally* and will rescue him from any predicament in which he finds himself. Apparently he seeks to replicate this interaction with other adults. It is so much a part of his belief system that he describes a good teacher as an individual who, among other things, "fusses" at him, as his mother does. As he sees it, an adult who fusses at him when he fails to do his schoolwork, which is almost all of the time, is one who really cares about him.

The underachieving females' responses at school are similar in many ways to the underachieving male students: they, too, use avoidance and defiance as a way of resisting dominant ideological claims. They also resist the silence attendant on female success (Tracy 1991:139). There are other gender-specific differences which will become clear in the individual case analyses that follow.

Sakay: "A Equals 7X Squared or Something like That."
Like Max, Sakay is the product of a middle-income background and is guilty of underachieving in school. Like Max, she tries to avoid representing the Other. But unlike Max's parents, hers do not insist on her participation in the advanced placement curriculum even though most of her friends have either opted to take most of their classes from that track or have been coerced into doing so. Sakay's parents' less demanding attitude enables her to decide not to become a member of the program though she does take some of the advanced placement courses, among them all the computer courses that are available. She decided on her own to take these courses and she likes them. On the other hand, because of her high score on the required English placement exam, she takes a section of English populated primarily by students who are official members of the AP program. She would rather not be taking this English course, and for the most part she avoids those courses that would suggest she is acting white.

In the Black community, Sakay's parents have middle-income status.[23] When asked, she insists that her family is middle class. Her father is a senior officer for the Metropolitan Police Department; earlier he was a member of the Marine Corps for nine years. Her two siblings both completed high school. Although her mother and father are divorced, their individual incomes are above the official poverty line, and they are able to buy her most of the material goods she wants.

Sakay's mother, formerly a salesperson for a new computer firm, and now temporarily unemployed, performed very well when she was in school. In fact, Sakay found her mother something of a role model, at least for a time:

> My mother, she was real smart in high school. I wanted to be just like her, and she had never *seen* a C in her [school] life— until her eleventh-grade year, and she had got a C, and almost got killed! [Laughter] I wanted to be just like my mother. My mother skipped second grade, and I wanted to do that *so* bad!—but I couldn't. And after a while, I figured, "This is getting too *hard* for me to try to skip, I think I'll just go ahead

and go forward to my regular grades and stuff." And I'm kind of glad. I wouldn't have skipped anyway, 'cause I would have missed a lot of my friends that I met. (Interview, February 4, 1983)

Further, Sakay reports:

My mother's *always* pressuring me. She doesn't do it as much now, I guess she figures I'm old enough, I'm going to do whatever I want to anyway. But she does put a lot of input, still. And my father, even though he doesn't live with us, the first thing he asks me whenever he sees me is, "How you doing in school? What are your grades like?" And I'll tell him, you know, if I'm not doing good in a subject I won't lie to him, because he's gonna find out sooner or later anyway, so I'll just go ahead and tell him. (Interview, February 4, 1983)

Sakay's insistence that "my mother's *always* pressuring me" should not be interpreted to mean that her parents demand good grades the way many of the parents of the high-achieving females do. Sakay's mother's "pressure" for good grades is manifested as support for her daughter's academic goals; her father's inquiry about her current academic effort is interpreted as a perfunctory rather than a real concern. If Sakay wants to take an advanced computer or math class, her mother talks with her about her choices, counsels her regarding how she can best obtain her desired goals, and advises her about some of the likely outcomes of the choice. Ironically, it is her mother's support—not her pressure—that is exacerbating Sakay's conflict. And her mother's own superior academic performance is implicated in Sakay's response. Like a protective shield, her genetic linkage to academic excellence reassures her. At the same time, however, she is riddled with conflict. Her mother's lack of substantive achievement as an adult, in spite of her accomplishments in high school, indicates that high academic achievement does not necessarily translate into adult achievement. And the fact that many of her peers are actively avoiding what they identify as acting white behaviors, including working for good grades, seems to suggest that high academic achievement should be avoided.

As is true of at least half of her underachieving cohorts, Sakay's grades in elementary school were well above average. This enabled her to maintain membership in her school's chapter of the National Honor Society. Sakay's academic achievements are reflected in her outstanding performance on standardized examinations. She recognizes her skills and, with hindsight, recalls her good fortune.

It seems likely that Sakay experienced virtually no conflict between academic success and racial identity: she could do well in school without seeing that performance as a breach of her sense of who she is. It was not until she reached high school that conflict arose. However, her official excuse for why her grades began to fall does not include this explanation. At the conscious level, Sakay is only aware that her academic performance began to decline when she was in the ninth grade.

Sakay's performance on the administered standardized exams—PSAT, CTBS, and LSE—was so high that she was one of only five students at Capital selected for possible designation as an Outstanding Negro Merit Scholar. But though her scores demonstrate unqualified mastery of the subject matter, her GPA indicates that she is failing or almost failing most of the courses she is taking as an eleventh-grade student.

Sakay's performance on standardized measures of school success has been virtually ignored at Capital because her grades are so low. Her contradictory performance led many of her peers as well as teachers and other adults to describe her as "lazy," a euphemism for an unwillingness on her part to put forth the effort necessary to perform well in class on a day-to-day basis. This is not a valid explanation.

When asked to explain the discrepancy between her exceptional performance on standardized measures of school success and her dismal GPA, Sakay implied that avoidance is the key.

> I figure that I do better on the standardized tests because it just goes over general stuff—you know, stuff that I think tenth- and eleventh-graders are *supposed* to know. And in my classes, it's—when I go over the work or something, like, if I do work in class, I have the examples right there before me, and I get lazy, because, okay, I have the formula—maybe A equals 7X squared or something like that—I have the formula sitting right in front of me, so if I forget it, I can just refer back to it. But when I take a test for my class, it's like, "Oh-oh, you forgot the formula. You should have remembered it, you should have went over it." And then I start panicking, and then I *know* I'm not going to remember it. So I just say, "Well, I'll just do it the next time." And after a while I'll start trying to improve, but by then it's affected my grade already. (Interview, February 4, 1983)

Like most of the underachieving students, Sakay admits that the primary reason for her unacceptably low grades is lack of effort or time-on-task. Like Art, Max, and Sidney, she attends most of her classes most of the time. However, as with them, the time devoted to homework and studying is severely limited.

> I *hate* studying. It's just going home, and opening your book—I think the problem is, not just with me, but with a lot of Black kids—they need a lot of . . . somebody looking over their shoulder all the time, saying, you know, you know, pushing to make sure you do your homework, and you do your classwork . . . In classwork, I feel my classwork is pretty good. But the homework brings it down—or not doing the homework brings it down. And, I don't know, I'm just going to have to work with it. (Interview, February 4, 1983)

There is more than mere abhorrence of the idea of studying involved here. She does not believe that her performance on school measures of success will lead to rewards commensurate with that effort. She also asserts that other African-American adolescents share her perception. Either this implies that they disbelieve the efficacy of potential academic accomplishments to erase a stigmatized Self, or it implies that they choose to avoid erasing the Self and accepting Otherness. Kaela admits that most Capital students are not self-starters in the academic arena; many have to be literally "compelled" to perform academically assigned tasks. This suggests resistance. Sakay is only partially conscious of why she and the other Black students at Capital do not put forth the effort necessary to achieve academic distinction. But her lack of awareness in no way diminishes her involvement in the conflict between White and Black worldviews operating at Capital High.

Kaela: "I Stayed Out for Almost All of October"

Kaela offers still another example of how the underachieving students' efforts to avoid critical components of the school curriculum adversely affect their school performance. She is also an example of how their resistance enables them to retain their perception of the school as creating an invalid African-American Self.

Kaela's family is Catholic, and all of her seven siblings obtained at least a portion of their education in Catholic schools. Prior to this year, she too attended a Catholic school. Her records show that she was a good student and a high achiever. In ninth grade, she earned high honors and received a full scholarship, easing the financial burden for her mother.

Recently, Kaela's mother lost her job as a midlevel employee of a poverty program in the Capital Community, where she had worked for nine and a half years. The family had experienced severe financial hardship. Kaela's mother had mixed feelings about allowing her daughter to attend a public school. But Kaela's failure to maintain her tuition scholarship, coupled with her mother's loss of her job, forced her mother to relent and enroll her at Capital.

Kaela had become disillusioned with what she viewed as the hypocrisy at the Catholic high school she had gone to. Still, she attended regularly. But once she enrolled at Capital she began to skip school, not just for a day but for extended periods. She attributes her anxiety to the decision of school officials to place her in the advanced placement program. They did this, she reasoned, because she had been at a Catholic school where, with the exception of her last year, she had performed extremely well. Unfortunately, Kaela did not share this perception of her capabilities. She was terrified at the high-level math and science courses she was expected to take in the program. Her much-ballyhooed Catholic-school training, she says, had not prepared her for the rigorous advanced placement curriculum at Capital. When she voiced her concerns to her counselor, Ms. Yanmon, and several of her teachers, they all summarily dismissed her anxieties, expressing great confidence in her. She was less sanguine. Because of her fears and her inability to get anyone to heed her apprehensions, she avoided school during most of October.

> I stayed out for almost all of October. And then Ms. Yanmon called my mother, and my mother asked me what I was doing, because she thought I was coming to school because she went to work part-time at, like, seven in the morning, so she didn't know. So then I just stayed home. While she was there, I'd get up and, you know, get dressed like I was going to school. And then when she left, I'd get back in the bed. So Ms. Yanmon called and so she set an appointment up for me. So I came up here and we talked. We had a nice long talk, and so she told me that, you know, there were other alternatives—to come back and get out of the program. And then I told her that I would want to, you know, maybe try just plain Algebra II. So I tried that and I couldn't keep up in that either. So now I don't take math at all, but I'm going to take, like, a course over the summer, and then I want to take it, you know, next year. So she told me, you know, I came in and we talked and she, you know, made a whole new . . . I got my whole sched-

ule changed, and . . . I came back to school, and now I'm
back. (Interview, January 6, 1983).

When questioned directly about her repeated absences, Kaela says
she does not know why she and other Capital students do not come to
school:

> I don't really know why. I don't even know why I don't come
> to school, when I know I should come. It's just that we Black
> students don't have that much support. We don't get—I know
> we know we should do things, but it's—you know, you know
> something pushing you. And when you don't have that, some-
> times you feel like nobody cares, so why should you care? It
> gets like that sometimes. But then other times, I don't know
> why. Sometimes I don't want to come if I haven't done my
> homework. And then—I don't understand, I don't know why.
> I think we're scared to take responsibility and stuff. And that's
> because of the people we keep company with, you know. And
> it's just—I don't know—people—when we see people, you
> know, and they're like role models. But they don't necessarily
> have to be good role models. And then we settle for that. And
> we—I know that I don't want to settle for that, but it's just
> something in me that won't let me do more. So I settle. I
> know I could make the honor roll . . . (Interview, April 18,
> 1983)

At some level, Kaela appears to have a fairly cogent understanding
of why she and other African-American students do not try to do better
in school. At another, she is totally baffled not only by her peers' lack
of motivation to do well in school but also by her own often bizarre
actions and reactions. She is also keenly aware of the African-American
community's uncompromising insistence on high academic performance
as a form of resistance to claims of inadequacy in the Black Self.

The resulting ambivalence, the liminality of being both Black and
academically successful, propels African-American students into a kind
of reactive posture in which prestige and stature are defiantly anchored
to the African-American community. This is particularly poignant for
the underachieving students in this study. The effort to retain a positive sense of the African-American Self invariably leads—often fortui-
tously—to a violation of most of what is considered virtuous and merito-
rious in both the school context and the larger society. The ambivalence
and liminality also leads to allegations of acting white. Kaela acknowledges this:

I mean . . . like every weekend you have to go, and you have
to go to a club or something . . . I mean, we don't take advantage of the free things, like, "Let's go to the Smithsonian," or
something. I mean, all you have to do is pay 65 cents to get
on the bus and go down there, and it's free, and come
back—or a couple of dollars, if you want to eat lunch down
there or something . . . A friend of mine and I went down
there, and so when we got back home, everybody was saying,
"Where you all coming from?" And we didn't even want to
tell them, because, you know, they look at you like, "What!
Down there with all those White people?" (Interview, April
18, 1983)[24]

Kaela acknowledges what is becoming increasingly apparent: commingling with White Americans, once celebrated as a positive indicator
of one's humanness, has come to be looked on as evidence of disloyalty.
This response is unique to African-Americans who were born and reared
during the Second Emancipation era. Kaela admits that she and her
friend were ashamed to tell their families that they had been down at
the Smithsonian because, in this era of integration, "cozying up" to
White America brings one's identity into question.

Like most African-Americans, Kaela is familiar with the internal
"civil war" that rages around issues of color in the Black community.
Very fair-skinned herself, she is extremely aware that her color is an
asset that minimizes the stigma of being Black. This is particularly true
when it comes to getting the attention of African-American men. Indeed,
she notes how the most benign greeting on her part is often misinterpreted as a signal of sexual interest when none is intended:

I don't like boys talking to me all the time and stuff. 'Cause I
think I'm a nice person, and when they speak to me, I speak
back and stuff. And just because I might speak back, say
hello, they think that I want to get involved with them or
something. And I just want to walk around, and they say
hello, I just keep walking, and they start—they will cuss you
out if you don't speak to them. They will cuss you out: "Who
do you think you are?" or something. "Forget you. I was just
trying to make you feel good, anyway, by speaking. Don't do
me any favors." (Interview, April 18, 1983)

She insists that avoiding school empowered her by making it possible
for her to escape that kind of male attention, the unrealistically high
expectations of teachers and administrators, and her own feelings of
inadequacy.

Kaela did not take the PSAT this fall, chiefly because she is convinced that she will be financially unable to go to college. Nor did she take the CTBS, because she was absent during the two days this exam was administered. She did, however, take the standardized Life Skills examination. She and Katrina were the only students in the research group to achieve a perfect score on that test.

Kaela's teachers insist that she not only has the ability to do the work required in their courses, but that she is also more capable than most of their other students. Yet Kaela failed nearly all her major courses during her first semester at Capital High. The primary reason for this wholesale failure was her *avoidance* of school and her repeated absence from her assigned classes. Testimony from her teachers in English and history indicates that poor attendance, not poor academic performance, is strongly implicated in her failure.

An examination of Kaela's schooling history shows that her problem probably began back in Catholic school, when she developed a sense of collective identity with the Black community. Prior to that time, her contact with people of African ancestry was limited primarily to the few who were members of her parish school and to the other members of her own family, who could also pass for White. She maintains that she began to lose interest in her schoolwork when she became aware of what she viewed as hypocrisy. The parochial administrators were treating her differently from the way they treated other Black students—as if she were special, a different breed of Black person. Since she *is* a Black person and wants to maintain her identity as a person of African ancestry, she began to cut down on her schoolwork and could not be persuaded by her teachers or her mother that she was unlike the other Black students.

> *Kaela:* My sister and I went to the same Catholic high school. And the first year I really liked it. I liked it—you know, that was my home away from home. And I did really good—I was on high honors, and, you know, I did so well that they gave me a scholarship, and I went in the tenth grade free; I didn't have to pay anything in the tenth grade. But then in the tenth grade I met—you know, it's a all girls' school, and I stopped doing my work. I stopped coming to school because, you know, I just—I didn't—you know, the people changed so much because when I passed from ninth to tenth grade, the friends that I had in ninth grade, they [school officials] put 'em out. And, you know, it wasn't fair because the reason they put 'em out was because, like, okay, they were average, and they didn't have, you know, high grades. But, you know,

it wasn't fair because the reason they did that, they were trying to make room because a school not too far from there had
just closed and, you know, a lot of people were applying from
that school. So they were letting, you know, all them people
come in, and the people who were in there, they weren't re-
serving their seats; they were putting them out instead. Right?
So I felt, you know, I was kind of angry with that.

Anthro: Were your friends mostly Black . . . that they put
out . . . ?

Kaela: You know, I tried to think that wasn't the reason they
were doing it. You know, I was trying to think, well, maybe
the people coming in had better grades than the ones they put
out. But the ones they put out, they were, you know, Black;
and the ones that came in were White. And, you know, the
school is a Catholic and it's, you know, headed by . . . you
know, the principal and everybody, mostly all the teachers are
White. I tried to think that it wasn't that, you know. So, you
know, I went there, and felt kind of hostile towards the teachers because I was, you know, I was angry because it wasn't
fair. But, you know, I was also angry at my friends because I
think if they had, you know, said something, if they had stood
up, I think they could have stayed there. But most of them,
you know, they just, you took it—they left, and most of them
went to public school. (Interview, January 6, 1983)

Prior to that experience, she had believed in the American dream.
Her efforts in school had resulted in her achieving high honors and a
tuition scholarship. It was not until the removal of most of the Black
students from the school that she began to doubt the value of what she
was learning. Kaela's inability to tell anyone at the school or elsewhere
about her indignation and have them respond to how she felt made her
bitter and hopeless. These feelings also led her to avoid most of what
school officials had defined as necessary for success both at school and
in the larger society.

Kaela's apparent indifference to curricular requirements at the Catholic school seriously threatened her survival there and led her to pressure
her mother to allow her to attend Capital High. During the last semester
of her sophomore year at the Catholic high school, she failed English
and nearly failed her other courses. Her academic record finally convinced her mother that a change of venue was probably appropriate. By
attending Capital High, she was in some ways being like her erstwhile
friends at the Catholic school and avenging their dismissal because, she
reasoned, when her friends were dismissed from that school, they were

forced to attend public school rather than any other Catholic school in the area.

Ironically, Kaela's decision to leave the Catholic school that had dismissed her Black classmates to make room for White students and had sought to reconstruct her in an image that minimized her Black heritage destabilized her sense of identity in ways that were manifested in the avoidance behaviors she began to practice once she was admitted as a student at Capital.

While the teachers and administrators at the Catholic school insisted on treating her as an individual with virtually no connection to the Black community, Kaela defined herself first and foremost as a Black person, despite her very light, freckled complexion. Probably it is her growing sense of racial identity, with its attendant anger and indignation, that has negatively affected her school performance. She appears convinced that opportunities for Black Americans are few and her personal future very limited because she is Black, her family cannot pay for her college education, and the competition for highly valued positions in the work-place is too keen for her.

Kaela attributes the behaviors and low academic achievement of other Black students at Capital to the same factors as those operating in her situation: no matter what they do at school, they are judged primarily on the basis of their socially stigmatized racial identity.

The formal interviews on which this analysis is based were occurring at a time when students were selecting classes for the following year. Kaela pointed out the effects of the students' perceptions of dismal futures on their course selections. She was convinced that they would try harder to make good grades if they thought they had a real chance.

> I know that. Because I've heard a lot of people say, "Well, I don't know why I'm taking all these hard classes. I ain't never going to see this stuff again in life! Why am I going to sit here and make my record look bad, trying to take all these hard classes and get bad grades? I ain't going to need this stuff. I'm just going to take what I need to get my diploma. Forget all that other stuff." And, you know, *I thought like that for a while too*. But [that's] not the right way. I mean, we should try to better ourselves in any possible way. But a lot of people don't think that way. (Interview, April 22, 1983)

Nekia: "People Get Away with Murder Up Here"
Nekia is one of the underachieving students who "play for time" in order to avoid the subject matter in their classes. She readily admits that she attempts to "stall so we won't have to take the test" (interview,

March 9, 1983). This is a strategy she has used since elementary school where, during one year, she was suspended eleven times. This pattern continues even in high school. Last year, her first year at Capital, she was again suspended several times. She explains why, as she sees it, she got into trouble her first year at school:

> Last year. I got up here, you know, had to get adjusted to that change from junior high to high school, and changing classes and all that, and had to learn my way around the building. But after I really got into it, I liked all my teachers, I liked the work. There was nothing I—there was no work they gave me that I couldn't do, and everything was fun. I liked it. (Interview, January 15, 1983)

Nekia's response captures only a small portion of the picture. She is an extremely bitter student, far more acquainted with the brutality of life than her innocent response would suggest. Her indignation and bitterness are partly a response to the absence of her father and her abandonment by her alcoholic mother. At some level she thinks that her mother never loved her; at another she refuses to acknowledge what is so painful. In fact, several of her teachers assured me that Nekia knew she was conceived as a result of rape. Yet she repeatedly denied any knowledge of why her mother allowed her aunt to rear her. One of her former teachers claimed that Nekia also has been raped. She was not sure about the alleged rape of Nekia's mother.

Nekia is the most devastated female in the underachieving group. Her avoidance behaviors are more visible and more debilitating than those of most of her peers. She feels keenly the pain of her life. But instead of admitting that she is in pain and seeking help to cope with her wretched situation, she denies the pain while lashing out at those who are most vulnerable. Avoidance in her personal life as well as in response to the school's demands is clearly a critical element in her life. Indeed, it is the only way she can even begin to cope with the indignation she feels. For example, she maintains that she wants to become a gynecologist and help teenage girls escape unwanted pregnancies. But at the same time she asserts that she hates science and math, two subjects she must master in order to obtain that goal, and she expends a great deal of her academic energy seeking to avoid these required courses. When avoidance is impossible, she resorts to behavior that borders on the bizarre. Her ongoing feud with her science teacher, Mr. Walkerson, is a case in point. Nekia has fought with Mr. Walkerson more than with any other teacher at the school. She tends to attack this rather proper, mild-mannered man with a vengeance.

Only person that I had a problem [with] was Mr. Walkerson . . . I used to get put out of his class every week. *Every
week*. I got put out of his class . . . But as the year went
along, we smoothed our problems out, after my father and my
mother [her aunt and uncle] came up here a few times, it was
all right. 'Cause I was taking advantage; he gave me a inch
and I took *three* miles. I just went off, I just *went* off. He just
gave me a little bit of leeway, and I just took it and went . . . I
don't know why; it was just something to do. His class was
boring. He had a lot of advanced placement students in there,
right? You could hear a cotton ball hit the floor. That's just
how quiet it was, you could hear a cotton ball. And I like to
talk . . . So I was sitting in there, and it was so boring, so I
had to do *something*. By the end of the year I was trying to
settle down a little bit, 'cause I knew that wasn't right. And
he's *still* nice to me after all those incidents. He's still nice.
And I said, no, that's not right for me to take advantage of
him like this. (Interview, January 15, 1983)

Virtually everyone at the school, both staff and students, feared
Nekia's caustic tongue. While some of the adults took her verbal attacks
personally, most realized that her hostility was a plea for help. But this
realization was frequently hard to act on because, as the following excerpt from my fieldnotes shows, Nekia's behavior was so difficult to
take, and she often misread kindness for weakness. If she thought you
were weak, she was merciless in her scathing indictments.

Nekia, who had agreed just before the Christmas holidays to
complete a pilot interview with me but did not, was scheduled
to talk with me today at the lunch hour. Surprisingly, she
came to her counselor's office at 11:40 (the beginning of the
lunch period). Her counselor and one of her colleagues tried
to talk with her. They attempted to make light conversation.
Nekia was totally unresponsive, even hostile or at least impo-
lite. I hurriedly tried to get her out of the office to the room
on the next level where the interview was to take place . . .
Nekia and I sat down, and she continually prodded me, "Let's
get started, Ms. Fordham." Her desire to control the activities
surrounding her can make one very nervous. There are thou-
sands of aggressive people, but many of them have developed
strategies to camouflage their aggression . . . Nekia has not developed this kind of finesse. Instead, her aggression is unfil-
tered and undiluted, which turns off a lot of people who do

not know or do not try to understand her pain. (Fieldnotes, January 4, 1983)

Nekia's avoidance strategies were too blunt for most of the adults at the school to handle. Virtually none were able to meet her greatest needs—acceptance, love, and appreciation—because they were so busy trying to drive her away. Mr. Walkerson, her science teacher, realized that her hostility was a cover for a greater problem; nonetheless, her extreme behavior in his class forced him to respond in ways that were counterproductive in changing her behavior—dismissing her from his science class every week.

While most of the adults experienced guilt at their inability to address her need for love, appreciation, and acceptance, Nekia perceived her behavior as helping her to avoid what she did not want. At the same time, however, she realized that the pain she was experiencing was not going away. This knowledge heightened her anxiety and increased rather than diminished her caustic behavior. Like many of the adults at the school, she knew she was hemorrhaging emotionally. She also knew that virtually no one was attempting to help her. In response, she became still more angry and hostile, further undercutting the possibility of getting help from those who under different circumstances would have been able to help her. She either did not understand or refused to recognize that her strategy of stalling for time was more harmful than helpful to her. Accordingly, she appeared totally unwilling or unable to change.

In summary, Nekia is a very sad Black female whose sadness and loneliness are camouflaged by her behavior and, in fact, her behavior contributes to her rejection (see Fordham 1990, 1993; Mullings 1994).

Shelvy: "They Used To Say We Was Brainiacs, and No One Really Liked Us"

More than most of the female underachieving students in the study, Shelvy seeks to avoid detection as a brainiac. She is absolutely terrified that some of her classmates might take it upon themselves to so identify her. She loves going to school and learning most of what is traditionally taught in school. Yet her earlier experiences at the elementary and junior high school levels have taught her some very unpleasant lessons—one of which is the high cost of being known as a brainiac. Avoidance, then, is a major strategy she uses in her efforts to remain encapsulated within the fictive kinship system at Capital High.

Like nearly all of the students involved in the ethnographic study at the school, Shelvy is growing up in an impoverished environment. During the first year of the study, she was living with her mother, an older sister, and a nephew in an apartment in the Capital community. This represented an enormous change in the structure of her family, which, not long before, had included her father and two older siblings, one male and one female. Her father no longer lives with them full-time, if he ever did. Apparently, according to Shelvy's mother, he returns periodically. Shelvy views her father's absences as further evidence of his lack of responsibility vis-à-vis his family.

Shelvy is the youngest of four. All of the others are high school graduates. Her brother is in the Navy; her oldest sister is married; her other sister is trying to get into the Navy. A single parent, this sister must find someone to list as having custody of her son; her mother is willing to serve in this role. Shelvy has decided that she too wants to be in the Navy, though she does not plan to take the ROTC classes offered at Capital.

> Well, for one, my brother went in there, and my father was in the Army, my uncle was in the Army, and my sister's going to the Navy, and it's just like something that's in the family, and I figure if I go to college and I pay them to give me an education, and I don't get a job—well, I can go into the Navy, and *they* pay *me* to get an education, and they'll *give* me a job. (Interview, March 7, 1983)

In elementary school her grades were "mostly VGs, As, Bs, and stuff like that." Despite the resistance of her peers in the schools she attended prior to coming to Capital, she continued to obtain good grades. In fact, in junior high she was placed in the only honors section of the ninth-grade class. This made it much easier for her because everybody had been identified as a potentially good student. As she recalled it:

> I went to Garden [Junior High School]. That was fairly well, but in the eighth grade when I had the problem of the same thing—everybody saying, "Well, she thinks she's smart," and all this. I had the same problem in the eighth grade. But in the ninth grade, they placed me in an all-academic section and, you know, everyone in there was smart, so it wasn't recognized—they recognized everybody as being part of a smart section, instead of an individual. (Interview, March 7, 1983)

Shelvy's pattern of academic success continued during her first year at Capital High, when she earned two As, two Bs, and two Cs.

Speaking of her earlier school experiences, Shelvy says that her first contact with success as risky was in the elementary school; and it hit home during the sixth grade when, for the first time in her life, she was called "teacher's pet" and "brainiac."

When I was in kindergarten, I wasn't really like most of the students, because they felt as though I was smart and I was the teacher's pet, and, you know, they hated people like that . . . I guess they figure, if you make good grades and the teacher like you—hm, you just want to be the teacher's pet and everything, and then they just . . . something they build up. They don't really . . . like, it's just something that's there. (Interview, March 7, 1983)

She is somewhat baffled by the persistence of these pejorative terms. She insists that all the students at the school, including the underachieving students, want to be brainiacs, but no one wants to be so identified. Realizing that such a dream is impossible, most of the underachieving students respond in ways comparable to the way in which she has responded: by turning their backs on success. Her own academic performance reflects the pain and frustrations associated with trying to hide one's academic abilities.

In the sixth grade, it was me and these two girls, we used to hang together all the time. They used to say we was brainiacs, and no one really liked us . . . It's not something—well, *it's something that you want to be, but you don't want your friends to know* . . . Because once they find out you're a brainiac, then the first thing they'll say is, "Well, she thinks she's cute, and she thinks she's smart, she thinks she's better than anyone else." So what most brainiacs do, they sit back and they know the answer, and they won't answer it . . . 'Cause, see, first thing everybody say, "Well, they're trying to show off." So they really don't—they might answer once in a while, but . . . Because if you let all your friends know how smart you are, then when you take a test or something, they're going to know you know the answer and they're going to want the answers. And if you don't give them to them, then they're going to get upset with you. And then everybody just . . . Well, they might start rumors about you, might give you a bad name or something like that. (Interview, March 7, 1983)

Shelvy had experienced the wrath of her peers when she behaved in ways which suggested that she was acting white. Her most recent experience was in junior high school. She has never forgotten it:

And so, like, I really didn't get in trouble until one time where this girl, she felt as though, you know, I thought I was smart, and she wanted to fight me. But, you know, I didn't have no reason to fight her. But she wanted to fight me, and I wasn't

going to stand there and let her fight me and not do anything.
So my sister came up there. To keep me from fighting, my sister just say, "Don't nobody put their hand on my sister." And
that was that. You know, ain't nobody else really said anything 'bout it, but—like, well, we had a lot of matches and
stuff like that. I was in double dutch, and I won a trophy, and
I brought it to school, 'cause we was required to bring it back
to school to show everybody . . . first thing they say, "She
brought her trophy to show off." I mean, if the teacher
wouldn't have asked me to bring it back, I would have left it
at home. And, you know, at the end of the year, I got awards
in geometry, math, for being on honor roll for four advisories.
But people just took that and turned up their nose. (Interview,
March 7, 1983)

Shelvy acknowledges that members of the community whose efforts
make them stand out above the crowd get clobbered. Her analysis of
the dilemma of the brainiac—how each one tends to go through a metamorphosis into an underachieving student—suggests that the academically successful Black student's life is fraught with conflict and ambivalence. Fear of being labeled a brainiac often leads to the emergence of a
social self that is unrecognizable. Essentially, Shelvy's analysis suggests
that a student who is identified as a brainiac is more vulnerable to what
Paterson (1982) calls "social death" than one who is not. Hence, her
goal has become to avoid this fate.

At the time of this study, things changed drastically for Shelvy. She
was no longer enthusiastic about school, no longer willing to brave the
resistance of her peers. She is not making any concerted effort to improve
the level of her academic performance. The reasons for this development
are possibly anchored in her experiences in school and her perceptions
of the limitations confronting African-Americans.

Black people always feel as though White people are superior
to them. But they won't always be superior. It's time to
change. I was always told that Black people was once superior. But this Black king, he told his people that they could
walk off the top of a mountain. And they tried to walk up to
the heavens, and they died! How true it is, I don't know. And
then the White man say, "Well, look, he's stupid. He's going
to tell his people that they can walk to heaven," so since then,
I was always told White people were superior.[25] But I don't
feel as though a White person is superior to me. I feel as
though we're equal, or either *I* might be superior to *them*. It's
not your color, like Martin Luther King said. It's not the creed

or your skin, it's like what you *know*. If you know this, and this White person don't, don't make no difference. (Interview, March 8, 1983)

Like most of the underachieving students, Shelvy is resisting the pervasive negative stereotypes regarding African-Americans by refusing to participate in the critical academic activities at the school, including the core curriculum. By refusing to become involved in the academic centerpieces at the school, she can avoid being judged and inevitably found inadequate in some way. Despite her claim that she does not "feel as though a White person is superior to me," parts of her statement negate this assertion, as does her sudden, drastic lessening of academic effort. She has performed well in school in spite of negative peer pressure, but the full realization of the limitations affiliated with her racial identity has suddenly stymied her academic effort.

Since elementary school, Shelvy has been constantly bombarded with messages indicating that it is not okay to be accused of acting white. As a high-achieving student, she was constantly derided by her peers and classmates. But none of this negative pressure stopped her from seeking academic success. Apparently she ignored or endured the teasing and harassment of her classmates and peers because she believed that her achievements in school would lead to a drastic change in her future life. During the last academic year, however, she has begun to believe what many of her classmates have been trying to tell her: seeking school success does not lead to acceptance or endorsement by the Other. This realization has transformed her academic effort into sullen resistance.

Shelvy's academic history reflects the pain and frustrations associated with coming to grips with a constructed reality in which race is both celebrated and stigmatized, and where both conformity and avoidance lead to the same undesired end: continuation of the status quo. She is more aware than many of her peers as to why she is not performing as well as she could. She realizes that seeking school success at Capital High is riddled with contradictions. Having learned from negative experiences associated with success in the elementary and junior high contexts, and, more important, from her emerging awareness of the power of the existing social order, she limits her academic effort in order to minimize bringing attention to herself.

EIGHT

Reclaiming and Expanding Humanness: Overcoming the Integration Ideology

I remember the very day I noticed that my blackness made me different. There was this girl named Marsha on whom I had what you could call a crush, young as I was. Her hair was white as sunlight on a web, her eyes were as blue as plums. This was so long ago, thirty years or better, that I can't remember the context within which all of this took place, but I do remember that it happened in school, and I remember that we were indoors, queued next to a row of windows that cast light only on Marsha. I stood in line dead next to her, inhaling her Ivory soap and whole-milk scent, watching the light set fire to that delicate hair. Some kid behind me had been trying to engage me in a conversation for more than five minutes, but I was having little of it. I only wanted to consume Marsha's presence. But, through sheer persistence, the kid broke through. I heard him say, ". . . born in California, just up the road. Where was you born?" "Germany," I answered, and drifted back to Marsha, her elbows, the backs of her knees, the heels of her saddle shoes. Then she turned around . . . to look at me . . . to speak to me . . . to cast her radiance my way. She said, "Coloreds can't be born in Germany." Of course I felt humiliated, embarrassed, angered. My stomach folded in on itself, my hands trembled, my face burned. I couldn't have explained it to you then, but I had never felt this way before, never felt singled out on account of my color, and at first I thought Marsha had misunderstood me, so I replied, "I didn't say I was German, I said I was *born* in Germany." But she stuck to her guns, empty as their chambers were, saying, "You're just a liar! Colored people do not come from Germany." And I told Marsha, as gently as I could, of course, that I most certainly had been born in Germany. Just ask my mother, etc., etc. But the more I asserted my claim, the more incredulous Marsha, and then a growing number of my schoolmates, became. I remember one boy telling me that he was Catholic, and that, ". . . um, in the Catholic Church? um, if you lie? um, you'll, ah go to H.E.L.L." I had only one supporter that morning, a kid whose name I can no longer recall. She tried to defend me by announcing that though she was Chinese she'd been born in Tennessee. Marsha, for some reason, saw no logic in this, and said, "Well, maybe so, but that doesn't mean a colored can be born in Germany."

I was six, I think. (McKnight 1993:95–96)

RECLAMATION OF AFRICAN-AMERICAN HUMANNESS

The humanness of peoples who were a part of the enormous African Diaspora was unilaterally and summarily expropriated by the Euramerican colonialists who took them from their homelands and enslaved them here in America (Blassingame 1979; Genovese 1972; Woodward 1957). Denying the humanness of the people they enslaved was an essential prerequisite of the colonization process. To enslave another people who were human in a way that was indistinguishable from their own humanness would have negated the emerging ideological claims of democracy by the colonialists. In other words, the enslavement of peoples whose status as part of the human family could not be challenged would have exposed the falsity of the dialectic integral to the democratic achievement ideology constructed by the Euramericans. It was therefore imperative that persons considered appropriate for enslavement be designated nonhuman or at least in some ways less human.

According to Trask (1991:161), "Modern westerners [tend to] appropriate what is outside of themselves in order to become what they are not." Friedman's argument parallels Fanon's claim that "the white man [en]slaves to reach a human level" (1967:9). It can therefore be argued that European colonialists appropriated the humanness of African peoples in order to elevate and reinforce their own uncertain human status. By defining another human population as inferior to themselves and concurrently expropriating from them what was deemed essential to humanness, their membership in the human family was assured. Gutted of what made them more than what the Europeans saw in themselves, Africans could then be defined as devoid of human status and therefore ineligible for the normal rights and responsibilities of citizens in democratic societies. Africans could be enslaved and subsequently reconstructed in ways that established and maintained their newly acquired nonhuman status.

While the dehumanization of African peoples took many forms and varied considerably from context to context, the most common feature of the process was (and still is) the systematic, continuing divestiture of what affirms their humanness: their inalienable right to the same. To support the declaration of their nonhuman status, it was claimed that their brain size and capacity were inadequate (Dreger 1973; Herrnstein and Murray 1994; Jensen 1969, 1973) and their intellect inferior (Herrnstein and Murray 1994; Jensen 1969; Shockley 1970). They were said to be innately lazy, oversexed, promiscuous, and so forth. It is against this backdrop that African-American adolescents at Capital High confront the issues of identity and academic success. It is also against this backdrop that Capital students seek to reclaim their appropriated humanness and weld it to their African origins.

Even though the official curriculum at Capital High deliberately steers clear of any perspective that might help matriculating students understand how and why their African ancestors' humanness was appropriated, mutilated, and reconstructed, the students have an acute awareness of and a permanent curiosity about this issue. They bring to the high school context a growing understanding of how the Black Self has been and continues to be fraudulently crafted. They also bring strong resistance to this reigning stereotype, backed by an unswerving desire to reclaim and reconfigure their African humanness.

Conformity as Resisting Otherness: The High Achievers

The high-achieving students at Capital High resist dominant claims of Black intellectual inadequacy by conforming to existing norms and values. They work hard to disprove Black *lack*. Attacked by all segments of the society, this segment of Capital's student population struggles with its "split personhood," its imaging as "acting white," as book-black Blacks. These "student-'halfies'" are acutely aware of the cultural imperative to "internalize what is outside of themselves in order to become more than what they are" (Trask 1991:161), because being who they are is not sufficient. They see themselves as having to become more than "mere" African-Americans. Conforming to school norms propels them to a place where they are constructed by their classmates as representing the dominant Other. They appropriate this Other because academic success and Otherness are inextricably linked in American society. In those instances when there is even a "partial [racialized] consciousness" (Weis 1985; Willis 1981), the high-achieving students' psyches are infested with apprehension and uncertainty, with fear and trepidation, juxtaposed with what Carter describes as a "burning drive to prove the racists wrong" (1993:76). At the level of consciousness, this uncertainty is most clearly manifested in the development of strategies that camouflage and minimize their academic effort and accomplishments. Unconsciously (and sometimes consciously), many of them come to valorize and internalize Otherness primarily because it is associated with success, purity, and a presumed superior humanness.

Acting white, as in pretending to be or masquerading as (an)Other, becomes the appropriated medium that high achievers use to become more than mere African-Americans. This appropriated identity is double-sided in that they are compelled both to be and not be (an)Other. Many of them seek to convey the impression that they are not concerned with academic excellence, that they are not status seekers. Conversely, in imaging the dominant Other, they appropriate an external persona, essentially mutating and in the process becoming book-black Blacks, individuals whose identity as African-Americans is decontextualized, constructed largely from academic and popular texts rather than consistent, intimate interactions with familial and nonfamilial African-Americans.

There are many ways by which the high-achieving students appropriate a non-Black identity or, in the vernacular, act white and become obsessed with issues of power and control. At Capital High, one of the more salient ways by which one can be accused of acting white is to become a member of the advanced placement program.

Ultimately, the high-achieving students are motivated by two critical factors. First, they believe that if they are able to demonstrate that African-American students can perform in ways that are comparable to those of their White counterparts ("prove the racists wrong"), they will be able to reclaim the rightful identity of African-Americans and obtain the same opportunities and rewards as their White cohorts. Second, they believe they will be able to avenge the dehumanization of their Black ancestors by appropriating and inverting the myth of intellectual inferiority. This is most evident in their verbalizations and in their development of strategies to minimize conflict with their less successful peers and with the staff at Capital High. Ironically, many of the strategies they develop to cope with the lack of peer support for academic excellence, as well as the lack of adequate reward for the scholarly achievements of their parents and other Black adults, are often misinterpreted by the staff as a lack of serious commitment to their espoused reclamation goals.[1] A more detailed examination, however, indicates that the conforming behaviors of these students are intended to reclaim the appropriated identity of African-Americans that was pilfered during the great African Diaspora, and to limit the negative response of their classmates to their efforts to behave in ways that violate existing racial and cultural boundaries.

The high-achieving students tend to minimize the impact of race and gender-related obstacles. By conforming to existing norms and expectations, they often override the barriers to their achieving their dreams. Even when they acknowledge the existence of strong barriers to equality of opportunity, they resist internalizing them, believing that if they can just prove that as individuals they can achieve the academic goals associated with the White Other, they can change the larger society's responses to the Black Other.[2] They also act as if they believe that they can overcome whatever obstacles are placed in their way. Hence, they defy the academic limitations by pushing upward, beyond the established ceiling, to the stratosphere.

The high-achieving students personify the "soldiers in the struggle" response, in that they believe they personally possess the skills and inner resources to overcome socially constructed boundaries and race-specific limitations. These students are more apt to reflect this orientation than those at the low end of the continuum. The fact that many of the parents of the high-achieving students are poor and therefore unlikely to be able to send their children to college does not impede their sons' and daughters' pursuit of good grades. Most of these students are convinced that if they resist the dominant society's low expectations of African-Americans, that is, if they study hard and do well in school, they will be able to work, receive academic scholarships, student aid, or other sources of support that will enable them to accomplish their goals. These youngsters' perceptions of their potential for success are buttressed by the significant adults in their lives. These adults—at home and school—constantly reassure them of their distinctiveness and their ability to overcome whatever might deter or discourage them, thereby reinforcing their commitment to resistance as conformity.[3]

Gender is also an important variable in both resistance and academic success at Capital. There are, obviously, gender-specific ways of acting white and gender-specific constraints on academic achievement. While the male and female high- and underachievers tend to identify and define the gender roles of African-Americans in similar ways, there are significant differences. Female students, regardless of level of performance, are much more likely to attend school on a regular basis than their male peers. They are also far more likely to resist systematic efforts to push them out of school, teenage pregnancy notwithstanding.[4] Most classes therefore have a much larger number of female students than male students. And most students are aware of this gender-linked variation.

Gender variation in the Black community does not parallel gender patterns in the White community, despite areas of overlap. At Capital, where gender diversity is manifested in a variety of ways, achieving academic excellence appears to be much more appropriate for female students than for males, a pattern that differs drastically from that reported in the dominant community (Best 1983).

High-achieving females appear to be very much aware of the ideological claims of the larger society and the societal limitations they suggest, yet they appear much more likely to ignore the existence of limitations no matter how formidable, acting as if they don't exist, even in the face of irrefutable evidence that they do. Such optimism may be encouraged by the fact that identity empowers and undermines them in ways that are both unavailable and unfamiliar to their Black male peers and the White female Other. Moreover, because the barriers facing African-American males are somewhat suppressed for African-American females, who are often perceived by the Other in a neutered role, they are motivated to persevere even when there is virtually no sign of hope. The fact that they face a "doubly-refracted" existence[5] does not stymie them in the way similar perceptions of limitations appear to hamper the pursuit of academic achievement on the part of their male peers. Their childhood socialization appears to have prepared them in such a way that they both "know" the larger society's low perception of them, and are willing and able to resist the "nothingness" ascribed to their lives (Christian 1990; Fordham 1990, 1993; Mullings 1994; Walker 1982). Hence, these female students are also much more adept at appropriating the image of (an)Other while "pretending" that the social reality they experience every day is not real. They are also capable of acting as if the texture of their lived reality is an aberration and not endemic to the lives of African-American people.

Persistence is the correct term for the response pattern of these females because it embraces continuing when there is seemingly little or no logical reason to continue. Furthermore, it is the appropriate term because, as Spicer (1971), Castile and Kushner (1981), and many other anthropologists have noted, groups that exhibit this characteristic tend to survive despite herculean efforts by a more powerful group to destroy them. African-Americans can surely be classed as a persistent people (V. Green 1981). African-American adolescents at Capital have to be willing to persevere because expectations at Capital are not high.

In general, the high-achieving students readily acknowledge that the lives of their family members have been negatively affected by the racially differentiated opportunity structure in America. They do not, however, appear to believe that conditions confronting them personally and individually are as restricting as they were and are for their siblings, their parents, and other African-American adults. Both males and females seem to believe that obtaining excellent school skills will mitigate the negative effects of race in a color-coded opportunity structure. Hence, even when they are imitating the Other, they are reclaiming African-Americans' appropriated humanness. Their perseverance suggests a conscious or unconscious commitment to the reclamation of African-Americans' humanness in the school context.

Refusing to Liquidate the "Self": The Underachievers
The underachieving students respond in a drastically different way to the larger society's construction of Blackness. Indeed, the textures of their lives and the lives of their significant adults appear to be much more influential in structuring both their defined and evolving perceptions. Unlike their high-achieving cohorts, who can often either dismiss evidence of racial discrimination or use it as motivation to prove the racists wrong, the underachieving students see such evidence as motivation to oppose and resist the dominant society's appropriation efforts. Their general response is to shun all efforts perceived as impersonating or imitating the Other. Instead of viewing perceived limitations as fuel for embracing Otherness and subsequently demonstrating to everyone that they are human because they can achieve the same or similar academic feats as their White counterparts, the underachieving students view race-specific limitations as the reason to reject claims made for schooling. Their reclamation goals are based on resistance through avoidance.

Underachieving students avoid obligatory school norms despite their upbeat, normative, verbal rejoinders in interviews which suggest that discrimination is not a major problem in the lives of Black Americans in contemporary Washington, DC. The widespread poverty and the underemployment of their parents, siblings, and other Black adults are too close to home to be summarily dismissed in words that approximate those of their high-achieving peers. Max was one of several underachieving students who acknowledged that their parents, siblings, and peers had tried but failed to achieve the American Dream.

The underachieving students internalize widely held perceptions of the capabilities and limitations of African-American people. A central goal in a capitalist society is learning to exploit resources, including other people, in order to make money. However, Max and his brother and most African-American adolescents are systematically taught to eschew such exploitation. In most instances, anything connected to capitalism is proscribed. Max's brother's efforts to develop an entrepreneurial relationship with other Black people is rejected not only by his family members, who define it as seeking "fast money" and therefore inappropriate, but also by other nonfamilial African-Americans, who likewise do not and will not support his efforts to become a small businessperson.

There is also the issue of how a particular people obtain prestige within the group. As Max's discussion of his brother's business efforts suggests, Black people perceive a job ceiling for African-Americans in Washington, DC. And, like White America, the Black community resists individual efforts to alter existing boundaries. The best indication of this perception is the students' choice of courses: generally they avoid those that represent the values of the larger society. The harder school officials work to persuade them to adopt existing educational norms and expectations historically reserved for White students and the dominant White community, the more they resist.

Although the resistance of these students is partial rather than complete, it differs from Willis's description (1981) of English working-class students' "partial consciousness" not so much because the response differs, but because the students' understanding and interpretations of their responses differ. Stigmatized race is not a consideration in the response of White working-class students in England. It is, however, central in the response of African-American students at Capital High.

While Capital students' perceptions of the narrowness of their life options are only partial, they are, nevertheless, often validated by the actual practices of the school. Students officially enrolled in the advanced placement program are generally given first priority for (1) morning classes—the most desired time; (2) exclusive homeroom sections; (3) extended and special counseling services; (4) free bus transportation to and from school;[6] and (5) the "best" teachers, that is, the teachers with the most teaching experience, and those who teach the courses and subject matter central to a perception of Otherness, such as high-level math, physics, foreign languages—especially German, Latin, French—and sections of English with a high literature content rather than a focus on grammar.

The underachieving students understand that assignment to the advanced placement program entitles the individual to all of the perquisites listed and many others. Assignment to the regular curriculum at the school invariably means a kind of second-class existence. But the underachieving students regularly choose that program in defiance of these known limitations.

Curiously, the underachieving students' response does not include coveting the perks offered the students who are members of the advanced placement program. Rather, their response represents a kind of resistance in which avoidance and inversion are the linchpins. Moreover, as the confidence of the underachieving students plummets, they become sullen, morose, and surly. This response is gender-differentiated, with females generally becoming more passive and silent, and males becoming more hostile, aggressive, and belligerent.[7]

The underachieving students appear to prefer teachers who are at least able to commingle aspects of a Black Self with Otherness, and they are apparently repelled by those who equate the reflection of Otherness with a superior humanness. Again, the male underachievers appear to be more adversely affected than the females by the total exclusion of the Black Self and the obligatory celebration of Otherness, although ultimately both sexes are severely injured by their gender-specific perceptions and their responses to these perceptions.

The male underachievers' responses reflect their perceptions of who they are as individuals as well as who they are as Black males. Their sense of who they are appears to be centered in their racial and cultural identity. The high-achieving males indicated that gender was more important to them than their identity as African-Americans.[8] Conversely, the underachieving males claimed that their racial identity was the primary way they identified themselves.

The future plans of the underachieving males were vague to nonexistent. When they were asked to describe their lives as adult males in the society, their responses were not grounded in a connectedness to what they were accomplishing or not accomplishing in the school context. All the underachieving males express a desire to achieve success and wealth, but they appear not to believe that schooling will empower them to achieve their dreams. At another level, it may be that these males do not believe they are capable of achieving the wealth and success that they claim they desire, nor that they have even developed the strategies needed to begin to achieve their verbalized aspirations.

As with their male counterparts, the female underachievers have not identified postsecondary goals, nor are they taking courses that will prepare them for challenging careers. Like many of the males, they expend a great deal of their academic energy seeking to avoid what they claim they want to achieve.

The conflicting forces and perceptions that are so much a part of the lives of the underachieving students are reflected in their understanding of what it means to be Black in contemporary America. The underachieving girls "know" the democratic ideology and tend to give standard responses to questions about opportunities in America. In general, they *verbally* maintain that discrimination is not the debilitating factor it once was for Black Americans. At the same time, they appear to disbelieve most of what the school teaches them about democracy and human equality. As they see it, virtually every feature of the school curriculum, including textbooks, celebrates Otherness. Perhaps unwittingly, it also vilifies the Black Self.

The underachieving females are also very much aware of the social conditions under which they are forced to function, leading to the readily apparent conflict between their espoused goals and objectives and their school behavior. Their academic effort makes an unambiguous political

statement: they do not see the opportunity structure as being characterized by unlimited access to existing jobs, goods, and services. Moreover,
their unwavering commitment to their identity as African-American
women means that they are unwilling to compromise their perceptions
of the collective Black Self. Unlike the majority of the high-achieving
females, the underachieving females reject the mandate to act white in
exchange for academic success; they are unwilling to masquerade as the
White female Other. They are also clearly reluctant to participate in a
process that demands their appropriation of the varied personas of the
female Other.

School Officials as "Book-black Blacks"

In general, the academic practices of the staff at Capital High force its
members to conform in order to resist. This is their dilemma in their
role either as teacher-parents or as teachers. Even teacher-parents are
generally rearing children who are resisting the reigning construction of
the Black Self through avoidance of, rather than conformity to, established school norms. Moreover, if Capital's school officials have any
faults as parents, it is on the side of overindulgence, one of the undesired
costs associated with being Black and having a middle-class income.

There is nothing new or strange about human populations creating,
changing, and maintaining their world. This is predictable. What is problematic for most of the teachers and administrators at Capital is that
they were born and reared African-Americans and continue to claim this
racialized identity (see Morrison, quoted in E. Washington 1987; Carter
1993:55–79). At the same time, they are being schooled as if their racial
and cultural origins are inconsequential. More important, in their pedagogical training, this "miseducation" was compounded: they were taught
to teach students as if *their* racial and cultural identity also did not
matter (Woodson 1933).

For a significant segment of the Black community, representing Otherness inevitably consists of expunging the Black Self. Staff members at
Capital are often defined and define themselves as Other, their Blackness
and African origins notwithstanding. Consequently, for many of the students being identifiably Black or African-American is not to be equated
with a commitment to the well-being of Black people. The amount and
level of schooling appears to be a strong influence in the students' assessment of who is appropriately Black. The lack of certainty regarding one's
Black identity is implicated in the quest of students and their teachers
for the space to maintain connectedness to the imagined Black community while pursuing careers identified with (an)Other. The desire to remain connected to their African-American ancestry compels many of the
teachers and some of the other school officials at Capital to engage in a

psychological migration in which the Black Self meanders, struggling to remain Black while appearing to appropriate (an)Other.

The saliency of Otherness in the school context has come to mean that activities generally linked to the Black community are not embraced. Not surprisingly, then, the students are not allowed to have pep rallies or dances either during or after school hours. Talent shows are also severely limited, as are any other community-connected/related activities. Such activities, it was said, were banned because they were too closely aligned with Black life and culture, and therefore were almost certain to be prohibited, minimized, and/or distorted.[9] This genre of activities is generally identified and defined as "wasteful" and as "taking students away from the important aspects of the school curriculum." Capital students must not be allowed to waste precious school time pursuing and embellishing what they already know, that which is generally associated with the Black Self. Rather, Capital students must learn and celebrate that which is generally external to the Black community and, at the same time, clearly affiliated with (an)Other. The more the students are able to masquerade as (an) Other, the more likely they are to be academically successful.

In summary, African-American teachers and other school officials are often tormented by the duality or multiplicity of their lives and their apparent commitment to what is frequently associated with (an)Other and Otherness. It is in fact the dual nature of their lives as well as their bifurcated identity that leads them to be characterized as book-black Blacks. Their comfort and familiarity with the Other and Otherness bring into question their identity as African-Americans.

Looking at the Black Self and Choosing Otherness

Reclaiming African-Americans' pilfered identity, culture, and history involves a reassessment and, in some instances, a reconstruction of the Black Self. For many members of the Capital community, this is a "partial" activity in perpetuity. Nevertheless, as Willis (1981) points out, "partial consciousness" suggests both insight and blindness, wisdom and ignorance, including an incomplete understanding of how race and various social forces are coupled and interconnected. Many of the students, especially high achievers, are not impressed with what they perceive to be the unique life of African-Americans; others do not think that African-Americans have a viable, autonomous cultural system. Still others argue that the culture of African-Americans is a caricature of the dominant, intrusive culture of the larger American society. All of these disparate segments of the ethnographic sample constitute the "voice" of the Capital student population.

The existence of these divergent, contradictory perspectives at the school suggests that what it means to be African-American is widely debated, contested, and challenged. How people behave or interact is the measure most often used in determining whether the Black Self is celebrated or denigrated. The lack of consensus and the existence of multiple voices often leads to debates and philosophical collisions. Many of the students therefore seek—often unknowingly—to be consumed by the Other, not only because it is officially sanctioned in school but because it is a way of minimizing their affiliation with the disparaged Black Self.

A significant segment of the high-achieving students see African-Americans as largely responsible for their own current lowly status. They have come to this understanding of existing social conditions in the Black community because in their schools they have been carefully taught the integration ideology, with its built-in denigration of the Black Other, and they have uncritically accepted its central premises. Thus, they blame the victim (Ryan 1976; Margolis 1982). Members of this segment of the student sample valorize greater individualism in the African-American community. Ironically, they also valorize group solidarity and communitas as an ideal (M. Williams 1974), and they reject the argument that preoccupation with individual "status needs" (Poussaint and McLean 1968) hampers group unity and the attendant collective orientation.

Most Capital students, high-achieving and underachieving, consistently lament the low academic *effort* of African-Americans.[10] They describe their peers as lacking the willingness and perseverance to continue striving to achieve academic excellence. These students' views are shaped by adult Black Americans, who, as demonstrated above, generally do not teach them about the possible impact of race and racism on their lives—at least not verbally. Their silence denies that racism exists.

A good many students take a different view of how African-Americans perform in the adult world. There they have to work hard in order to survive.[11] Moreover, they argue, African-Americans, male and female, have historically had no choice in this matter. Their reason for being in America was to labor for a social group whose members needed vast numbers of unpaid workers to develop the newly proclaimed nation. Nevertheless, several of the students suggested that if Black people would just work harder at those things that are good for America, they too, like European immigrants, would be able to change their lowly status in the existing social system. Apparently, these students have bought the unreconstructed message regarding African-American identity that to be human is to be of Euramerican ancestry.

In constructing this ethnographic text, I was compelled to recognize that I was "embroiled, compromised, [and] entangled in [a multitudinous] affair" (Berge, cited in Stoller 1994) with the people in the Capital community. This dilemma is not unique to me, to my diasporic condition, or to my "split personhood." In ethnographic research, *the ethnographer is the primary research instrument*. Nevertheless, as Narayan (1993:679) accurately asserts, even when the ethnographer is a "purported insider [a 'native'], it is clearly impossible to be omniscient: one knows about a society from particular locations within it." The resulting analysis is invariably filtered through the lens of the ethnographer.

Inherent in the ethnographic lens is watching. In the Capital community, I watched by focusing my anthropological gaze on the "entangled tension" of the diasporic people living there, including their articulation of the "copresence of a 'here and there'" in their nonlinear resistance practices (Clifford 1994:318). I watched them as they meandered from one cultural site to another, inevitably confronting the issue of acting white. In braiding these different cultural frames, I watched their contradictory interactions and behaviors and heard their verbalized claims, highlighting in the process the school as a social arena where success and failure are alloyed, continuously manufactured, and controlled by the larger American society, where most norms and values, including success and failure, are implanted by the larger society, and where containment and constraints of the Black Other are rampant. Consequently, the Capital community is perhaps best seen as a diasporic population, characterized by displacement, hybridity, and other boundary-blurring phenomena.

In my study of the Capital community residents, my initial gaze was bleached of its "split personhood" and hybridity, its conflated African *and* American origins. I watched the residents using resistance both to conform to and to avoid the ideological claims of the larger society. I scrutinized and evaluated their seemingly illogical responses—students who did not study or attend school systematically, parents who did not teach their children about race and racism, teachers and other school officials whose lives on paper appeared "white" but who were compelled to live "black," high-achieving students whose conforming behaviors masked their avoidance of dominant ideological claims—silently screaming as I watched: "You are doing it wrong! Why can't you get it right?" I winced when I observed the students' almost total lack of academic effort; I cringed in the presence of parental linguistic practices[1] that did not shroud their sense of power and control (Delpit 1988; M. Foster 1989); I mourned the practice of teachers revisiting the students' seemingly unalterable commitment to depth over breadth in school-sanctioned subject matter (B. Williams 1988; Snead 1984); and so on ad infinitum, my gaze inevitably negating the residents' humanness.

In violation of the widely extolled anthropological principle that cultural rules are arbitrary, I invariably found something sacred about existing school norms and practices that compelled me to conclude that the students' responses were "abnormal." Hence, the violence and terror attendant on the act of watching (see Chow 1993; Jameson 1990) was unavoidable and inevitable, inherent in my school-learned normalizations and celebrations of (an)Other.

Fortunately, the theoretical claims of my discipline merged with my perceptions, making it impossible for me to put my initial analyses on paper. I struggled with the weighty issue of why the abnormal responses at Capital were so prevalent and persistent, why they both did and did not make sense. I was continually troubled by how these "abnormal" responses resonated in my own life, while connecting me to my own school experience and the seeming vacuousness of my generation's conformity. Indeed, I have wasted years paralyzed with my own fears of representation, my worries about how my (re)presentations would be policed and subsequently interpreted.

In hindsight, this "down time" was not idly squandered. I am almost able to forgive myself for the inactivity because I now feel that this "absence" gave me the necessary space and distance to correct my near-sightedness, my penchant for ethnocentric responses to cultural rules and practices that are inevitably arbitrary. Apparently I needed this time in order to unlearn conventional explanations of African-Americans' academic performance and to reflect on the meanings embodied in the behaviors I observed. I needed to be able to come to terms with the findings emerging from the study, to report what I initially could not accept, what I initially rejected. Essentially, I needed this time to contemplate and ponder what I could not understand and appreciate during the time I was actually collecting the data.

This was a difficult process, made even more difficult by the dominating ideologies penetrating and impregnating school discourse. Thus, as I began the study, I struggled with my existing perceptions: academic failure as evidence of lack of agency and academic success suggesting absence of resistance. I clung to these perceptions, discounting—as my schooling had taught me—my experiential knowledge and what I observed as well as what I was told for a major portion of the study period. What I was observing at Capital High made me extremely uncertain, for it supported none of my prior beliefs. How could I convince my intended audiences that at Capital High academic failure is constructed as agency, and academic success is forged as resistance to dominant discourses regarding the academic abilities of the Black Other?

Initially, my nearsightedness, my internalized diasporic schooling and its attendant penchant for the parochial and provincial propelled me to construct the Capital community residents as if they were in an "other-land" (Stoller 1994:357), naked and devoid of the humanness that is gratuitously associated with visions of the American Self.

Like most other researchers, when I initially observed the massive resistance to school-sanctioned learning so prevalent among Capital High adolescents, I wanted to label and attribute their behaviors to an absence, deficit, shortage, or some other *lacking* argument. The usual constructions came immediately to mind: Capital students were *lacking in* proper middle-class American values, adequate parental training, appropriately trained and caring teachers. Even when the emerging data pointed overwhelmingly to the students' reluctance to forgo their sense of agency as a central explanation for both underachievement and academic success at the school, I resisted describing it in those terms.

Failure as a sign of agency does not mesh with conventional explanations. As I ended my fieldwork, academic failure as agency certainly did not emerge as an acceptable explanation in either my belief system or my evolving analyses. Nevertheless, resistance as an explanation for academic failure (Giroux 1983a, 1983b; Gilmore 1985; Weis 1985; Solomon 1992) as well as a form of agency for dominated populations (see J. Scott 1985, 1990; Scott and Kervliet 1986; Haynes and Prakash 1991) offered insights into the academic performance of the students at Capital High that propelled me to the analysis offered here. I am, therefore, intensely conscious of the centrality of resistance as a theoretical claim in the academy and the tensions and contestations evoked by this discourse. At the same time, I am also aware of its widespread meaninglessness (that is, lack of acceptance) outside the academy.

The residents of the Capital community helped me get a stronger sense of my own identity. They propelled me to a broader image of African-Americans, compelling me to magnify my ethnographic lens, to accept as legitimate the *"meanings that [African-Americans] themselves give to what is going on"* (Kochman 1981:3; emphasis added). Throughout the study, I struggled with the issue of how to textualize a critical ethnography that did not give center place to my presence.

This is not an insignificant concern. It is not inconsequential because, as I noted above, the idea of "ethnographies as texts" is a dominant postmodern issue in anthropology, with "writing up data" a central component of the meaning of "ethnographic authority" (Clifford 1983). As is generally true of ethnographic analyses, my involvement in the Capital community went well beyond mere participant observation. I watched these people intently, becoming in some sense a griot, "implicated and embodied" in the Capital community. My multiple subjectivities did not (and still do not) permit me to be either disengaged or disembodied. Unlike most ethnographers, who are "shielded from the complicated negotiations of social life in other-land" (Stoller 1994:357), in textualizing my study at Capital High I am unable to avoid responsibility for my words, images, and actions. This reality initially robbed me of the will to write, to construct written images of the Capital community residents and the meanings they gave to what was occurring. My discursive writing practices were extremely problematic because, as noted above, writing and anthropology are in many ways synonymous. Erase writing as a component of the discipline, and anthropology is effaced. Disappears. Consequently, the discipline demands that in order to be known as a "real" anthropologist, I must write—not just talk—about the people I studied. However, my initial inability to accept as legitimate the Capital community residents' existing meaning system, as evidenced in the resistance practices reported here, bludgeoned any preexisting notions I had about what was implicated in the academic performance of Second Emancipation African-American adolescents. At the same time, my ethnographer-as-griot status (Stoller 1994) compelled me to construct a text that reflected how I was and am "implicated and embodied" in the Capital community, including how I interacted with the participants.

Not surprisingly, then, the analysis presented here reflects the way I watched and was watched at Capital High and within the Capital community. It documents how I became implicated and even "overimplicated" in a network of relationships. My involvement is not laminated by textual claims of scientific objectivism or lack of engagement. I *was* engaged, and in far more than classroom observations. Indeed, I was involved in the school and community. I cannot pretend otherwise; that is what transpired. Hence, in addition to classroom observations, formal interviews with the key informants, the daily recording of fieldnotes and so forth, I was often smothered in the crosscutting and shifting alliances and allegiances. At the surface level, I actively participated in the key informants' activities in and out of school.

My research activities followed the guidelines and mirrored the practices anthropologists have traditionally followed, with possibly one exception. Mine did not take place in an exotic context among the exotic Other outside North America but in the Capital community, where the "stickiness" of crosscutting and shifting social relationships complicated my involvement. Moreover, because many of the central issues affecting their lives had resonance in my own schooling and in my racialized, genderized Self, I first rejected and subsequently internalized many of their perceptions of Blackness.

As Van Maanen (1988) declares, *culture* is a slippery, elusive concept that emerges for most of us—especially with regard to (an)Other—in "black and white" or written form. Because a culture is constantly changing while texts are inevitably static, the ethnographer can only seek to represent accurately in narrative form those whom she studies at a particular time. Ethnography then is "a means of representation," as much a way of creating culture or a cultural practice as it is a way of determining the writing itself (Van Maanen 1988:6).

Regardless of the historical era, race, gender, and resistance have been and continue to be key issues in the lives of people in America who identify themselves and/or are racially identified as Black. Indeed, I began this book by asserting that the common denominator in the response pattern of all segments of the Capital community, including both the high- and the underachieving students, is a commitment to resist dominant imaging and imagining of the Black Other. I hope this primary issue is adequately addressed in this ethnography.

Finally, like most ethnographers, I trust that I have been successful in "teas[ing] from the tangled threads of social life insights that will make a contribution to social theory" (Stoller 1994). At the same time, I am not sure that offering such insights is more important than trying to decipher and understand the impact of the dreaded R-word—representation—on Americans' racialized perceptions. As I have documented in this analysis, the power of written representations is unmatched. Those empowered to use one of society's most powerful weapons—the pen—can permanently shape or transform our thinking. If this premise is accurate, our perceptions of an entire generation could be permanently altered as a result of these ethnographic images.

How can the findings reported here spawn social policies that minimize the massive resistance evident in the academic responses of the Capital High students? What is to be done? Can we and should we seek to intervene in cultural practices in order to produce a desired response? What are the possible unintended outcomes? Are they likely to exacerbate the existing response pattern?

As I have argued in the preceding chapters, the primary factor fueling the massive resistance—as conformity or avoidance—so prevalent at Capital High is the social practice of assigning to the Black Self the lowest status in America's racialized hierarchy. As a population historically represented as Other, the residents use resistance as an ongoing strategy to avoid colluding in legitimizing the extant oppressive system. I have documented how the residents of the community construct and maintain this resistance, as well as the enormous price they pay for trying to invalidate "official transcripts." And I have chronicled Black students' attempts to reclaim what they see as their appropriated humanity undermine their academic performance. The questions thus become: What are the implications of such a widespread, persistent strategy? For the members of the community? For the larger society? For Black adolescents' academic performance? Should we—the nation—actively seek to interrupt this process? Indeed, the central question is whether the nation should intervene or, alternatively, redirect its focus to include finding ways to minimize both the students' sense of alienation from the nation and its public system of education and the school's tendency to (mis)represent these students as Other.

The findings emerging from this ethnographic study indicate that the site of the problem is much broader than what occurs between the school walls. In order to penetrate the unadulterated resistance described in this research, dismantling the existing opportunity structure is central. The dismantling must be the first order of business because, as these data demonstrate, the nature and configuration of the opportunity structure   343 compels Capital High students to resist the dominant society's oppressive hegemonic claims. The Capital community's struggle is embodied in their resistance, their refusal to accept the dominant society's representations of the Black Self. Their fear of being consumed by both the norms and values of (an)Other and by (an)Other that historically appropriated Black humanness propels them to seek a space where individual perceptions of the Black Self are safe. As presently constituted, the American educational system is not that safe space.

Dismantling the existing opportunity structure will entail more than discontinuing the practice of Black exclusion from that which is quintessentially American. If America wants to transform the practice of avoidance as resistance among Second Emancipation African-American adolescents—the biggest deterrent to academic success at Capital High—while concurrently expanding the nation's desire to increase conformity, our emerging social policies must entail becoming assertive about including people who are more than just phenotypically African-American; these policies must also promote the inclusion of culturally identifiable African-Americans as more than mere tokens who are constantly watched and found lacking. Moreover, the opportunity structure will have to do more than reflect the norms and values of the historically dominant Other; it must accept as normal what is generally associated with African-Americans and other peoples of color. Eliminating those symbols that suggest hostility will liquidate the resistance strategies identified and discussed in this ethnography.

In schools, a parallel kind of restructuring is necessary, primarily because the pasting-on now practiced does not work. A poorly planned course in Black History or a Black History Month celebration in March rather than February (or even every day in February) will not quell the resistance reported here. The goal, as Castenell and Pinar (1993) suggest, is to transform existing practices in such a way that the Other is internalized in the school's curriculum and programs; the Black Self becomes embodied in what is defined as normal. Anything less will only exacerbate existing resistance strategies.

At the same time, much greater attention and validation must be given to the ways African-American adults use language in the rearing of their children. As I have indicated here, linguistic practices in the Black community differ drastically from those sanctioned in the academy and by the upper strata of the society.[1] The failure of school officials and policymakers not only to acknowledge this difference but to continue to resist altering teaching practices to reflect this linguistic pattern will not only exacerbate but promote resistance as avoidance and thus Black students' continuing academic failure.

PROLOGUE

1. For a fuller discussion of the role of emotions in social life see H. Geertz (1959); Lutz (1988); Lutz and White (1986).

2. Verification of this claim can be found in many ethnographic sources, including Malinowski (1987[1929]); Chagnon (1968); and Mead (1961[1928]).

3. I use the word *suddenly* advisedly. I do not mean to convey that this debate started yesterday. Rather, I am trying to juxtapose the relative recency of the ongoing debate about a long-standing practice in the discipline to suppress or ignore ethnography as a process (see Agar 1980; Clifford 1983, 1986:2; Freilich 1978; Van Maanen 1988).

4. Castile and Kushner (1982) and Spicer (1980) have developed a definition of what it means to be a people and have identified a litany of issues affecting peoplehood, including "continuity of a common identity" based on "common understandings concerning the meaning of a set of symbols" (Spicer 1980:347). My primary concern here is with how a population that is identified as a people responds to the idea of "writing culture" and their own, perhaps unwitting, collusion in the construction of themselves as the Other.

5. For an explanation of "book-black Black," see introduction, n. 10.

6. In some countries in precolonial Africa, griots were social outcasts who possessed knowledge not shared by the other members of the community. The price griots paid for their *uncommon* knowledge was permanent estrangement from both their community of origin and the community where such knowledge was eagerly sought and valued. Thus, in exchange for the transformation of their pariah status, they were permanently consigned a marginal status, neither members of their former caste nor full-scale members of the lineage to which they were attached or assigned (see Chinweizu 1987; Tate 1992). In that regard, Stoller (1994) argues that, like griots, ethnographers consume and are partially consumed by otherness. There appear to be parallels between the roles of griots in traditional Africa and contemporary African-American adolescents' perceptions of how they must function as schooled members of the Black community. I believe that their desire to bypass this liminal status is in part responsible for their reluctance to engage in the academic writing process.

INTRODUCTION

1. All proper nouns identifying the school, its curriculum, and its personnel are pseudonyms.

2. My wombmate and I shared teachers, homework, and academic goals during elementary and junior high school. We were not allowed to share the same homeroom when we became high school students. Our competition, collaboration, and support for each other made us much better students than either one of us would have been alone.

3. Throughout this text, I use the term *Other* in two radically different ways. First, I use it to refer to the historical or traditional construction of those peoples who are not Euramerican in origin and who are, regardless of their accomplishments, "inevitably . . . perceived unidimensionally" (Madrid 1992:8). Second, I use it to refer to those peoples who were initially responsible for creating cultural boundaries by labeling and defining peoples who were seen as culturally or visibly different as *Other*. Hence, I offer the reader the opportunity to understand the othering process from two different perspectives: (1) a social group that has always been "othered," and (2) the way the traditional Other perceives those who have consistently "othered" them. When I note, for example, that my classmates defined my response to academic learning as representing the Other, I am acknowledging my dual status. What I struggle to represent throughout the text are (1) the "enactment of hybridity" (Narayan 1993:681), that is, deliberately imposing a multifaceted perspective on the residents in the community, which I then textually juxtapose with their struggle to create an uncontaminated racialized identity, and (2) my fractured, racialized identity as an African-American (a "halfie") who is also an anthropologist, wrestling to represent a non-monolithic population that, ironically, idealizes collectivity, egalitarianism, and an imagined cultural past. In this sense, I am both "Us" and "Other"; "We" and "Them."

4. Appadurai (1992:35) insists that anthropologists need to examine their assumptions regarding people who are categorized and labeled "native." This is necessary, he asserts, because people so identified are constructed as "not only persons who are from certain places" but also as "those who are somehow *incarcerated*, or confined, in those places."

5. A nontraditional student in one of my classes shared with me the unanticipated response of her daughter to her parents' decision to have her pursue her education in a predominantly White suburb in the Washington area. The practice of not hiring teachers of African ancestry prior to and during the early 1960s had conveyed to her the unacceptable notion that Black people should not be employed in such positions. She cried and even threatened to kill herself when she was assigned to a Black teacher's classroom—the result of a change in the school system's policy in response to the Civil Rights Movement. My student tried to console her distraught daughter by assuring her that people of African ancestry could be excellent teachers and that, indeed, when she was a student in a segregated school system, nearly all of her teachers had been Black. Her daughter remained convinced that she, along with her unfortunate classmates,

was going to receive an inferior education as compared with those whose teachers were White.

6. At Capital High, African-American adolescents generally framed their verbal responses to the notion of "acting white" in behavioral terms such as speaking standard English, going to the Smithsonian, having a party with no music, dancing to the lyrics rather than the beat of the music, studying hard in school, hiking in the mountains. These kinds of responses, though not unexpected, captured only a small portion of what they meant. My incessant participant watching confirmed the need for a broader definition. As I shall document throughout this ethnography, the students at Capital High intuitively understood that acting white celebrated an ethic that was enshrined in the valued practices of the school's curriculum and that, as Black people, their own futures were constructed in ways that differed from those of their White cohorts in suburban Maryland and Virginia. Hence, while they were not as sophisticated as Gramsci (1971) and other theorists, their constructions suggest a rudimentary understanding and conflation of Gramsci's notion of hegemony.

7. Traditionally, the term *resistance* has been used to describe a struggle endemic to the schooling of students of nondominant groups, to indicate their marginality as well as their opposition to this marginality. Most often it conveys a sense of the lack of fit between the middle-class norms of the school and the culture and values of those who are relative newcomers to the schooling process (Castenell and Pinar 1993; Cusick 1973; Everhart 1983; Solomon 1992; Weis 1985; Willis 1977). In my use of the term, resistance is not just the struggle of the individual, nor is it mere ritual (McLaren 1986:80–81). It has "sociopolitical significance," suggesting opposition to perceived acts of subordination and degradation by both the high-achieving and underachieving students (Solomon 1992; Giroux 1983). As thus constructed, resistance is a culturally significant process within the African-American community.

8. Here I am referring to my status as an anthropologist and an African-American. The residents were not fearful of my identity as an African-American. It was the anthropology component that was problematic for most of them. Most residents had never met an anthropologist; some had never heard of the discipline. Those who knew something of it associated it with White people. I evoked suspicion because I was connected to a "Whitie" discipline and, more important, because I would be *watching* them.

9. "Black voice" is not be to equated with one voice. There are many ways to speak in "Black voice." My use of this concept is at least somewhat analogous to what hooks means when she speaks of "coming to voice as an act of resistance" (1989:12).

10. The term *book-black Blacks* is here used to describe an internal sorting process—a dilemma in which Americans of African ancestry who have obtained school credentials and a modicum of success in the dominant community are pilloried by both the Black and the White communities. Their economic separation from the plight of most African-Americans leads some members of the Black community to construct them as "Other"—individuals who have "passed over" to the other side. That is, they have obtained a new identity, one which makes

them less than *totally* Black. A similar perception is held by non-Black people: this category of Black Americans is not like the Black masses; their schooling, Carter's "professionalism" (1993:67–76), has transformed or marginalized them, making them raceless (Fordham 1988, 1991a, 1991b) or race-neutral (Meri Danquah, *Washington Post*, 3 July 1994, C9). In both the Black and the White communities, then, these group members are perceived as having been reborn. *Within* the Black community, their rebirth defines them as socially or symbolically dead and forever lost to the African-American community; in the White community they are seen as having been literally "born again" and thereby transformed into raceless entities that are not Black. Consequently, as Black people who have "passed over" (the Black community's perception) or been reconstructed (the White community's perception), these group members' cultural knowledge and understanding of the conditions confronting the majority of Black people is frequently devoid of firsthand contact. It is obtained from books or other literary sources, not from living with the folks. Hence the term *book-black Blacks.*

11. The trips to the pornography store were always with one of the high-achieving males. No underachieving male indicated that going to a sex shop or pornography store was a typical part of his after-school routine. When I went to the store in Georgetown, the high-achieving male student and I never went alone; there were always at least two other high-achieving males in the group.

12. In order to both protect and disguise the actual geographical location of the Capital community, I have deleted those aspects of the U.S. Census data that might make it possible to identify the geographical area that I here label the Capital community. I have also disguised Census data or other data that are not of a composite nature.

13. A small percentage of the parents come to every PTA meeting, but though the administrative staff at the school send notices and invitations, they do not succeed in getting large numbers of the students' parents to alter their view of the school and become engaged in the PTA and other school-sponsored activities. Parental absence from these formal meetings is not to be equated with a lack of interest, but rather the fear of being exposed and judged by school officials on the basis of preexisting stereotypes.

14. Behaviors are not to be equated with cultural knowledge, even though all behavior is culturalized (Bohannan 1992). Culture is not merely behavior. It is the acquired, socially transmitted knowledge that people use to interpret experience and to generate behavior (Spradley and McCurdy 1989). Moreover, as R. Rosaldo (1989:26) asserts: "Culture lends significance to human experience by selecting from and organizing it . . . It encompasses the everyday and the esoteric, the mundane and the elevated, the ridiculous and the sublime. Neither high nor low, culture is all-pervasive."

15. "Advanced placement" is a fictitious name I give to the rigorous academic program offered at Capital High. This appellation is not intended to suggest an analogous relationship with the program bearing the same name sponsored by the Educational Testing Service in Princeton, New Jersey. Nevertheless, there are parallels and ways in which the two programs overlap.

16. Strawberry Hill is only a short distance away, but it might as well be on

the other side of the earth. It is characterized by affluence and by businesses and support services designed to enhance and promote the well-being of its members. There are huge, single-family homes, modern apartment buildings, school and recreational facilities, all designed to make life meaningful and enjoyable for its residents. There are also numerous colleges, art galleries, museums, theaters, libraries, shopping malls, and restaurants. The streets are all paved and maintained. Every support service imaginable is available, either at city expense or as one of the many entrepreneurial services offered in the community.

17. As many researchers have suggested (see, for example, Benjamin 1991; Cox 1948; Dollard 1937; Frazier 1939; Landry 1987; Ogbu 1978), race undercuts class in the Black community. For example, Ogbu (1978), argues quite convincingly that there is a lack of congruence among the various classes in Black and White communities. That is, "middle class" in the White community is not analogous to "middle class" in the Black community. The same is true of the working class, lower class, upper middle class, and so forth. In analyzing the quantitative data collected during the Capital High Study, I am overwhelmed by the unanimity of the response to the question, "How would you describe yourself?" Almost invariably, the students chose "middle class" rather than "upper class" or "lower class."

18. The value assigned to the advanced placement program is manifested in the nature and configuration of course offerings and other perquisites and services made available to these students. In making up the academic calendar, nothing took precedence over this component of the school's curriculum. Every other academic track—the humanities, regular curriculum, and special education—had to defer to it. This worked a major hardship on the students in the other academic tracks. In the case of English, which was required of everyone, the decision to assign as many sections as possible of college-level English courses to the morning meant that students in the regular curriculum were forced to take their assigned English classes in the afternoon, thereby presenting three-fourths of the student body with a huge problem: how to obtain work permits that enabled them to work afternoons. Moreover, since the teachers assigned to teach eleventh- and twelfth-grade English classes were entitled to at least one planning period, many of the students assigned to the lower track at the school found themselves forced out of gainful employment because the official school policy gave first priority to the smallest group of students and the students least likely to seek employment during school hours—students enrolled in the advanced placement program.

19. For a detailed discussion of African-American females' school success, see Fordham 1993.

ONE

1. Elsewhere I have identified major periods in the cultural life of people of African ancestry in America (Fordham 1991a). My purpose was to suggest a schema that would broaden our understanding of how and why contemporary Black adolescents at Capital High School are responding as they are to the possibility of unlimited opportunities in the school context and the larger society. Here I suggest a four-layer topology rather than the three-layer one presented

earlier. It includes the following historical periods: (1) official enslavement—ca. 1609–1865, for which the harshness and dehumanization has been well documented: Blassingame 1979; Genovese 1972; Painter 1995; Van Woodward 1957; (2) the First Emancipation—a three-hundred-year time period when people of African descent were forbidden to "act white"; (3) the Second Emancipation—the 26-year-transition period, roughly 1960–1986—when Black Americans were obligated to "act white" in order to compete with white Americans; and (4) the emerging time period, which I label neosegregation and others label the new racism. In this book, my focus is the Second Emancipation period (1960–1986) and its impact on the academic performance and behavior of contemporary Black adolescents. I argue that this historical period is critically important because it enables us to look, for the first time, at a generation of Black people born and reared in a maelstrom of cultural forces, all of which claimed to support the humanness of Black people. Prior to the Second Emancipation, there existed both legal (de jure segregation) and extralegal (de facto segregation) ways of denying the humanness of people of African descent. This was the case despite legal documents and other ideological props (such as the Dred Scott Decision, the U.S. Constitution, and the Declaration of Independence coexisting with the Three-Fifths Clause and the Supreme Court's decision in *Plessy* v. *Ferguson*). In short, the Second Emancipation is the first historical period in American history in which African peoples are both legally and morally declared to be indistinguishable from their White American counterparts.

In this typology, I go on to point out that today's Black students are both victims and recipients of a cultural heritage which is rich in opportunities but riddled with limitations to a degree unmatched in the history of Black people in America. Unfortunately, in the various analyses presented by social scientists, greater emphasis is generally placed on the opportunities than the limitations that are imposed both externally and internally. Black adolescents are growing up in a social context that purports to value integration of all segments of the American society. In many ways this is their social reality. At the same time, however, there are definite indications of continuing racism and other forms of human degradation which their parents did not face. In a sense, then, these students' parents can neither teach them nor share with them certain experiential survival skills. Regrettably, in many instances these students' parents do not understand nor do they see the problems their children see and with which they must contend on an ongoing basis. Many of these parents do not fully appreciate how actively their children are engaged in both creating and maintaining a racialized and culturalized identity that is affiliated with peoples whose self-proclaimed ancestry is African.

2. Baltimore and St. Louis also had large free Black populations, but they were not as large as that of Washington, nor did they influence the development of these respective cities in comparable ways (L. Brown 1972).

3. A central point of B. Anderson's (1991:6) argument is that states and state systems lack real geographical boundaries. Their existence is an *invention*—"imagined as both inherently limited and sovereign." Following Anderson (1991), I argue that Black people's perception of the Black community is also an invention. It is *imagined* because we—the members—"will never know most

of [our] fellow-members, meet them, or even hear of them, yet in [our] minds . . . lives the image of [our] communion" (p. 15). Hence, the centrality of writing and written forms of communication in the imagined (Black) community. I speculate that in the imagined (Black) community it is the privileging of music and song, orality and forms of visual communication, that are pivotal.

4. Though some readers will argue that the policy issue was about desegregation rather than integration, I think it is important to call this process integration, the language of the "public transcripts," which, as J. Scott (1990:2) reminds us, are "unlikely to tell the whole story."

5. As Farhi (1990) notes, Washington is the "yuppie capital," the context where both Black and White Washingtonians live beyond the income levels of most Americans. Nevertheless, "taking orders" is a reality for large numbers of Black Washingtonians. It refers to a whole cadre of jobs characterized by individual workers' lack of autonomy in deciding whether these tasks are worthy of completion. Workers who "take orders" generally occupy jobs that are distinguished by monotony, repetition, lack of autonomy, and so forth.

6. Willie Horton is an African-American male who was convicted of a felony in Massachusetts. He became the symbol of fear and violence during the 1988 presidential election when the Bush campaign developed a political advertisement depicting how Dukakis's decision to offer him a furlough led to the rape and killing of a White woman. America's criminal justice system was thus constructed as a revolving door, and Horton was constructed as the quintessential thug or outlaw.

7. Following Smith (1992: ix), I make a distinction between imaging and imagining. Central to the idea of imaging is memory as well as constructive skills, sensation, and perception. Imagining or imagination in all its multiple forms is grounded in "irreducible perceptual components." In imaging, one "constructs an image in the presence of an object from which the image is fashioned." One does not have to be "in direct sensory contact with the object from which the imagery of the imagining is constructed."

8. The garnering of political power by African-Americans in Washington is often mistakenly equated with the existence of a meritocracy, or, at the very least, the deconstruction of race in the American political arena. Such a conclusion is not warranted. Race is still a significant signifier in who gets elected in Washington, a context steeped in a diasporic history. Indeed, virtually nothing has changed except that the people who get elected during the post-Civil Rights eras are Black rather than White. A major reason African-Americans are elected to political office in Washington is that a majority of the voters in the city are Black, just as a major reason why African-American politicians are not elected to political office in Birmingham, Alabama, is that the majority of the voters in Birmingham are *not* Black. Historically, race and gender of voters have been central elements in who gets elected in the United States. Indeed, as manifested in American society, one could argue that democracy and/or majority rule has been a euphemism for race loyalty. There are a few exceptions to this generalization, notably the election of Douglas Wilder as the first Black governor of Virginia.

9. In this book, I am positing that a racialized identity can be either Black

or White. For some peoples, a racialized identity confers status and privilege; for some other peoples, such an identity suggests limitations and contestation.

10. Elsewhere I have outlined ways in which "suffering" affects African-American females' academic performance (Fordham 1993). More recently, E. Brown describes how her efforts to assimilate caused her horrific childhood agony and confusion (1992:31).

11. Essentialized identities are disparaged in contemporary academic discourse, particularly in anthropological discourse. No one wants to be accused of making essentialist claims (Fuss 1989; Said 1978, 1986; Stoller 1994) regarding race or gender. Indeed, it is currently fashionable to argue that much of what is written relating to race or gender can be dismissed as essentialist, that is, related to some "true essence—that which is most irreducible, unchanging, and therefore constitutive of a given person or thing" (Fuss 1989:2). I am not positing that there is some "pure or original [race], a [race] outside the boundaries of the social and thereby untainted by a [racist] order" (Fuss 1992:2; see also Said 1978, 1986). Instead, I try to convey the Capital community's response to a constructed reality in which they perceive themselves and their ancestors as having been defined racially in ways that diminished their human status. Moreover, I argue, this historicized nonhuman status is the linchpin of Capital's students' response to academic demands.

12. While I prefer the term *schooling* to *education,* I shall sometimes use *education* because it is more popular. Nevertheless, the technically correct term is *schooling.* As Cohen (1970, 1971) and many other scholars, including Whitehead (1957), have noted, education is much broader in scope, indicating what a culture mandates its members learn in order to reflect the "acquired knowledge" necessary to function in a particular culture (Spradley and McCurdy 1989). Schooling, on the other hand, is the formal, bureaucratized knowledge sanctioned by the state (Watkins 1963).

13. Class and racial differences in the Capital community are extremely troublesome, with what is generally thought of as class differences being partially subsumed under the more inclusive notion of race. Class distinctions exist in the African-American community, but they do not appear to have the same import and meaning in this African-American community that many researchers claim they have in the dominant community (see, for example, Langston 1988; for validation of the kind of "deviation" noted here, see also Benjamin 1991; Cox 1945; Dollard 1957; Landry 1987; Ogbu 1978). The saliency of race in the Capital community ruptures the often identified linear pattern of class demarcations in America in favor of the "master status" nature of race in the community (Hughes 1945). The residents' internal conflict relating to these concepts—race and class—is everywhere apparent. For example, even when the parents of the students at Capital explicitly taught their children to separate themselves from the collective ethos so rampant in the community, that is, seek distinction rather than blending into the crowd, the students often breached established class etiquette.

14. I am not positing that there is an essentialized "Whiteness." As is true in the case of "Blackness," there are obviously many variations of "Whiteness."

In spite of these, I am postulating that each of them is generally elevated above all variations of Blackness.

15. The irony embodied in this perception of race should not be dismissed. Race is not a neutral category. Obviously, if it is marked as a virtue for some people, it is also seen as a stigma for some people. A stigma only has meaning in its juxtaposition with another cultural category: virtue. Prior to the Civil Rights Movement, Blackness as a racial category was almost unanimously defined as a stigma, in both the Black and the White communities. During the Civil Rights Movement, Black Americans unilaterally decided to invert the meaning of Blackness (see, for example, popular music, the Civil Rights anthems). Their decision to transpose the culturally prescribed meaning of Blackness and recast it as a privilege rather than a stigma has had and continues to have a profound impact on the academic performance of African-American adolescents, including the genesis of their systematic effort to reclaim Black Americans' presumed appropriated humanness.

TWO

1. Academic success among African-American students is not widely reported in the research literature. In contrast to the large number of studies devoted to Black children who do poorly in school, studies of Black students who perform well in school are relatively rare. For exceptions, see Fordham 1987, 1988, 1991a, 1991b, 1993; Fordham and Ogbu 1986; Edwards 1976; Mackler 1970, 1972; Shade 1978, 1981; and Trotter 1981.

2. A perception among contemporary African-Americans is that a primary "achievement" of White Americans is their ability to dominate other population groups. Among those who have been dominated are African-Americans who were enslaved and transformed from a human to a property, or nonhuman, status. Thus, I argue, contemporary African-American adolescents generally seek to avoid accomplishing this "achievement."

3. The "Black Self" is a self-definition that surfaces in social spaces that are presumed safe (see Collins 1993). Within the Capital community, the Black Self is envisioned as the construction and valorization of a racialized image decorated with the appropriate(d) humanness that their resistance personifies. It is subversive and unadulterated. The Black Self then embodies and reflects the most highly idealized cultural features of the fictive kinship system: sharing, egalitarianism, collectivity, and so on.

4. My characterization of fictive kinship as the dominant organizational structure in the African-American community represents a central tendency, more a statistical probability than a monolithic certainty. Fictive kinship is a dominant, though certainly not the only, organizational form in the African-American community. Therefore, I am in no way arguing for uniformity— cultural, economic, or political—of goals, beliefs, or values among African-Americans or any other human population. As I envision it, there is enormous complexity of social life in the Capital community. This complexity scrapes up against two competing, idealized organizational frames. In the African-American community, it is the fictive kinship system; in the school context, it is the integra-

354 NOTES TO PAGES 71–90

tion ideology of the larger society. In this analysis, the totalizing and/or essentializing nature of these idealized organizational forms is bludgeoned by my self-conscious efforts to make the text reflect the hybridity we are all compelled to live in modern state systems.

5. Like many other long-standing anthropological concepts, the term *hierarchy* (see Dumont 1970) is undergoing a backlash primarily because of its affiliation with essentialism and essentialists' claims and exoticizing and totalizing critiques (Appadurai 1992; Dumont 1986). Consequently, throughout this text I use the term cautiously and guardedly.

6. I am not suggesting that African-Americans do not compete with each other. They do, sometimes violently. My assertions here are applicable only to competition and the competitive ethos *between* Black and White Americans; it is not intended to address the pattern of interaction *within* the Black community or among Black people. The critical distinction is work vs. nonwork. In arenas not defined as work (e.g., "play"), African-Americans compete with each other in ways that replicate the dominant society's notions of competition (Gay and Abrahams 1972). But in arenas defined as work, African-Americans do not use an individualistic approach to tasks assigned. What seems to dominate instead is a kind of group-centered ethos or approach in which collaboration and cooperation are defined as prestigious. (For further elaboration of this claim, see Abrahams and Gay 1972; Haskins 1975.)

7. Resistance also appears to be one of the quintessential characteristics of that genre of peoples Spicer (1971, 1980), Castile and Kushner (1981), and a whole litany of other anthropologists (Adams 1981; V. Green 1981; Leone 1981) have identified as "persistent peoples." (See also Blassingame 1979; Gutman 1976; Hine and Wittenstein 1981:291–298; Holt 1972; Johnson 1934; McGary 1992:35–54; Rawick 1972; J. Scott 1985; Solomon 1992).

8. As Rohrer and Edmondson (1960) note, *uppity* was the derogatory term coined and used by the White community to describe the small middle-class segment of the African-American community. Interestingly, this term is used to label the middle-class segment of only the Black community. No parallel term exists for the middle-class segment of the White community.

9. I add the caveat that while the income of the parents of African-American students is likely to produce different levels of academic performance, what some researchers euphemistically label "survivors' guilt" often erases this differential.

10. For example, African-American students often insist that they experience prejudice on the part of their classroom instructors. This perception either motivates them to greater conformity or, alternatively, to shut down academically. At Capital High, if they chose the second option, efforts to get them to reengage the textual information were invariably unsuccessful in such a teacher's classroom because, as the students perceived it, they had experienced prejudice. Hence, their experienced reality (experiential knowledge) took precedence over any other kind of knowledge (see Hill Collins 1991; Rushforth 1994).

11. At Capital High, one of the most frequently voiced complaints on the part of teachers and other school officials was the students' reluctance, and in some instances downright refusal, to write short-answer responses to test questions and to complete written assignments such as book reports and term papers.

12. I am arguing that these views are idealized by African-Americans; group members hold them up as the model to which they should aspire. They may or may not be able to practice them in their own personal lives. Nevertheless, I am arguing, these are the *ideals* that guide their assessment of each other and the contexts in which they are forced to function.

13. In the public school system, the only sharing that is socially approved is that which is intended to "tell" another about the speaker's accomplishments. For example, in most elementary schools "show-and-tell" is an obligatory component of the early morning activities. Its approval, however, is not to be equated with the kind of sharing that exists among African-American people, both in and outside school. In the former case, information is shared. Among African-Americans, sharing one's sense of self is culturally approved.

14. Identity implosion was evident in the music and songs generated by the Civil Rights revolution. Perhaps the best-known example of how African-Americans inverted the meaning of stigmatized race can be found in the lyrics of a song sung by James Brown, a rhythm and blues singer known as the "godfather of soul": "Say it loud/I'm black and I'm proud." "Say it loud/I'm black and I'm proud." "Say it loud/I'm black and I'm proud."

15. Under noncoercive conditions, officials are unlikely to implement social policies that they can anticipate will produce social chaos and/or widespread undesired responses on the part of those for whom the policies are intended. Therefore, the integration ideology was envisioned as a social policy that, at the very least, would suggest a positive—accepting—response on the part of African-Americans.

16. I am not unmindful of the fact that among this segment of the African-American population, real cultural change might possibly have taken place. These teachers and other school officials may have actually revised their former cultural knowledge. Here I am following Spradley and McCurdy (1989:302), who insist that cultural change is a process whereby a population revises its former "cultural knowledge and use[s] it to generate and interpret new forms of social behavior." They go on to argue that "at the heart of all cultural change are new patterns of thinking, new ideas and new cognitive maps." What I observed among some of the teachers and officials at Capital may be evidence of cultural change, as described here. While I am pointing out that this is the more prevalent response, it is just as important to note that it is not the only response. As I hope will become clear in the chapters that follow, many teachers and some other school officials were deeply conflicted by their roles at the school. Among this group were many people who were engaging in behaviors and practices as conscripts. Thus, as Spradley and McCurdy assert: "A forced change in social behavior does not necessarily involve culture change" (1989:305).

17. These officials' responses suggest either (1) the denial of cultural change as an active ongoing progress, or (2) a population's total encapsulation in the idea of cultural change as always being characterized by lineal rather than nonlineal processes (see D. Lee 1987; Staiano 1980), a highly unlikely possibility.

18. For a detailed discussion of this phenomenon see my article, "Peer-Proofing Academic Competition among Black Adolescents: 'Acting White' Black American Style" (Fordham 1991a).

19. The need to belong is not more intense among African-Americans than among other social groups. As Maslow (1954) notes, belonging is one of the basic human needs. This is validated by Tracy (1991:176), who asserts that as a group "human beings are so terrified of isolation that we will literally shut off conscious awareness of individual reality in order to be part of the group."

20. The openness and fluidity clearly visible in Black people's within-group interactions must be contrasted with the secrecy and silence characteristic of their responses to and interactions with text-derived knowledge and the voice of the Other. These different ways of responding are implicated in the flotilla of contradictions observed in the tautness and artificiality of Black students' behaviors while at school (Gwaltney 1980; Collins 1990).

THREE

1. In an article in the *New York Times Magazine,* Tannen (1994) describes the issue as an exploration of the distinction between indirectness and directness in language usage, noting that in addition to being extremely confusing, these categories often overlap and contradict each other.

2. I am indebted to Paglia (1994) for the concept *dressage.* She attributes it to Jacqueline Bouvier Kennedy Onassis: "'the closest thing to royalty' that America has ever seen." Paglia (1994:12) asserts that "dressage is a form of radical minimalism, of hierarchial stillness and repose," so entrenched, so well synchronized in the personhood of the aristocratic horseperson that "the rider's signals to the horse are completely invisible." Her analysis is analogous to Tracy's argument (1991) regarding how to measure success and power among academic women: silence and invisibility.

3. As Kaela's mother defined it, a "finishing school" was an institution where young women matriculated in order to learn to be ladies, that is, to learn how to juggle the roles of hostess, wife, and mother. Because her sister had graduated from an institution without skills that she could trade in the market-place—she could not get a teaching job because she did not have teaching credentials—Kaela's mother viewed Smith as a "finishing school."

4. Shortly after the passage of the *Brown* v. *Board of Education* decision in 1954, Washington's public school officials implemented a four-track system at the high school level (Hansen 1964, 1968). This track system sealed the fate of the students in the system, depending on the option they wisely or unwisely chose as they began to matriculate at the high school level. As someone who chose the business track, Kaela's mother was somewhere near the middle, smothered in the rigidity of the track system.

5. I use the phrase "first learned cultural system" rather than the more familiar "indigenous" or "authentic" because of their affiliation with essentialism and essentialist claims (Asad 1973; Carrier 1992; Fuss 1989; Said 1978, 1989).

6. Note that Alice never answered this question, at least not verbally, no doubt because she was too embarrassed to acknowledge that her mother would spend most of the remaining money in any way she wanted.

7. I have struggled with this construction. My struggle is ensconced in my fear that these textual representations are likely to be constrained by a pervasive normative understanding of what it means to be supportive, loving, and caring.

I do not wish to give the impression that Capital High parents are not supportive of their daughters' academic goals. What I hope to convey instead is that the parents of female students in the Capital community were often ambivalent about the implicit or unstated goals of schooling, especially as they penetrated and interrupted their daughters' connectedness to the imagined Black community and the Black fictive kinship system. These parents' ambivalence and ambiguities were often manifested as resistance—both as conformity and avoidance—to the ideological claims of schools and schooling. The direct speaking style of African-American adults (and their children) is not to be equated with lack of support, hostility, etc. Indeed, it might be useful to see Capital parents' direct speaking style as being reflective of both a lack of power in the larger dominant community and their efforts to amass power and self-actualization.

8. *Most* does not mean *all*. Not every one of the females in the underachieving sample was sexually active. Nonetheless, each of them was able to test the waters regarding her desirability as a female love object, if she so desired. This test was rarely available to the high-achieving females.

9. Dawn's mother refers to the night shift. The White females on this shift appear to be leaving offices rather than custodial jobs. No such identity confusion existed regarding the Black workers leaving the building in the morning. They were invariably identified as the janitorial staff.

FOUR

1. Accepting subordination is not to be interpreted as acquiescence. Black parents who are deemed successful in rearing males display a nuanced understanding of when resistance as conformity or resistance as avoidance is appropriate. These parents know when they must demand unconditional conformity to certain rules and/or expectations and when it is possible to allow their sons to avoid or evade certain social expectations. Not fully understanding these subtle differences can have devastating consequences. Indeed, in patriarchal societies, it appears to be the shame and degradation of humiliation that fuels the resistance of Black males—and perhaps all males. African-American males are committed to resistance (as avoidance) to the norms and precepts which assign and consign them to a secondary status in America's gendered hierarchy and, in their perception, the negation or erasure of their claim to manhood. More research is needed.

2. I am concerned about how this statement might be interpreted. Nevertheless, I have decided to include it because Norris was so adamant about how he currently felt about what he perceived as his father's lack of involvement in the family unit. I suggest caution in reading this and similar statements on adult gender roles.

3. Some of the mothers who were rearing their children without the active financial support of the father had to make a choice between two equally unacceptable options: work and provide food and shelter, or stay at home and seek public assistance. Norris's mother exemplifies this cruel dilemma. Unlike Martin's father, who went to work every day to the low-status job he occupied as a parking-lot attendant, Norris's father would not sell his labor in such a job. Acknowledging the presence of these two responses to the existence of a peren-

nial *job ceiling* (Ogbu 1978)—that is, built-in limitations in how high people of African ancestry can rise in dominant organizations—is not meant to suggest that one response is superior to the other. Apparently, it is not.

4. Black males' consignment to this secondary status is tantamount to a kind of intra-gender sexism in which male-on-male domination is both unnamed and legitimated.

5. Sidney is in the advanced placement program because his parents insist on it. He has the intellectual ability to be a high achiever in the program. His greatest deterrent in achieving this goal is his effort to avoid that which is unavoidable. Among the high-achieving males, he and Max share this dilemma.

6. Norris's mother equates "Uncle Tomming"—that is, being dependent on a White person—with a lack of intelligence.

FIVE

1. Ms. Aster's use of *overachiever* is not to be confused with Gates's description (1994) of his doctor's use of this term to both deprecate and minimize the seriousness of his insistence that when he grew up he wanted to be a doctor: "The doctor shook his head and walked over to my mother, who was waiting in the corridor. 'Pauline,' he said, his voice kindly but amused, 'there's not a thing wrong with that child. The problem's psychosomatic. Because I know the type, and the thing is, your son's an overachiever'. . . . In 1964 'overachiever' designated a sort of pathology: the dire consequence of overstraining [one's] natural capacity. A colored kid who thought he wanted to be a doctor—just for instance—was headed for a breakdown" (Gates 1994:140–141).

2. For most adults at Capital, class status is job-linked. If one has a stable job, one can claim middle-class status (this is irrefutably documented in the students' responses to a survey question about class status in which virtually everyone identified himself or herself as belonging to the middle class). This differs from the situation in the larger society, where one's class status is more closely aligned with a professional position (Sennett and Cobb 1972) or, as Ostrander (1984) postulates, the length of time one *has* been wealthy.

3. Elsewhere (Fordham 1988) I have labeled this phenomenon "racelessness." As I then perceived it, racelessness was best seen as a strategy the high-achieving students utilized in their efforts to "make it" in the school context. The irony here is that Capital is a predominantly African-American school where greater attention is given to the celebration of St. Patrick's Day than to Black History Month. Ladson-Billings (1991:151) outlines the impact of this monocultural schooling by describing what she calls "multicultural illiteracy": "the inability to be conversant with basic ideas, issues, personalities, and events that reflect the perspectives and experiences of people other than White, middle class-males." She describes "multicultural illiteracy" among the undergraduate students she was teaching at Santa Clara University who were preparing to become classroom teachers. She asked them to recall the "activities they remember doing in grade school to commemorate" certain holidays. For most of her respondents, "long and elaborate lists were submitted for St. Patrick's Day including 'singing Irish songs,' 'making shamrocks,' 'reading stories about the legend of St. Patrick's

Day and leprechauns,' 'wearing green,' and 'having shamrock-shaped cookies or Irish soda bread with milk that was tinted green with food coloring.'" She insists that her respondents' "lists for the other holidays were either not as long or nonexistent." The students she taught were predominantly White and were apparently taught to celebrate that which reflected their schooling. This was not the message conveyed to the students at Capital High.

4. Identity as something that implodes, centralizes, and grows rather than dissipating and disappearing is a relatively new phenomenon in the Black community. Despite its recent arrival, it is wreaking havoc with many of our previously held ideas about how to create and maintain a raceless society of unhyphenated Americans (see Lieberson 1985; Peshkin 1991).

5. I do not mean to suggest that the view of African-American adolescents as deficient or inadequate was the only one or the predominant one of the teachers at Capital High. As Foster (1990:123) notes, "Studies of teacher thinking do not consider the influence of the racial identity of teachers on their belief systems and teaching practices" (see also Lightfoot 1973, 1978). Moreover, she cites case after case of how the teachers she studied were victimized by their identity as African-Americans. "Ella Jane went on to say that though she and her cousin, each of whom possessed master's degrees, reported to [the desegregated] school [to which they had been assigned] each day, neither of them was given a class. Instead, because the townspeople were unwilling to accept them as teachers of their children, they sat in a classroom for half of the school year without teaching a single student. Finally, after the white teachers complained, the school board created classes of remedial reading students, composed of 9 or 12 students, all of whom were Black or poor white, for them to teach. For three years, they continued teaching remedial reading classes" (Foster 1990:131; see also Foster 1989).

6. "Mental health day" is a popular phrase used to convey an effort on the part of the user to retain his or her good health. Hence, one takes time off in order to be able to cope effectively with the stress affiliated with one's work.

7. Building seniority has increased in importance since the firing of teachers in the District of Columbia in 1983. Retaining seniority minimizes the possibility of losing one's teaching position or being transferred from Capital to another school where one would have to start at the bottom of the seniority system.

8. My data and the subsequent analysis are premised on a perspective which suggests that people cannot be understood apart from their history. Therefore, since every people's history is different, the fact that they may engage in the same or similar experiences does not mean that they bring to them the same understandings, nor do they necessarily have the same meaning. Consequently, the "free enterprise system" as practiced by the White teachers at Capital had vastly different meanings for them than it did for their Black colleagues. Many Black teachers at the school refused to support the business activities of their White colleagues because they understood it to mean exploitation. The White teachers were baffled by such a "ludicrous" perspective.

9. Membership in the lunch group varies. There are, however, some teachers who appear to be critical for its survival. Ms. Mentor is absolutely essential. In

fact, they usually meet in her room. Many of the other members share with her membership in the mathematics department. Several other departments are represented, including foreign language, English, history, social studies, physics.

10. These teachers' prestige items differ somewhat from what might be the most valued items among the vast majority of the parents of the students at Capital. Obtaining the right kind of schooling for their children is likely to take precedence over home ownership, for instance, because for many of the Capital parents, home ownership is definitely beyond their reach. But because public education is virtually free in this country, they eagerly seek its presumed benefits for their children, constantly admonishing them to get all they can get from the public school system so they may aspire to owning a home. In this way, the parents feel that they will have achieved a modicum of success by ensuring that their children's lives will not be a replication of theirs.

11. Harris (1989[1974]) revises Ruth Benedict's notions of the function of the potlatch. In her book, *Patterns of Culture* (1934), which predates his analyses, Benedict argued that among the Kwakiutl Indians of Vancouver Island the potlatch was part of a megalomaniacal lifestyle characteristic of the Kwakiutl culture in general.

12. Some readers will not see a distinction in the behavior of these middle-income Black Americans and middle-class White Americans vis-à-vis the desire for home ownership. I am not claiming that there is a difference. What I am trying to make clear is that even when African-Americans and White Americans share class status, they do not have the same opportunities.

13. As idealized, as opposed to realized in the African-American community, is the belief that the quintessential feature of humanness among African-Americans is encapsulation in the Black fictive kinship system and the celebration of the indigenous "Self." I am not claiming that there is some kind of essentialized "Self"—a pure, untainted, or original African-ness that survives outside existing social boundaries. Rather, I am trying to account for the community's shared, albeit uneven, perceptions of what is appropriate and inappropriate behavior.

14. For a discussion of the importance of reputation among African peoples, see Margaret Gibson's article "Reputation and Respectability: How Competing Cultural Systems Affect Students' Performance in School" (1982).

15. In general, the students constructed Mr. McGriff in unflattering ways, missing and/or erasing his complexity, and hence his resistance to the dominant imaging of the imagined black community. Most students envisioned him as an uncritical conformist to the ideology of the larger society. They generally do not envision adult behavior as resistance to the hegemony of the larger society. Hence, for Capital students, teachers and other school officials are book-black Blacks.

16. Mr. McGriff tended to dismiss this invariable complaint because he had assigned the scheduling responsibilities to one of the assistant principals—Mr. Madison. It was, in his view, Mr. Madison's professional responsibility to make sure that every student was properly registered before school began and to have in place the infrastructure to enable newcomers to enroll without delay. Mr. Madison did not get the schedule done on time.

17. In the existing patriarchy, similar role expectations were imposed upon

women regardless of whether they were African-American or White women. One of the major exceptions was that White women were generally expected to avoid employment outside the home. When they had to work for pay, the structural constraints confronting them as women were similar to, although not the same as, those imposed upon African-American women (see Palmer 1989; see also Rollins 1993). Similar structural limitations meant that their labor was bid and sold for similar wages. This was not the case for African-American and White males; there the differential was much greater.

SIX

1. Clifford (1994:307) asserts that "resistance to assimilation can take the form of reclaiming another nation that has been lost, elsewhere in time and space, but powerful as a political formation here and now." My use of *reclamation* is broader than that proposed by Clifford. I am not constrained by the notion of a lost *nation* but an entire *continent:* Africa. Since most African-Americans do not know the specific country or region of their origin, my argument regarding reclamation is more global, intended to suggest both a connectedness to Africa and an effort to reclaim the presumed appropriated Black Self.

2. *Brainiac* is a term widely used and understood by the students at Capital. Outside of Capital High, it is often erroneously equated with the term "nerd," so popular among White American adolescents. It is not appropriate to describe non-Black students as "brainiacs." The terms are not synonyms. It is appropriate to describe academically successful African-American adolescents as "brainiacs" because the term captures the unique meanings and understandings that Second Emancipation African-American adolescents bring to an obligatory and oppressive dominant-group institution whose core curriculum is understood as "racial text" (see Castenell and Pinar 1993). Thus this term embodies and reflects the numerous conflicts, tensions, and contestations African-American students bring to the contemporary schooling experience. Depending on how it is used, it can be either derisive or respectful, but in most instances is used to convey derision. A "pervert brainiac" takes the term to a new level of contempt.

3. A well-developed body of literature exists outlining the impact of stigma on achievement and identity formation (see, for example, Zweigenhaft and Domhoff 1991; Granfield 1991; Goffman 1963, 1967; Willis 1977; Sennett and Cobb 1973).

4. Among the four student groups making up the research sample—high-achieving males and females and underachieving males and females—the parents of the high-achieving females were the most impoverished, with the lowest annual income. By all indicators, this group of students was the most disadvantaged economically.

5. This conclusion is based on a complete analysis of the ethnographic data and a preliminary, incomplete analysis of a segment of the quantitative data.

6. Anthropologists (see, for example, V. Turner 1969) have long recognized the importance of every culture's color-code system and its impact on a people's worldview.

7. English is the one exception both because it is an annual requirement and because it is tracked in ways that the other courses are not. Since every student

at the school has to take an English requirement *every year,* school officials have developed and implemented a system that enables them to place students in certain sections based on their individual performances regardless of their academic "track."

8. Like Wendell, several of the other students indicated that they were initially recruited by school officials and asked to become members of the advanced placement program. This was true of both the high- and underachieving student sample. Among the high-achieving students, Martin, Kent, and Adam were also invited to become members of the program. For reasons similar to the ones offered by Wendell, they refused. Among the underachieving males, only Sidney and Max are members of the advanced placement program. The grades of Manley, Art, and Karl in junior high did not bring them to the attention of officials managing the program.

9. The Life Skills examination is a D.C. Public School System examination which is intended to assuage the public's discontent with a widely held perception that the students who graduate from the system are inadequately prepared for the ordinary challenges of living. This exam tests the students' ability to write a check, locate a desired television program in *TV Guide,* read an apartment lease, etc. In short, while it is not the most challenging academic test in the world, it serves an important political function: mitigating the fears of parents and other adult Washingtonians that they are not getting an appropriate return on their tax dollar—a basic education for their children.

10. Katrina's parents would not describe their response in this way. Indeed, they repeatedly assured me that they supported their daughter's academic goals. For example, her father insisted that she prepare to apply for a scholarship to one of the military academies, an option Katrina deplored. He interpreted his support for this postsecondary option as evidence of how much he endorsed her high school performance and future goals. Katrina and her parents, however, did not agree on an undifferentiated definition of what it means to be supportive. Her parents gave it a gender-specific meaning. Katrina idealized parental support as being universal and undifferentiated in either race or gender terms. She used the normalized larger society meaning of support; her parents' understanding of support for their daughter's educational goals embraced African-Americans' gender-specific ideals regarding female achievement.

11. I do not wish to convey the impression that for some of the high-achieving females "othering" or "acting white" is free of conflict. Even among the segment of the student population that is less conscious of the controversy surrounding this issue, conflict and ambiguity are apparent.

12. Mr. McGriff owned an enormous old Cadillac. Despite the fact that it was a very old car, as many of the students constructed it, the car was symbolic of his acceptance of a life largely extraneous to the African-American community. Students' criticism of his efforts to amass wealth did not mean that they did not aspire to own the same or a similar car. They probably didn't know that he bought some of his clothes from Goodwill and other consignment shops.

13. "Joning" is similar in form to what has traditionally been identified in the African-American community as "playing the dozen" (see H. Foster 1974). Here Martin is rationalizing his tendency to harass his homosexual classmates

by claiming that unlike the heterosexual males at the school, the "gay guys" can take "joning" about their sexual orientation.

14. As the reader will recognize, Paul's understanding of culture is rather embryonic, and his definition of culture is relatively concrete. He tends to equate behavior with the meaning of culture rather than the more abstract notion that while culture is manifested in behavior, it is not just behavior (see Spradley and McCurdy 1989; see also Bohannan 1992; Kottak 1994).

SEVEN

1. These students' perceptions are not totally inaccurate. Most of the obligatory school knowledge is external to both their immediate community and the Black community at large. Further, what they are compelled to learn in school is legally and socially sanctioned.

2. For many of these students, White Americans are identified almost exclusively with slavery and the oppression of people of African ancestry. That part of their history they "know," even if it is only given cursory attention in their history and social studies classes. The fact that in school very little attention is given to the broad history of African-Americans suggests that the school is perhaps unwittingly colluding in this limited perception of the accomplishments of Africans in the Americas and White Americans' involvement in the slave trade and the oppression of African peoples.

3. Blackness and success are not mutually exclusive. Nevertheless, the culturally conditioned practice of seeing blackness as a stigma and, in striking contrast, success or virtue as whiteness makes it more difficult for students who are racially identified as Black. The central issue is how to hybridize these cultural categories in such a way that Black students can overcome the stigma assigned to blackness in order to achieve the virtue affiliated with success and/or whiteness.

4. Like most Americans, these visitors equate the absence of physical violence with the absence of human degradation. As I document throughout this book, human degradation is rampant at Capital although virtually no one fights or engages in other forms of physical violence.

5. "All students play hooky. It is not a practice unique to African-American students." To these responses to the claims I am making here, I would point out that *uniqueness* is not a prerequisite for a practice to have a special meaning to one group of people (see, for example, Castile and Kushner 1981). Indeed, as I am defining it, culture is not a material phenomenon (Goodenough 1957); it is not behavior. It is instead the knowledge people have acquired that enables them to interpret experience and generate behavior (Spradley and McCurdy 1989:2).

6. As I have indicated, the high-achieving student sample included 12 students: 6 males and 6 females. The underachieving sample consisted of 21 students, 12 of whom are included in this analysis. The underachieving sample was much larger than the high-achieving sample for several reasons: there were far more of them at Capital than there were high-achieving students; they were much more willing to participate in the study; and many of the teachers and other school officials urged me to include a larger number of the underachieving students because they were more likely to leave Capital before the end of the school year. Hence, a predicted high attrition rate is strongly implicated in the

size of the underachieving sample. As it turned out, the predicted attrition did not occur. In fact, all of the underachieving students, save one, followed through on his or her commitment to participate in the study.

7. Art's observation does not negate the centrality of the claim I am making in this book: peer pressure is not the real problem in Capital High students' lack of academic effort. Negative peer pressure is the marked category, but it is not more important than the structure of the curriculum, the stigma of race and its manifestation at Capital, and the students' perception of the school's nonverbalized mandate to become (an)Other.

8. Intellectually, I also have to admit that as I write these words, I have overcome much of my provincialism, that is, my belief in the rightness or superiority of my views. This has led me to accept the validity of what the residents taught me about their lives and the meanings they assign to them. In that sense, I have come closer to anthropology's ideal, if not to its actual practices.

9. School as a masculine environment dominated by male values conflicts with a widely held view initially espoused by Patricia Sexton (1969). Sexton argued that males do not do as well as females in school because school is a "feminized institution." Further, males who do well in school become "feminized," primarily because, as she put it, "society turned education over to women and feminized males" (p. 199). Following Cohen (1971); Friedl (1975); K. Scott (1990); Pagano (1990); and Rich (1979a, 1979b), I am arguing that in a male-dominated society, the major societal institutions—including schools—are designed to reproduce rather than transform the existing patriarchy.

10. Tracy (1991) argues that in the domestic sphere "women bond with each other by sharing bad news" (p. 138). She goes on to postulate that in the workplace, "it is the women who lose who speak . . . [Women] have helped foster a very powerful lie about women's work: the lie that their success at [work] *depends* on their invisibility . . . Ideals of grace and elegance interfere with visibility. They coincide with another lie: that women who complain or ask for recognition are shrews" (p. 139).

11. It is widely acknowledged that in White America, the whiter members of the group are most highly valued. Group members who are blue-eyed and blond are likely to be given more privileges and, at least among female members, are the more desired date and marriage partners. Unlike Black Americans, whose descriptions of the most valued members of the community explicitly designate light skin color as the most desirable sexual characteristic, this same phenomenon among White Americans is euphemistically known as a preference for those persons who are blond with blue eyes (see Holland and Eisenhart 1990; Podlesney 1991; Schillinger 1994; Simpson 1993; Turim 1990). This preoccupation has led to the development of a business in the beauty industry based on changing hair color, so much so that blonds are designated either "lockie" (after Goldilocks) or "boxie" (out of a box; see Schillinger 1994). It is also manifested in the phenomenon that there are "blondes with black roots," meaning that White American women—as well as some non-White women—are pretending to be blondes. It is virtually unheard of, for example, to have women whose hair is naturally blond be accused of being "brunettes with blond roots." This is unlikely because White women whose hair is naturally blond do *not* dye it another color;

they do not pretend to be "brunettes with blond roots." This would be an oxymoronic activity.

Not surprisingly, then, little girls, Black and White, are deliberately taught to idealize and idolize "Barbie," an extremely thin, blue-eyed blonde doll that virtually every prepubescent female covets or owns. In an article describing the upcoming Miss America pageant, a *Washington Post* reporter referenced a study conducted at the University of Louisville. According to Joel Achenbach, the five-year-old study came to these conclusions: "The perceived ideal female face has eyeballs one-fourteenth the height of the face, chin length one-fifth that same height, and a nose that covers only 5 percent of the area of the face. And so on . . . The judges (at the pageant) are looking for a woman who is the best "composite" of all the right attributes of womanhood. According to studies by Judith Langlois at the University of Texas, a beautiful face is one that most resembles the average face of a given society. No wonder Jenna Wms Hashway, a former Miss Rhode Island who comes back every year to watch, says, "I always get all the blondes mixed up" (Achenbach, *Washington Post,* 14 September 1991, G1).

The dominance and prominence of Euramerican standards of beauty are widely documented; see, for example, Morrison's discussion (1970) of its implication in the lives of Black women in the novel *The Bluest Eye* (1970). In an article in the *New York Times,* Elisabeth Rosenthal (1991) acknowledges that "esthetics surgery has [historically] been tailored to Caucasian faces." Consequently, even when non-White Americans seek plastic surgery, "surgeons [perform] the same operations for all groups." Rosenthal cites Dr. Song as making the following statement about traditional plastic surgery practices: "If a surgeon uses Western textbook measurements to guide his scalpel, the result can also be poor [on non-European faces] since such books frequently specify dimensions for European faces [only]" (quoted in Rosenthal, *New York Times,* 25 September 1991, C11).

Hence, to be human is to embody and reflect Euramerican features. However, as Rosenthal points out, this practice is slowly changing. Traditionally (and continuing today), African-Americans and other non-Euramericans sought plastic surgery in order to be perceived as more human, to look more like the embodiment of beauty as portrayed and normalized on the dominant population—Euramericans.

What I am emphasizing here is that African-Americans are not unique or "weird" in their preoccupation with "light skin color." Colorism or colorphobia is a central fixation within the dominant White community as well, with the blond, blue-eyed type being most valued and the dark-haired, brown-eyed White person being the least valued. Schillinger (1994), an erstwhile blonde, notes the centrality of her blonde tresses in her male friend's mind: "Not long ago, a dark-haired male friend took me out for drinks. As he escorted me to my taxi afterward, he reminded me a little sentimentally that we had drinks on the same day, at the same place, a year earlier. Teasing him on his good memory, I joked, "So what was I wearing?" He looked at me in confusion and said, "Well, I don't remember—you were blonde then" (Schillinger 1994:C4).

12. Preoccupation with skin color is not a new phenomenon in the Black

community. It emerged during the period of Black enslavement and continues even today. While it is unofficially recognized, it is both censured and promoted among African-American women; that is, it is more important for a Black woman than for a Black male to be light-skinned in order to attract the attention of the opposite sex. Though less important for male than for female acceptance, it, too, is an issue that promotes success and the pursuit of the good life among African-American males. Hamilton (1991) describes how an icon of the Black community, one of the most revered African-American politicians, Adam Clayton Powell Jr., manipulated his light skin color to promote his acceptance and economic well-being while a student at Colgate University. "The first year at Colgate presented Powell with his first serious confrontation with the color problem and racism . . . When he enrolled it was assumed that he was white, and he made no effort to inform anyone otherwise. Even the few Negro students did not suspect he was a Negro. To say that he was "passing" for white would imply a deliberate intent to conceal his racial identity, but it is clear that he knew that he was being treated differently than the other Black students who, for example, were never housed with whites. The final stroke came when Powell attempted to join an all-white fraternity. As was customary, the fraternity checked the family background of each prospective member, and his race became known. The fraternity immediately dropped him, and his white roommate insisted that he be required to move. The university, of course, consented and told Powell he would have to find other living arrangements. The incident became widely known, and Powell was ostracized by most white and Negro students" (Hamilton 1991:49).

13. I have already pointed out that Kaela is such an extremely light-skinned African-American that even Ms. Costen took her for White. In an interview that occurred during the next year, Kaela vividly detailed how she was invariably objectified, her individual identity subsumed and submerged under the pale haze of her very light skin. This objectification, she argued, compelled her to confront her lack of individuality in the eyes of her male peers. Moreover, as she noted, it was a very uncomfortable experience to always be the object of the male gaze, not because of some special characteristics she possessed, but primarily because she was born "light, bright, and damn near white."

14. I am grateful to Terry (1970) for this concept. The central claim posited here is that male African-Americans are compelled to mimic the behaviors of what Theweleit (1987) describes as the "soldier male." In this case, African-American males adopt the ideals espoused by White American males. However, the hierarchical structure of the existing patriarchy, buttressed by racism and the attendant social barriers, block their efforts to compete on an equal basis with this group of males. Therefore, the "whiteness of maleness" acts as a barrier to the pursuit of academic excellence among African-American male students.

15. The Capital High study was a multiyear study. The first year was devoted entirely to the collection and analysis of ethnographic data. During the second year, I administered a 55-page, 201-item questionnaire to a random sample of students in grades nine through twelve. Only a small segment of those data has been analyzed. It is this small segment that I refer to here.

16. Conflict regarding the supremacy of race or gender issues is quite promi-

nent among the male students at Capital. This response stands in stark contrast to that of the female students in the sample, who apparently do not experience this friction. The female students appear to value their racial identity much more than their male counterparts do. Among the male students, conflict surfaces when they are forced to have to choose between their identity as men and their racial identity.

17. Ms. Blumberg has taught at Capital for over twenty years. She received her undergraduate degree from an Ivy League university. Her teaching style and curriculum focus are definitely traditional. She makes her teaching more up-to-date by including many references to non-White writers and authors. Nevertheless, from her course outline one could conclude that she is what Rich (1979b) characterizes as a "male-identified woman." Moreover, even though she is female, her celebration of that which is patriarchal and not female, that which is Eurocentric and not affiliated with African-Americans, reflects the kinds of professional compromises she has had to make in her construction and consumption of knowledge. Her English classes are therefore heavily weighted toward the students' consumption of the male dominant Other. She does include two African-American male writers: Langston Hughes and Richard Wright. However, as I postulate in chapter 2, the African-American and/or female epistemologies do not simply parallel the Eurocentric epistemology in Black or female face. African-American or female "ways of knowing" (Belenky 1986) are more than simply attaching examples of African-Americans who have achieved what White Americans have achieved. While Ms. Blumberg tends to favor the more traditional approach to teaching, she admits that over the years she has had diminishing success with it.

18. Following Ogbu (1978), in this analysis jobs above the ceiling are identified as (1) executive, administrative, and managerial; (2) professional specialty; and (3) technicians and related support occupations. Those below the job ceiling include sales, administrative support service, labor, and others. The inclusion of administrative support positions, which encompass a larger number of clerical jobs, in the category of jobs below the job ceiling, differs from Ogbu's typology (1978), which classified administrative support positions as being above the job ceiling. The vast majority of the adults in the Capital High community who were employed during the last census were working in jobs which are below the job ceiling: 86.9 percent compared with 62.7 percent citywide (U.S. Census 1980).

19. Ironically, the efforts of Max's brother to appropriate what is generally perceived as the exlusive domain of White America were perceived by Max and many others as an inappropriate arena for him. Because the community defined his business ventures as inappropriate, he was not successful in his efforts to become an entrepreneur. In discussing African-Americans' lack of entrepreneurial success, this response to capitalism is vastly understudied and misunderstood.

20. There are numerous plausible scenarios for why African-Americans respond as they do to the development of individual or small businesses. Many of these reasons are embedded in historical, structural, and cultural factors. It is no secret that the world of business has been extremely hostile to the entry efforts of African-Americans. If, for example, an African-American sought to establish a business outside the confines of the Black community, he or she was

not able to obtain the necessary papers and capital to do so. They were also unable to acquire the clientele necessary to support a business. The same response is not a part of the history of White Americans. African-Americans have been repeatedly and systematically denied access to capital and customers primarily because they are Black. As descendants of an enslaved people, they have been consistently discriminated against in their efforts to obtain money and capital. Also, when they sought protection for their invested capital, they were declared ineligible and therefore not entitled to the government funds that made it possible for other groups to succeed in what is the American free enterprise system.

21. There *are* African-American astronomers. The fact that Max does not know of their existence is an indictment of both the curriculum and the counseling program at the school.

22. Art is sometimes late for his first period class, but most often he just misses the fifteen-minute homeroom period. This means that he comes in late and advises Ms. Raye, his homeroom teacher, that he is present and then goes on to his first period class. Ms. Raye was his homeroom teacher his first year at Capital and she now knows his pattern, so she expects him to be present every day and she waits to turn in her attendance roster in anticipation that he is going to come in and tell her that he is present. Thus, Art loves Ms. Raye because her actions suggest that she accepts him for who he is, not for who he should be or become.

23. Ogbu (1978) emphasizes in his analysis that Black and White class attributes are not contiguous. Indeed, he notes that "a large portion of the middle class in the white caste ranks above the entire upper class in the black caste, while a good portion of the middle class in the black caste, ranks at the same level as the lower class in the white caste" Ogbu (1978:102). Hence, he argues, middle class in the Black community does not necessarily mean the same thing in the White community.

I decided to emphasize income rather than class factors because class has such drastically different meanings in the Black and White communities. I have selected this option despite Ortner's claim that "class is central to American social life" (1991:164; see also Gardner 1993; Gardner, Dean, and McKaig 1989; Langstron 1993; Tokarczyk and Fay 1993). My fear is that to designate some of the students in the sample as middle class would breach their understanding and interpretation of that concept. Hence, I center on family income. The primary criterion I have used in ascribing middle-class status to these students is that their parents make more money than the average adult in the Capital community. (This differs drastically from the conclusion of Ostrander [1984] that class status hinges on how long one's family has been wealthy.) I also do not mean to imply that these students' belief system and/or worldview differs from that of the other members of the Capital community. In most instances, these components of their lives are indistinguishable from the Capital community residents who have access to far less earned income.

24. Kaela was not alone in this observation. Most of the students described how their peers and some Black adults resisted acting white, violating widely accepted standards regarding what is and is not the right way to live. They repeatedly delineated how African-Americans' lack of frugality or perseverance,

and their general unwillingness to hoard is implicated in their ongoing impover-ished existence in America. Most of them lamented this fact and mourned the existence of such practices within the Black community. Rita, for example, talks about it extensively, including how her family tends to cling to a way of life traditionally identified with African-American peoples.

25. I am totally unfamiliar with this story. To date, I have been unsuccessful in verifying Shelvy's claim.

EIGHT

1. Lack of adequate reward for scholarly achievements is gender-differentiated, with female students' academic accomplishments severely mini-mized and underrepresented in the school and immediate community (see exam-ples cited in chapter 7). Ironically, as the male and female students leave Capital and the immediate community in order to seek *entry-level* jobs and careers, the larger society inverts this practice, generally embracing the females and dis-playing greater hostility toward the males. Fortunately, the female students' mar-ginal acceptance in school empowers them in some ways that make it possible for them to adjust to the new context in which they are forced to function: accomplishments are minimized and their racialized female bodies are marginally accepted. The same is not true for the males. To the extent that gender was a factor in their gender-favored status *within* the Black community, their loss of this status disempowers them. As racially distinct males seeking to compete with White ones, African-American males become victims of their gender in ways comparable to the victimization experienced by African-American females and other females who enter this White male-dominated context. Hence, gender bias is a serious, although unnamed, issue for African-American males.

The fact that in competing for entry-level jobs, African-American females benefit from this inversion of gender preference does not mean that they are protected from job discrimination. They are not. As an African-American female who has been repeatedly harmed by the negative effects of both race and gender bias, I want to disavow any association with such a position. In the workforce, it is widely documented that African-American females evoke dual discrimination practices (see Allen 1988; C. Epstein 1973; Hendrickson 1991; Leggon 1980; Lewis 1977). At the same time, however, I want to describe the effects of the intersection of a complex of social forces in which maleness is honored and celebrated in the Black community, but when fused to a Black body in the White community, this gender bias is nullified, exposing the African-American male—for the first time—to systemic intra-gender sexism. While African-American males are more highly valued in the Black community than their female counterparts, they are repeatedly and continually marginalized and even rejected as they attempt to gain entry-level jobs in the White-male-dominated larger society. Hence, it seems clear to me that as a result of having been the recipients of gender preference all of their lives *within* the Black community, African-American males are ill-prepared for the sudden and irrevocable lack of preference they encounter in the dominant work community. More research is needed.

2. For many of the high-achieving students, the social changes evoked by the Civil Rights Movement and its attendant legislation are prima facie evidence of

social change. They assume that the world they have inherited is simultaneously drastically different and unchanged from that of their parents. It is the duality of the diasporic American experience embodied in the bleeding of the Civil Rights Movement that compels the high-achieving African-American students to seek change through resistance to dominant claims of Black lack.

3. Regrettably, adult encouragement often includes the destructive idea that high-achieving students are not like other Black students. A similar message is often conveyed by the dominant community in explaining why a few African-Americans are successful in the larger society (see, for example, Carter 1993; Cose 1993). This message is widely rejected by the students at Capital High, or, if not, it has negative consequences in further marginalizing the affected students.

4. I am cognizant of the politically charged nature of the term *pushout* rather than the more benign *dropout* (see Fine 1983, 1991). *Dropout* suggests a voluntary act on the part of the student. *Pushout,* on the other hand, implies involuntary removal on the part of the institution.

5. Elsewhere (Fordham 1993) I have described African-American females as being victimized by having to become the "doubly-refracted" Other in the academy. Apparently, African-American females do not experience the same level of estrangement from the normalized American female role as their male counterparts experience vis-à-vis the normalized male role. In addition, as these data show, African-American females' learned passivity lends itself to greater conformity to the school curriculum. This greater passivity appears to be implicated in African-American females' higher academic performance at Capital High.

6. While the students officially participating in the advanced placement program were provided free transportation to and from school by the District of Columbia Public School System, all other students attending Capital were expected to make it on their own. How these other students got to school was their problem. Also, while free transportation was available to the students officially participating in the program, those who lived outside the designated bus zone were compelled to provide their own transportation. Not surprisingly, the conditions for riding the bus were regularly ignored. Indeed, violating them appeared to be one of the most highly valued ways of breaching parental and school officials' petit bourgeois class expectations and producing, at the same time, an evolving communitas or sense of group solidarity. Consequently, none of the students riding the bus—and they varied daily—ever reported another student for being a scofflaw.

7. This general pattern is not unique to African-Americans. Rather, it replicates the gender-differentiated pattern of the dominant society. In general, women—regardless of racial or ethnic background—are enculturated to be passive. Harris (1974), for example, asserts that in male-dominated societies, passive women assure their indemnification as barter. Some anthropologists have made other claims, including Friedl (1992:125), who postulates that in such contexts, status goes to those group members "who control the distribution of valued goods and services *outside* [emphasis added] the family."

8. This conclusion is based on both the ethnographic data and a partial analysis of the quantitative data that were collected during the second year of the study.

9. Mr. McGriff was able to implement a program of denial because he had the almost unanimous support of the students' parents. They too often defined such activities as frivolities, unimportant and unnecessary to the development of an authentic academic curriculum and a socially integrated person. Their support of the principal's principled stand on this aspect of school life meant that the students were forever consigned to a school reality that deprived them of even the remote opportunity to pursue the idea of Self-production (Trask 1991).

10. "Most Capital students" are not "all" of them. While many of the high-achieving students unwittingly come to see what is Black and of African origin as essentially lacking in what is critical to success, many of them—including some of the previous subset—also interpret their actions to mean that they are resisting the prevalent perceptions regarding African-American adolescents' intellectual capabilities. Indeed, some of them are so conflicted by their unilateral assignment to this unacceptable status that they eventually internalize or consume the Other, to the extent that is possible.

11. Students' point of reference was the labor of their parents, siblings, and other adults. They argued that these persons' labor is often appropriated in that they are underpaid for what they do on their jobs and are systematically denied promotions and other rewards routinely awarded their White counterparts. Hence, Capital students resent the dominant society's appropriation of the work ethic from the African-American cultural repertoire. Many of the students referenced slavery, implying that to enslave a human population is to bestow on them the idea of work—that is, appropriation of labor—as a quintessential symbol. At the same time, their contested responses indicated an inchoate understanding of how the White community's appropriation of this and other work-correlated symbols has detonated African-Americans' humanness.

AFTERWORD

1. What I have suggested here conflicts in many ways with Tannen's (1994a, 1994b) general claims regarding linguistic practices among dominant and subordinate individuals. I am aware of this conflict and would like to remind the reader that my analysis is limited primarily to the language usage of Black parents in rearing their children. In that context, it is the powerful (parents) versus the less powerful (their children).

Abrahams, Roger D., and Geneva Gay. 1972. Talking Black in the Classroom. In *Language and Culture Diversity in American Education*, ed. Roger D. Abrahams and Rudolph C. Troike. Englewood Cliffs, NJ: Prentice-Hall.

Abu-Lughod, Lila. 1991. Writing against Culture. In *Recapturing Anthropology: Working in the Present*, ed. Richard G. Fox. Santa Fe, NM: School of American Research Press.

Adams, Jacqueline. 1994. Hers: The White Wife. *New York Times Magazine*, September 18.

Adams, William Y. 1981. Dispersed Minorities of the Middle East: A Comparison and a Lesson. In *Persistent Peoples: Cultural Enclaves in Perspective*, ed. George P. Castile and Gilbert Kushner. Tucson: University of Arizona Press.

Agar, Michael H. 1980. *The Professional Stranger: An Informal Introduction to Ethnography*. New York: Academic Press.

———. 1986. *Speaking of Ethnography*. Qualitative Research Methods, Series 2. Beverly Hills, CA: Sage.

Allen, Walter R. 1988. Family Roles, Occupational Statuses, and Achievement Orientations among Black Women in the United States. In *Black Women in America: Social Science Perspectives*, ed. Micheline R. Malson, Elizabeth Mudimbe-Boyi, Jean F. O'Barr, and Mary Wyer. Chicago: University of Chicago Press.

Anderson, Benedict. 1991. *Imagined Communities: Reflections on the Origins and Spread of Nationalism*. Rev. ed. London: Verso.

Anderson, Elijah. 1990. Streetwise: Race, Class, and Change in an Urban Community. Chicago: University of Chicago Press.

Anderson, James D. 1973. Education for Servitude: The Social Purposes of Schooling in the Black South, 1870–1930. Ph.D. diss. University of Illinois.

———. 1975. Education as a Vehicle for the Manipulation of Black Workers. In *Work, Technology, and Education: Dissenting Essays in the Intellectual Foundations of American Education*, ed. Walter Feinberg and H. Rosemont Jr. Chicago: University of Illinois Press.

Andrews, Adrianne R. 1993. Balancing the Personal and Professional. In *Spirit*,

Space and Survival: African American Women in (White) Academe, ed. Joy James and Ruth Farmer. New York: Routledge.

Anson, Robert Sam. 1987. *Best Intentions: The Education and Killing of Edmund Perry.* New York: Random House.

Appadurai, Arjun. 1990. Disjuncture and Difference in the Global Cultural Economy. *Public Culture* 2(2):1–24.

———. 1991. Global Ethnoscapes: Notes and Queries for a Transnational Anthropology. In *Recapturing Anthropology: Working in the Present,* ed. Richard G. Fox. Santa Fe, NM: School of American Research Press.

———. 1992. Putting Hierarchy in Its Place. In *Rereading Cultural Anthropology,* ed. George E. Marcus. Durham: Duke University Press.

Aptheker, Herbert. 1963. *American Negro Slave Revolts.* New York: International Publishers.

Asad, Talal, ed. 1973. *Anthropology and the Colonial Encounter.* London: Ithaca Press.

Associates for Renewal in Education. 1983. *City of Magnificent Intentions: History of District of Columbia.* Washington, DC: Intac.

Bailey, F. G. 1971. *Gifts and Poison: True Politics of Reputation.* Oxford: Blackwell.

———. 1977. *Morality and Expediency: The Folklore of Academic Politics.* Chicago: Aldine.

Bakhtin, Mikhail M. 1981. *The Dialogical Imagination: Four Essays,* ed. Michael Holquist. Austin: University of Texas Press.

Baratz, Stephen S., and Joan C. Baratz. 1970. Early Childhood Intervention: The Social Science Base of Institutional Racism. *Harvard Educational Review* (1): 29–50.

Barth, Frederick. 1974. *Ethnic Groups and Boundaries: The Social Organization of Culture Difference.* Boston: Little, Brown.

Beals, Melba Pattillo. 1994. *Warriors Don't Cry: A Searing Memoir of the Battle to Integrate Little Rock's Central High School.* New York: Pocket Books.

Behar, Ruth. 1992. *Translated Woman: Crossing the Border with Esperanza's Story.* New York: Beacon Press.

Belenky, Mary Field, Blyth Clinchy, Nancy Goldberger, and Jill Tarule. 1986. *Women's Ways of Knowing: The Development of Self, Voice, and Mind.* New York: Basic Books.

Bell, Derrick. 1992. *Faces at the Bottom of the Well: The Permanence of Racism.* New York: Basic Books.

Benedict, Ruth. 1934. *Patterns of Culture.* Boston: Houghton.

Benjamin, Lois. 1991. *The Black Elite: Facing the Color Line in the Twilight of the Twentieth Century.* Chicago: Nelson-Hall Publisher.

Berry, Mary F., and John W. Blassingame. 1982. *Long Memory: The Black Experience in America*. New York: Oxford University Press.

———. 1992. American Archipelago: Blacks and Criminal Justice. In *Race, Class, and Gender: An Anthology*. ed. Margaret L. Andersen and Patricia Hill Collins. Belmont, CA: Wadsworth.

Best, Raphaela. 1983. *We've All Got Scars: What Boys and Girls Learn in Elementary School*. Bloomington: Indiana University Press.

Bhabha, Homi K. 1990a. DissemiNation: Time, Narrative, and the Margins of the Modern Nation. In *Nation and Narration*, ed. Homi K. Bhabha. London: Routledge.

———. 1990b. Introduction to *Nation and Narration*, ed. Homi K. Bhabha. London: Routledge.

Blascoer, Frances. 1970 (1915). *Colored School Children in New York*. New York: Negro Universities Press.

Blassingame, John W. 1979. *The Slave Community: Plantation Life in the Antebellum South*. 2d ed. New York: Oxford University Press.

Bohannan, Paul. 1992. *We, the Alien: An Introduction to Cultural Anthropology*. Prospect Heights, IL: Waveland Press.

Bond, Horace Mann. 1966. *The Education of the Negro in the American Social Order*. New York: Octagon Books.

Bourdieu, Pierre, and J. C. Passeron. 1977. *Reproduction in Education, Society and Culture*. Translated by Richard Nice. London: Sage.

Bowles, Samuel, and Herbert Gintis. 1976. *Schooling in Capitalist America: Educational Reform and the Contradictions of Economic Life*. New York: Basic Books.

Brain, James J. 1972. Kinship Terms. *Man* 7(1):137–138.

Breines, Wini. 1992. *Young, White, and Miserable: Growing Up Female in the Fifties*. Boston: Beacon Press.

Bretell, Caroline B. 1993. *When They Read What We Write: The Politics of Ethnography*. Westport, CT: Bergin and Garvey.

Brown, Elaine. 1992. *A Taste of Power: A Black Woman's Story*. New York: Pantheon.

Brown, Elsa Barkley. 1988. African-American Women's Quilting: A Framework for Conceptualizing and Teaching African-American Women's History. In *Black Women in America: Social Science Perspectives*, ed. Michelene R. Malson, Elizabeth Mudimbe-Boyi, Jean F. O'Barr, and Mary Wyer. Chicago: University of Chicago Press.

Brown, Letitia W. 1972. *Free Negroes in the District of Columbia, 1790–1846*. New York: Oxford University Press.

Bullivant, Brian M. 1987. *The Ethnic Encounter in the Secondary School: Ethnocultural Reproduction and Resistance: Theory and Case Studies*. London: Falmer Press.

Bullock, Henry Allen. 1967. *A History of Negro Education in the South: From 1619 to the Present.* New York: Praeger.

———. 1982. Negro Education as a Way of Life. In *The School in the Social Order: A Sociological Introduction to Educational Understanding,* ed. F. Cordasco, M. Hillson, and H.A. Bullock. Washington, DC: University Press of America.

Carby, Hazel. 1987. *Reconstructing Womanhood: The Emergence of the Afro-American Woman Novelist.* New York: Oxford University Press.

Carrier, James G. 1992. Occidentalism: The World Turned Upside-down. *American Ethnologist* 19(2):195–209.

Carter, Stephen L. 1993. The Black Table, the Empty Seat, and the Tie. In *Lure and Loathing: Essays on Race, Identity, and the Ambivalence of Assimilation,* ed. Gerald Early. New York: Allen Lane, Penguin Press.

Cary, Lorene. 1991. *Black Ice.* New York: Alfred A. Knopf.

Cary, Willie Mae. 1976. *Worse Than Silence: The Black Child's Dilemma.* New York: Vantage Press.

Castenell, Louis A., and William F. Pinar. 1993. Introduction to *Understanding Curriculum as Racial Text: Representations of Identity and Difference in Education,* ed. Louis A. Castenell and William F. Pinar. Albany: State University of New York Press.

Castile, George P. 1981. Issues in the Analysis of Enduring Cultural Systems. In *Persistent Peoples: Cultural Enclaves in Perspective,* ed. George P. Castile and Gilbert Kushner. Tucson: University of Arizona Press.

Castile, George P., and Gilbert Kushner (eds.). 1981. *Persistent Peoples: Cultural Enclaves in Perspective,* ed. George P. Castile and Gilbert Kushner. Tucson: University of Arizona Press.

Center for the Study of Social Policy. 1983. *A Dream Deferred: The Economic Status of Black Americans.* A Working Paper. Washington, DC: The Center for the Study of Social Policy.

———. 1984. *The "Flip-Side" of Black Families Headed by Women: The Economic Status of Black Men.* Washington, DC: The Center for the Study of Social Policy.

Chagnon, Napoleon A. 1968. *Yanomamo: The Fierce People.* New York: Holt, Rinehart and Winston.

Chinweizu. 1987 (1975). *The West and the Rest of Us: White Predators, Black Slavers, and the African Elite.* New York: Random House.

Chow, Rey. 1993. *Writing Diaspora: Tactics of Intervention in Contemporary Cultural Studies.* Bloomington: Indiana University Press.

Christian, Barbara. 1990. What Celie Knows That You Should Know. In *Anatomy of Racism,* ed. David T. Goldberg. Minneapolis: University of Minnesota Press.

Clark, Reginald. 1983. *Family Life and School Achievement: Why Poor Black Children Succeed or Fail.* Chicago: University of Chicago Press.

Clark-Lewis, Elizabeth. 1994. *Living In, Living Out: African American Domestics in Washington, D.C., 1910–1940.* Washington: Smithsonian Institution Press.

Clifford, James. 1983. On Ethnographic Authority. *Representations* 1:118–146.

———. 1986. Partial Truths. In *Writing Culture: The Poetics and Politics of Ethnography,* ed. James Clifford and George E. Marcus. Berkeley: University of California Press.

———. 1988. *The Predicament of Culture.* Cambridge: Harvard University Press.

———. 1994. Diasporas. *Cultural Anthropology* 9(3):302–338.

Clifford, James, and George E. Marcus. 1986. *Writing Culture: The Poetics and Politics of Ethnography.* Berkeley: University of California Press.

Cohen, Yehudi A. 1970. Schools and Civilizational States. In *The Social Sciences and the Comparative Study of Educational Systems,* ed. Joseph Fischer. Scranton, PA: International Textbook Company.

———. 1971. The Shaping of Men's Minds: Adaptation to the Imperatives of Culture. In *Anthropological Perspectives on Education,* ed. Murray L. Wax, S. Diamond, and F. Gearing. New York: Basic Books.

Cole, Robert. 1967. *Children of Crisis: A Study of Courage and Fear.* Boston: Little, Brown.

Coleman, James S., Ernest Q. Campbell, Carol J. Hobson, James McPartland, Alexander M. Mood, Frederic D. Weinfeld, and Robert L. York. 1966. *Equality of Educational Opportunity.* Washington, DC: United States Department of Health, Education, and Welfare.

Collins, Patricia Hill. 1986. Learning from the Outsider Within: The Sociological Significance of Black Feminist Thought. *Social Problems* 33(6):514–531.

———. 1991. *Black Feminist Thought: Knowledge, Consciousness, and the Politics of Empowerment.* New York: Routledge.

Condit, Celeste. 1993. *Crafting Equality: America's Anglo-African World.* Chicago: University of Chicago Press.

Cose, Ellis. 1993. *The Rage of the Privileged Class.* New York: HarperCollins.

Coughlin, Ellen K. 1988. *Chronicle of Higher Education* 30, November 30.

Cox, Oliver C. 1948. *Caste, Class, and Race: A Study in Social Dynamics.* New York: Monthly Review Press.

Crosby, Edward W. 1970. The Nigger and the Narcissus (or Self-Awareness in Black Education). In *Black America,* ed. John F. Szwed. New York: Basic Books.

Cusick, Philip. 1973. *Inside High School: The Student's World.* New York: Holt, Rinehart and Winston.

Davis, Angela. 1971. Reflections on the Black Woman's Role in the Community of Slaves. *Black Scholar,* December: 3–15.

de Certeau, Michel. 1980. Writing vs. Time: History and Time in the Works of Lafitau. *Yale French Studies* 59:37–64.

deLone, Richard H. 1979. *Small Futures: Children, Inequality, and the Limits of Liberal Reform.* New York: Harcourt Brace Jovanovich.

Delpit, Lisa. 1988. The Silenced Dialogue: Power and Pedagogy in Educating Other People's Children. *Harvard Educational Review* 54(3):280–298.

Derrida, Jacques. 1974. *Of Grammatology.* Baltimore: Johns Hopkins University Press.

DeVita, Philip. 1992. Introduction. *The Naked Anthropologist: Tales from around the World,* ed. Philip R. DeVita. Belmont, CA: Wadsworth.

DeVos, George. 1967. Essential Elements of Caste: Psychological Determinants in Structural Theory. In *Japan's Invisible Race: Caste in Culture and Personality,* ed. George A. DeVos and H. Wagatsuma. Berkeley, CA: University of California Press.

Diamond, Stanley. 1971. Epilogue. In *Anthropological Perspectives on Education,* ed. Murray L. Wax, S. Diamond, and F. Gearing. New York: Basic Books.

Dizard, Jan. 1970. Black Identity, Social Class, and Black Power. *Psychiatry* 33:195–202.

Dollard, John. 1957. *Caste and Class in a Southern Town.* 3d ed. Garden City, NY: Doubleday.

Drake, St. Clair, and Horace R. Cayton. 1970. *Black Metropolis: A Study of Negro Life in a Northern City.* 2 vols. New York: Harcourt.

Dreger, Ralph Mason. 1973. Intellectual Functioning: In *Comparative Studies of Blacks and Whites in the United States,* ed. Kent S. Miller and Ralph Mason Dreger. New York: Seminar Press.

DuBois, William E. B. 1970 (1903). *The Souls of Black Folks: Essays and Sketches.* New York: Simon and Schuster.

Dumont, Louis. 1970. *Homo Hierarchicus: The Caste System and Its Implications.* Chicago: University of Chicago Press.

———. 1986 (1983). *Essays on Individualism.* Chicago: University of Chicago Press.

Dyson, Michael Eric. 1993. *Reflecting Black: African-American Cultural Criticism.* Minnesota: University of Minnesota Press.

Edwards, Ozzie L. 1976. Components of Academic Success: A Profile of Achieving Black Adolescents. *Journal of Negro Education* 45(4):408–422.

Embers, Carol R., and Melvin Embers. 1990. *Anthropology.* 6th ed. Englewood Cliffs, NJ: Prentice Hall.

Epstein, Arnold L. 1978. *Ethos and Identity: Three Studies in Ethnicity.* London: Tavistock.

Epstein, Cynthia Fuchs. 1973. Positive Effects of the Multiple Negative: Explaining the Success of Black Professional Women. *American Journal of Sociology* 78(3):912–935.

Erickson, Eric. 1968. *Identity, Youth, and Crisis.* New York: W.W. Norton.

Evans, Grace. 1988. Those Loud Black Girls. In *Learning to Lose: Sexism and Education.* London: The Women's Press.

Everhart, Robert B. 1983. *Reading, Writing, and Resistance.* Boston: Routledge and Kegan Paul.

Fanon, Frantz. 1967. *Black Skin, White Masks.* New York: Grove Press.

Ferguson, Russell, et al. 1990. *Out There: Marginalization and Contemporary Cultures.* Cambridge: MIT Press.

Fine, Michelle. 1983. Dropping Out of High School: The Ideology of School and Work. *Journal of Education* 165(3):257–272.

———. 1991. *Framing Dropouts: Notes on the Politics of an Urban High School.* Albany: State University of New York.

Fishkin, Shelley Fisher. 1993. *Was Huck Black? Mark Twain and African-American Voices.* New York: Oxford University Press.

Flanagan, James G. 1989. Hierarchy in Simple "Egalitarian" Societies. *Annual Review of Anthropology* 18:245–266.

Folb, Edith A. 1980. *Runnin' Down Some Lines: The Language and Culture of Black Teenagers.* Cambridge: Harvard University Press.

Foley, Douglas E. 1990. *Learning Capitalist Culture: Deep in the Heart of Tejas.* Philadelphia: University of Pennsylvania Press.

Fordham, Signithia. 1982. Cultural Inversion and Black Children's School Performance. Paper presented at the 81st Annual Meeting of the American Anthropological Association, Washington, DC. December 5.

———. 1985. Black Students' School Success: Coping with the Burden of "Acting White." Paper presented at the 84th Annual Meeting of the American Anthropological Association, Washington, DC. December 5.

———. 1987. Black Students' School Success as Related to Fictive Kinship: An Ethnographic Study in the District of Columbia School System, 2 vols. Ph.D. diss. The American University.

———. 1988. Racelessness as a Factor in Black Students' School Success: Pragmatic Strategy or Pyrrhic Victory? *Harvard Educational Review* 58(1):54–84.

———. 1989. "The Whiteness of Maleness": Spawning Racial and Cultural Identity in a Predominantly Black High School. Paper presented in the Visiting Minority Scholar Lecture Series. The School of Education and the Wisconsin Center for Education Research, University of Wisconsin, Madison. February 8.

———. 1990. Spawning the "Doubly-Refracted Other": African-American Females' Academic Achievement at Capital High. Paper presented at the 3d

Biennial Meeting of the Society for Research on Adolescence, Washington, DC.

———. 1991a. Peer-Proofing Academic Competition among Black Adolescents: "Acting White" Black American Style. In *Empowerment through Multicultural Education,* ed. Christine E. Sleeter. New York: State University of New York Press.

———. 1991b. Racelessness in Private Schools: Should We Deconstruct the Racial and Cultural Identity of African-American Adolescents? *Teachers College Record* 92(3):470–484.

———. 1991c. Suffering, Silence, and "Female Infanticide": The Untold Story of African-American Women's Academic Success. Paper presented at American Education Research Association Annual Meeting. Chicago, IL. April 4.

———. 1993. "Those Loud Black Girls": (Black) Women, Silence, and Gender "Passing" in the Academy. *Anthropology and Education Quarterly* 24(1):3–32.

Fordham, Signithia, and John U. Ogbu. 1986. Black Students' School Success: Coping with the "Burden of 'Acting White.'" *Urban Review* 18(3):176–206.

Fortes, Meyer. 1969. *Kinship and the Social Order: The Legacy of Lewis Henry Morgan.* Chicago: Aldine.

Foster, Herbert. 1974. *Ribbin,' Jivin,' and Playin' the Dozens: The Unrecognized Dilemma of Inner City Schools.* Cambridge, MA: Ballinger.

Foster, Michele. 1989. "It's Cookin' Now": A Performance Analysis of the Speech Events of a Black Teacher in an Urban Community College. *Language and Society* 18:1–29.

———. 1990. The Politics of Race: Through the Eyes of African-American Teachers. *Journal of Education* 172(3):123–141.

Foucault, Michel. 1977. Intellectuals and Power. In *Language, Counter-Memory, Practice,* ed. and trans. Donald F. Bouchard. Ithaca: Cornell University Press.

Fox, Richard G. 1991. Introduction to *Recapturing Anthropology: Working in the Present,* ed. Richard G. Fox. Santa Fe, NM: School of American Research Press.

Fox-Genovese, Elizabeth. 1986a. Strategies and Forms of Resistance: Focus on Slave Women in the United States. In *Resistance: Studies in African, Caribbean, and Afro-American History,* ed. Gary Y. Okihiro. Amherst: University of Massachusetts Press.

———. 1986b. The Claims of Common Culture: Gender, Race, Class, and the Canon. *Salmagundi* 72:131–43.

Frankenberg, Ruth. 1993. *White Women, Race Matters: The Social Construction of Whiteness.* Minneapolis: University of Minnesota Press.

Frazier, E. Franklin. 1939. *The Negro Family in the United States.* Chicago: University of Chicago Press.

Freed, Stanley. 1973. Fictive Kinship in a North Indian Village. *Ethnology* 2(1):86–103.

Freilich, Morris. 1970. *Marginal Natives*. New York: John Wiley and Sons.

———. 1978. The Meaning of Sociocultural. In *The Concepts and Dynamics of Culture*, ed. B. Bernado. The Hague: Mouton.

Friedl, Ernestine. 1975. *Women and Men: An Anthropologist's View*. New York: Holt, Rinehart and Winston.

———. 1992. Society and Sex Roles. In *Anthropology: Annual Editions 92/93*. 15th ed. Edited by Elvio Angeloni. Guilford, CT: Dushkin Publishing Group.

Friedman, Jonathan. 1992a. Myth, History, and Political Identity. *Cultural Anthropology* 7(2):194–210.

———. 1992b. The Past in the Future: History and the Politics of Identity. *American Anthropologist* 94(4):837–859.

Fuss, Diane. 1989. *Essentially Speaking: Feminism, Nature, and Difference*. New York: Routledge.

Gadsden, Vivian L. 1994. Understanding Family Literacy: Conceptual Issues Facing the Field. *Teachers College Record* 96(1):58–86.

Gardner, Saundra. 1993. "What's a Nice Working-Class Girl Like You Doing in a Place Like This?" In *Working-Class Women in the Academy: Laborers in the Knowledge Factory*, ed. Michelle M. Tokarczyk and Elizabeth A. Fay. Amherst: University of Massachusetts Press.

Gardner, Saundra, Cynthia Dean, and Deo McKaig. 1993. Responding to Differences in the Classroom: The Politics of Knowledge, Class, and Sexuality. *Sociology of Education* 62(1):64–74.

Gates, Henry Louis, Jr. 1994. *Colored People: A Memoir*. New York: Alfred A. Knopf.

Gay, Geneva, and Roger Abrahams. 1972. Black Culture in the Classroom. In *Language and Culture Diversity in Amerian Education*, ed. Roger D. Abrahams and Rudolph C. Troike. Englewood Cliffs, NJ: Prentice-Hall.

Geertz, Clifford. 1973. *Interpretation of Culture: Selected Essays*. New York: Basic Books.

———. 1988. *Works and Lives: The Anthropologist as Author*. Stanford: Stanford University Press.

Geertz, Hildred. 1959. The Vocabulary of Emotion: A Study of Javanese Socialization Processes. *Psychiatry* 22(3):225–237.

Genovese, Eugene. 1972. *Roll, Jordan, Roll: The World the Slaves Made*. New York: Random House.

Gibbs, Jewelle Taylor (ed.). 1988. *Young, Black, and Male in America: An Endangered Species*. Dover, MA: Auburn House.

Gibson, Margaret A. 1982. Reputation and Respectability: How Competing Cultural Systems Affect Students' Performance in School. *Anthropology and Education Quarterly* 13:3–27.

Giroux, Henry. 1983. *Theory and Resistance in Education: A Pedagogy for the Opposition.* Westport, CT: Bergin and Garvey.

Glasgow, Douglas E. 1980. *The Black Underclass: Poverty, Unemployment, and Entrapment of Ghetto Youth.* San Francisco: Jossey-Bass.

Goffman, Erving. 1963. *Stigma: Notes on the Management of Spoiled Identity.* Englewood Cliffs, NJ: Prentice-Hall.

————. 1967. *Interaction Ritual: Essays in Face-to-Face Behavior.* Chicago: Aldine.

Goldfield, David R. 1990. *Black, White, and Southern: Race Relations and Southern Culture, 1940 to the Present.* Baton Rouge: Louisiana State University Press.

Gossett, Thomas F. 1963. *Race: The History of an Idea in America.* Dallas: Southern Methodist University Press.

Gramsci, Antonio. 1971. *On Intellectuals: Selections from the Prison Notebooks,* ed. Quintin Hoare and Geoffery N. Smith. New York: International.

Granfield, Robert. 1991. Making It by Faking It: Working-Class Students in an Elite Academic Environment. *Journal of Contemporary Ethnography* 20(3):331–351.

Green, Constance. 1967. *The Secret City: A History of Race Relations in the Nation's Capital.* Princeton: Princeton University Press.

Green, Vera M. 1981. Blacks in the United States: The Creation of an Enduring People? In *Persistent Peoples: Cultural Enclaves in Perspective,* ed. George P. Castile and Gilbert Kushner. Tucson: University of Arizona Press.

Grier, George, and Eunice Grier. 1985. *The Washington Labor Force: An Asset in a Changing Economy.* Washington, DC: Greater Washington Research Center.

Grier, William H., and P. M. Cobbs. 1968. *Black Rage.* New York: Basic Books.

Griffin, Susan. 1981. *Pornography and Silence: Culture's Revenge against Nature.* New York: Harper and Row.

Gutman, Herbert. 1976. *The Black Family in Slavery and Freedom, 1750–1925.* New York: Pantheon Books.

Gwaltney, John Langston. 1980. Drylongso: A Self-Portrait of Black America. New York: Random House.

Hale, Janice. 1977. De-mythicizing the Education of Black Children. *First World* 1:30–35.

————. 1982. *Black Children: Their Roots, Culture and Learning Styles.* Provo, Utah: Brigham Young University Press.

Haley, Alex. 1976. *Roots: The Saga of an American Family.* Garden City, NY: Doubleday.

Hamilton, Charles V. 1991. *Adam Clayton Powell Jr.: The Political Biography of an American Dilemma:* New York: Atheneum.

Hansen, Carl F. 1964. *The Four-Track Curriculum in Today's High Schools*. Englewood Cliffs, NJ: Prentice-Hall.

———. 1968. *Danger in Washington: The Study of My Twenty Years in the Public Schools in the Nation's Capital*. West Nyack, NY: Parker Publishing Company.

Haraway, Donna J. 1989. *Primate Visions: Gender, Race, and Nature in the World of Modern Science*. New York: Routledge.

Harris, Marvin. 1974. *Cows, Pigs, Wars, and Witches: The Riddles of Culture*. New York: Vintage Books.

———. 1989. *Our Kind: Who We Are; Where We Came from; Where We Are Going*. New York: Harper and Row.

Haskins, Kenneth. 1975. You Have No Right to Put a Kid Out of School. In Arthur Tobier, Four Conversations: The Intersection of Private and Public. *The Urban Review* 8(4):273–287.

Haviland, William A. 1989. *Anthropology*. 5th ed. New York: Holt, Rinehart and Winston.

Haynes, Douglas, and Gyan Prakash (eds.). 1991. *Contesting Power: Resistance and Everyday Social Relations in South Asia*. Berkeley: University of California Press.

Heath, Shirley Brice. 1983. *Ways with Words: Language, Life, and Work in Communities and Classrooms*. London: Cambridge University Press.

Heller, Celia S. 1969. *Structured Social Inequality: A Reader in Comparative Social Stratification*. New York: Macmillan.

Henry, Jules. 1963 (1957). *Culture Against Man*. New York: Random House.

———. 1971. Is Education Possible? In *Anthropological Perspectives on Education*, ed. Murray L. Wax, Stanley Diamond, and Fred O. Gearing. New York: Basic Books.

Herrnstein, Richard J., and Charles Murray. 1994. *The Bell Curve: Intelligence and Class Structure in American Life*. New York: Free Press.

Herskovits, Melville J. 1958. *The Myth of the Negro Past*. Boston: Beacon Press.

Hine, Darlene. 1993. "In the Kingdom of Culture": Black Women and the Intersection of Race, Gender, and Class. In *Lure and Loathing: Essays on Race, Identity, and the Ambivalence of Assimilation*, ed. Gerald Early. New York: Allen Lane, Penguin Press.

Hine, Darlene Clark, and Kate Wittenstein. 1981. Female Slave Resistance: The Economics of Sex. In *The Black Woman Cross-Culturally*, ed. Filoma Chioma Steady. New York: Schenkman Publishing Company.

Holland, Dorothy C., and Margaret A. Eisenhart. 1990. *Educated in Romance: Women, Achievement, and College Culture*. Chicago: University of Chicago Press.

Holt, Grace Sims. 1972. "Inversion" in Black Communication. In *Rappin' and Stylin' Out*, ed. Thomas Kochman. Urbana: University of Illinois Press.

Holtzclaw, William Henry. 1970. *The Black Man's Burden.* New York: Negro Universities Press.

hooks, bell. 1981. *Ain't I a Woman: Black Women and Feminism.* Boston: South End Press.

———. 1989. *Talking Back: Thinking Feminist; Thinking Black.* Boston: South End Press.

———. 1992. *Black Looks: Race and Representation.* Boston: South End Press.

———. 1994. *Teaching to Transgress: Education for the Practice of Freedom.* New York: Routledge.

Hughes, Everett. 1945. Dilemmas and Contradictions of Status. *American Journal of Sociology* 50:353–359.

Hunter-Gault, Charlayne. 1992. *In My Place.* New York: Vintage Books.

Hutchinson, Louise. 1977. *The Anacostia Story, 1608–1930.* Washington, DC: Smithsonian Institution Press.

Inkeles, Alex. 1968. Social Structure and the Socialization of Competence. *Harvard Educational Review,* Reprint Series, no. 1:50–68.

Jackson, Jacquelyne J., and Larry C. Harris. 1977. "You May Be Normal When You Come Here, But You Won't Be Normal When You Leave," or Herman the Pushout. *The Black Scholar,* April: 2–11.

Jameson, Fredric. 1990. *Signatures of the Visible.* New York: Routledge.

Jencks, Christopher. 1972. *Inequality: A Reassessment of the Effects of Family and Schooling in America.* New York: Basic Books.

Jensen, Arthur R. 1969. How Much Can We Boost IQ and Scholastic Achievement? *Harvard Educational Review,* Reprint Series, no. 2:1–123.

———. 1973. *Educability and Group Difference.* London: Methuen.

Jewell, K. Sue. 1993. *From Mammy to Miss America and Beyond.* New York: Routledge.

Johnson, Charles S. 1934. *Shadow of the Plantation.* Chicago: University of Chicago Press.

———. 1941. *Growing Up in the Black Belt: Negro Youth in the Rural South.* New York: Schocken Books.

Johnson, Walton. 1994. *Dismantling Apartheid: A South African Town in Transition.* Ithaca: Cornell University Press.

Kadi, Joanna. 1993. A Question of Belonging. In *Working-Class Women in the Academy: Laborers in the Knowledge Factory,* ed. Michelle M. Tokarczyk and Elizabeth A. Fay. Amherst: University of Massachusetts Press.

Kaprow, Miriam Lee. 1992. Celebrating Impermanence: Gypsies in a Spanish City. In *The Naked Anthropologist: Tales from around the World,* ed. Philip R. DeVita. Belmont, CA: Wadsworth.

Kardiner, Abram, and Lionel Ovesey. 1972. *The Mark of Oppression: Explorations in the Personality of the American Negro.* New York: World.

King, Joyce E. 1991. Dyconscious Racism: Ideology, Identity, and the Miseducation of Teachers. *Journal of Negro Education* 60(2):133–146.

Kohl, Herbert. 1994. *"I Won't Learn from You" and Other Thoughts on Creative Maladjustment.* New York: The New Press.

Kondo, Dorrine K. 1986. Dissolution and Reconstitution of Self: Implications for Anthropological Epistemology. *Cultural Anthropology* 1(1):74–88.

———. 1990. *Crafting Selves: Power, Gender, and Discourses of Identity in a Japanese Workplace.* Chicago: University of Chicago Press.

Kottak, Conrad. 1994. *Cultural Anthropology.* 6th ed. New York: McGraw-Hill.

Kozol, Jonathan. 1966. *Death at an Early Age.* Boston: Houghton Mifflin.

———. 1991. *Savage Inequalities.* New York: Crown.

Ladson-Billings, Gloria. 1991. Beyond Multicultural Illiteracy. *Journal of Negro Education* 60(2):147–157.

Landry, Bart. 1987. *The New Black Middle Class.* Berkeley: University of California Press.

Langston, Donna. 1988. Tired of Playing Monopoly? In *Changing Our Power: An Introduction to Women's Studies,* ed. Jo Whitehorse Cochran, Donna Langstron, and Carolyn Woodward. Dubuque, IA: Kendall-Hunt.

———. 1993. Who Am I Now? The Politics of Class Identity. In *Working-Class Women in the Academy: Laborers in the Knowledge Factory,* ed. Michelle M. Tokarczyk and Elizabeth A. Fay. Amherst: University of Massachusetts Press.

Larson, Tom E. 1988. Employment and Unemployment of Young Black Males. In *Young, Black and Male in America: An Endangered Species,* ed. Jewelle Taylor Gibbs. Dover, MA: Auburn House.

Leacock, Eleanor B. 1969. *Teaching and Learning in City Schools: A Comparative Study.* New York: Basic Books.

———. 1970. Education, Socialization, and "The Culture of Poverty." In *Schools Against Children: The Case for Community Control,* ed. Annette T. Rubinstein. New York: Monthly Review Press.

———. 1982. The Influence of Teacher Attitudes on Children's Classroom Performance: Case Studies. In *The Social Life of Children in a Changing Society,* ed. K. M. Borman. Norwood, NJ: Ablex.

Leap, William L. 1993. *American Indian English.* Salt Lake City: University of Utah Press.

Lee, Dorothy. 1987. Codifications of Reality: Lineal and Nonlineal. In *Freedom and Culture.* Prospect Heights, IL: Waveland Press.

Lee, Richard. 1969. Eating Christmas in the Kalahari. *Natural History Magazine.* December.

———. 1974. What Hunters Do For a Living; or, How to Make Out on Scarce

Resources. In *Man in Adaptation: The Cultural Present.* 2d ed. Edited by Yehudi A. Cohen. Chicago: Aldine.

Leone, Mark. 1981. Mormon "Peculiarity": Recapitulation of Subordination. In *Persistent Peoples: Cultural Enclaves in Perspective,* ed. George P. Castile and Gilbert Kushner. Tucson: University of Arizona Press.

Lewis, Diane K. 1977. A Response to Inequality: Black Women, Racism, and Sexism. In *Black Women in America: Social Science Perspectives,* ed. Micheline R. Malson, Elizabeth Mudimbe-Boyi, Jean F. O'Barr, and Mary Wyer. Chicago: University of Chicago Press.

Lewis, Magda, and R. I. Simon. 1986. A Discourse Not Intended for Her: Learning and Teaching within Patriarchy. *Harvard Educational Review* 56(4):457–472.

Lieberson, Stanley. 1985. Unhyphenated Whites in the United States. *Ethnic and Racial Studies* 8(1):159–180.

Liebow, Elliot. 1967. *Tally's Corner: A Study of Negro Streetcorner Men.* Boston: Little, Brown.

Lightfoot, Sara Lawrence. 1973. Politics and Reasoning: Through the Eyes of Teachers and Children. *Harvard Educational Review* 43(2):197–244.

———. 1978. *Worlds Apart: Relationships between Families and Schools.* New York: Basic Books.

Limon, Jose E. 1991. Representation, Ethnicity, and the Precursory Ethnography: Notes of a Native Anthropologist. In *Recapturing Anthropology: Working in the Present,* ed. Richard G. Fox. Santa Fe, NM: School of American Research Press.

Lutz, Catherine. 1988. *Unnatural Emotions: Everyday Sentiments on a Micronesian Atoll and Their Challenge to Western Theory.* Chicago: University of Chicago Press.

Lutz, Catherine, and Geoffrey A. White. 1986. The Anthropology of Emotions. *Annual Review of Anthropology* 15:405–436.

Mackler, Bernard. 1970. Blacks Who Are Academically Successful. In *Urban Education* 5:210–237.

———. 1972. Up from Poverty: The Price of "Making It" in a Ghetto School. In *Opening Opportunities for Disadvantaged Learners,* ed. Harry A. Passow. New York: Teachers College Press.

MacLeod, Jay. 1987. *Ain't No Makin' It: Leveled Aspirations in a Low-Income Neighborhood.* Boulder: Westview Press.

Madrid, Arturo. 1992. Missing People and Others: Joining Together to Expand the Circle. In *Race, Class, and Gender: An Anthology,* ed. Margaret Andersen and Patricia Hill Collins. Belmont, CA: Wadsworth.

Majors, Richard. 1986. Cool Pose: The Proud Signature of Black Survival. *Changing Men: Issues in Gender, Sex, and Politics* 17:5–6.

———. 1987. Cool Pose: *A New Approach toward a Systematic Understanding and Studying of Black Male Behavior.* Ph.D. diss. University of Illinois, Urbana.

————. 1990. Cool Pose: Black Masculinity and Sports. In *Sports, Men, and the Gender Order: Critical Feminist Perspectives,* ed. Michael A. Messner and D. F. Sabo. Champaign, IL: Human Kinetics Books.

Majors, Richard, and Janet M. Billson. 1992. *Cool Pose: The Dilemmas of Black Manhood in America.* New York: Lexington Books.

Malinowski, Bronislaw. 1987 (1929). *The Sexual Life of Savages: An Ethnographic Account of Courtship, Marriage, and Family Life among the Natives of the Trobriand Islands, British New Guinea.* New York: Harcourt Brace and World.

Margolis, Maxine. 1982. Blaming the Victim: Ideology and Sexual Discrimination in the Contemporary United States. In *Researching American Culture.* Ann Arbor: University of Michigan Press.

Martin, Emily. 1987. *The Woman in the Body: A Cultural Analysis of Reproduction.* Boston: Beacon Press.

Martin, Verna E. 1983. *Socio-Economic Characteristics of the Black Population of Metropolitan Washington, 1980.* Washington, DC: Metropolitan Washington Council of Governments 1980 Census Reports, no. 4.

Masayesva, Jr., Victor, and Erin Younger. 1984. Kwikwilyaqa: Hopi Photography. In *Hopi Photographers/Hopi Images,* ed. Victor Masayesva, Jr. and Erin Younger. Vol. 8. *Sun Tracks: An American Indian Literary Series.* Tucson: Sun Tracks and University of Arizona Press.

Maslow, Abraham. 1954. *Motivation and Personality.* New York: Harper and Row.

Matusow, Barbara. 1989. Guess Who's Not Coming to Dinner? *Washingtonian* 25(2):152.

Maxwell, Joan Paddock. 1985. *No Easy Answers: Persistent Poverty in the Metropolitan Washington Area.* Washington, DC: Greater Washington Research Center.

Mays, Benjamin E. 1971. *Born to Rebel: An Autobiography.* New York: Scribner.

McBride, James. 1988. What Color Is Jesus? When Your Mother Is White and Your Father Is Black, the Questions Never Stop. *Washington Post Magazine,* July 31.

McCall, Nathan. 1994. *Makes Me Wanna Holler: A Young Black Man in America.* New York: Random House.

McGary, Howard. 1992. *Between Slavery and Freedom: Philosophy and American Slavery.* Bloomington: Indiana University Press.

McKnight, Reginald. 1993. Confessions of a Wannabe Negro. In *Lure and Loathing: Essays on Race, Identity, and the Ambivalence of Assimilation,* ed. Gerald Early. New York: Allen Lane, Penguin Press.

McLaren, Peter. 1986. *Schooling as a Ritual Performance: Towards a Political Economy of Educational Symbols and Gestures.* London: Routledge and Kegan Paul.

McPherson, James M. 1982. *The Negro's Civil War: How American Negroes Felt and Acted during the War for the Union.* Chicago: University of Illinois Press.

McRobbie, Angela. 1978. Working-Class Girls and the Culture of Femininity. In *Women Take Issue: Aspects of Women's Subordination,* ed. Centre for Contemporary Cultural Studies Working Papers in Cultural Studies. London: Hutchinson.

Mead, Margaret. 1961 (1928). *Coming of Age in Samoa.* New York: Morrow Quill.

Moone, Janet R. 1981. Persistence with Change: A Property of Sociocultural Dynamics. In *Persistent Peoples: Cultural Enclaves in Perspective,* ed. George P. Castile and Gilbert Kushner. Tucson: University of Arizona Press.

Morrison, Toni. 1972. *The Bluest Eye.* New York: Holt, Rinehart and Winston.

Morton, Patricia. 1991. *Disfigured Images: The Historical Assault on Afro-American Women.* Westport, CT: Greenwood Press.

Moses, Yolanda T. 1985. Black American Women and Work: Historical and Contemporary Strategies for Empowerment—II. *Women's Studies International Forum* 8(4):351–359.

Mullings, Leath. 1994. Images. Ideology, and Women of Color. In *Women of Color in U.S. Society,* ed. Maxine Baca Zinn and Bonnie Thornton Dill. Philadelphia: Temple University Press.

Murray, Pauli. 1978 (1965). *Proud Shoes: The Story of an American Family.* New York: Harper and Row.

Myrdal, Gunnar. 1944. *An American Dilemma: The Negro Problem and Modern Democracy.* New York: Harper.

Nakhleh, Khalil. 1979. On Being a Native Anthropologist. In *The Politics of Anthropology: From Colonialism and Sexism to the View from Above,* ed. G. Huizer and B. Mannheim. The Hague: Mouton.

Napper, George. 1973. *Blacker than Thou: The Struggle for Campus Unity.* Grand Rapids, MI: William B. Eerdmans.

Nayaran, Kirin. 1993. How "Native" Is a Native Anthropologist? *American Anthropologist* 95(3):671–686.

Neira, Christian. 1988. "Building 860." *Harvard Educational Review* 58(3):337–342.

Norbeck, Edward, and Harumi Befu. 1958. Informal Fictive Kinship in Japan. *American Anthropologist* New Series 60:102–117.

Ogbu, John U. 1974. *The Next Generation: An Ethnography of Education in an Urban Neighborhood.* New York: Academic Press.

————. 1978. *Minority Education and Caste: The American System in Cross-Cultural Perspective*. New York: Academic Press.

————. 1980. *Cultural Differences v. Alternative Cultures: A Critique of Cultural Discontinuity Hypothesis in Classroom Ethnographies*. Paper presented at the 79th annual meeting, American Anthropological Association, Washington, DC.

————. 1981a. Education, Clientage, and Social Mobility: Caste and Social Change in the United States and Nigeria. In *Social Inequality: Comparative and Developmental Approaches*, ed. Gerald D. Berreman. New York: Academic Press.

————. 1981b. On Origins of Human Competence: A Cultural Ecological Perspective. *Child Development* 52:413–429.

————. 1982a. Cultural Discontinuities and Schooling. *Anthropology and Education Quarterly* 13(4):290–307.

————. 1982b. Societal Forces as a Context of Ghetto Children's School Failure. In *Language of Children Reared in Poverty: Implications for Evaluation and Intervention*, ed. L. Feagans and D.C. Farran. New York: Academic Press.

————. 1982c. Socialization: A Cultural Ecological Approach. In *The Social Life of Children in a Changing Society*, ed. Kathryn M. Borman. Hillsdale, NJ: Lawrence Erlbaum Associates.

————. 1983a. Crossing Cultural Boundaries: A Comparative Perspective on Minority Education. Paper presented at a symposium, Race, Class, Socialization, and the Life Cycle, in honor of Allison Davis. Chicago: University of Chicago, October 21–22.

————. 1983b. Indigenous and Immigrant Minority Education: A Comparative Perspective. Paper presented at the 82d annual meeting of the American Anthropological Association, Chicago. November.

————. 1988. Understanding Cultural Diversity and Learning. *Educational Researcher* 21(8):5–14.

Ohnuki-Tierney, Emiko. 1984. "Native" Anthropologists. *American Ethnologist* 11:584–586.

Ong, Walter. 1982. *Orality and Literacy: The Technologizing of the Word*. London: Methuen.

Ortner, Sherry B. 1991. Reading America: Preliminary Notes on Class and Culture. In *Recapturing Anthropology: Working in the Present*, ed. Richard G. Fox. Santa Fe, NM: School of American Research Press.

Ostrander, Susan. 1984. *Women of the Upper Class*. Philadelphia: Temple University Press.

Pagano, Joanne. 1990. *Exiles and Communities: Teaching in the Patriarchal Wilderness*. Albany: State University of New York Press.

Paglia, Camille. 1994. Jackie's Ride. *New Republic* 210(24):4.

Painter, Nell Irvin. 1995. Soul Murder and Slavery: Toward a Fully Loaded Cost

Accountability. In *U.S. History as Women's History: New Feminist Essays.* Chapel Hill: University of North Carolina Press.

Palmer, Phyllis. 1989. *Domesticity and Dirt: Housewives and Domestic Servants in the United States, 1920–1945.* Philadelphia: Temple University Press.

Paterson, Orlando. 1982. *Slavery and Social Death: Comparative Study.* Cambridge: Harvard University Press.

Payne, Irene. 1988. A Working-Class Girl in a Grammar School. In *Learning to Lose: Sexism and Education.* Rev. ed. Edited by Dale Spender and Elizabeth Sarah. London: The Women's Press.

Peshkin, Allen. 1991. *The Color of Strangers, the Color of Friends: The Play of Ethnicity in School and Community.* Chicago: University of Chicago Press.

Podlesney, Teresa. 1991. Blondes. In *The Hysterical Male: New Feminist Theory,* ed. Arthur and Marilouise Kroker. New York: St. Martin's Press.

Poussaint, Alvin F., and L. R. McLean. 1968. Black Roadblocks to Black Unity. *Negro Digest* 17:11.

Rabinow, Paul. 1991. For Hire: Resolutely Late Modern. In *Recapturing Anthropology: Working in the Present,* ed. Richard G. Fox. Santa Fe, NM: School of American Research Press.

Ramos, Alcida R. 1992. Reflecting on the Yanomami: Ethnographic Images and the Pursuit of the Exotic. In *Rereading Cultural Anthropology,* ed. George E. Marcus. Durham: Duke University Press.

Rawick, George P. 1972. *From Sundown to Sunup: The Making of the Black Community.* Westport, CT: Greenwood Publishing Company.

Redcay, Edward E. 1935. County Training Schools and Public Secondary Education for Negroes in the South. Washington, DC: John F. Slater Fund.

Reiter, Rayna (ed.). 1975. *Toward an Anthropology of Women.* New York: Monthly Review Press.

Renan, Ernest. 1990. What Is a Nation? In *Nation and Narration,* ed. Homi K. Bhabha. London: Routledge.

Rich, Adrienne. 1979a. Taking Women Students Seriously (1978). In *On Lies, Secrets, and Silence: Selected Prose, 1966–1978.* New York: W.W. Norton.

———. 1979b. Toward a Woman-Centered University (1973–74). In *On Lies, Secrets, and Silence: Selected Prose, 1966–1978.* New York: W.W. Norton.

Rist, Ray C. 1970. Student Social Class and Teacher Expectations: The Self-Fulfilling Prophecy in Ghetto Education. *Harvard Educational Review* 40(3):411–451.

———. 1973. *The Urban School: A Factory for Failure. A Study of Education in American Society.* Cambridge: MIT Press.

Rodriguez, Richard. 1982. *Hunger of Memory: The Education of Richard Rodriguez, An Autobiography.* Boston: D. R. Godine.

Rohrer, John H., and Munro S. Edmonson. 1960. *The Eighth Generation Grows*

Up: Cultures and Personalities of New Orleans Negroes. New York: Harper and Row.

Rollins, Judith. 1993. *Between Women: Domestics and Their Employers.* Philadelphia: Temple University Press.

Rosaldo, Michelle. 1980. *Knowledge and Passion: Ilongot Notions of Self and Social Life.* New York: Cambridge University Press.

Rosaldo, Michelle Zimbalist, and Louise Lamphere (eds.). 1974. *Women, Culture, and Society.* Stanford: Stanford University Press.

Rosaldo, Renato. 1980. *Ilongot Headhunting, 1883–1974: A Study in Society and History.* Stanford: Stanford University Press.

———. 1989. *Culture and Truth: The Remaking of Social Analysis.* New York: Beacon Press.

Rosenfeld, Gerry. 1971. *"Shut Those Thick Lips!": A Study of Slum School Failure.* New York: Holt, Rinehart and Winston.

Rushforth, Scott. 1994. Political Resistance in a Contemporary Hunter-Gatherer Society: More about Bearlake Athapaskan Knowledge and Authority. *American Ethnologist* 21(2):335–352.

Russell, Kathy, Midge Wilson, and Ronald Hall. 1992. *The Color Complex: The Politics of Skin Color among African-Americans.* New York: Harcourt Brace Jovanovich.

Ryan, William. 1976. *Blaming the Victim.* Rev. Ed. New York: Vintage Books.

Said, Edward W. 1978. *Orientalism.* New York: Pantheon.

———. 1986. *After The Last Sky: Palestinian Lives.* New York: Pantheon.

———. 1989. Representing the Colonized: Anthropology's Interlocutors. *Critical Inquiry* 15:205–225.

Schofield, Janet W. 1989. *Black and White in School: Trust, Tension, or Tolerance?* New York: Praeger.

Scott, James C. 1985. *Weapons of the Weak: Everyday Forms of Peasant Resistance.* New Haven: Yale University Press.

———. 1990. *Domination and the Arts of Resistance: Hidden Transcripts.* New Haven: Yale University Press.

Scott, James C., and Princeton Kerkveleit. 1986. *Everyday Forms of Peasant Resistance in Southeast Asia.* London: Frank Cass.

Scott, John Finley. 1965. Sororities and the Husband Game. *Transaction* 2(6):137–146.

Scott, Kesho Yvonne. 1990. *The Habit of Surviving: Black Women's Strategies for Life.* New Brunswick, NJ: Rutgers University Press.

Segal, Lynne. 1990. *Slow Motion: Changing Masculinities; Changing Men.* New Brunswick, NJ: Rutgers University Press.

Sennett, Richard, and Jonathan Cobb. 1972. *The Hidden Injuries of Class.* New York: Vintage Books.

Sexton, Patricia Cayo. 1969. *The Feminized Male: Classrooms, White Collars, and the Decline of Manliness.* New York: Random House.

Seymour-Smith, Charlotte. 1986. *Dictionary of Anthropology.* Boston: G. K. Hall.

Shade, Barbara J. 1978. Social-Psychological Characteristics of Black Achieving Children. *Negro Educational Review* 29:80–86.

———. 1981. Personal Traits of Educationally Successful Black Children. *Negro Educational Review* 32(2):6–11.

Shanklin, Eugenia. 1993. *Anthropology and Race.* Belmont, CA: Wadsworth.

Shockley, William. 1970. A "Try Simplest Cases" Approach to the Heredity-Poverty-Crime Problem. In *Psychological Factors in Poverty,* ed. Vernon L. Allen. Chicago: Markham.

———. 1972. Dysgenics, Geneticity, Raceology: A Challenge to the Intellectual Responsibility of Education. *Phi Delta Kappan* 53(5):297–307.

Shuey, Audrey M. 1966. *The Testing of Negro Intelligence.* New York: Social Science Press.

Siddle Walker, Emilie V. 1993. Caswell County Training School, 1933–1969: Relationships between Community and School. *Harvard Educational Review* 63(2):161–182.

Simpson, Amelia. 1993. *Xuxa: The Mega-Marketing of Gender, Race, and Modernity.* Philadelphia: Temple University Press.

Smith, Bernard. 1988. Upscaling Downtown: Stalled Gentrification in Washington, DC. Ithaca, NY: Cornell University Press.

———. 1992. *Imagining the Pacific: In the Wake of the Cook Voyages.* New Haven: Yale University Press.

Snead, James. 1984. Repetition as a Figure in Black Culture. In *Black Literature and Literary Theory,* ed. Louis Henry Gates, Jr. New York: Methuen.

Solomon, R. Patrick. 1992. *Black Resistance in High School: Forging a Separatist Culture.* Albany: State University of New York.

Spicer, Edward H. 1961. Introduction to *Perspectives in American Indian Culture Change,* ed. Edward H. Spicer. Chicago: University of Chicago Press.

———. 1971. Persistent Cultural Systems: A Comparative Study of Identity Systems That Can Adapt to Contrasting Environments. *Science* 174:795–800.

———. 1980. *The Yaqui: A Cultural History.* Tucson: University of Arizona Press.

Spickard, Paul R. 1989. *Mixed Blood: Intermarriage and Ethnic Identity in Twentieth-Century America.* Madison: University of Wisconsin Press.

Spindler, George D. (ed.). 1955. *Anthropology and Education.* Stanford: Stanford University Press.

Spivey, Donald A. 1978. *Schooling for the New Slavery: Black Industrial Education, 1868–1915.* Westport, CT: Greenwood Press.

Spradley, James P., and David D. McCurdy. 1989. *Anthropology: The Cultural Perspective.* 2d ed. Prospect Heights: IL: Waveland Press.

Stack, Carol. 1974. *All Our Kin: Strategies for Survival in a Black Community.* New York: Harper and Row.

Staiano, Kathryn Vance. 1980. Ethnicity as Process: The Creation of an Afro-American Identity. *Ethnicity* 7(1):27–33.

Staples, Brent. 1989. The White Girl Problem: A Black Male Comes to Terms with His Politically Incorrect Taste in Women. *New York Woman*, March: 87–91.

Staples, Robert. 1981. The Black American Family. In *Ethnic Families in America: Patterns and Variations,* ed. C.H. Mindel and R.W. Habenstein. New York: Elsevier Scientific Publishing Co.

———. 1984. The Mother-Son Relationship in the Black Family: An Explosive Controversy. *Ebony* 39(12):74–78.

Stein, Annie. 1971. Strategies for Failure. *Harvard Educational Review* 41(2):158–204.

Stoller, Paul. 1994. Ethnographies as Texts/Ethnographers as Griots. *American Ethnologist* 21(2):353–366.

Szasz, Thomas S. 1970. Blackness and Madness: Images of Evil and Tactics of Exclusion. In *Black America,* ed. John F. Szwed. New York: Basic Books.

Tannen, Deborah. 1994a. How to Give Orders Like a Man. *New York Times Magazine,* August 26:46–49.

———. 1994b. *Talking from 9 to 5: How Men's and Women's Conversational Styles Affect Who Gets Heard, Who Gets Credit, and What Gets Done at Work.* New York: William Morrow.

Tate, Gregg. 1992. *Flyboy in the Buttermilk: Essays on Contemporary America.* New York: Simon and Schuster.

Tatum, Beverly Daniel. 1987. *Assimilation Blues: Black Families in a White Community.* Northhampton, MA: Hazel-Maxwell Publishing.

Taussig, Michael. 1987. The Rise and Fall of Marxist Anthropology. *Social Analysis* 21(1):101–113.

Terborg-Penn, Rosalyn. 1986. Black Women in Resistance: A Cross-Cultural Perspective. In *Resistance: Studies in African, Caribbean, and Afro-American History,* ed. Gary Y. Okihiro. Amherst: University of Massachusetts Press.

Terry, Robert W. 1970. *For Whites Only.* Grand Rapids, MI: William B. Eerdmans Publishing.

Theweleit, Klaus. 1987. *Male Fantasies: Women, Floods, Bodies, History.* Vol. 1. Minneapolis: University of Minnesota Press.

Tokarczyk, Michelle M., and Elizabeth A. Fay. 1993. Introduction to *Working-Class Women in the Academy: Laborers in the Knowledge Factory,* ed. Michelle M. Tokarczyk and Elizabeth A. Fay. Amherst: University of Massachusetts Press.

Torgovnick, Marianna. 1990. *Gone Primitive: Savage Intellects, Modern Lives.* Chicago: University of Chicago Press.

Tracy, Laura. 1991. *The Secret between Us: Competition among Women.* Boston: Little, Brown.

Trask, Haunani-Kay. 1991. Natives and Anthropologists: The Colonial Struggle. *Contemporary Pacific* 2:159–167.

Trotter, John Rhodes. 1981. Academic Attitudes of High-Achieving Academically Able Black Male Adolescents. *Journal of Negro Education* 50(1):54–62.

Trouillot, Michel-Rolph. 1991. Anthropology and the Savage Slot: The Poetics and Politics of Otherness. In *Recapturing Anthropology: Working in the Present,* ed. Richard G. Fox. Sante Fe, NM: School of American Research Press.

Turim, Maureen. 1990. Gentlemen Consume Blondes. In *Issues in Feminist Film Criticism,* ed. Patricia Erens. Bloomington: Indiana University Press.

Turner, Victor. 1969. *The Ritual Process: Structure and Anti-Structure.* Ithaca: Cornell University Press.

Tyack, David B. 1974. *The One Best System: A History of American Urban Education.* Waltham, MA: Blaisdell Publishing.

Tyler, Stephen L. 1992. On Being Out of Words. In *Rereading Cultural Anthropology,* ed. George E. Marcus. Durham: Duke University Press.

U.S. Census. 1980. U. S. Department of Commerce, Bureau of the Census. *1980 Census of Population and Housing, Census Tracts, Washington, D.C.-Md.-Va. Standard Metropolitan Statistical Area.* Washington, D.C.: U.S. Government Printing Office, 1983. Vol. 2, pp. H-1–H-23.

Van Gennep, Arnold. 1960. *The Rites of Passage.* Chicago: University of Chicago Press.

Van Maanen, John. 1988. *Tales of the Field: On Writing Ethnography.* Chicago: University of Chicago Press.

Vincent, Joan. 1991. Engaging Historicism. In *Recapturing Anthropology: Working in the Present,* ed. Richard G. Fox. Sante Fe, NM: School of American Research Press.

Walker, Alice. 1983. *In Search of Our Mothers' Gardens.* New York: Harcourt Brace Jovanovich.

———. 1982. *The Color Purple.* New York: Harcourt Brace Jovanovich.

Wallace, Michael. 1970–71. The Uses of Violence in American History. *American Scholar* 40(1):81–102.

Wallace, Michelle. 1990. Modernism, Postmodernism, and the Problem of the Visual in Afro-American Culture. In *Out There: Marginalization and Contemporary Cultures,* ed. Russell Ferguson, Martha Gever, Trinh T. Minh-ha, and Cornel West. Cambrige, MA: MIT Press.

Walton, Anthony. 1989. Willie Horton and Me. *New York Times Magazine,* August 20.

Washington, Elsie. 1987. Tony Morrison Now: Interview. *Essence* 18(6).

Washington, Mary Louise. 1987. *Invented Lives: Narratives of Black Women, 1860–1960*. Garden City, NY: Anchor Press.

Washington Urban League. 1985. *A Profile of Nonworking Black Males Aged 16–64 in Washington D.C*. 2 vols. Washington, DC: Washington Urban League.

Watkins, Mark Hanna. 1963. The West African "Bush" School. In *Education and Culture; Anthropological Approaches*, ed. George D. Spindler. New York: Holt, Rinehart and Winston.

Wax, Murray L., and Rosalie H. Wax. 1971. Cultural Deprivation as an Educational Ideology. In *The Culture of Poverty: A Critique*. New York: Simon and Schuster.

Weber, Max. 1978. *Economy and Society*. 2 vols. Berkeley: University of California Press.

Weinberg, Meyer. 1977. *A Chance to Learn: The History of Race and Education in the United States*. Cambridge: Cambridge University Press.

Weis, Lois. 1985. *Between Two Worlds: Black Students in an Urban Community College*. Boston: Routledge and Kegan Paul.

West, Cornel. 1990. The Cultural Politics of Difference. In *Out There: Marginalization and Contemporary Cultures*, ed. Russell Ferguson, Martha Gever, Trinh T. Minh-ha, and Cornel West. Cambridge: MIT Press.

———. 1993. *Race Matters*. New York: Beacon Press.

Wexler, Natalie. 1994. Babysitter in a *Strange* Land. *Washington Post Magazine*. May 22.

What It Means to Be Colored in the Capital of the United States. 1907. *Independent*.

White, Deborah Gray. 1985. *Arn't I a Woman? Female Slaves in the Plantation South*. New York: W.W. Norton.

———. 1990. Female Slaves: Sex Roles and Statuses in the Antebellum Plantation South. In *Unequal Sisters: A Multicultural Reader in U.S. Women's History*, ed. Ellen Carol DuBois and Vicki L. Ruiz. New York: Routledge.

Whitehead, Alfred North. 1957 (1929). *The Aims of Education and Other Essays*. New York: Free Press.

Williams, Brett. 1988. *Upscaling Downtown: Stalled Gentrification in Washington, D.C*. Ithaca: Cornell University Press.

Williams, Melvin. 1974. *Community in a Black Pentecostal Church: An Anthropological Study*. Pittsburgh: Unviersity of Pittsburgh Press.

Willis, Paul E. 1981 (1977). *Learning to Labour: How Working-Class Kids Get Working-Class Jobs*. Westmead, England: Saxon House.

Wilson, William Julius. 1987. *The Truly Disadvantaged: The Inner City, the Underclass, and Public Policy*. Chicago: University of Chicago Press.

———. 1978. *The Declining Significance of Race: Blacks and Changing American Institutions*. Chicago: University of Chicago Press.

Wolcott, Harry F. 1967. *The Kwakiutl Village and School.* New York: Holt, Rinehart and Winston.

———. 1973. *The Man in the Principal's Office: An Ethnography.* New York: Holt, Rinehart and Winston.

Woodson, Carter G. 1933. *The Miseducation of the Negro.* Washington, D.C.: Associated Publishers, Inc.

Woodward, C. Vann. 1957. *The Strange Career of Jim Crow.* New York: Oxford University Press.

Wright, Lawrence. 1994. One Drop of Blood: Annals of Politics. *New Yorker,* July 25.

Zinn, Maxine Baca, and Bonnie Thornton Dill. 1994. *Women of Color in U.S. Society.* Philadelphia: Temple University Press.

Zweigenhaft, Richard L., and William G. Domhoff. 1991. *Blacks in the White Establishment: A Study of Race and Class in America.* New Haven: Yale University Press.

For authors cited parenthetically but not discussed in text, see the Bibliography, pp. 373–96 above.